Time For

Halloween Decorations!

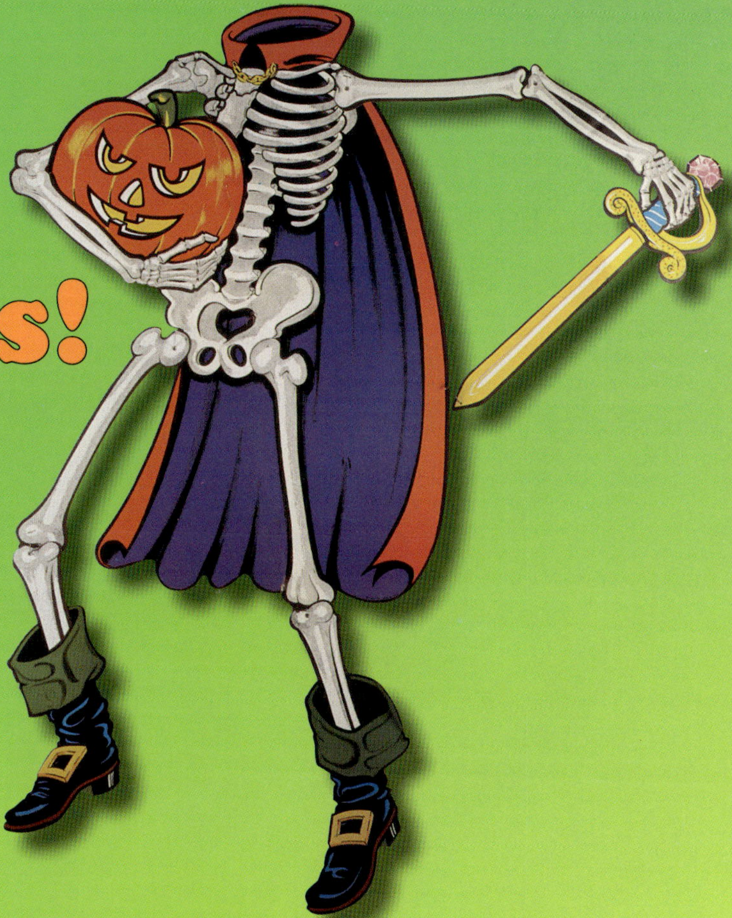

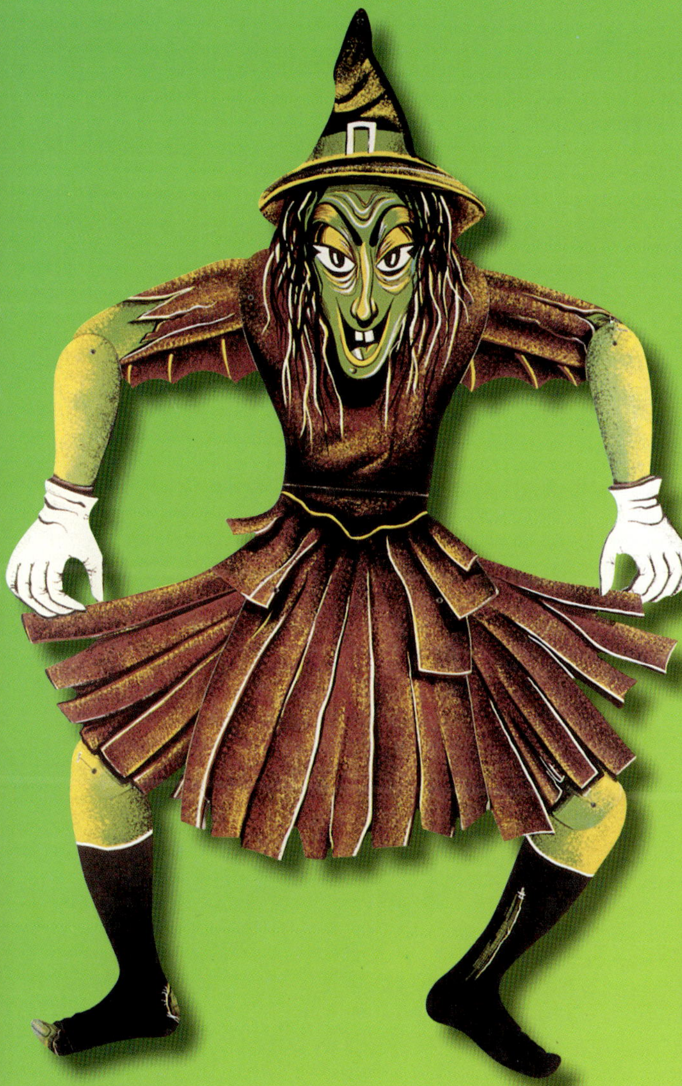

Claire M. Lavin

Schiffer Publishing Ltd®
4880 Lower Valley Road, Atglen, PA 19310 USA

I dedicate this work to my husband,
Philip Andrew Lavin.

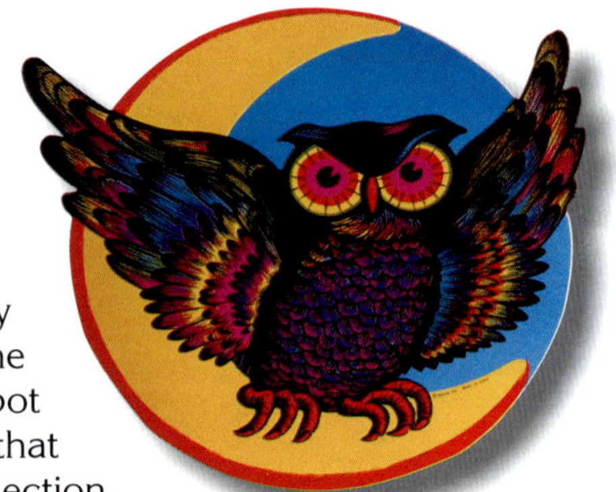

Phil is the person who stands out from all others. Through the years, he has trudged many miles through flea markets, antique co-ops, and auction houses digging through too many musty boxes to count trying to find elusive vintage Halloween pieces for me. There are many occasions when he's given up a rare day of fishing, a game of golf, or the big sporting event on TV just to tag along on the off-chance that I'll spot a bit of orange and black. The ultimate time was when I discovered that a well-known collector was selling at auction his entire Halloween collection in Minnesota. Barely containing my excitement at the prospect of adding some fabulous treasures to my growing collection, I asked if we could travel to Minnesota. The response? "Do you want to drive or fly?"

We are a team in every sense of the word. This was never more evident than our opportunity to photograph hundreds of pieces in the Beistle Company archives. You have to understand that Phil's interests lean in the direction of model trains. But the trooper that he is, he removed his engineer's cap and threw himself into the work, 100%. His talent with the camera is showcased here..

Another Schiffer Book by Claire Lavin:
Timeless Halloween Collectibles 1920-1949

Library of Congress Control Number: 2006936833

Designed by John P. Cheek
Cover design by Bruce Waters
Type set in Kabel Bd/Korinna BT

ISBN: 0-7643-2606-6
Printed in China
1 2 3 4

Published by Schiffer Publishing Ltd.
4880 Lower Valley Road
Atglen, PA 19310
Phone: (610) 593-1777; Fax: (610) 593-2002
E-mail: Info@schifferbooks.com

In Europe, Schiffer books are distributed by
Bushwood Books
6 Marksbury Ave.
Kew Gardens
Surrey TW9 4JF England
Phone: 44 (0) 20 8392-8585;
Fax: 44 (0) 20 8392-9876
E-mail: info@bushwoodbooks.co.uk
Website: www.bushwoodbooks.co.uk
Free postage in the U.K., Europe; air mail at cost.

A Note From The Author

Although the feeling of Halloween is with me year-round, it really gets kicked up a notch right after Labor Day. There are so many activities surrounding this wonderful holiday and I want to do everything! It's not unusual to see our home decked out for Halloween by mid-September. I'm a big believer in family traditions so each year both my husband and I set aside a day in October to build a scarecrow with Daniel, Elizabeth, and Jared, three of our six grandchildren. In addition to these activities, I also draw up plans for our yearly Halloween greeting card, which always includes my husband (the photographer) and various combinations of our grandchildren.

When I'm not lecturing during this time of year on the subject of Halloween collectibles, I can be found busy with other events such as the Halloween Opera in Jim Thorpe, Pennsylvania – either as a guest speaker or simply as an attendee. The latter is dangerous since that means I can shop! As an exhibitor at the October 2005 Atlantic City's Atlantique City Show, I wowed the dealers and public alike with my vintage Halloween display.

Besides numerous radio interviews, I have appeared on TV. My vintage Halloween crepe paper collection was featured on The Martha Stewart Show in October of 2003, and I appeared on CN8's Your Morning show, The Pinky Kravitz Antique/Collectibles Show as well as Collective Intelligence, a cable TV show on the Dish Network which featured the "20 Tips to Halloween Collecting."

The items in this book showcase the remarkable material found in the archives of one of the leading producers of holiday decorations, the Beistle Company, in Shippensburg, Pennsylvania. Because there is such a wealth of objects, the information was separated into two volumes. This book continues the story begun with Timeless Halloween Collectibles (Schiffer, 2005). It resumes the cataloguing of some of the most wonderfully graphic Halloween decorations ever to be seen. In this volume, a plethora of adornments are found that will surely make a Baby Boomer's nostalgic heart race.

The material here is derived from the Beistle company's archives and information about the Dolly Toy Company, of Dayton, Ohio, that made Fibro Toys. Vintage pieces from Mark Craven's collection are presented, as well as a few of my own. Since it is a Halloween collector's reference guide, all pertinent information is included.

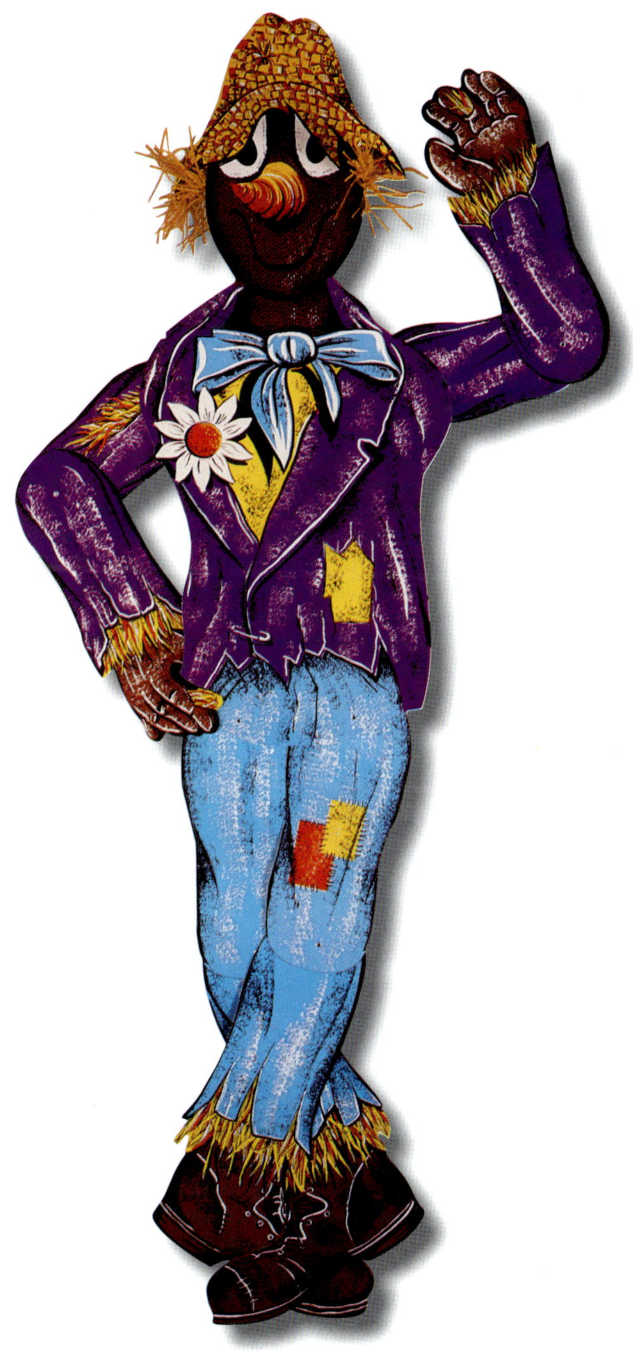

Acknowledgments

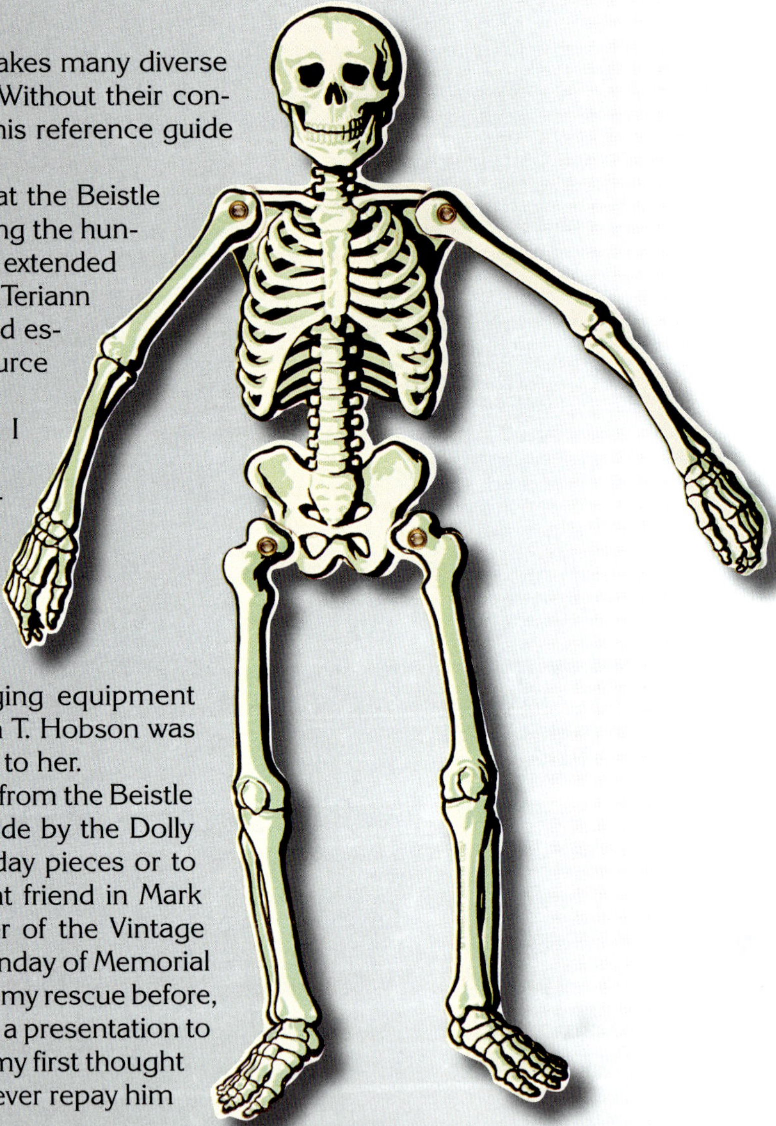

Writing a book is not a solo accomplishment; it takes many diverse contributors, each bringing their talents to the task. Without their contributed time, talent, perseverance, and assistance, this reference guide would not have been realized.

Heartfelt thanks goes to my kindhearted friends at the Beistle Company. I was treated like royalty while photographing the hundreds of items in their archives. My sincere gratitude is extended to Tricia Lacy, President; Rick Buterbaugh, Art Director; Teriann Hilbinger, Assistant Art Director; Tim Luhrs, Artist; and especially Bob Hansen, Artist, my host, guide, and resource for all things Beistle.

If it were not for the following faithful supporters, I couldn't have completed the writing and cataloging: Barbara Wachter is a very good friend, and her husband, Robert Wachter, gave his legal expertise. Philip A. Lavin strapped on a camera and created the breathtaking display of classic Halloween images. He has received compliments on his photography in the previous volume.

Gerard Gantert loaned us photography cataloging equipment that made the job of sorting the pictures easier. Maria T. Hobson was especially helpful with the text, and I am very grateful to her.

The objects shown in Chapters 1 through 6 come from the Beistle Company archives. The items in Chapter 7 were made by the Dolly Toy Company, which never thought to save the holiday pieces or to compile an archive collection. Luckily, I have a great friend in Mark Craven, a fellow Halloween aficionado and manager of the Vintage Holiday Show (which takes place every year on the Sunday of Memorial Day weekend, in Columbus, Ohio). Mark had come to my rescue before, when I needed plastic Halloween candy containers for a presentation to the Pennsylvania Auctioneers' Convention. Mark was my first thought when I needed to borrow the Fibro Toy items. I can never repay him for his generosity and kindness.

I also thank the following Halloween authoriti collectors, who have been a blessing to me throu my Halloween mission: Pamela Apkarian-Russell, Hugh Luck, Bob Kubicki, the staff of Alderfer Auctions, Tom Cabela, and Dawn Kroma.

Ellen T. Schroy, the editor of Warman's Antiques and Collectibles Price Guide and an invaluable friend, opened doors of opportunity for me. I am indebted to her and think of her as my Fairy Godmother!

The Halloween collecting community is a wide and varied one, yet closely knit and always available to lend a hand when the situations arise. There are many wonderful people I have met along the way at shows, auctions, my lectures, and book signing events. They share my desire to increase the collector's knowledge about vintage Halloween items. I am grateful for their enthusiasm, eagerness, interest, and passions for the most wonderful time of the year!

Contents

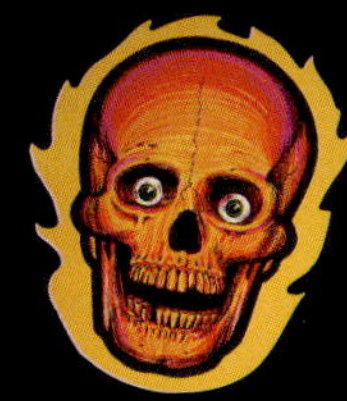

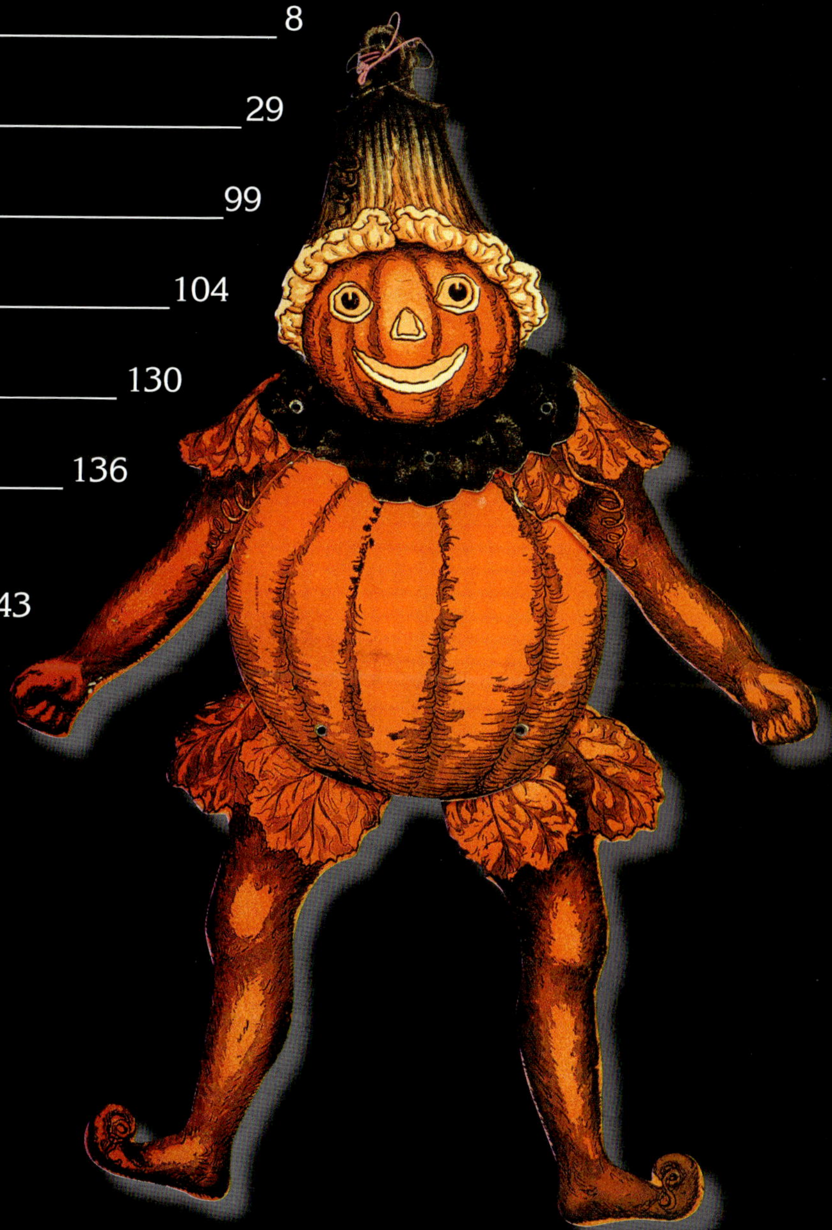

Foreword

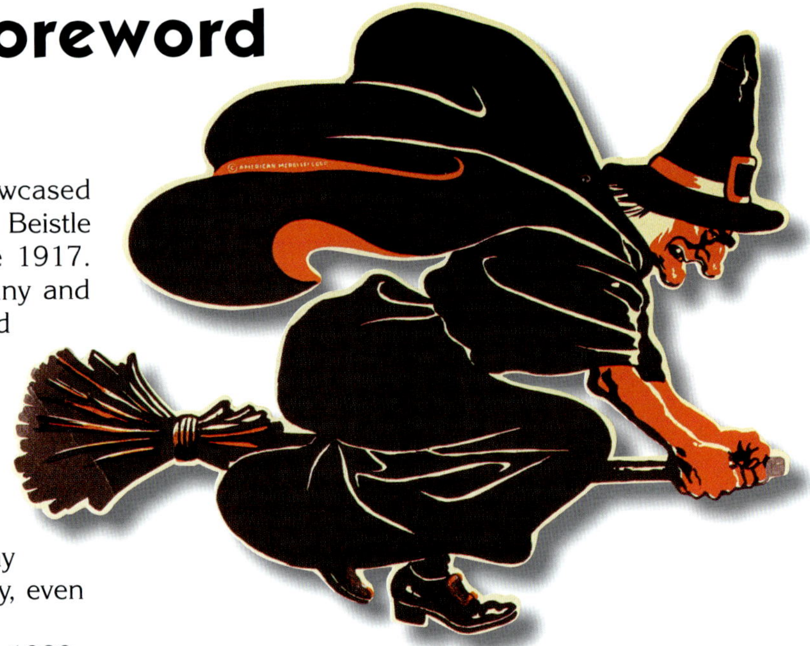

The Beistle vintage Halloween items showcased throughout this book are genuine Americana. Beistle has been producing Halloween goods since 1917. Personally, as an artist for the Beistle Company and a collector of vintage Halloween items, I find Claire Lavin's books to be both intriguing and informative about the company's involvement with October 31.

Halloween is the only holiday that permits you to be who or what you aren't. You can be a hippie, a ghost, a baseball player, or even a princess, anything you can imagine! That is why I love Halloween; it allows you to escape reality, even if it's just for a day.

My first Halloween memory is from the early 1980s. I dressed up as my favorite GI Joe character, a ninja named "Storm Shadow." I wore my white judo uniform, two pairs of my father's tube socks (one pair on my feet and the other I used as gloves), a folded t-shirt for my mask, and a four-foot plastic ninja sword I had purchased at the local party store. Of course, no Halloween costume was complete without a He-Man pillowcase for holding all the goodies that I would collect. There I stood, a 50-pound ninja, ready to take on the criminals of the world one house at a time, and nothing could stop me... well, maybe the 9:00 p.m. curfew.

As an adult, my career dream came true when I was hired in 2000 as an artist at the Beistle Company to design Halloween party goods. My first year was exciting because I witnessed the process of making and distributing party goods. I learned how each product begins with an idea and then is turned into reality. It was exciting to see my own ideas go from sketches on paper to actual decorations.

Today at Beistle, every decoration begins as a pencil drawing, just as it did 106 years ago when M.L. Beistle started the company. Coincidentally, it wasn't until 2003, that I received a true appreciation for the art of the Beistle Company, which resulted in my becoming a collector. I was given the responsibility of recreating some of the vintage pieces from the Beistle Halloween line. I was handed the key to the Beistle archives and was sent to research the products from the past. I dug through the filing cabinets for hours, flipping through records that dated back to the early 1900s. Some files contained original artwork, notes on the ideas, inserts from Beistle catalogues, and even the actual decoration in mint condition in its original packaging. This task made me feel like a kid on October 30 preparing my costume for trick-or-treating the following day.

As for the classic pieces I redesigned, Beistle brought back twelve items to its current Halloween line. When I see people decorating with party goods that I created and think that one day those items may become collectible, I am delighted beyond words.

In conclusion, I hope you enjoy Time for Halloween Decorations! The Beistle Company is proud of our past, and we look forward to creating new Halloween collectibles for the future. Maybe it will inspire you to become a collector of Beistle Halloween Americana items, too!

Bob Hansen
Artist and Beistle Historian

Introduction

For an avid collector, facts and information regarding the vintage pieces are eagerly sought. The descriptions here include the original date, or "inauguration," of a piece and the final year of production. If an item went by a particular name, which I discovered Beistle used more often than not, it is included. The exact measurements are given, and the values on today's market are included. The Stock Number information is not included in this book, because the Beistle company had a tendency to recycle numbers from discontinued pieces. I have come to the conclusion that these Stock Numbers do not add significantly to collecting knowledge.

Each Halloween item and set that appears here has information that includes the Beistle-assigned name in bold type followed by the initial release year and production run dates. The italicized paragraphs are taken directly from the Beistle Halloween Sales Catalogues. An asterisk (*) indicates comments made by the author. An assigned value for each piece is in bold type.

I was amazed to find that the majority of these pieces were marked only, "Made in U.S.A." without the benefit of a Beistle company mark. An exception was during the administration of Henry E. Luhrs, son-in-law of Martin Luther Beistle and president from 1949 through 1962. During presidency, Henry Luhrs' name appeared on every holiday and party item that was manufactured. This had led people to think that the names "Beistle" and "Luhrs" were from two separate companies. But now it is known that a decoration stamped "H. E. Luhrs – Made in U.S.A." is from the Beistle Company.

Beistle Company Marks

The Beistle Company's identifying mark is elusive. In the early 1920s, Beistle used the diamond-shape mark that resembles a honeycomb. It seems to refer to their signature products that were made with honeycomb tissue paper. New marks appeared later such as:

Printed in U.S.A.

Made in U.S.A.

Beistle – U.S.A."

"U.S.A."

You might think it is simple to date these Halloween pieces. Not so. For example, the diamond mark used in the initial years of production was retired, but appeared again on Halloween Trick or Treat bags in 1960.

I was notified, just before this book was completed, that a member of Beistle's staff had just begun work on the history of the company's marks. This is sure to be an exhaustive venture and obviously one that would not be completed before this book is printed. But, if a reader is interested in this additional information, contact me and I shall be happy to send it to you.

Using The Values Guide

The values listed with the descriptions represent the author's opinion of what the items, in excellent condition, might be valued by an educated collector. Any price paid for any particular article will, naturally, vary by geographical location and be affected by the buyer's enthusiasm, the disposition of the seller, and where the item is purchased (for example, at an antiques show, a retail show, a flea market, etc.).

Rare and especially desirable items in excellent or mint condition, which may include the original packaging (box, bag, wrapper, etc.), can, in some instances, be worth several times the value suggested.

A price paid for any particular piece depends on the buyer and the seller. The author does not claim to be the final authority on prices and, therefore, the publisher and/or the author assume no responsibility for financial loss or gain based on the use of this guide.

CHAPTER I
Party Helps

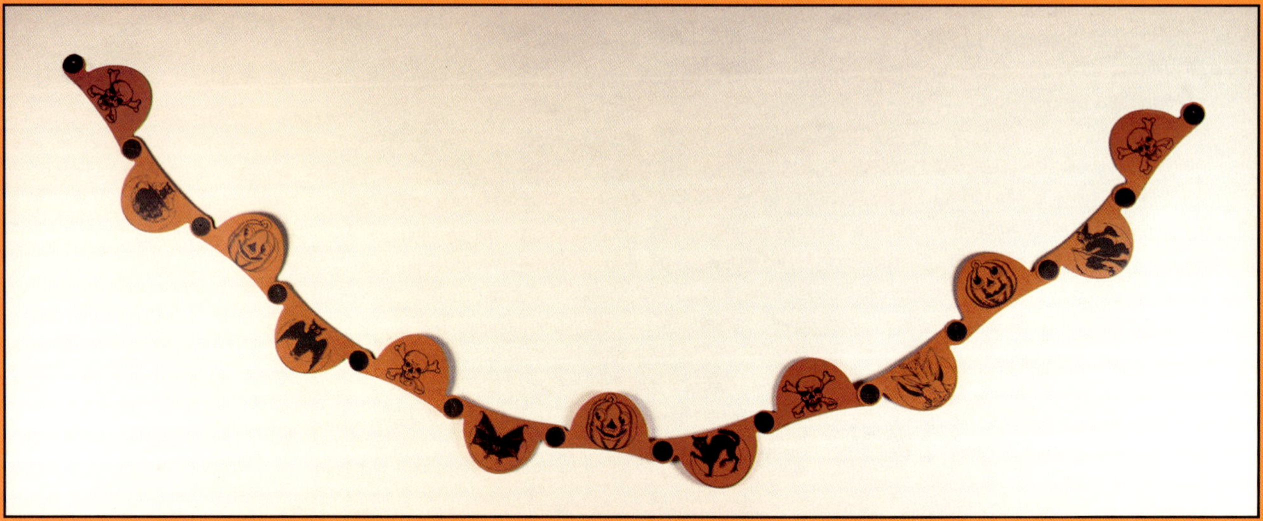

HALLOWEEN BANNER
Initial Release: 1941
Production Run: One year only: 1941
Varied designs printed black on eyeleted, folding, heavy orange paper sections. Opens to 6.75', 6" wide. String loop hangers at ends.
Value: $75

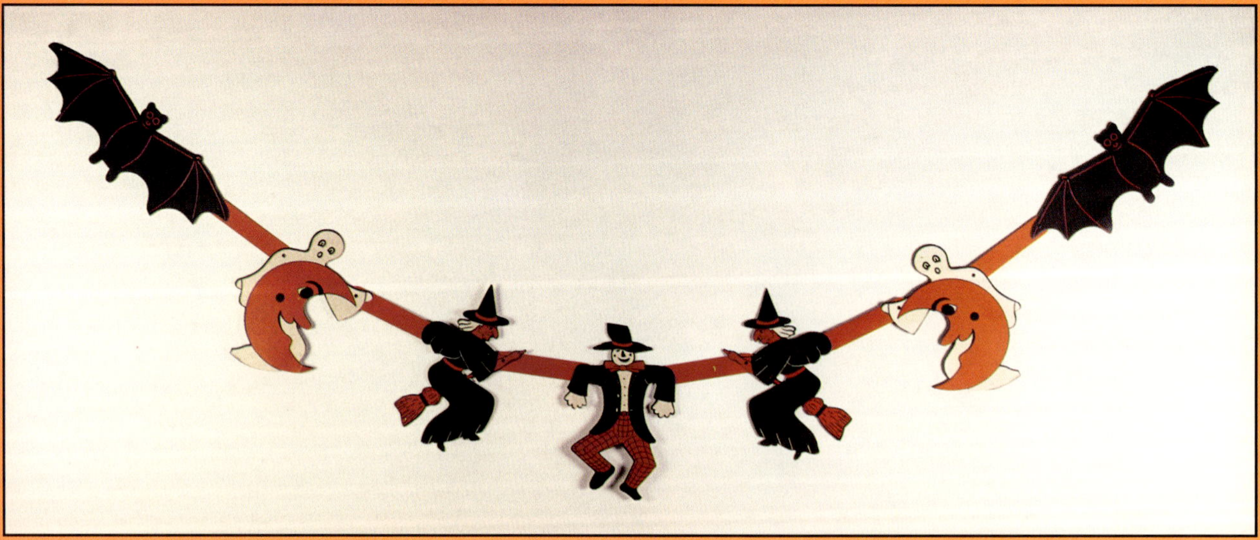

HALLOWEEN WALL STREAMER
Initial Release: 1952
Production Run: 1952 – 1959
A seven-foot banner of gay Halloween figures eyeleted together. Scarecrows, witches, bats and ghosts all combine to create Halloween party spirit. Ideal for large rooms and windows. Printed one side on heavy white stock in colors of orange and black and die-cut to shape. String loops at ends for hanging. Each banner banded.
Value: $55

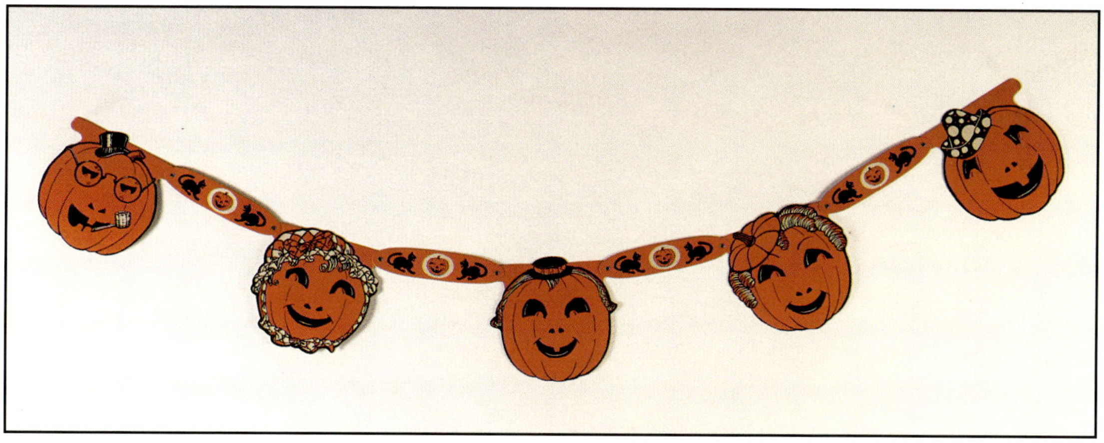

JACK-O-LANTERN BANNER
Initial Release: 1955
Production Run: 1955 – 1962
You're sure to create party spirit with these five different Jack-O-Lantern faces printed orange and black on heavy white stock and eyeleted together to form a banner 50" long. Size of each Jack-O-Lantern face about 6" x 6". One design.
Value: $55

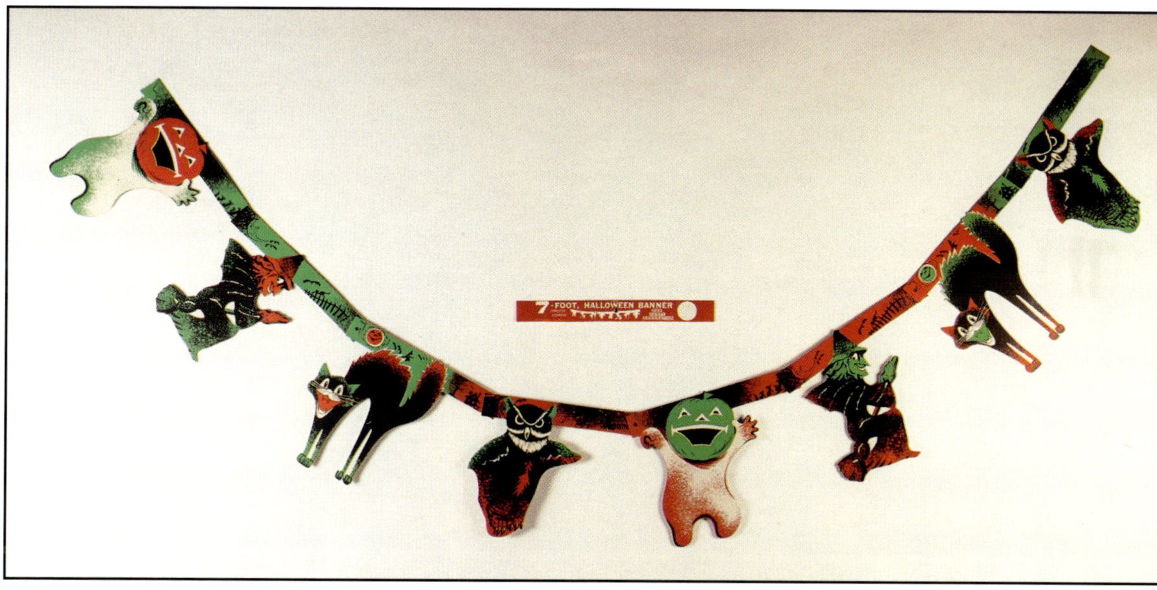

HALLOWEEN BANNER
Initial Release: 1960
Production Run: 1960 – 1963
A seven foot banner of Halloween characters eyeleted together. Ghosts, witches, cats and owls combine to create a gay Halloween party spirit. Ideal for party decorating and trimming stores. Each design printed in three colors on heavy white stock and die-cut to shape. String loops for hanging. Each banner packaged in a polyurethane bag with printed top.
Value: $60

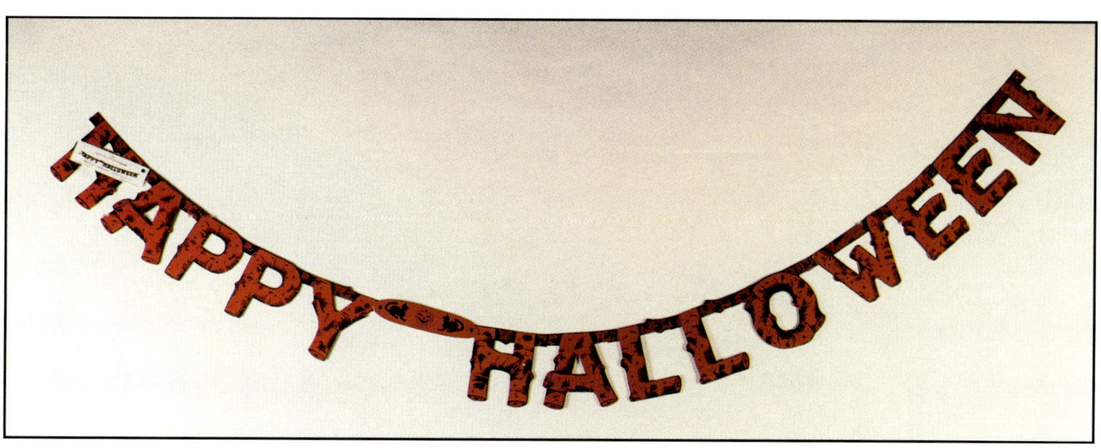

HAPPY HALLOWEEN STREAMER
Initial Release: 1960
Production Run: 1960 – 1963
An attractive streamer that will lend a gay new note to Halloween decorating. Letters printed in orange and black rustic design and die-cut to shape are eyeleted together to form a "Happy Halloween" greeting. String hangers. Size 4.5" x 6'.
Value: $45

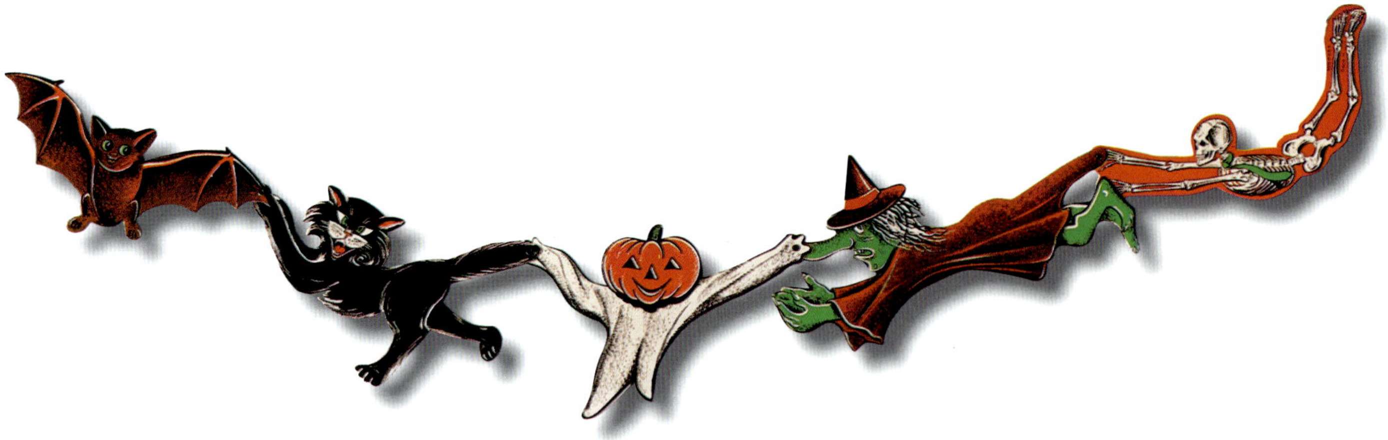

HALLOWEEN BANNER
Initial Release: 1966
Production Run: One year only: 1966
You're sure to create gay party spirit with these lively Halloween characters. Printed in bright three-color design and die-cut to shape, each piece is eyeleted together to form a 4-foot banner. Each banner is packaged in a clear poly bag with header.
Value: $45

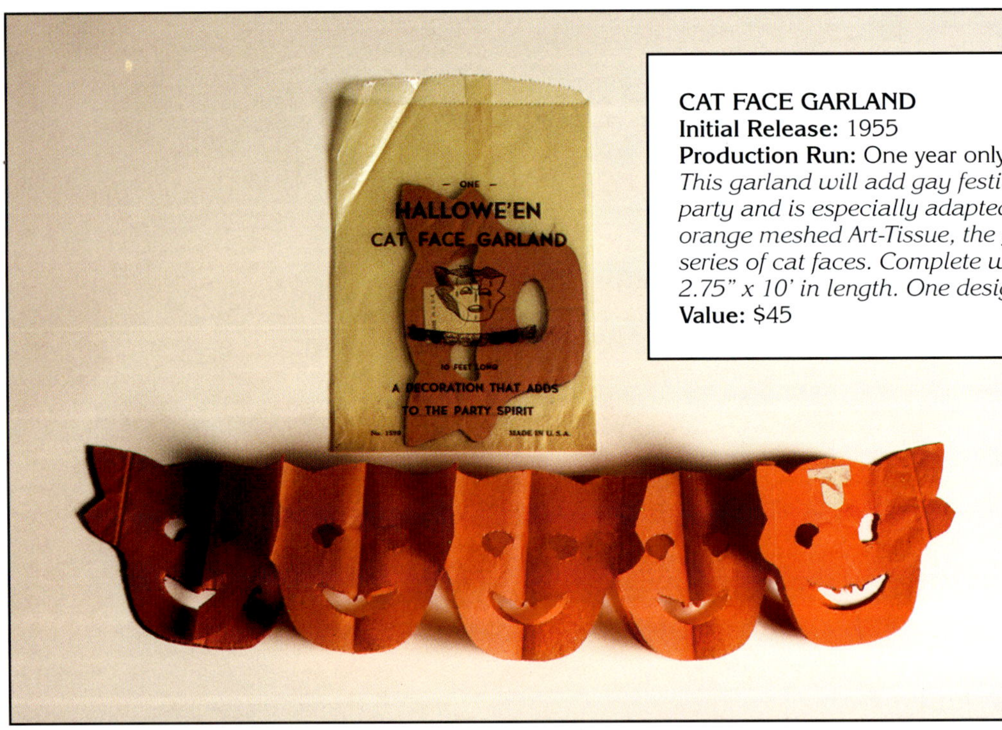

CAT FACE GARLAND
Initial Release: 1955
Production Run: One year only: 1955
This garland will add gay festive color to any Halloween party and is especially adapted to low ceilings. Die-cut from orange meshed Art-Tissue, the garland when opened forms a series of cat faces. Complete with tabs for hanging. Size 2" x 2.75" x 10' in length. One design. Packed flat for shipping.
Value: $45

Below:
SILHOUETTED WITCH BANNER
Initial Release: 1961
Production Run: One year only: 1961
Silhouetted witches die-cut from heavy stock in alternating solid colors of orange and black. Eyeleted together to form a banner 84" long. Size of each witch 10" x 14". Each banner packed in a polyurethane bag.
Value: $65

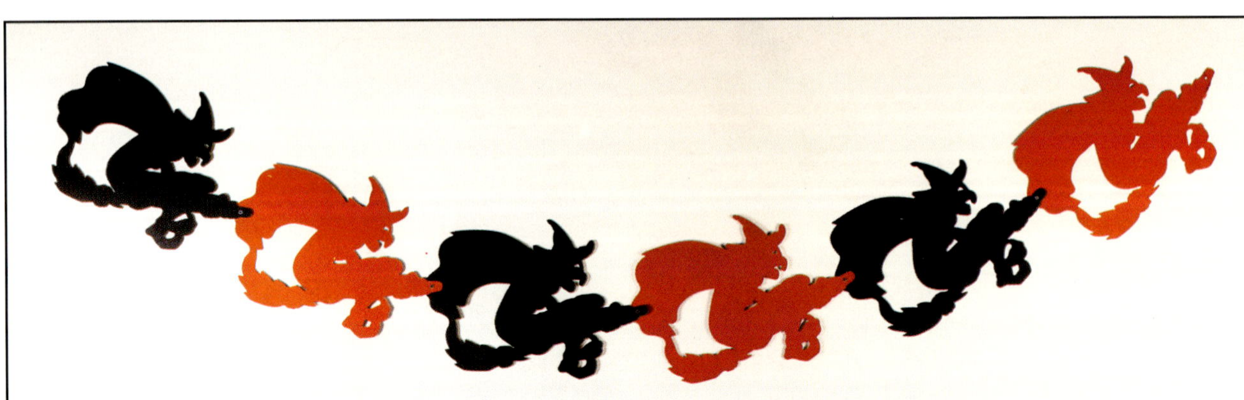

24-INCH HALL-O-LETTES

Initial Release: 1961
Production Run: 1961 - 1962
A clever assortment of ten Halloween faces with yellow 24" sunburst. Faces approximately 10" x 11.5" are printed in colors of orange and black. Packed equally assorted designs.
*The ten faces were first introduced by Beistle in 1948 as Halloween Masks. They had a long and healthy production run of 14 years. Showing seven of the ten faces here.
Value: $45 each

(Continued on following page)

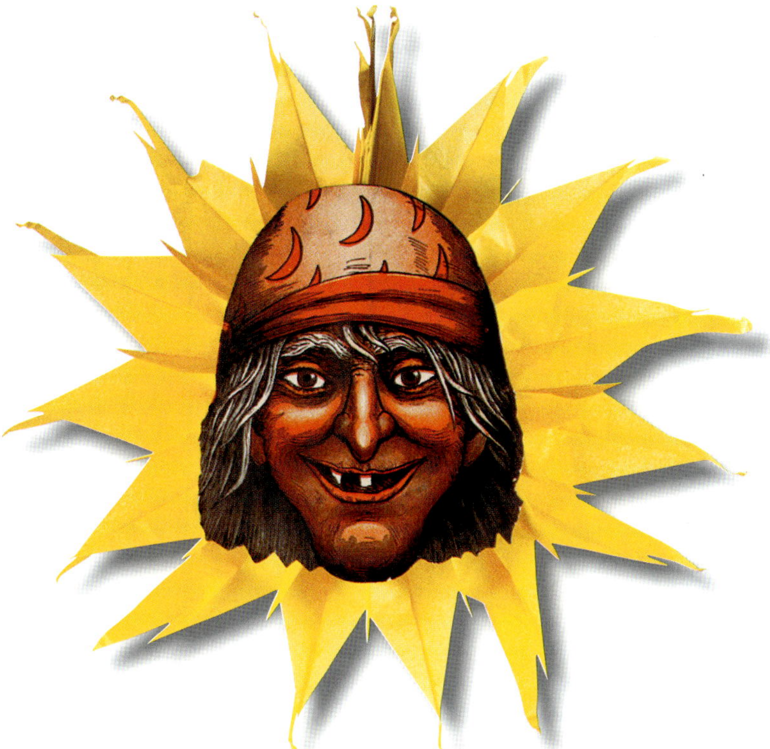

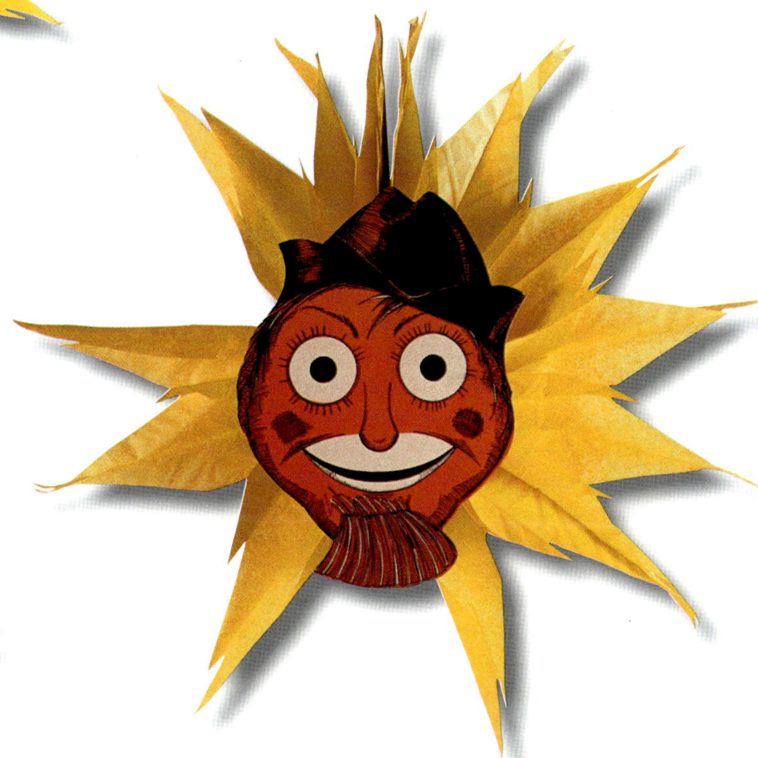

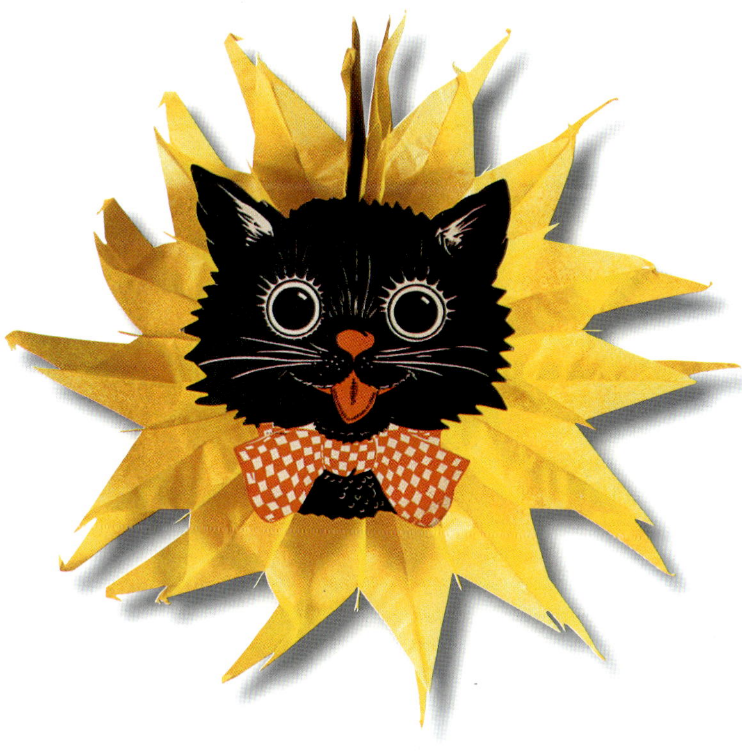

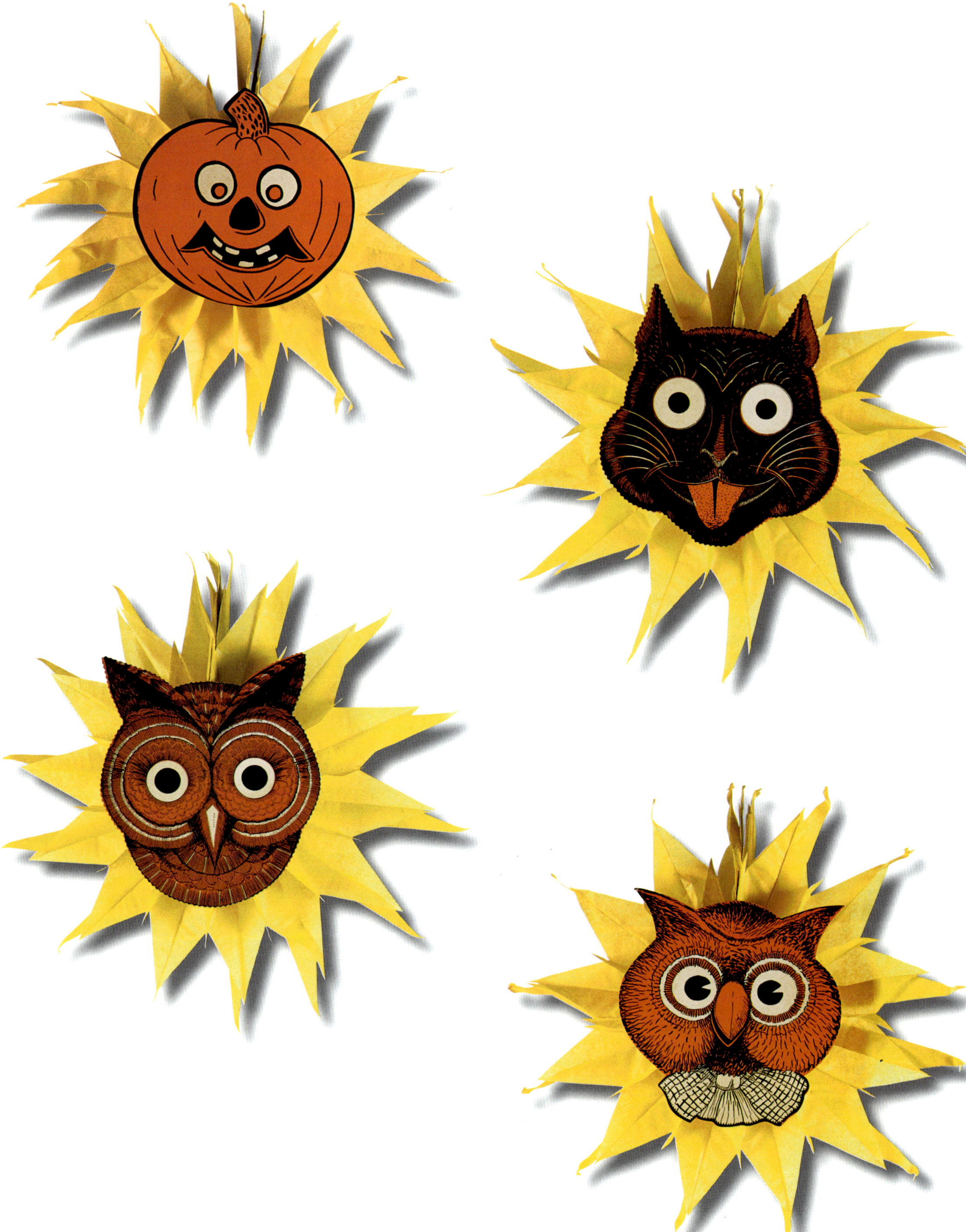

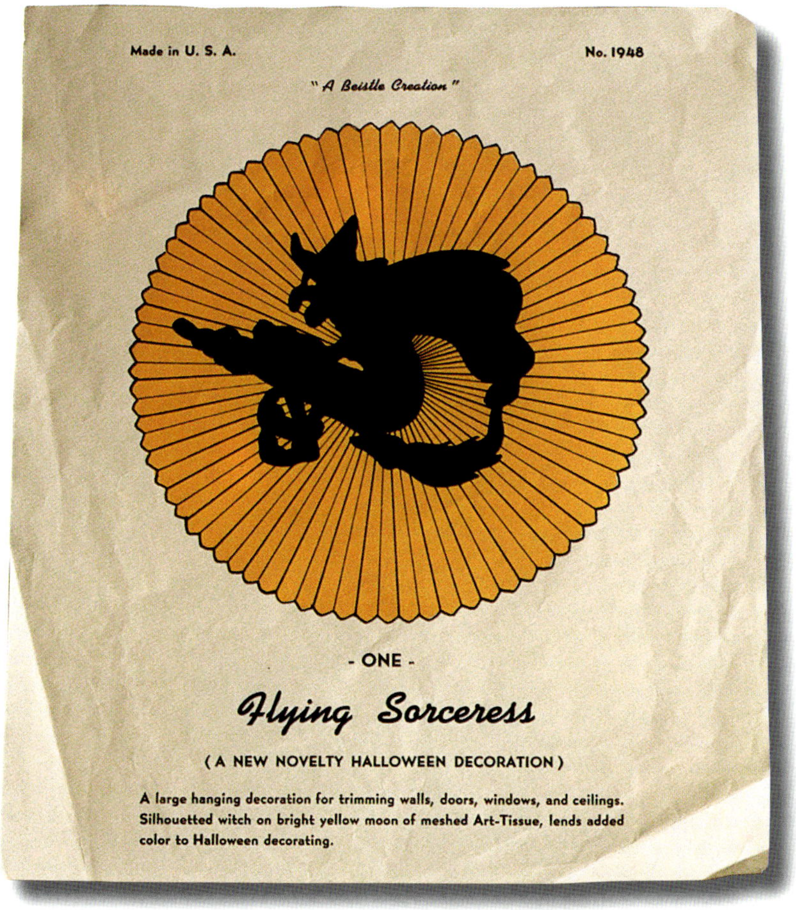

FLYING SORCERCESS
Initial Release: 1960
Production Run: 1960 – 1962
New idea lends added color to Halloween decorating. A Halloween witch die-cut from heavy black stock silhouetted on bright yellow moon of meshed Art-Tissue. Size 17". One design. Packed folded flat each in a polyurethane bag.
*The cover sheet included in the decoration's poly bag.
Value: $55

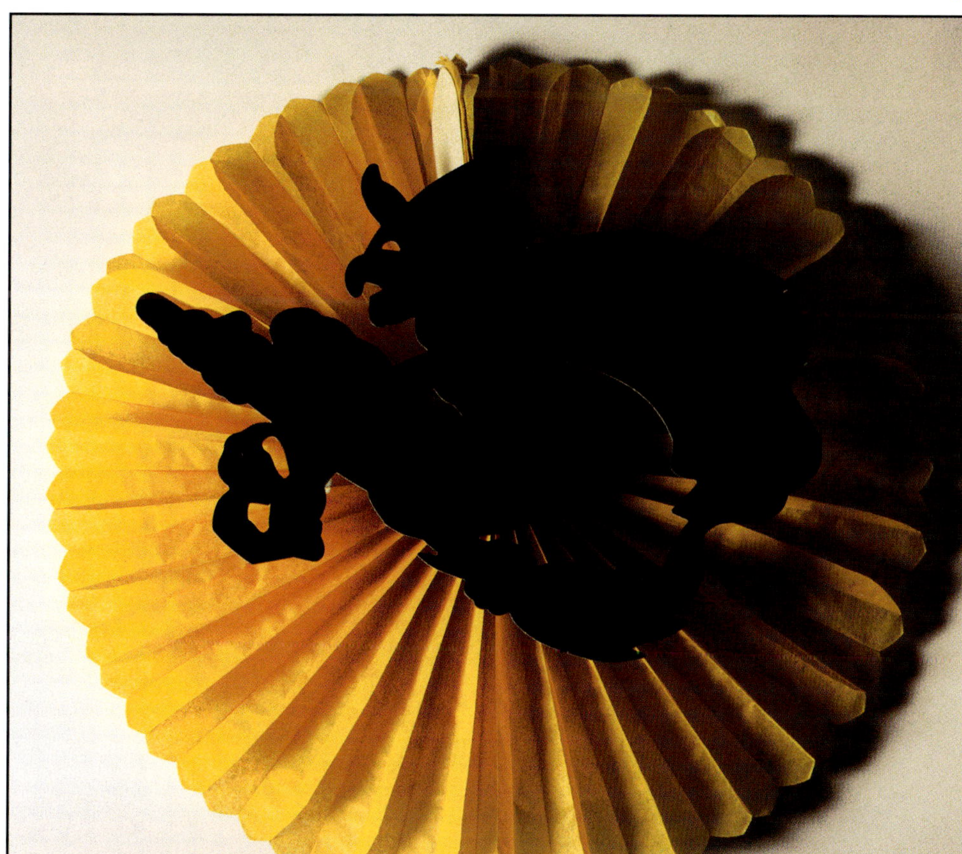

ROLY POLY
Initial Release: 1929
Production Run: 1929 – 1933
Assorted four designs, front and back of figures printed on cardboard stock with a 6.5" diameter heavy honeycomb tissue ball bottom, total height 11".
*Once again, the Beistle artistry at its best. Attention to detail was their trademark and it comes to the fore with these wonderful ephemeral pieces.
*Showing both front and back of each Roly Poly.
Value: $115 each

(Continued through page 17)

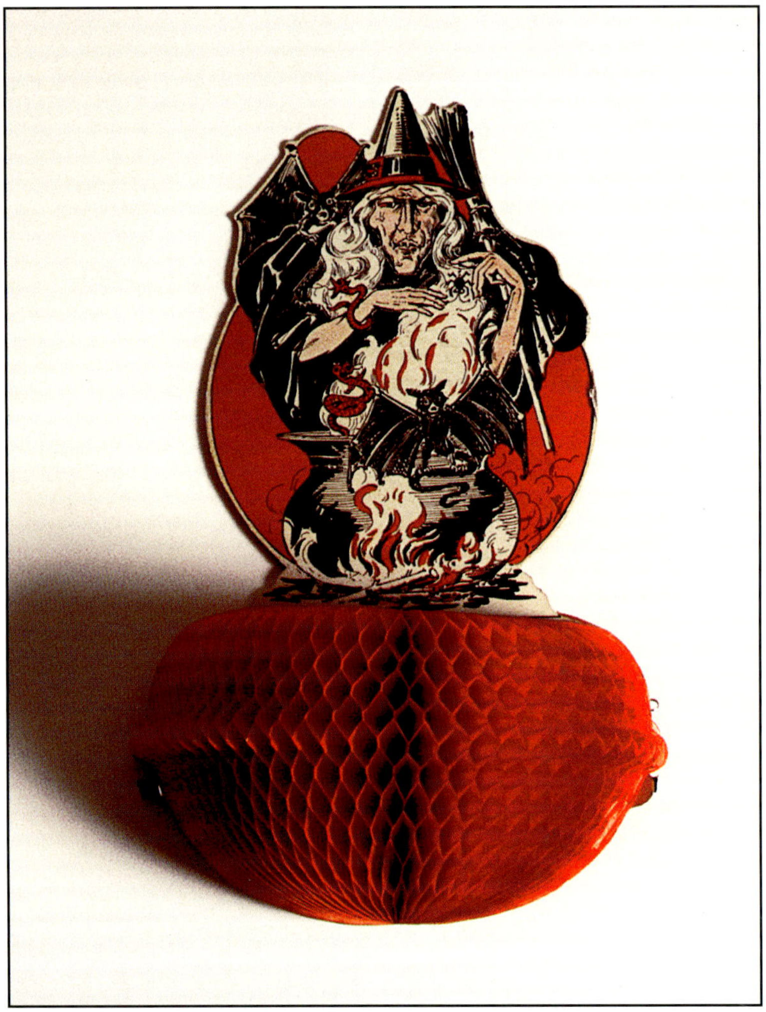

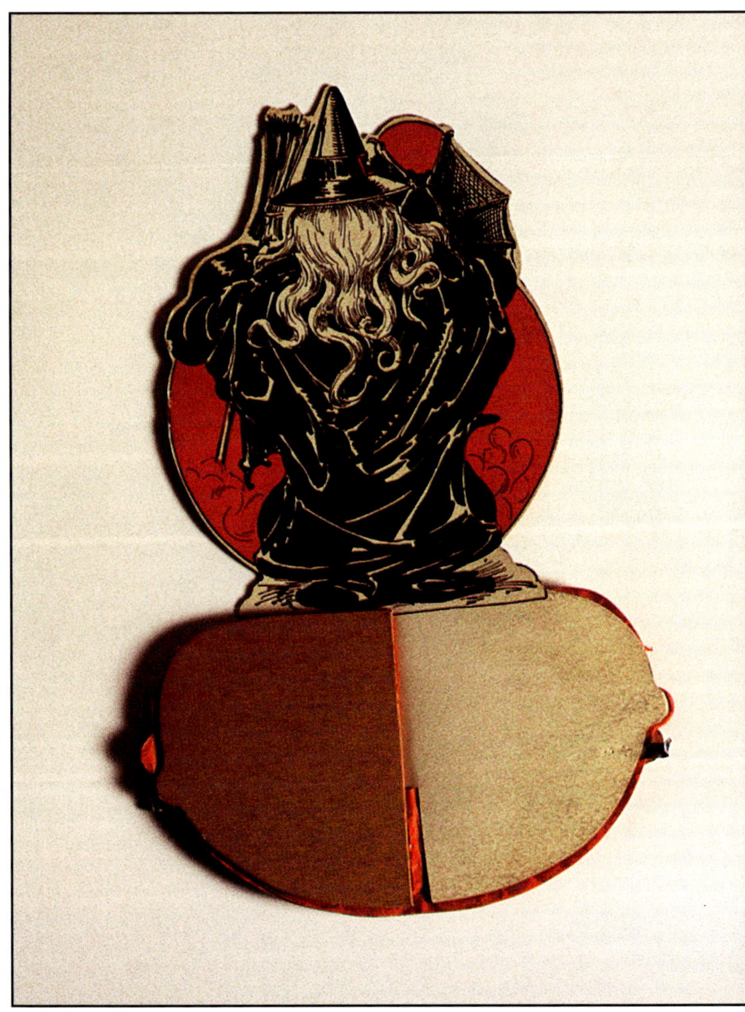

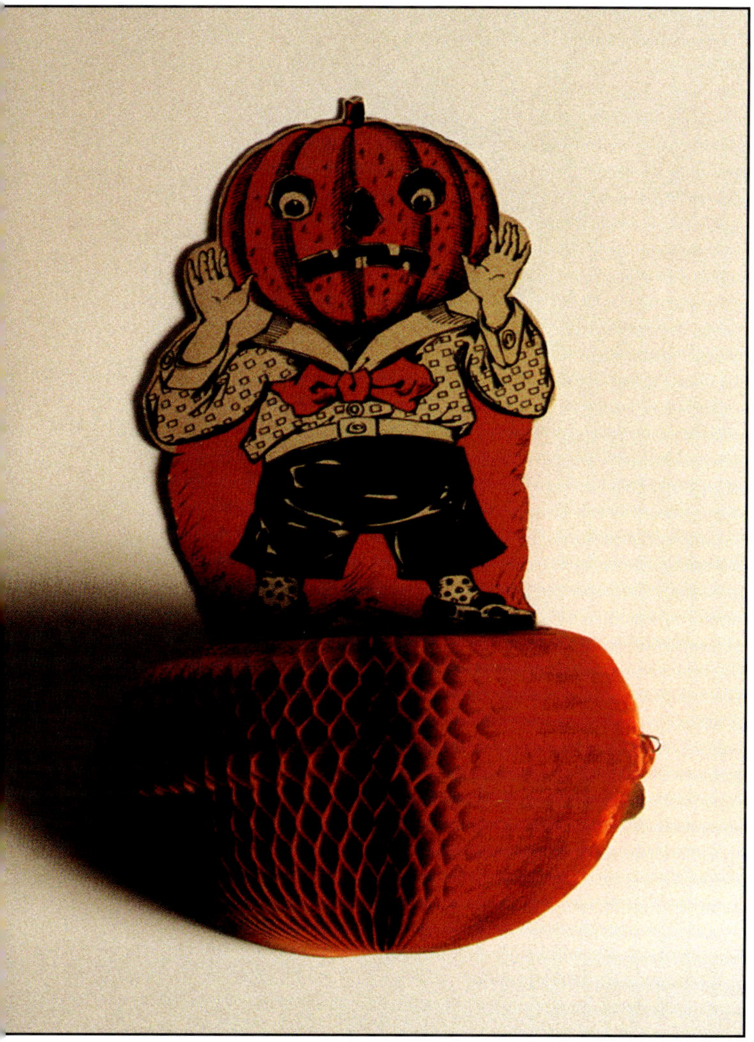

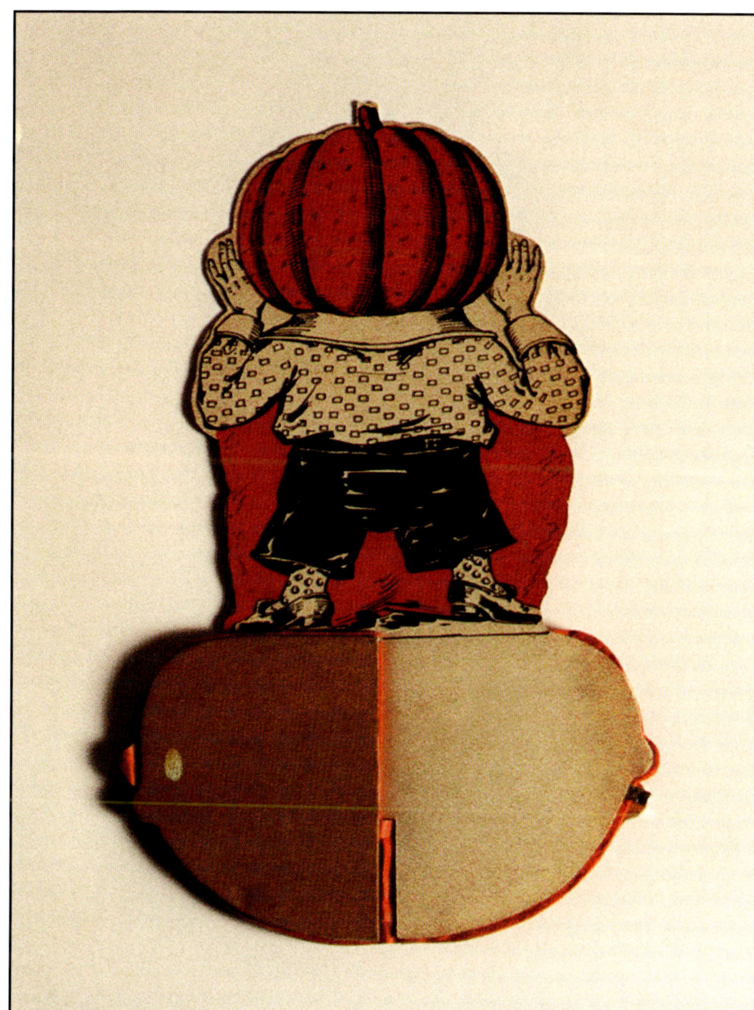

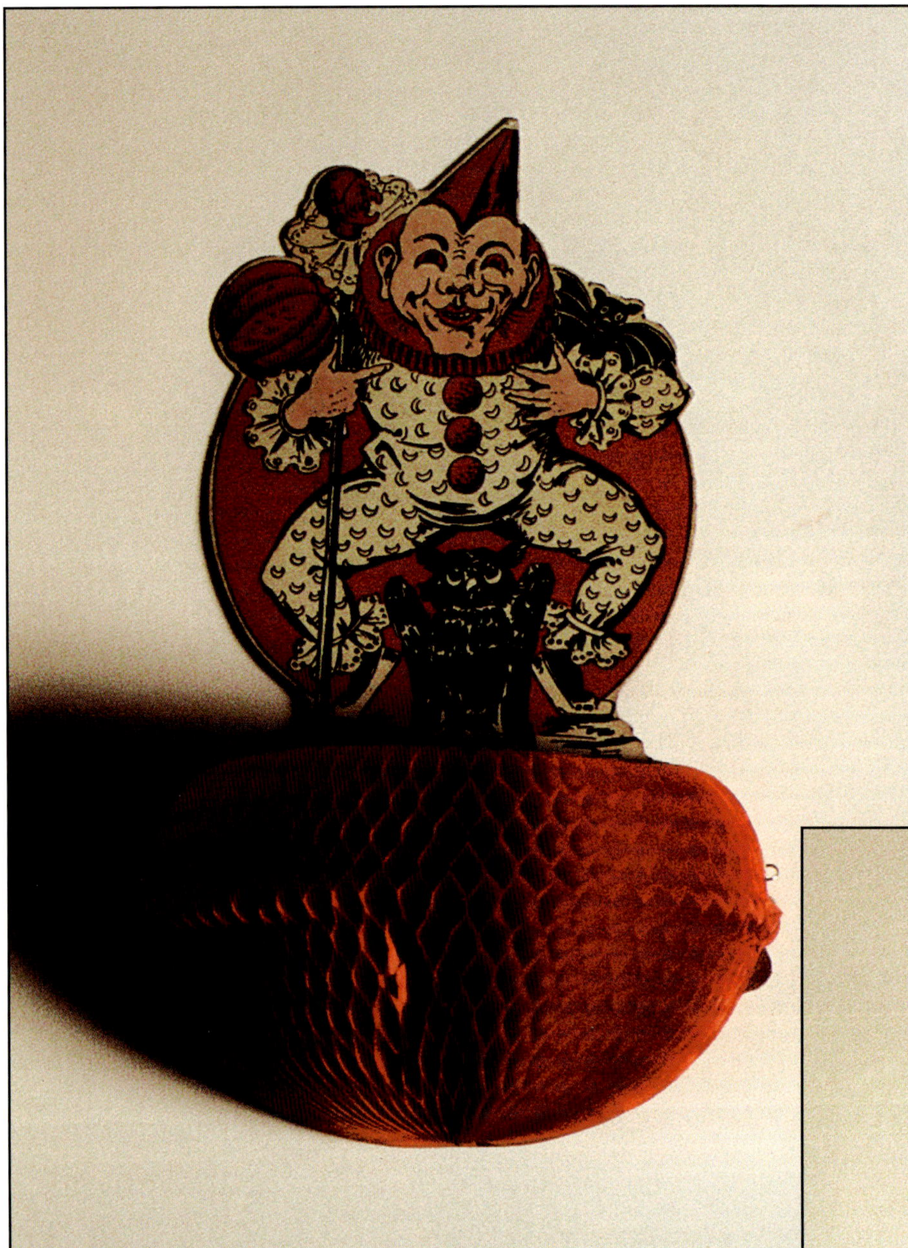

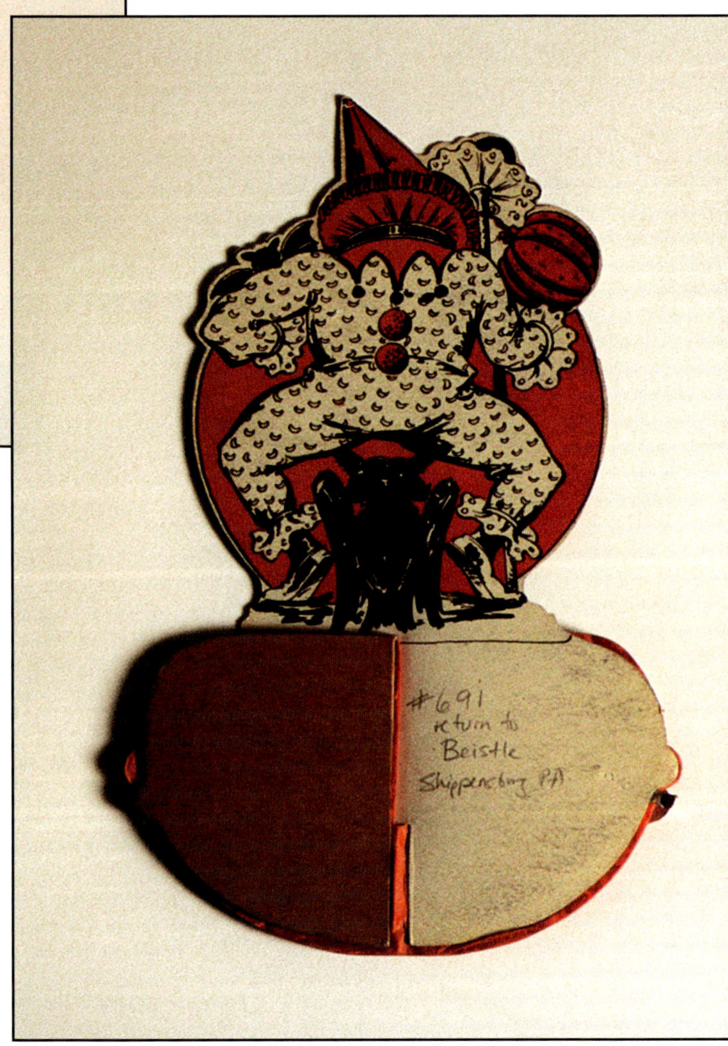
#691
return to
Beistle
Shippensburg PA

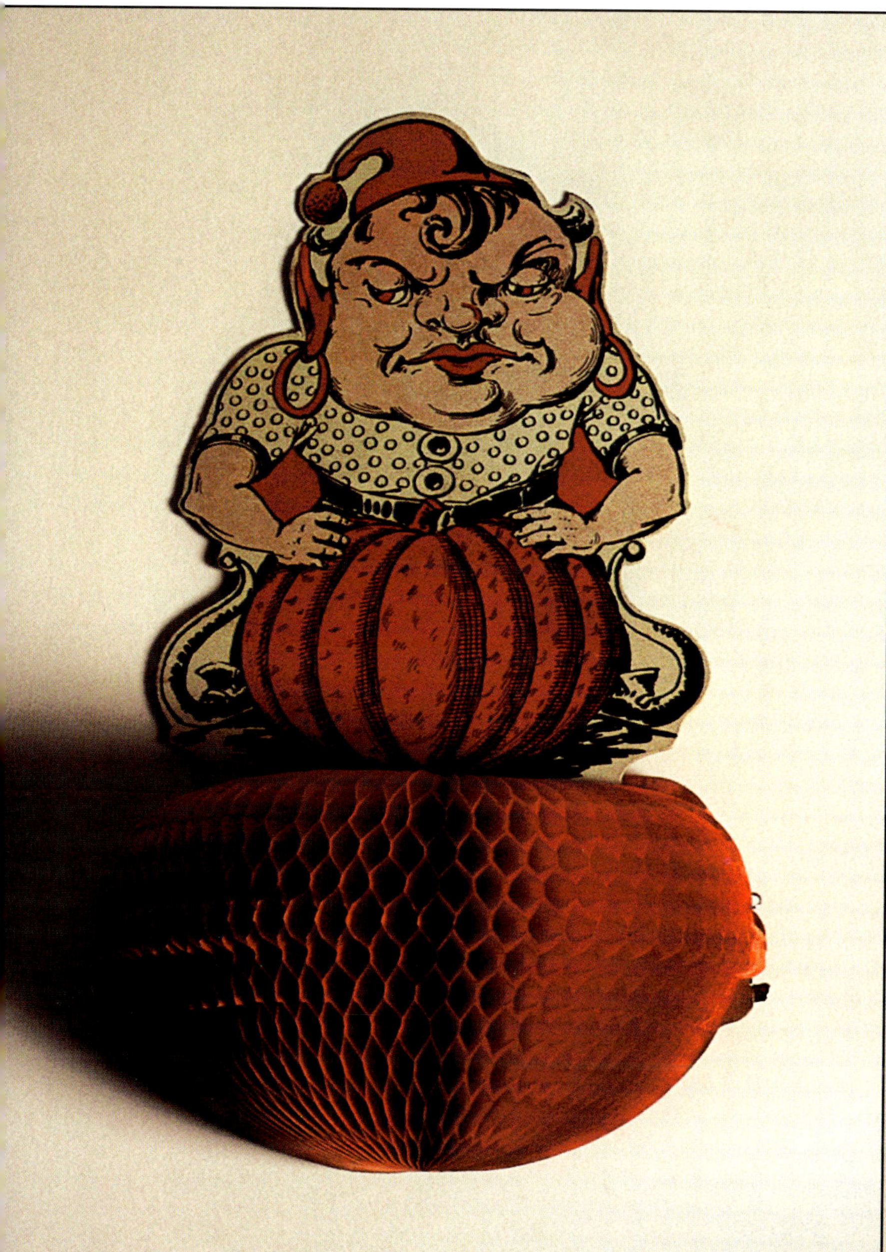

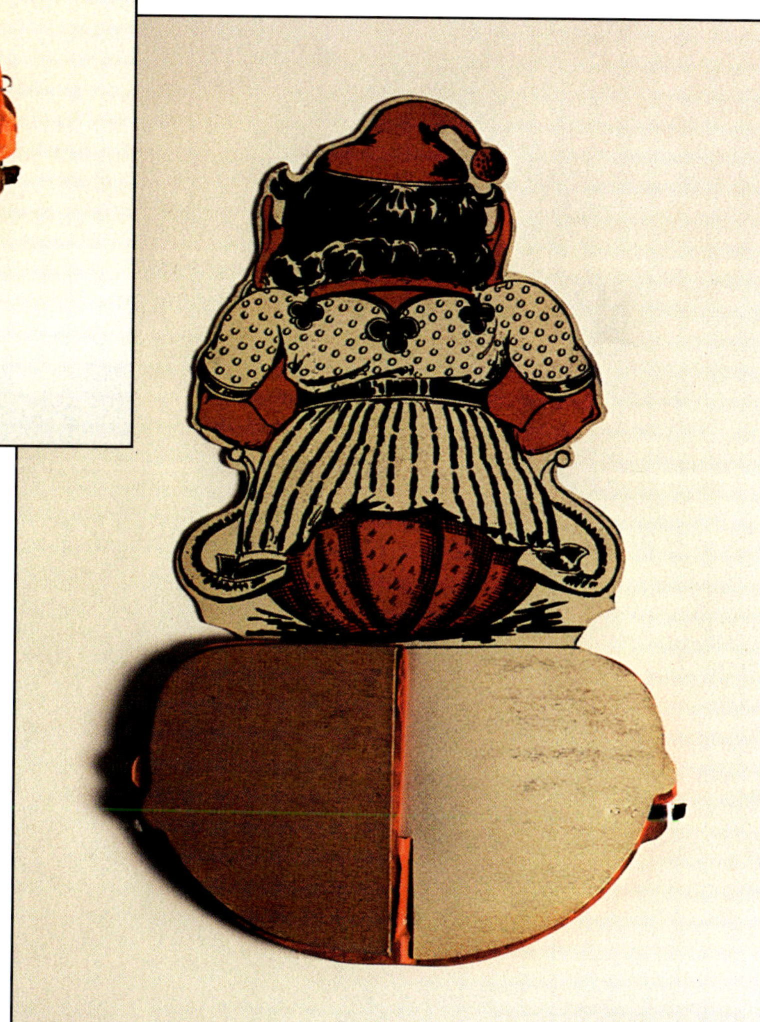

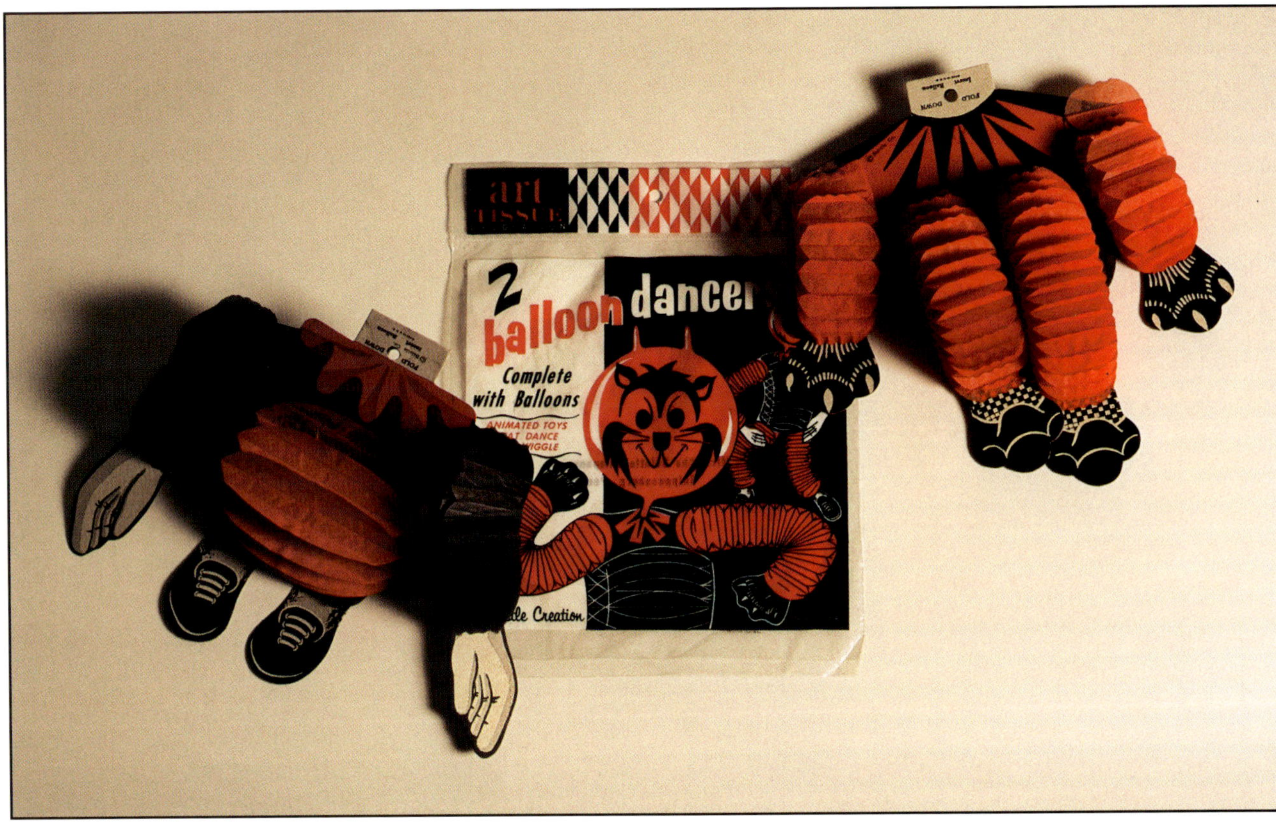

BALLOON DANCERS
Initial Release: 1964
Production Run: 1964 – 1969
Here's a real action novelty to delight children and adults as well. Bodies, arms and legs die-cut from bright colored orange and black meshed Art-Tissue. Cat and Jack-O-Lantern face designs are printed in black on orange colored balloons. Size 6.5" x 24". Packed two designs with balloons in a printed poly bag with header. Bodies completely assembled with directions for inflating and attaching balloons.
Value: $25 each

TOM-CAT
Initial Release: 1966
Production Run: 1966 – 1973
This jovial cat will lend a note of revelry and merriment to party decorating. Insert face and bow tie printed in two-color design and die-cut to shape. Black Art-Tissue body opens half-round with self-backing easel. A delightful new decoration or table centerpiece. Size 9.75" x 15". One design. Each packed in a printed poly bag with header.
Value: $35

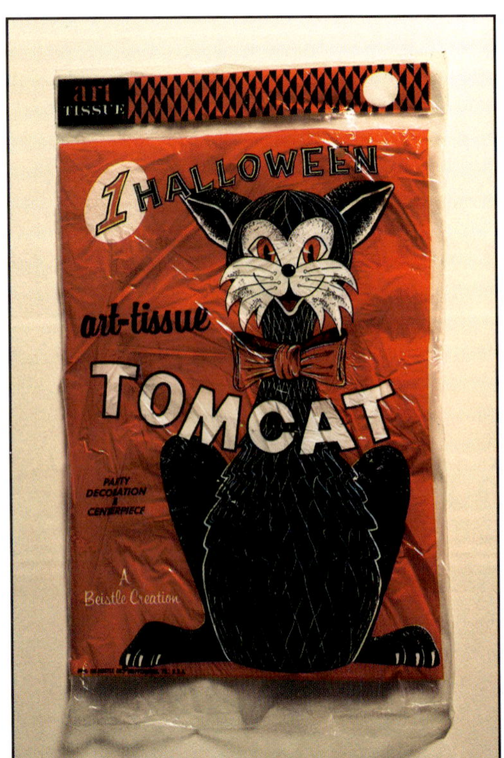

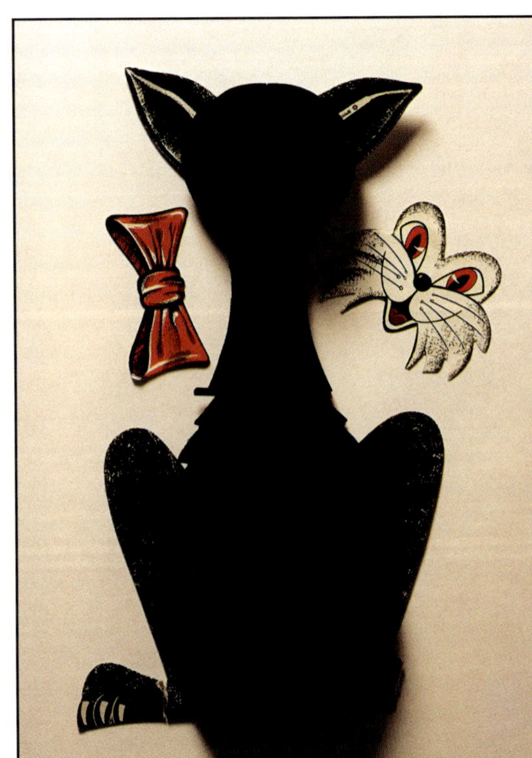

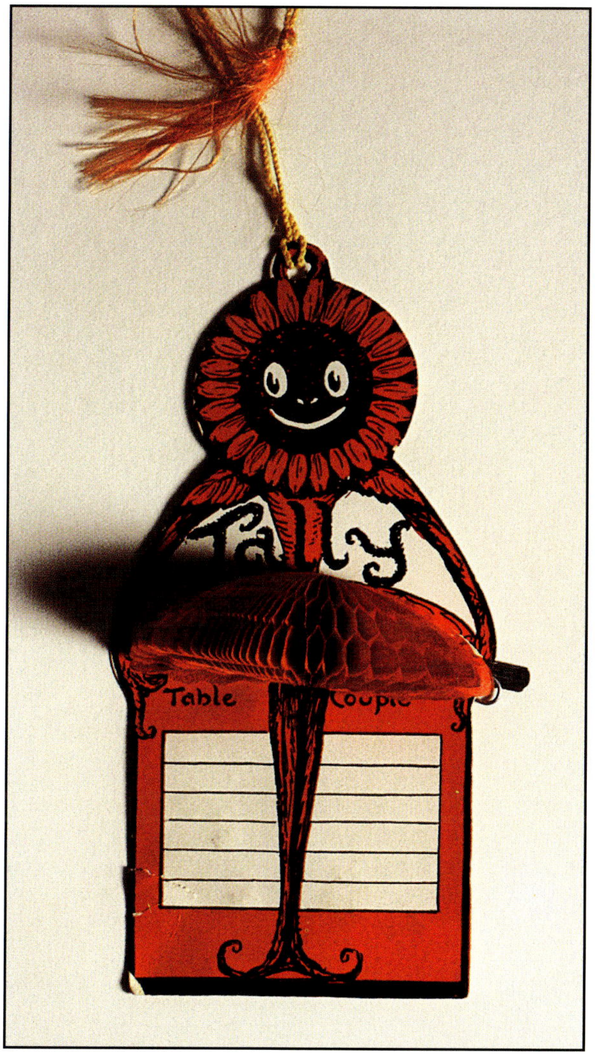

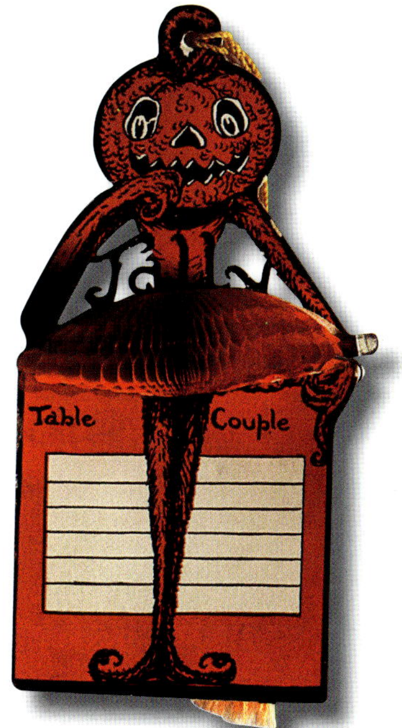

TALLY AND SCORE CARD SETS
Initial Release: 1929
Production Run: 1929 – 1932
Assorted two designs, size 2.5" x 5.5", printed on white stock with a 2.75" novelty orange honeycomb tissue skirt. Each with an orange cord and silk tassel. "Bridge" and "Five Hundred" scores printed on back.
*For something as commonplace as a bridge tally (the game was at its height of popularity from the 1930s through the 1950s), the Beistle Company artists really came through with many clever and unique ideas for their scorecards. When I commented on the variety offered to the public, Tricia Lacy, the Beistle Company president, exclaimed, "Grand-mom and Grand-pop loved their bridge!"
Value: $175 each

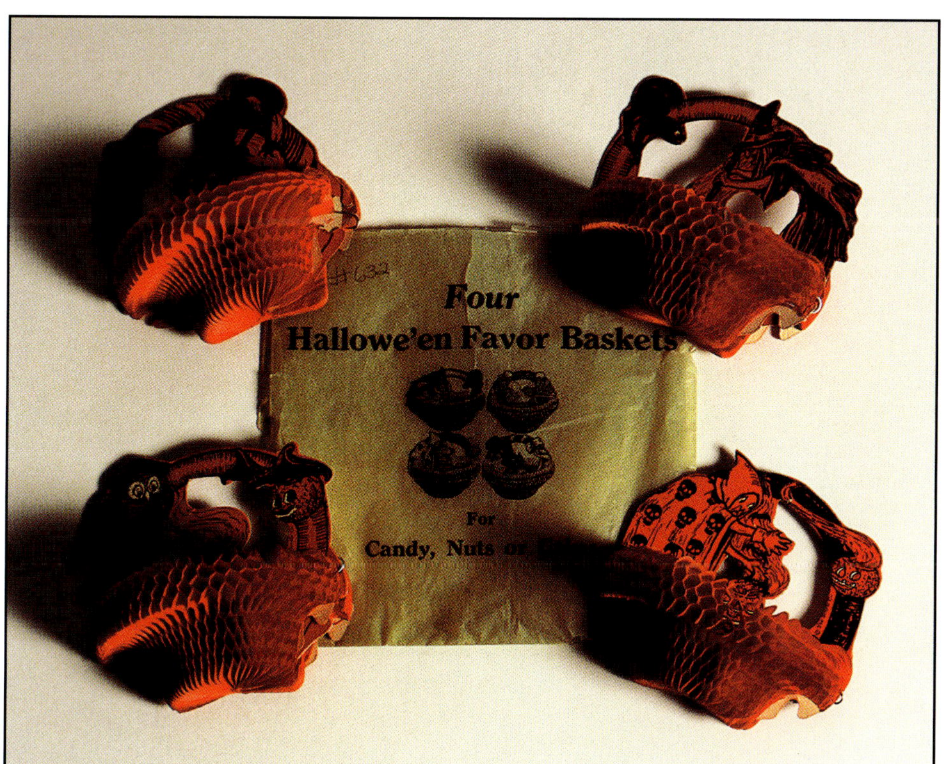

HALLOWEEN FAVOR BASKETS
Initial Release: 1928
Production Run: 1928 – 1932*
Assorted 3 designs, size 4" diameter, 3" high. Design printed on both sides on cardboard, die-cut and with orange honeycomb tissue basket attached to bottom. Packed 3 in printed transparent bag.
*This set is a true puzzlement! I found the set of three advertised in the Beistle Company sales catalogues beginning with 1928 and ending in 1932 under Stock Number 631. In the five catalogues, the only two designs shown are the black cat and the ghoul. I can only guess which one (the witch or the owl?) was the third to complete this set. In my latest venture of uncovering Halloween treasures from the Beistle archives, I came upon this set of four, marked Stock Number 632. I can't find this group advertised in any of their sales catalogues and yet I know these were distributed since I've seen this set of four in other collector's books.
Value: $135 each

TWO-COLOR ART-TISSUE ACORN
Initial Release: 1941
Production Run: 1941 – 1947
Something new in Art-Tissue decoration for Halloween and the Autumn season. Acorn shaped, the top is black, the bottom orange tissue. Folds flat.
*Artist's prototype of an acorn with black top, yellow bottom. This particular model was never marketed to the public.
Value: $15

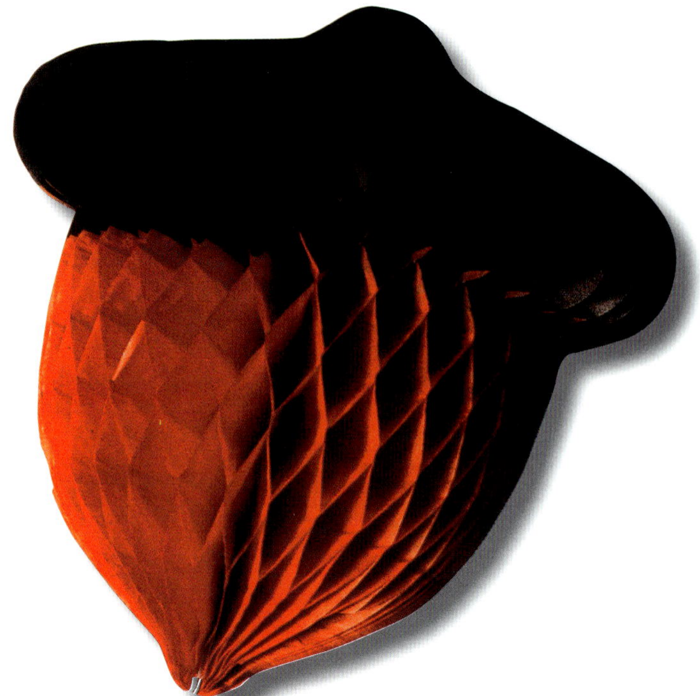

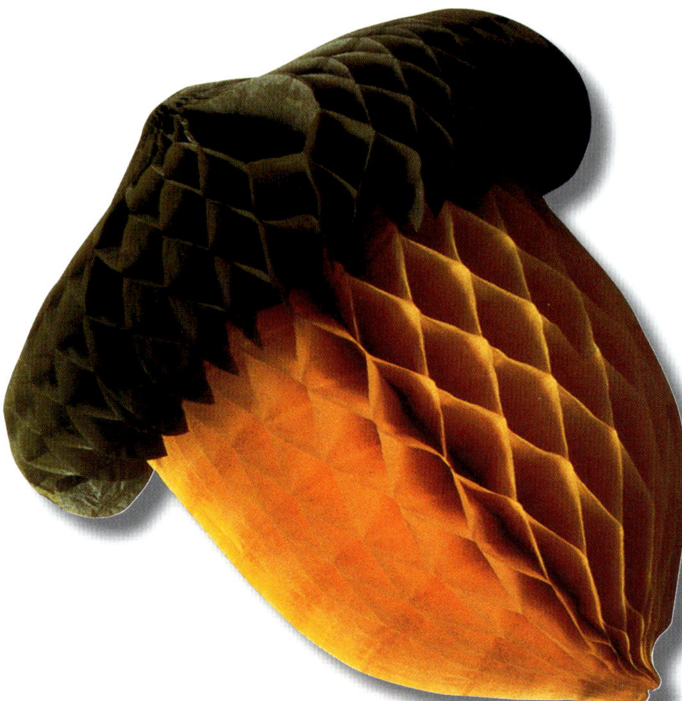

CAT PLACE-MATES
Initial Release: 1964
Production Run: 1964 – 1968
A new table favor that will lend a cheerful note to festive party decorating. Miniature black cats with body of finely meshed black Art-Tissue open full-round. Completely assembled with standing base and ribbon printed and die-cut from quality white stock. Size 2.5" high. Packed six pieces, one design, in a printed poly bag with header.
Value: $10 each

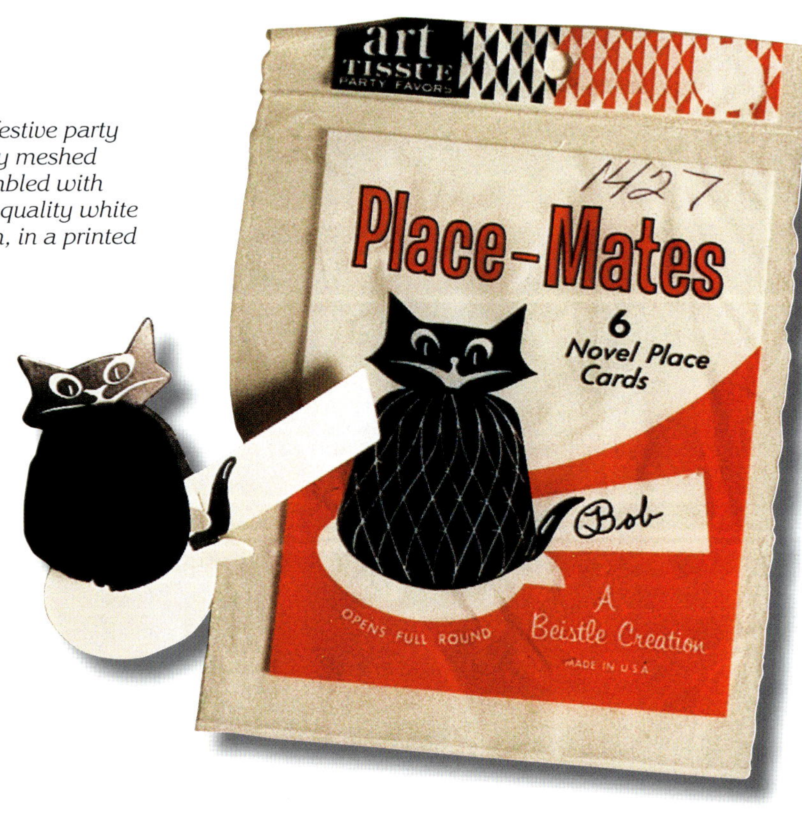

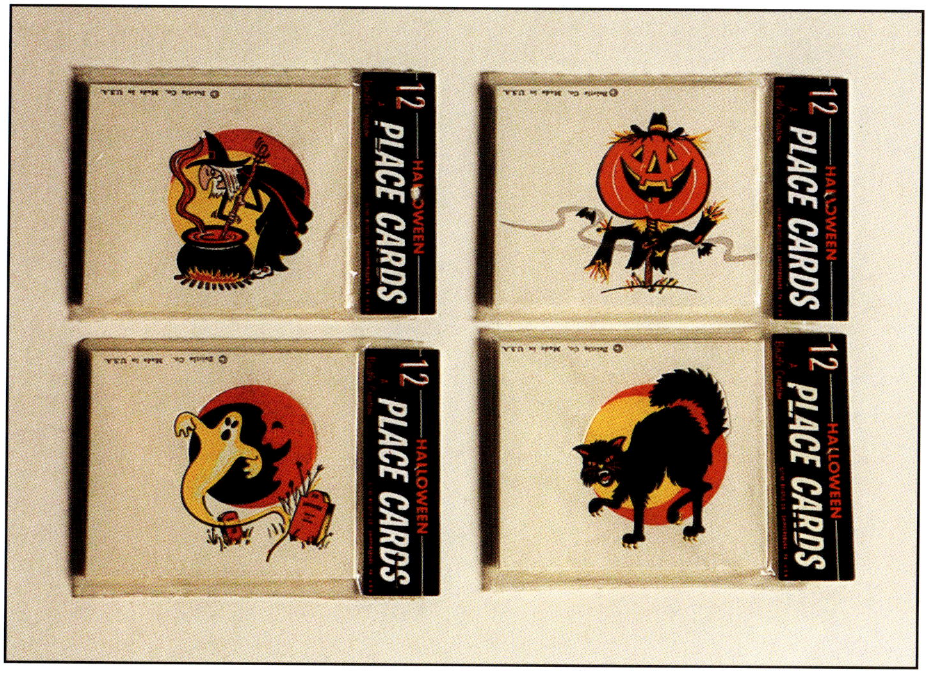

HALLOWEEN PLACE CARDS

Initial Release: 1969
Production Run: 1969 – 1973
Popular-priced table favors for individual party place settings printed in traditional Halloween designs. Colorful prints in four designs on quality card stock, creased and die-cut to shape. Size 2.5" x 3.5". Packed equally assorted twelve pieces in a clear poly bag with header.
Value: $5 a piece

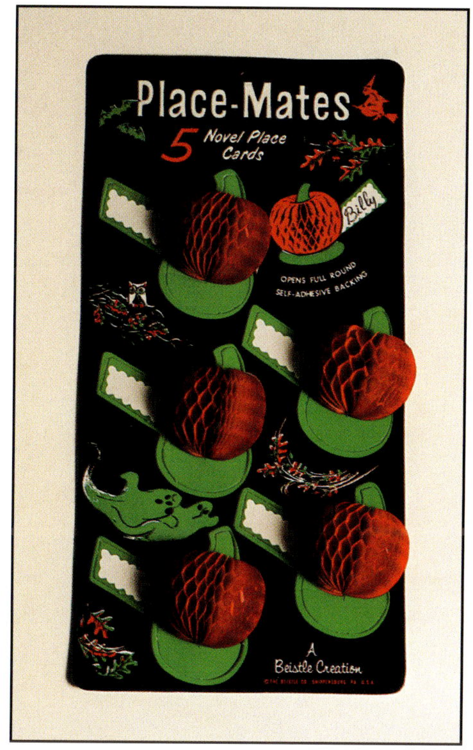

PUMPKIN PLACE-MATES

Initial Release: 1969
Production Run: 1969 – 1970
These novel table favors will add gay color and décor to any Halloween or fall season party. Miniature pumpkins in bright colored, finely meshed orange Art-Tissue opens all around. Completely assembled with standing base and die-cut ribbon. Size 2.25" high. Five pieces carded in a crystal-clear poly-shrink pack.
Value: $5 each

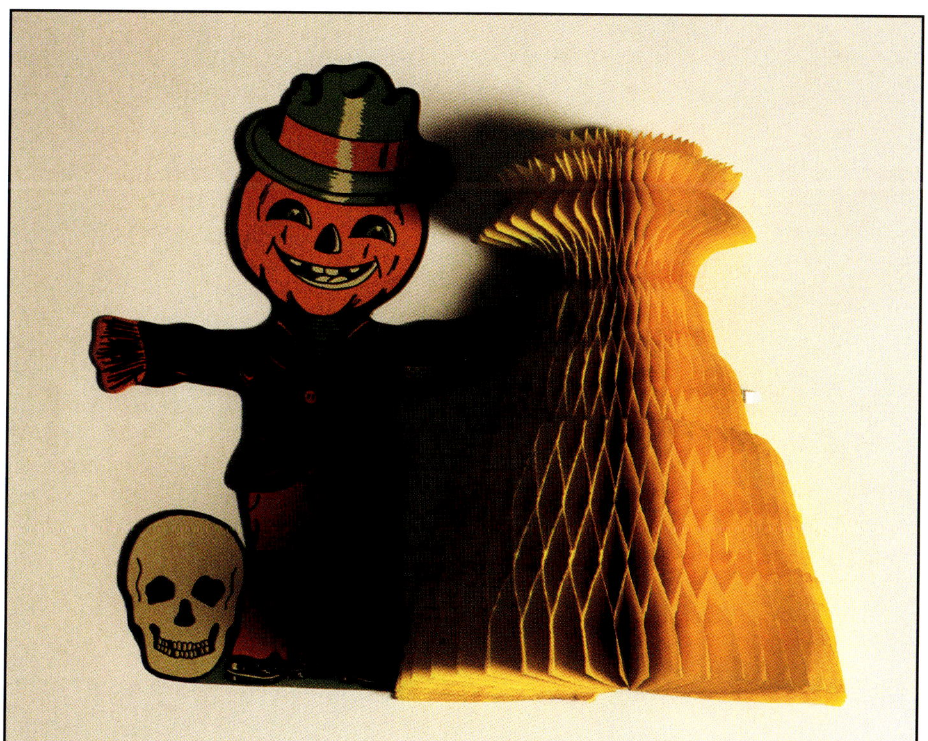

CORN SHOCK CENTERPIECE

Initial Release: 1956
Production Run: One year only: 1956
A popular priced Halloween centerpiece. Comical scarecrow and skull printed two sides in three colors on heavy card stock, and die-cut to shape. Corn shock of old gold meshed Art-Tissue opens full-round to complete the centerpiece and form a standing base. Approximately 10.5" x 12" in size. One design. Packs folded flat.
Value: $35

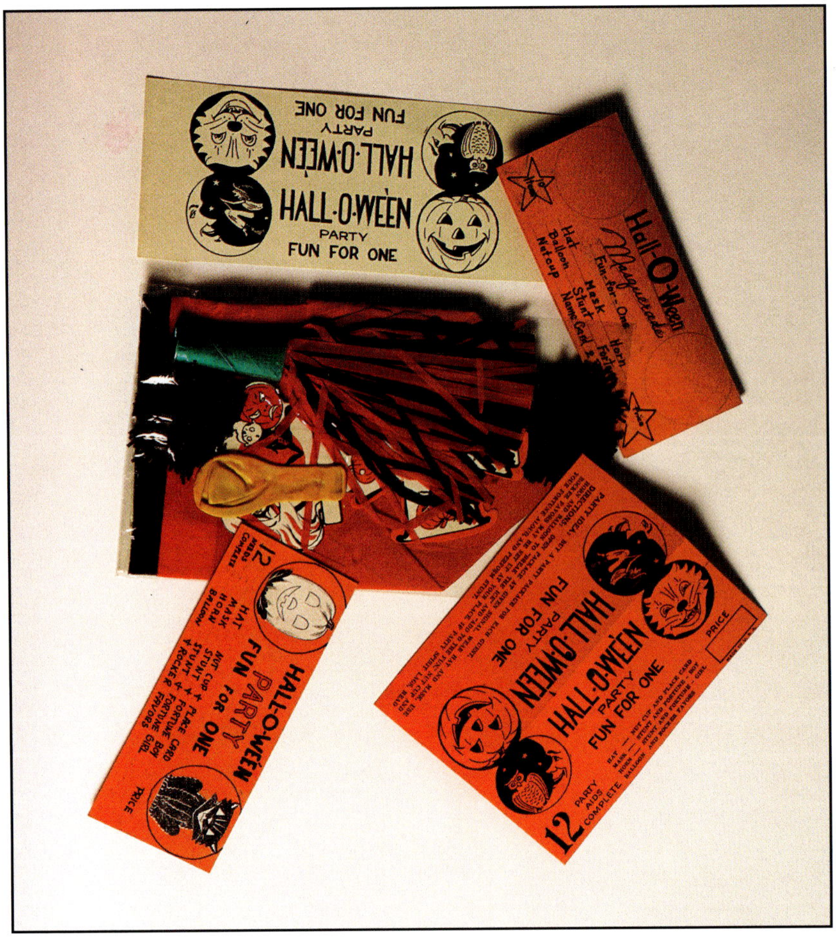

HALLOWEEN PARTY FUN-FOR-ONE

Initial Release: 1955
Production Run: 1955 – 1963
Popular new party package makes party planning easy. Your guests are sure to have a swell time and your Halloween party will be a real success with the help of these gay party packs. Each bag contains a colorful hat, horn, mask, and balloon, as well as nut cup, place card, rocker favors, and stunts and fortunes for each person. An inexpensive way to "break the ice," create a gay Halloween spirit, and assure everyone a good time and lots of fun.
*Here is the package with several prototypes of the header. The second photo displays the contents of each package. What a nifty idea!
Value: $45 for complete packaged set

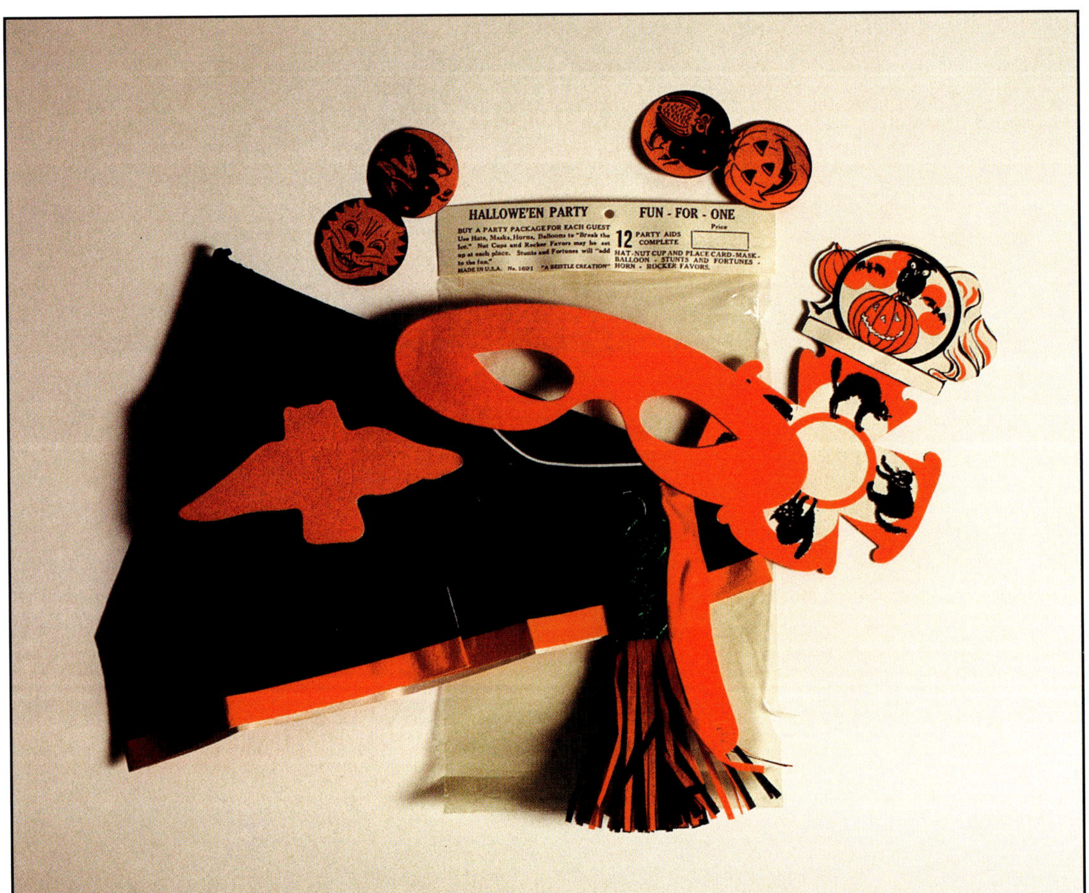

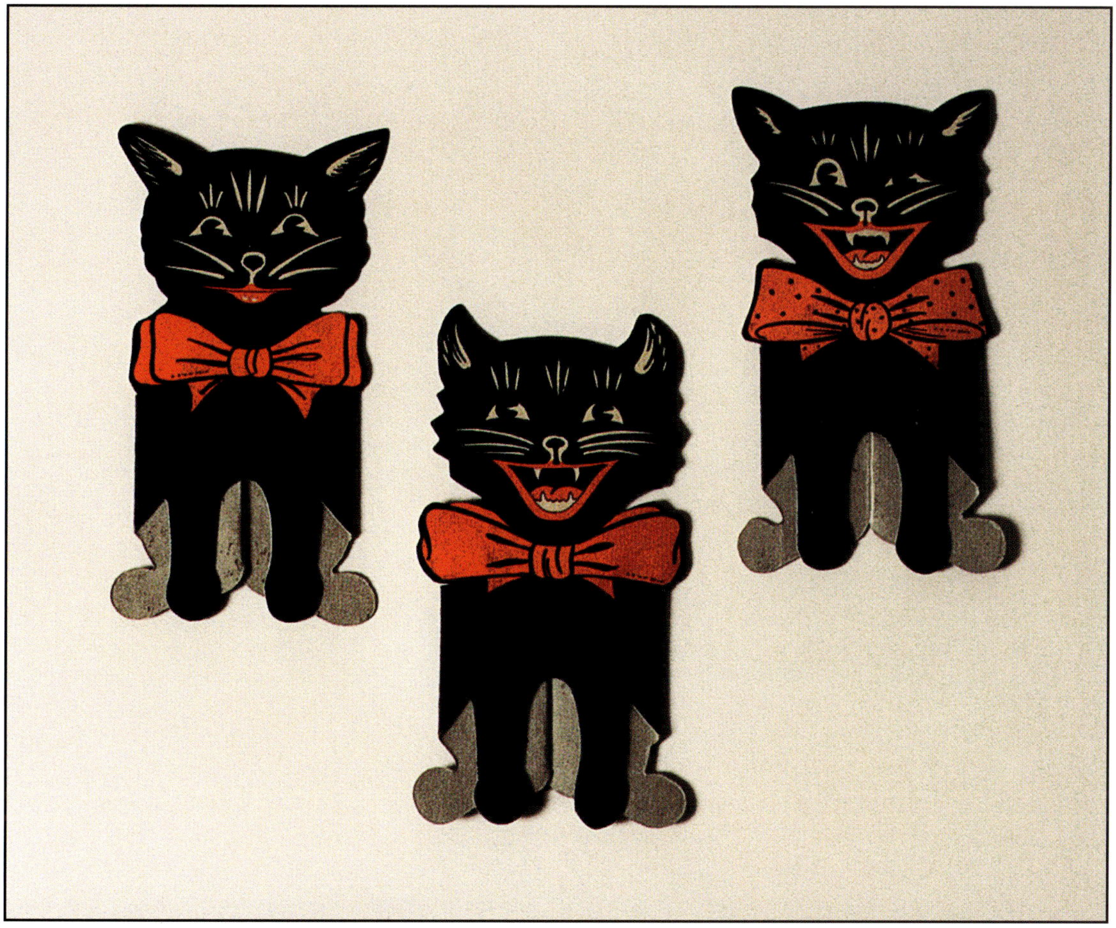

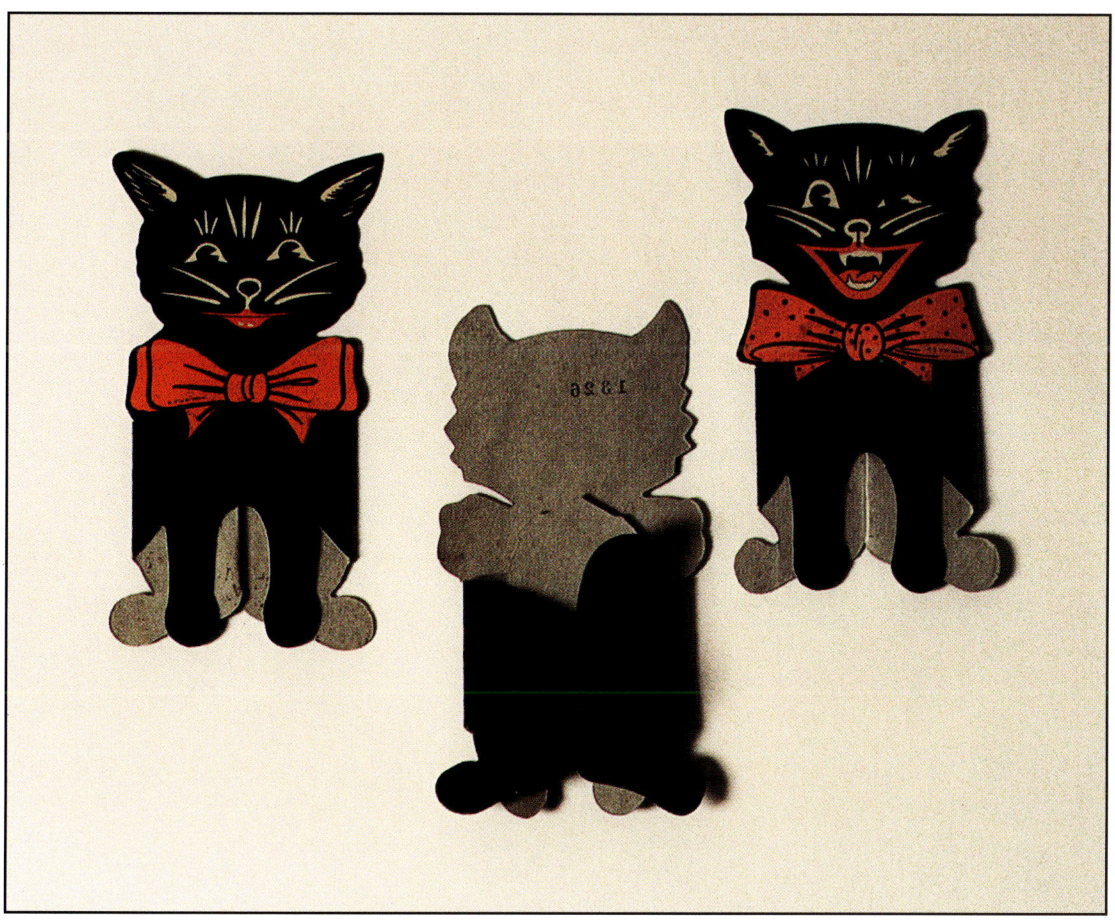

SITTING CAT NUT CUP
Initial Release: 1952
Production Run:
1952 – 1959
A swell party favor. Six designs of laughing cats, 5.5" tall. Printed orange and black on white stock. Blank space on the bows for name, and small cup for candy, nuts, etc. Fold flat for packing and shipping.
*I could only find three examples of these nut cups in the Beistle archives. The second photo, middle cat, shows the backside of the nut cup.
Value: $15 each

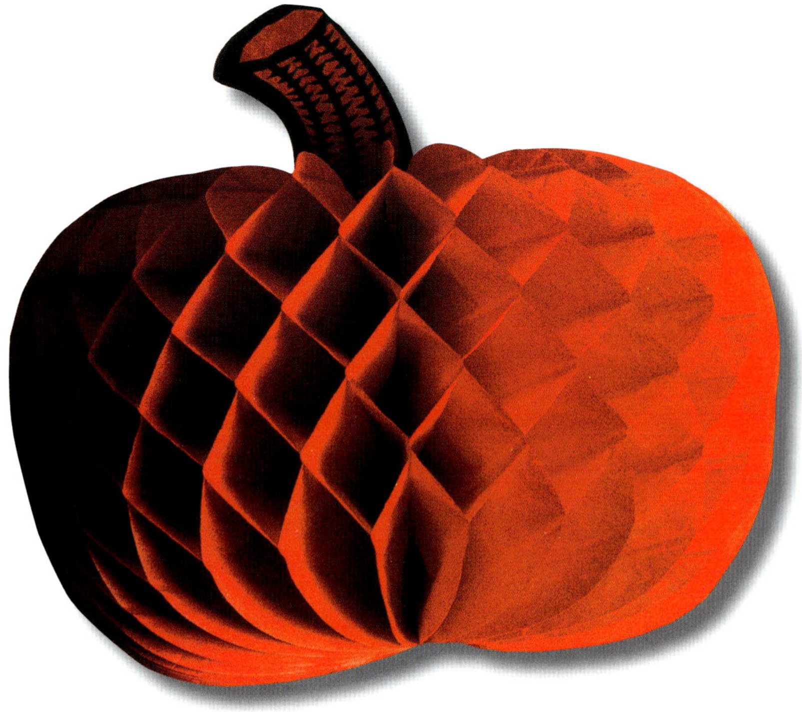

ART-TISSUE PUMPKINS
Initial Release: 1969
Production Run: 1969 – 1985+
Sensational Halloween decoration for window trims, table favors and centerpieces. Made of bright orange Art-Tissue with printed stems. Folds flat for shipping and is easily opened and displayed.
*Three varied views of this pumpkin – one ready for display, the illustrated display card, and an artist's model using white honeycomb tissue paper in place of the orange. Martha Stewart would have loved the white pumpkins!
*Also included in this lot is the artist's sketch of display card.
Value: $12 – $15 range

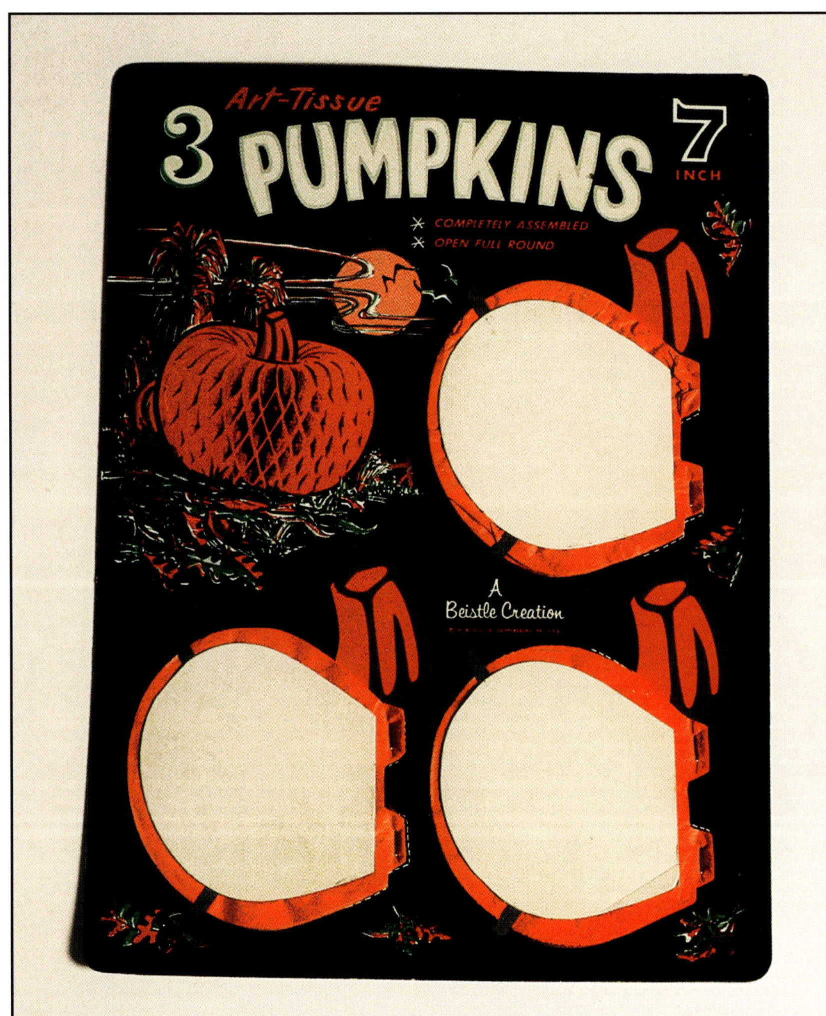

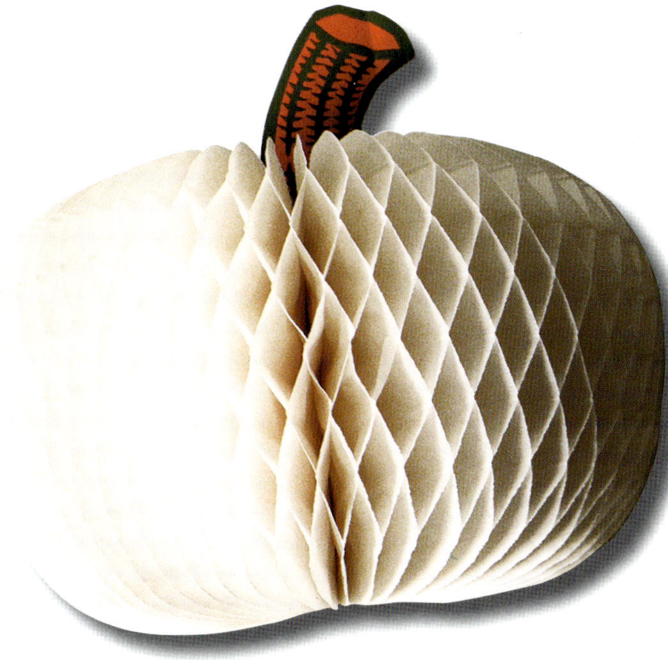

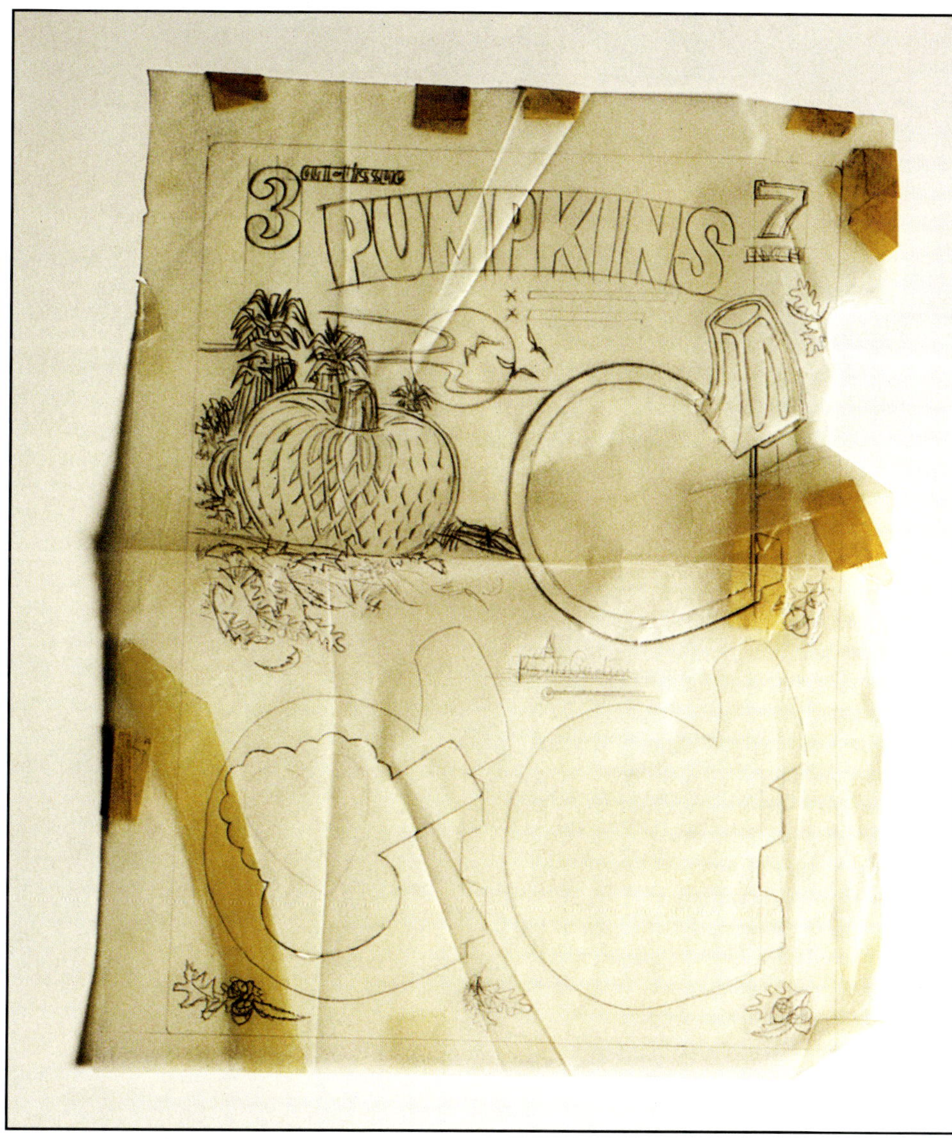
3
PUMPKINS
7

"SKEERIE" SPIDERS

Initial Release: 1966
Production Run: 1966 – 1968
These creepy spiders will provide a shivery Halloween feeling when used for party decorating. Spider's legs are die-cut from black craft stock. Orange and black Art-Tissue body opens half-round. Size 6.5" x 9". One design. Packed two pieces in a printed poly bag with header.
Value: $10 each

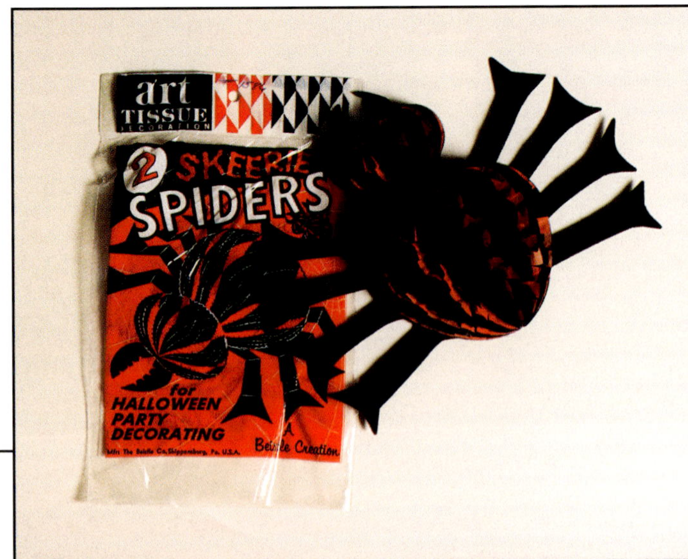

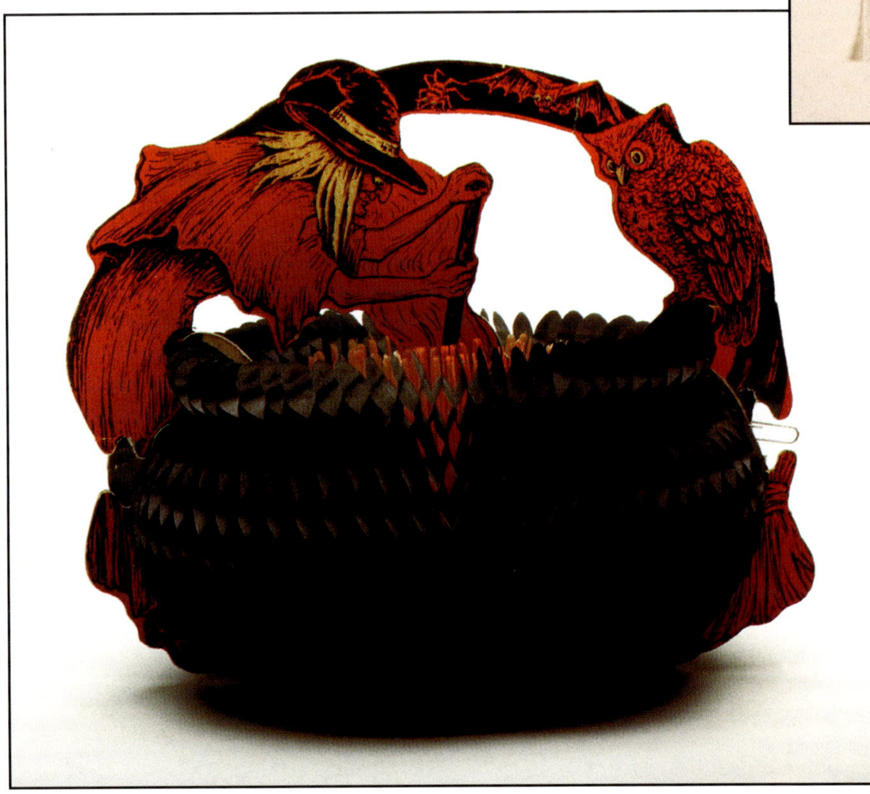

OLD WITCH'S KETTLE

Initial Release: 1928
Production Run: 1928 – 1932
Size 6.25" in diameter and 7.5" high. Made of close meshed orange tissue and when open the "flame" spreads around the old Witch's paddle.
*In 1928, along with the 6.25" model, Beistle offered the same caldron in an 8.5" in diameter x 7.5" high size. By 1931, only the 8.5" model was offered.
*In 1930, Beistle offered the public a color choice in caldrons: either black or orange.
Value: $275

RUSTIC FIREPLACE

Initial Release: 1929
Production Run: 1929 – 1932
Fireplace of imitation logs, printed on heavy card-board stock, total height 11", length 15", Old Witch stirring in a black tissue caldron, under which is imitation fire of red tissue. All packed in a heavy white printed envelope 9.5" x 13.25". Directions for use on back of envelope.
*To my utter disappointment, the caldron from the archives was in pretty rough condition, so much so that it was not suitable for photographing. However, the piece above (Old Witch's Kettle) was the model for this piece. The only additions would have been the imitation logs. Luckily the original envelope survived in great condition.
Value: $800 (with envelope)

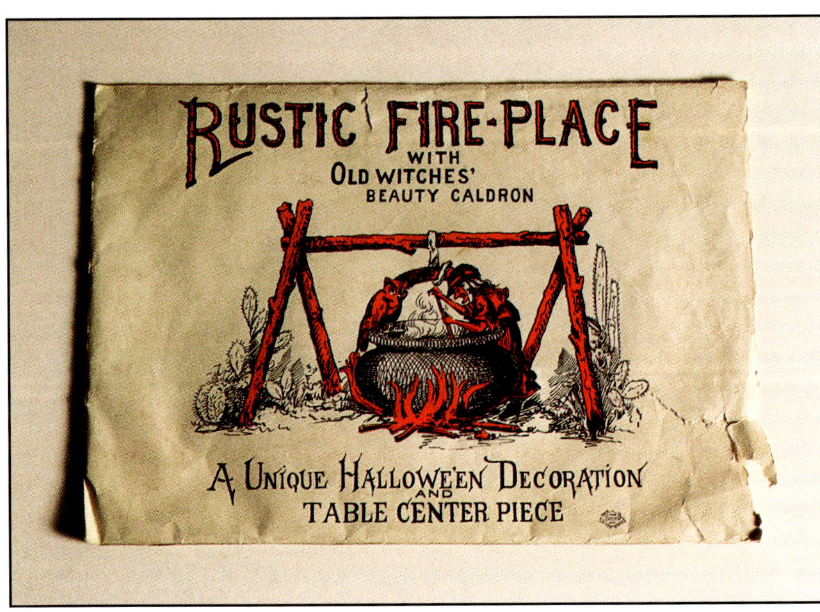

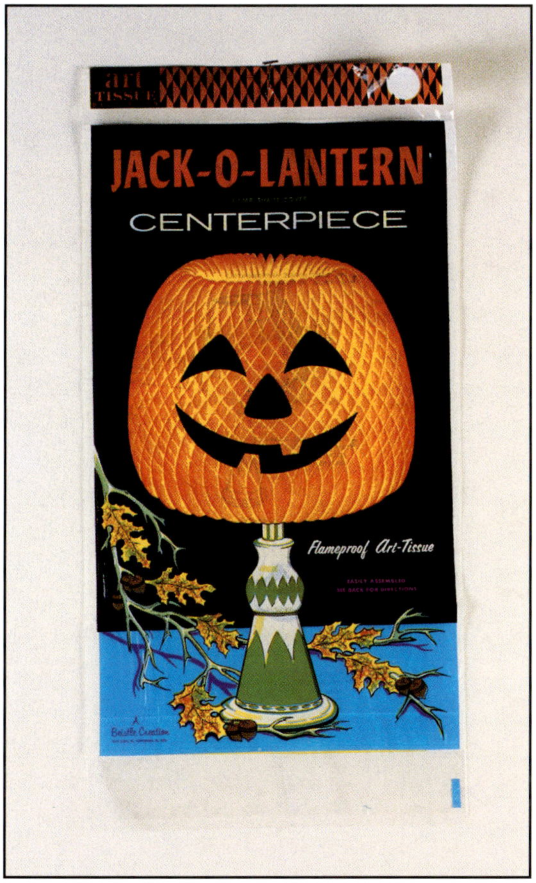

JACK-O-LANTERN LAMP SHADE
Initial Release: 1970
Production Run: 1970 – 1971
This bright orange flame-proof Art-Tissue lamp shade cover creates a novel Halloween party centerpiece or window decoration. Designed for use with any average shade approximately 12" to 15" in diameter. Soft glow from lamp will highlight the die-cut face features which insert easily into mesh to complete the Jack-O-Lantern. Each packaged complete with directions in a printed poly bag with header.
*The printed poly bag above the displayed shade.
*I don't recall this Beistle item but I do remember a similar lamp shade produced by Hallmark. One of our neighbors displayed this lighted shade on their glass-enclosed front porch on Halloween night only. I'm including a picture of the Hallmark package.
Value: $110

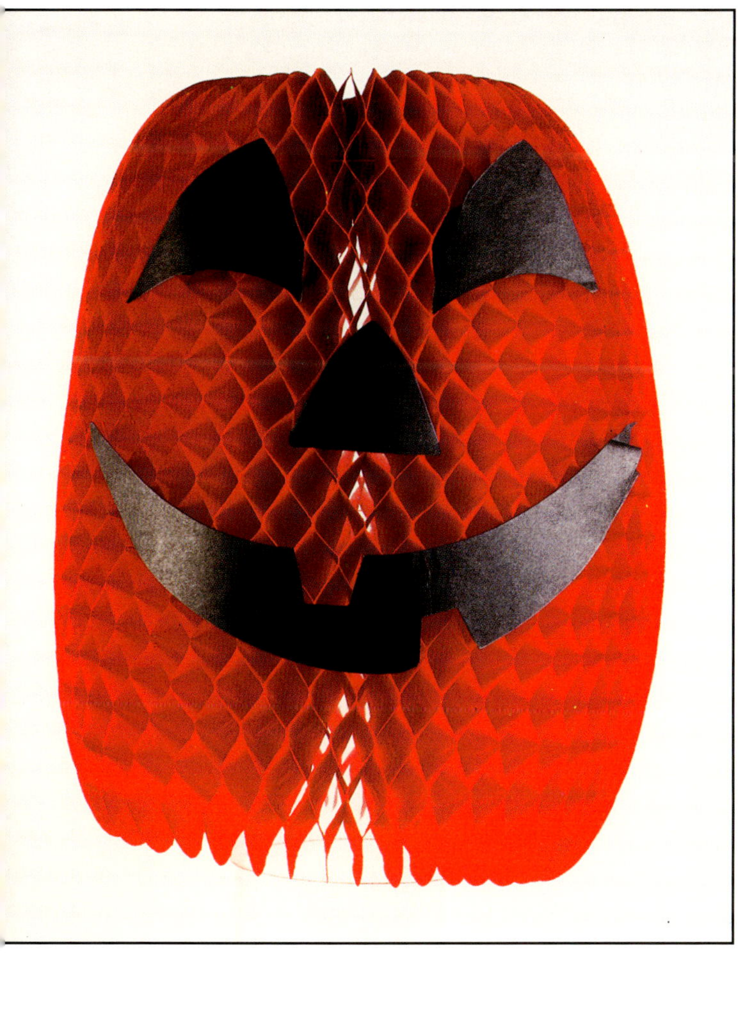

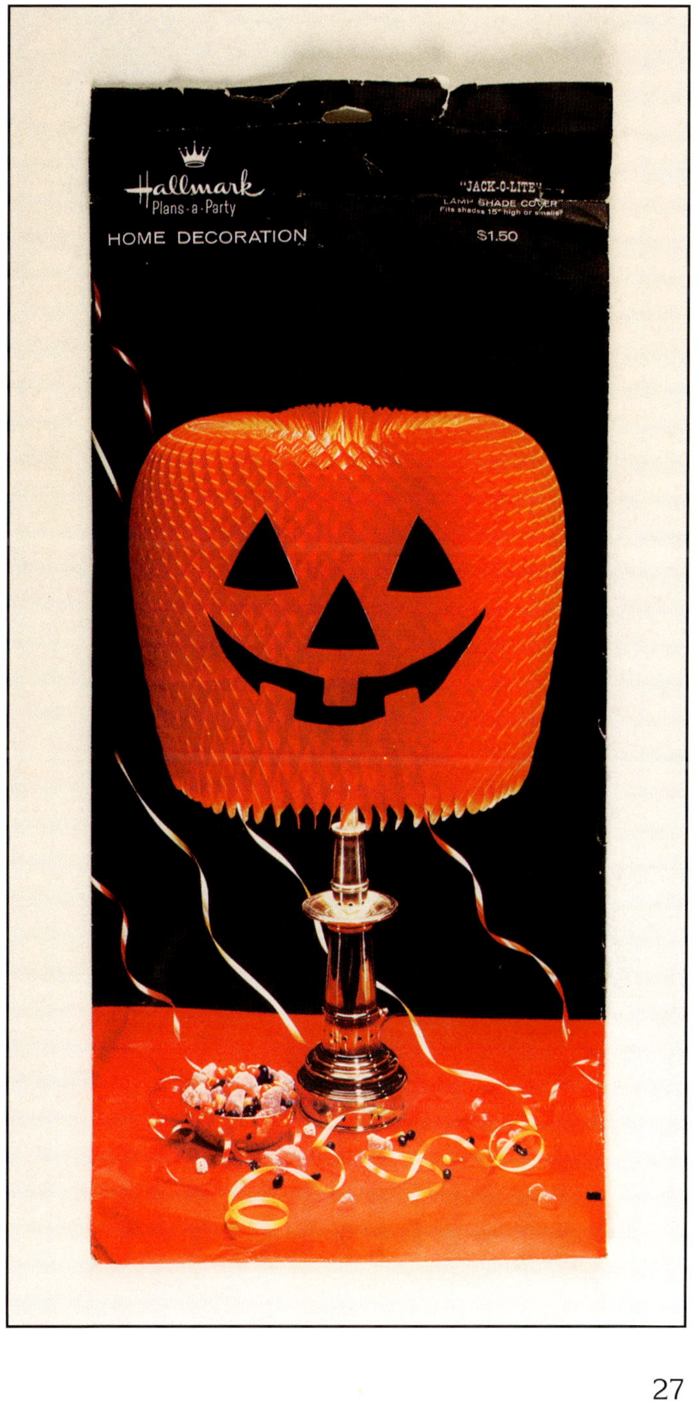

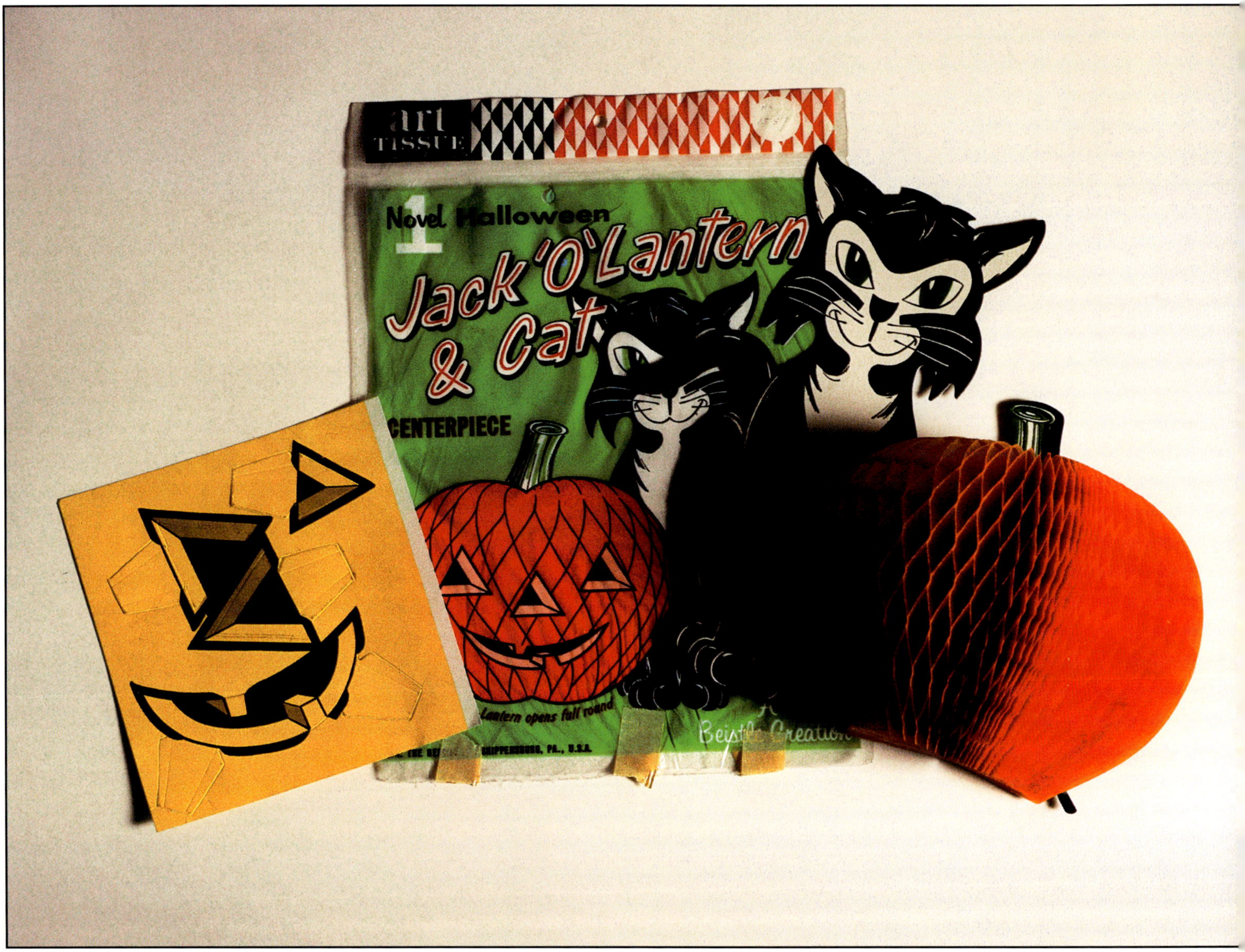

CAT AND JACK-O-LANTERN
Initial Release: 1966
Production Run: One year only: 1966
A bright, new table centerpiece that will lend a cheerful note to party decorating. A mischievous cat printed both sides in two colors. Golden-yellow pumpkin of meshed Art-Tissue opens full-round to form a standing base. Printed insert Jack-O-Lantern face may be added to complete the centerpiece design. Size 10' x 10". One design. Each packed in a printed poly bag with header.
Value: $55

CHAPTER 2
Die-cuts

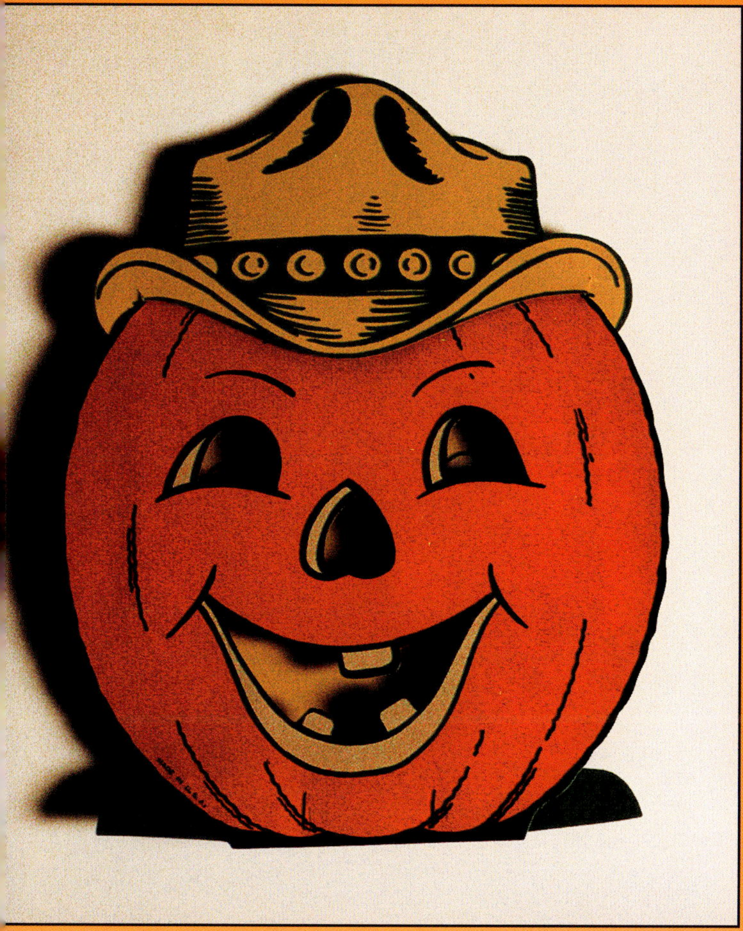

3-D HALLOWEEN PLAQUES
Initial Release: 1955
Production Run: 1955 – 1958
A new and sensational standing or hanging decoration that's sure to be a volume seller. Jolly Jack-O-Lantern faces printed in four gay colors. Eyes set in the third dimension, follow you as you move about. A real party thriller. Size 6.25" x 9.25". Four designs.
Value: $75 each

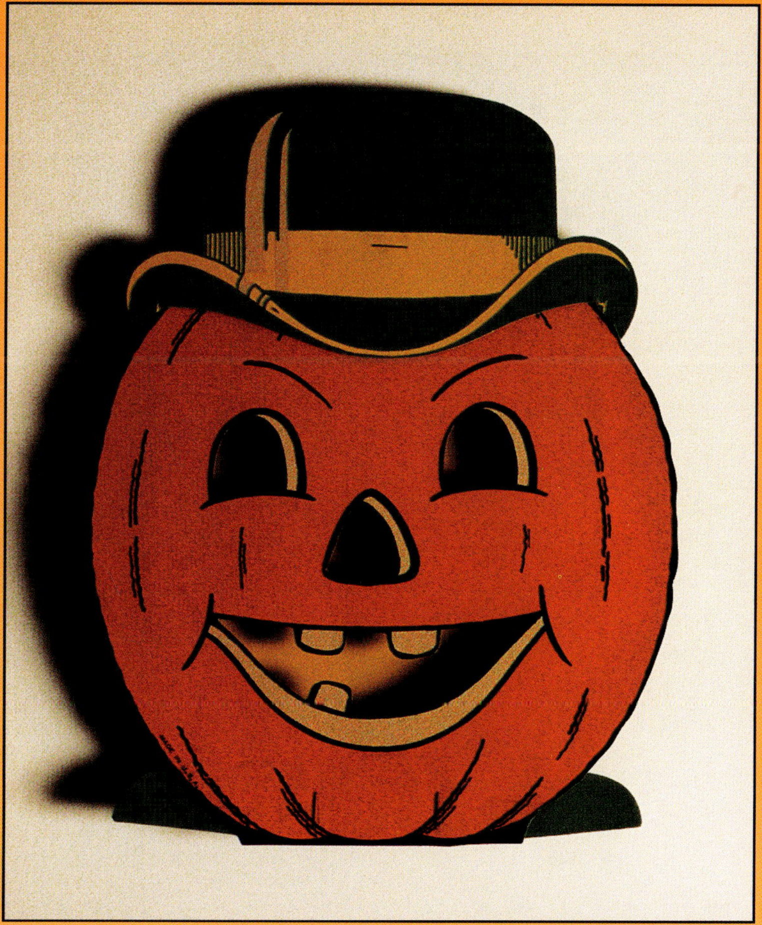

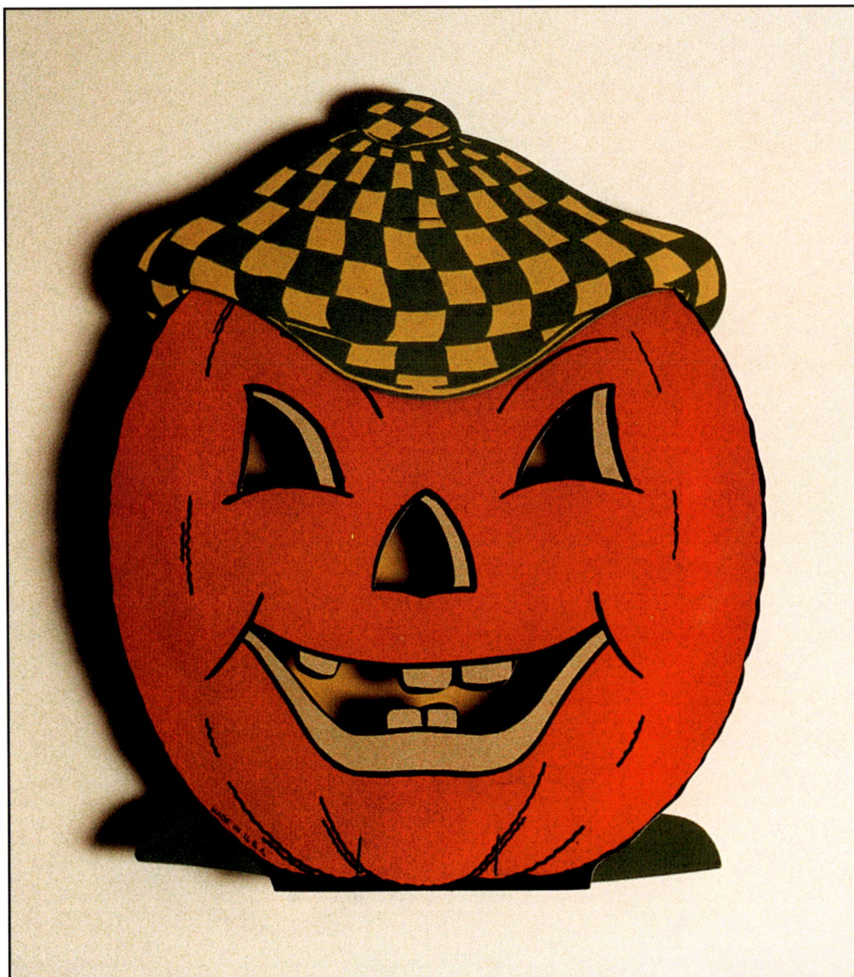

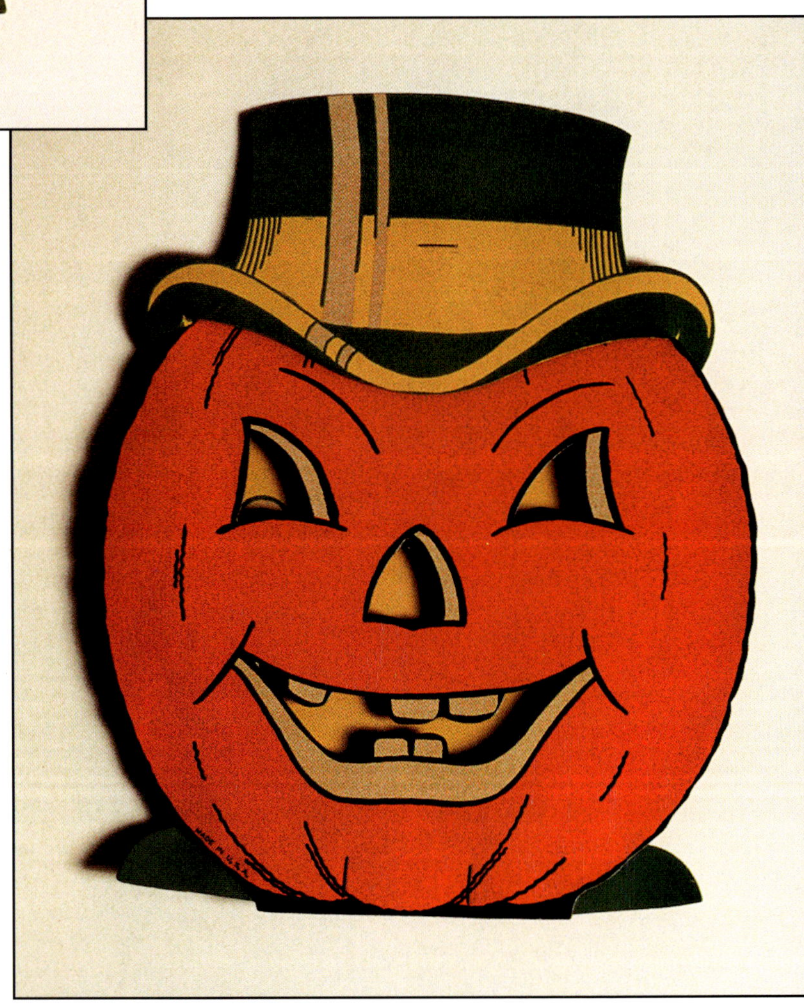

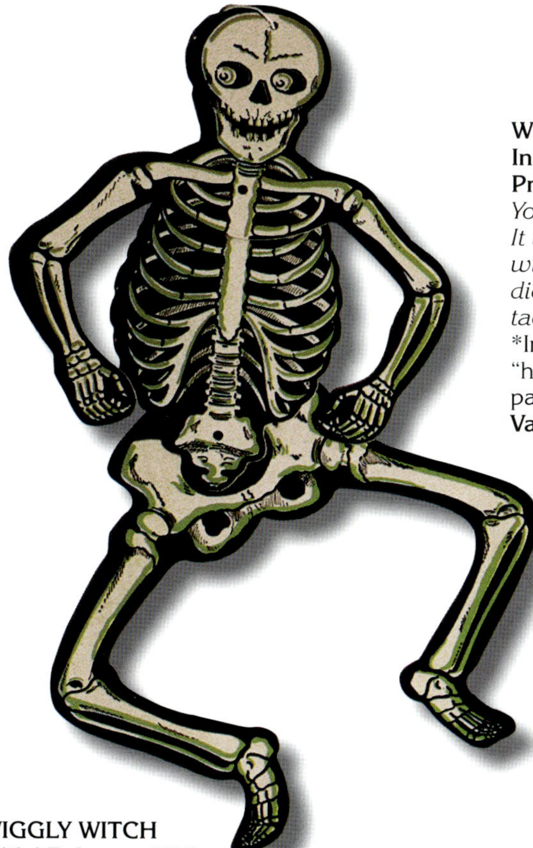

WIGGLY SKELETON
Initial Release: 1955
Production Run: 1955 – 1965*
You can have lots of fun and laughs with this amusing skeleton. It wiggles and dances and is sure to be a popular party favorite with everyone. Printed in two colors on quality white stock and die-cut to shape. Size 8" x 13". One design. String loop attached.
*In 1966, Beistle decided to modernize this fellow and give him a "hep" look to have more of an appeal for the Halloween-themed parties for teenagers.
Value: $25

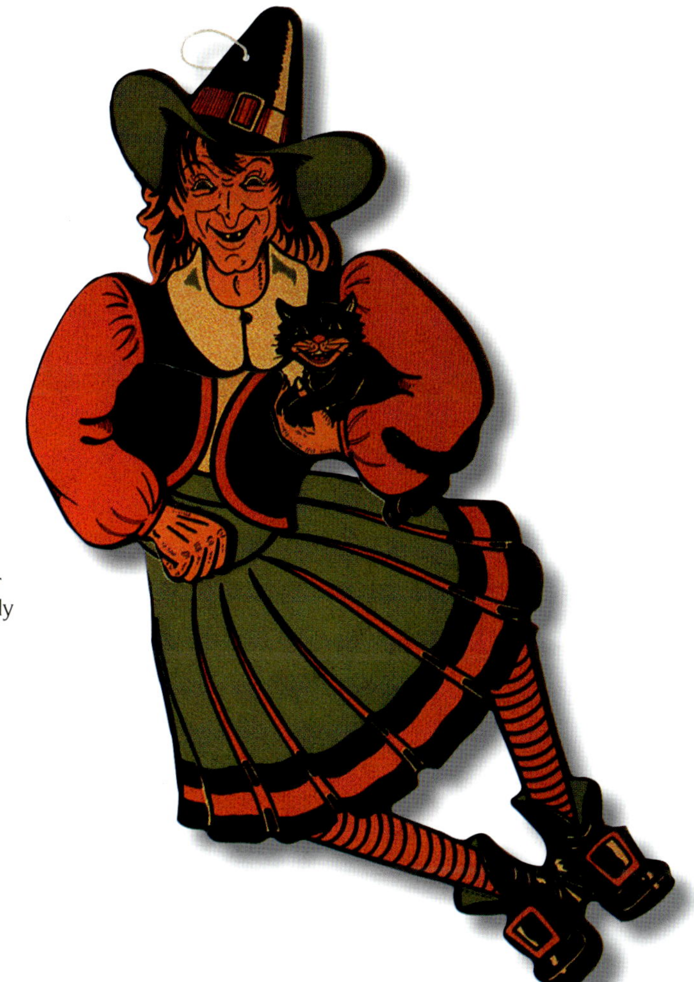

WIGGLY WITCH
Initial Release: 1955
Production Run: 1955 – 1966*
This grinning witch will amuse young and old alike. She wiggles and dances with a flick of your finger. Printed on fine quality stock in three colors and die-cut to shape. Size 6" x 14". One design. String loop attached.
*In 1966, Beistle decided to update this witch's look to be more in tune with 1960s. Her skirt was shortened and made to look flirty while her striped stockings were given the heave-ho and replaced by bare legs. Her clunky witchy shoes gave way to a pair of go-go boots. Her short, scraggly hair magically turned into a beautiful mane of long hair. Her features too took on a transformation – from crone to sweet young lass.
Value: $25

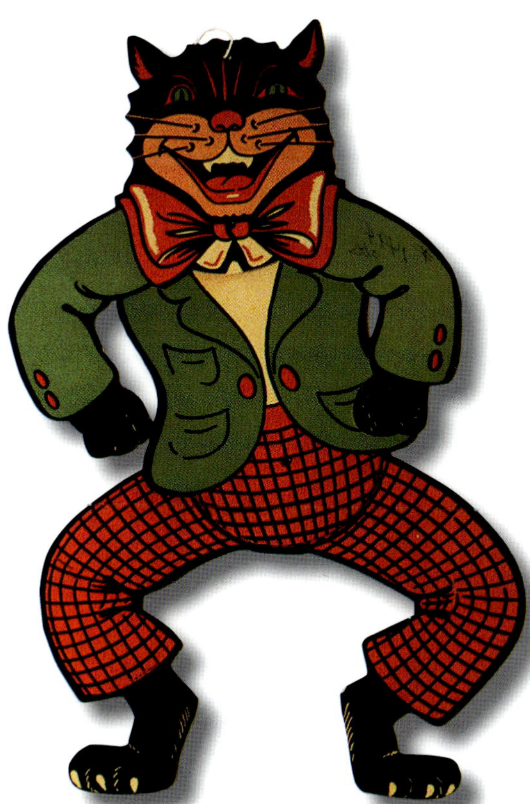

WIGGLY CAT
Initial Release: 1955
Production Run: 1955 – 1965
A new and unusual action toy. Free motion of body and legs enables the Halloween cat to wiggle and dance. Printed in three colors on quality stock and die-cut to shape. Size 7" x 11.5". One design. String loop attached.
*For whatever reason, Beistle decided not to update the cat's look in 1966 as they did for the witch and skeleton.
Value: $25

3-D FANTASIES
Initial Release: 1955
Production Run: 1955 – 1959
Unusual decorative Halloween plaques printed in two colors on fine white stock. Each plaque has three separate parts, die-cut, attached and projected to produce a three dimensional effect. May be used as a standing table or a window decoration, or wall plaque. Three designs equally assorted. Size 6.5" x 8". Folds flat for packing, and snaps into place.
Value: $75 each

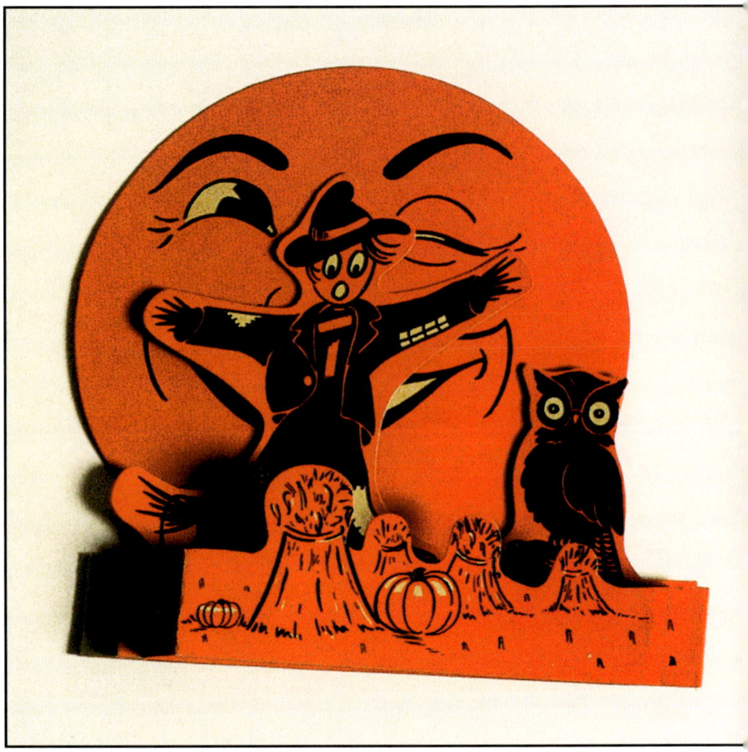

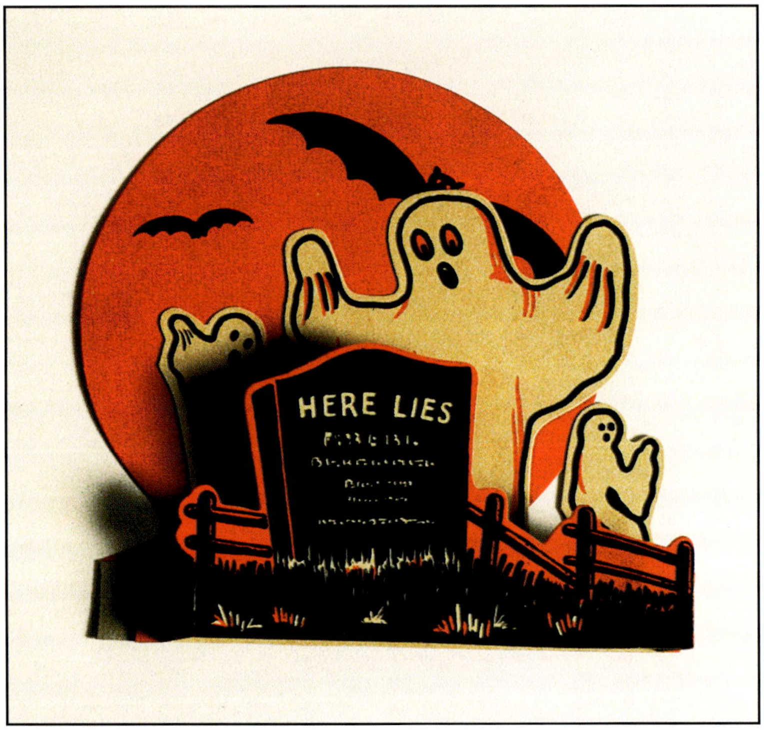

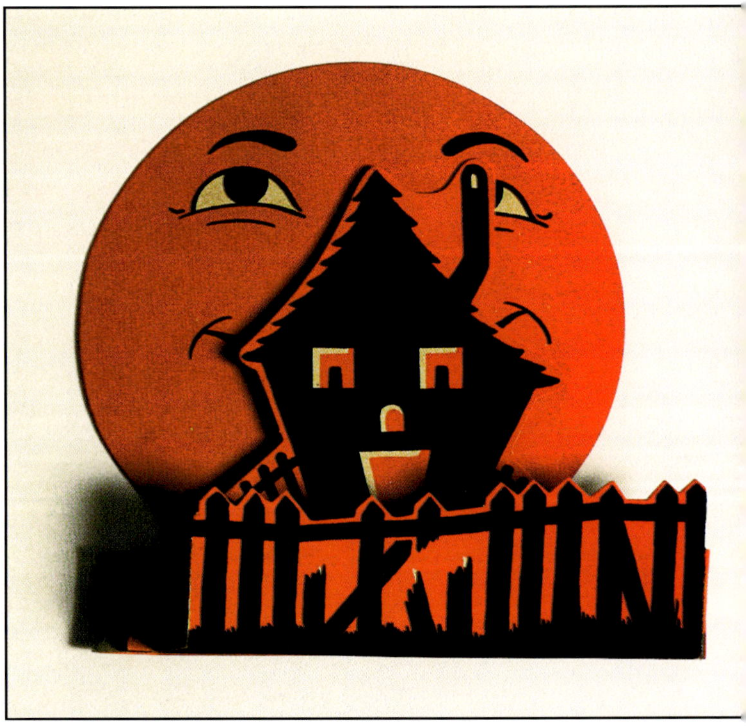

WINGY WHIMSIES
Initial Release: 1956
Production Run: 1956 – 1965
A combined decoration and novelty item with lots of sales appeal. This owl, witch, and scarecrow are expertly designed with expanding arms and wings of orange tissue eyeleted to orange and black body. Folded flat for packing, they cleverly open to the amusement of all and make a novel party favor as well as a favorite Halloween decoration. Three designs. Size opened 8" x 12".
Value: $40 each

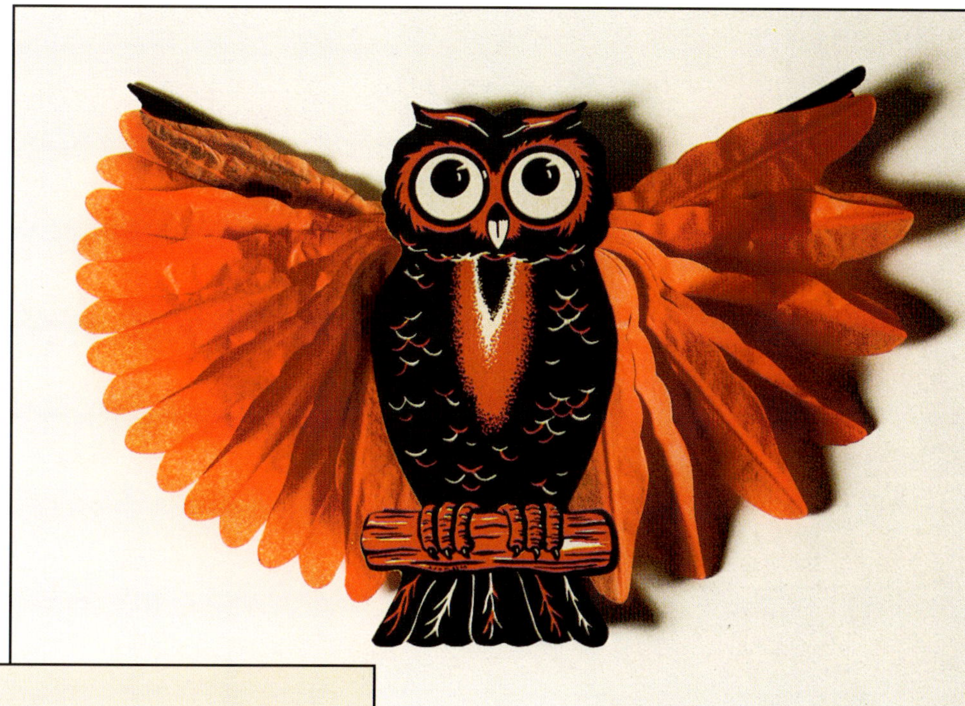

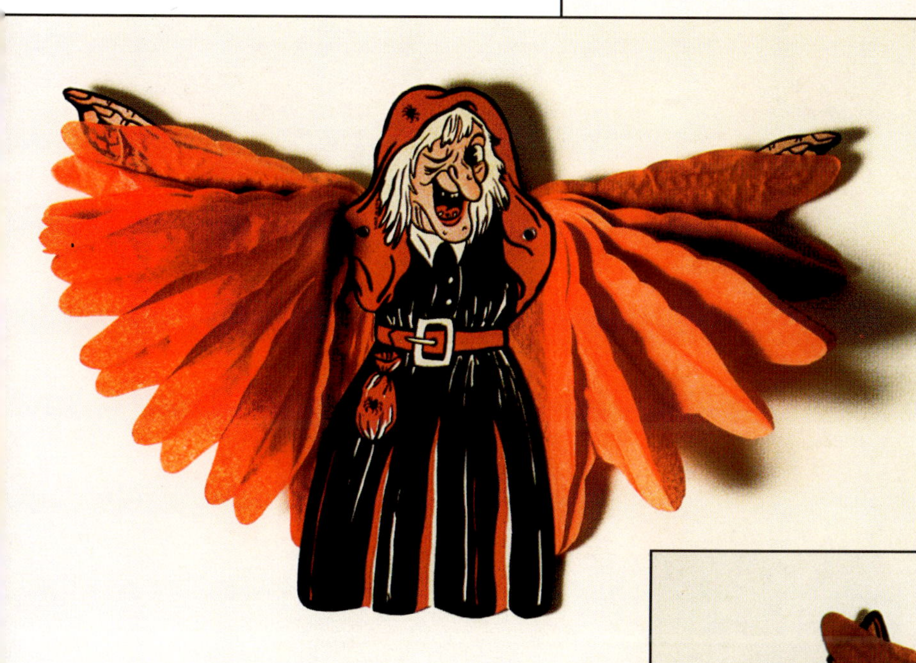

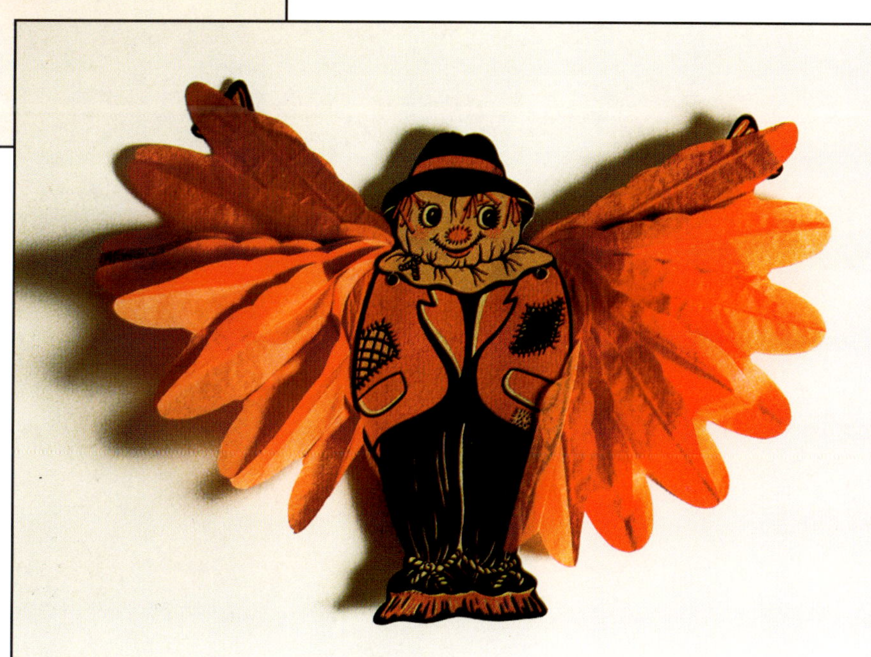

WITCH CUT-OUTS
Initial Release: 1956
Production Run: 1956 – 1962
Always a popular Halloween character and favorite for party decorating. Three spooky, grotesque witches printed in colors of orange, black, and green on fine stock and die-cut to shape. Three designs. Average size 8" x 18".
Value: $55 each

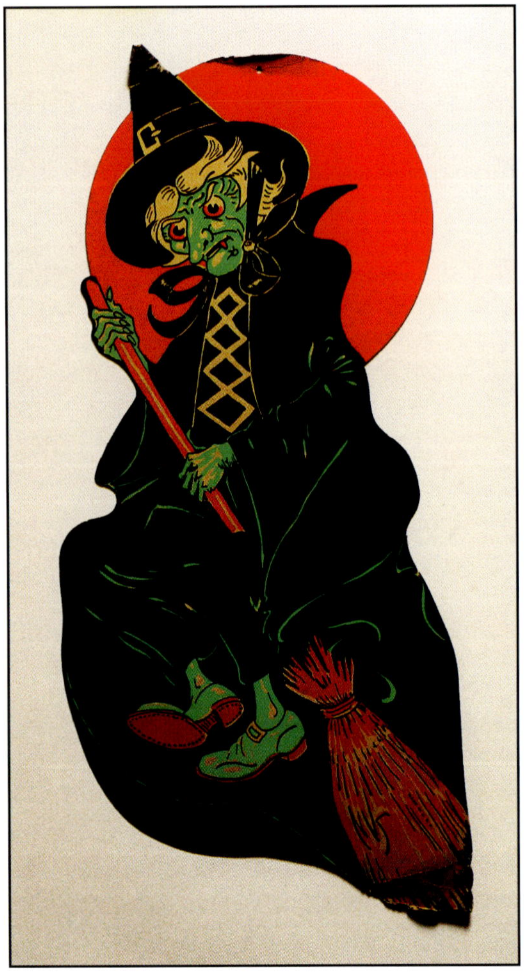

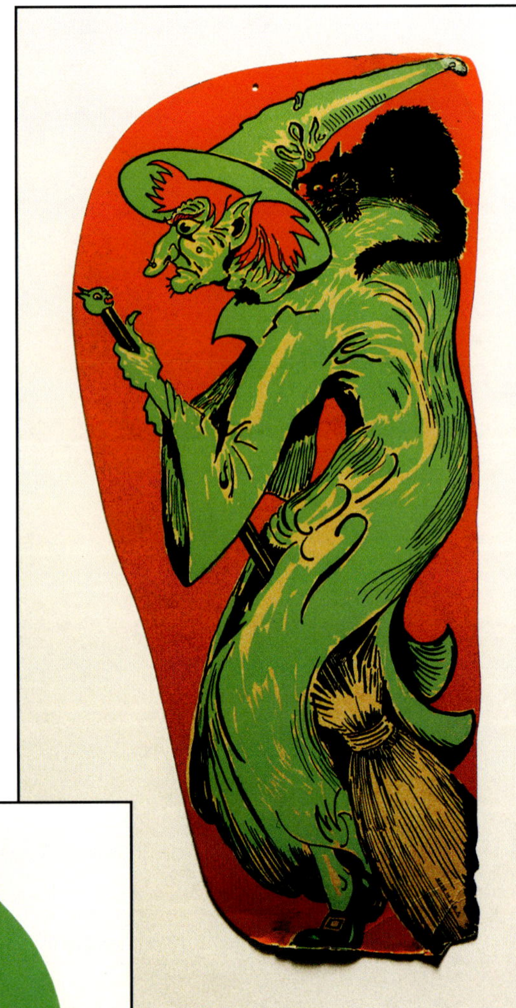

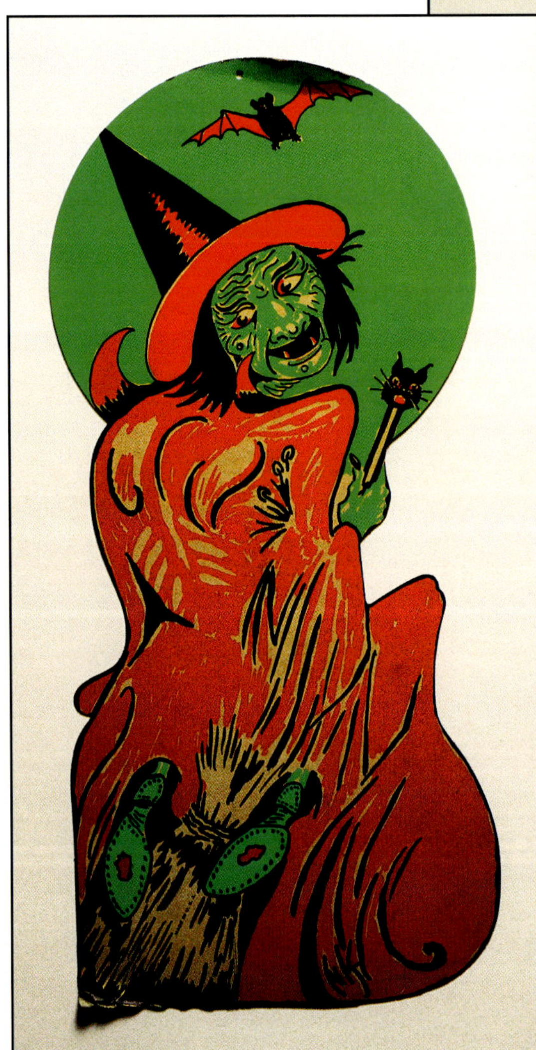

WITCH CENTERPIECE
Initial Release: 1964
Production Run: 1964 – 1974
A delightful new Halloween Party Centerpiece. A mischievous witch printed both sides in four colors. Caldron of black meshed Art-Tissue and printed die-cut flames open full-round to complete the centerpiece and form a standing base. Size 8" x 11". One design. Each packed in a printed poly bag with header.
*Three views of this piece: Removed from its plastic bag, shown flat. Removed from bag with honeycomb tissue paper caldron fully opened. Artist's model with notations.
**In 1969, Beistle offered a slightly different version of this witch along with the above. The newer version had the witch clutching her pointed hat with her left hand while in her right she dangled a spider over a steaming caldron.
Value: $65

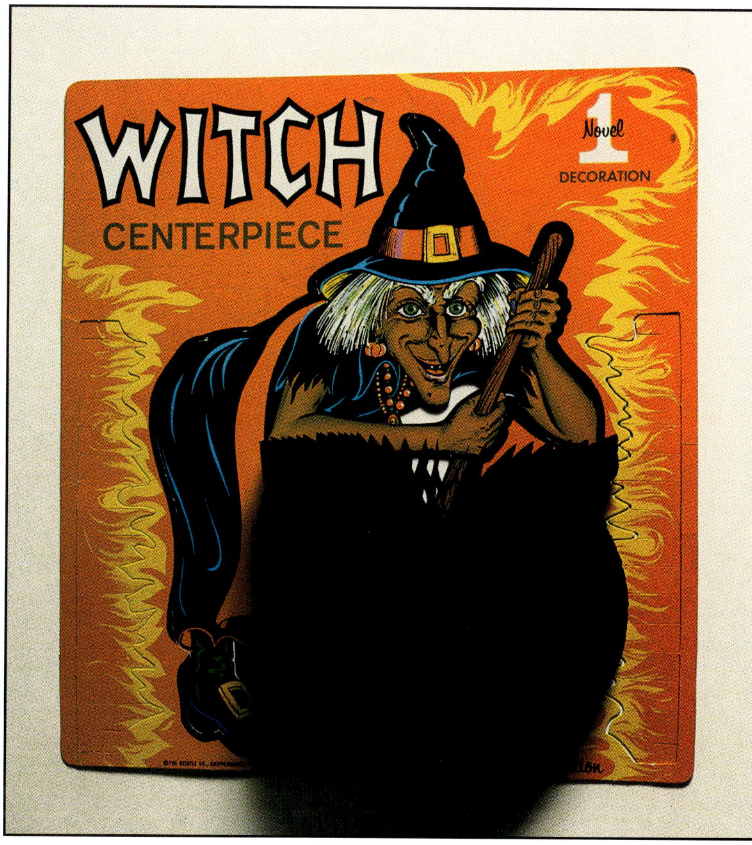

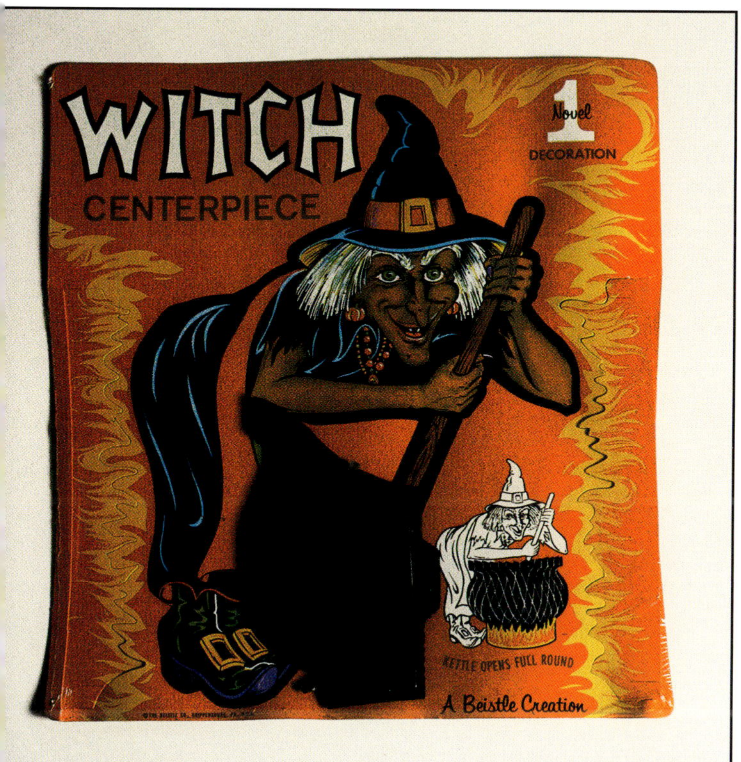

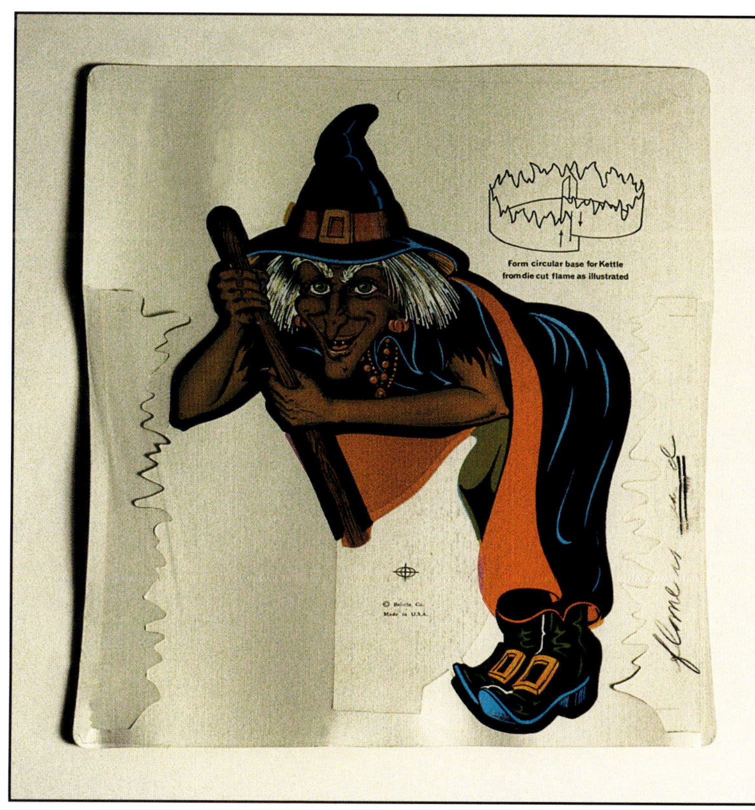

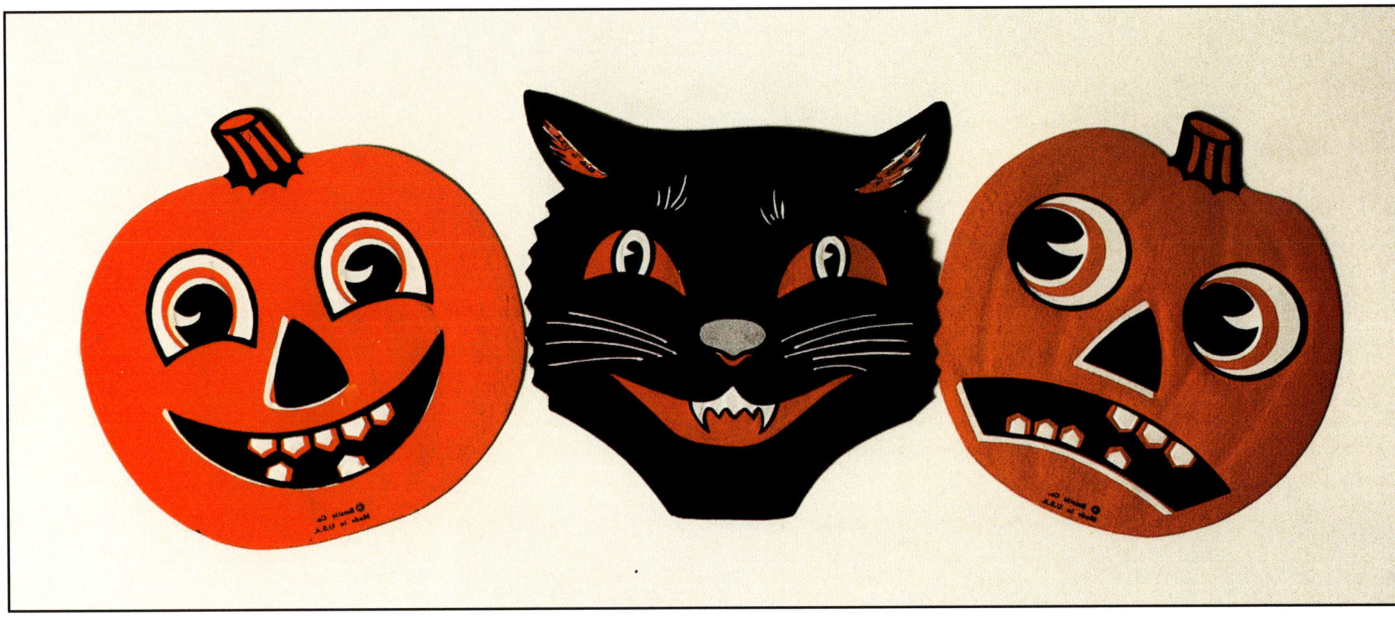

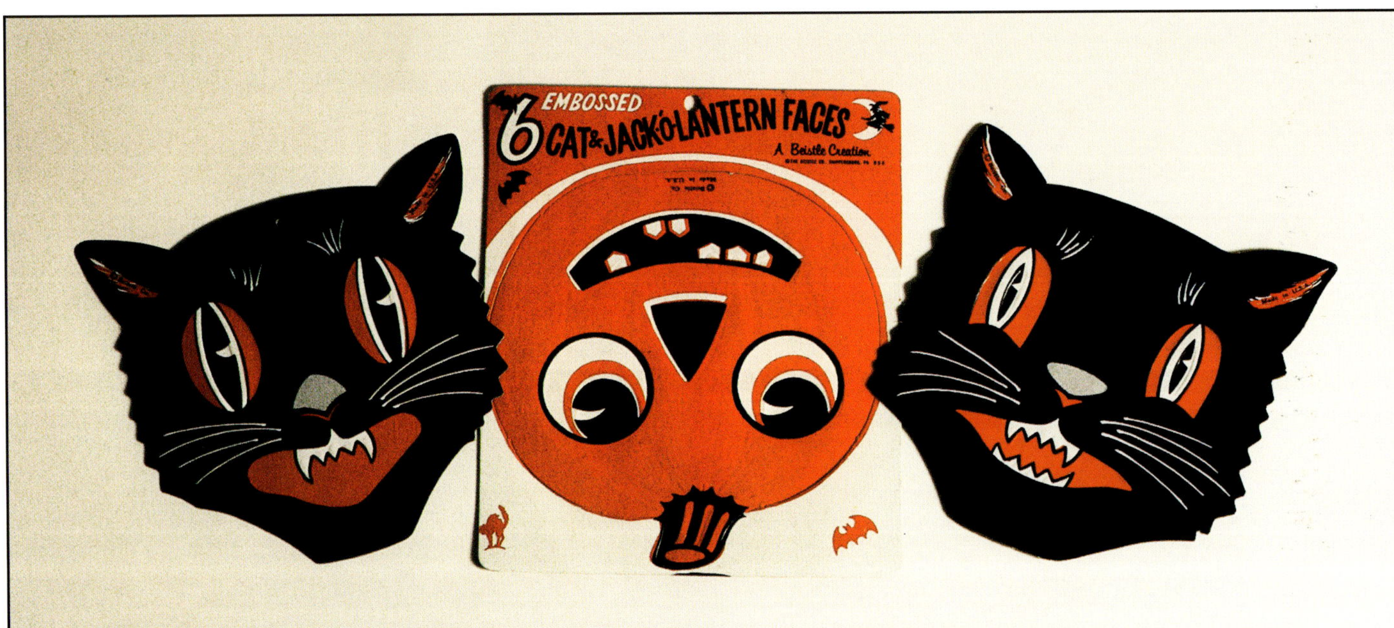

EMBOSSED CAT AND PUMPKIN HEADS
Initial Release: 1941
Production Run: 1941 – 1973
These six embossed cat and pumpkin heads will please the most particular customer. Each design in two colors, orange and black. Size 6" x 8.25". Packed 6 dozen assorted.
*I was quite surprised to discover how far back these pieces go. They had quite a healthy sales run. I think it's safe to say that these six pieces make up part of the dozen or so items that are true Halloween decoration icons.
*In 1960 Beistle introduced this same set of die-cuts, but the six pieces were packed in a clear polyethylene bag with a printed heat-sealed top. This set was marketed under a different Stock Number to differentiate between the two.
Value: $20 – $25 each

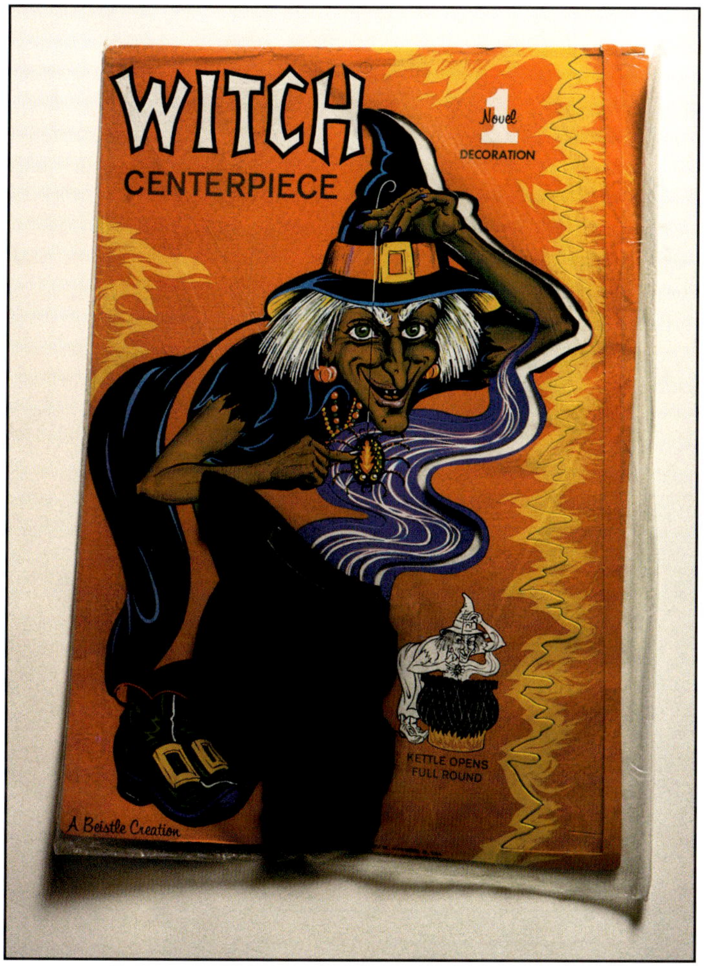

WITCH CENTERPIECE
Initial Release: 1969
Production Run: 1969 – 1973
An enchanting Halloween Party Centerpiece. A mischievous witch printed both sides in four-color design. Caldron of black meshed Art-Tissue and printed die-cut flames open full-round to complete the centerpiece and form a standing base. Size 8" x 11.5". One design. Each centerpiece carded in a crystal-clear poly shrink-pack.
*This is the updated version of Beistle's 1964 offering.
Value: $55 each

EMBOSSED CUT-OUTS
Initial Release: 1952
Production Run: 1952 – 1955
Popular priced for volume sales is this fine assortment of four designs. Deeply embossed on quality stock and printed in two colors, orange and black. Size 6" x 9".
*The four designs are shown along with three artist's models incorporating three colors into the design. The three-color design was never sold to the public.
Value: $75 each

(Continued on following 2 pages)

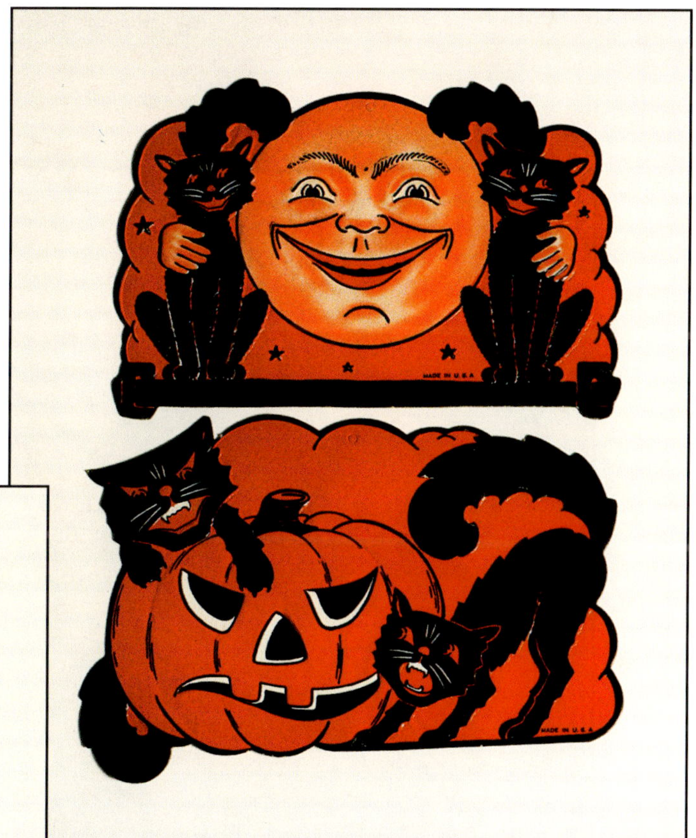

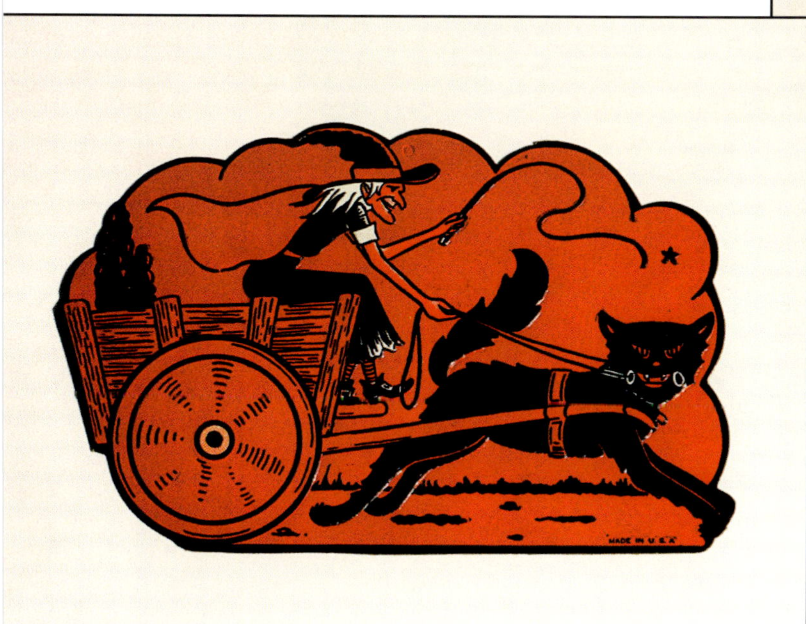

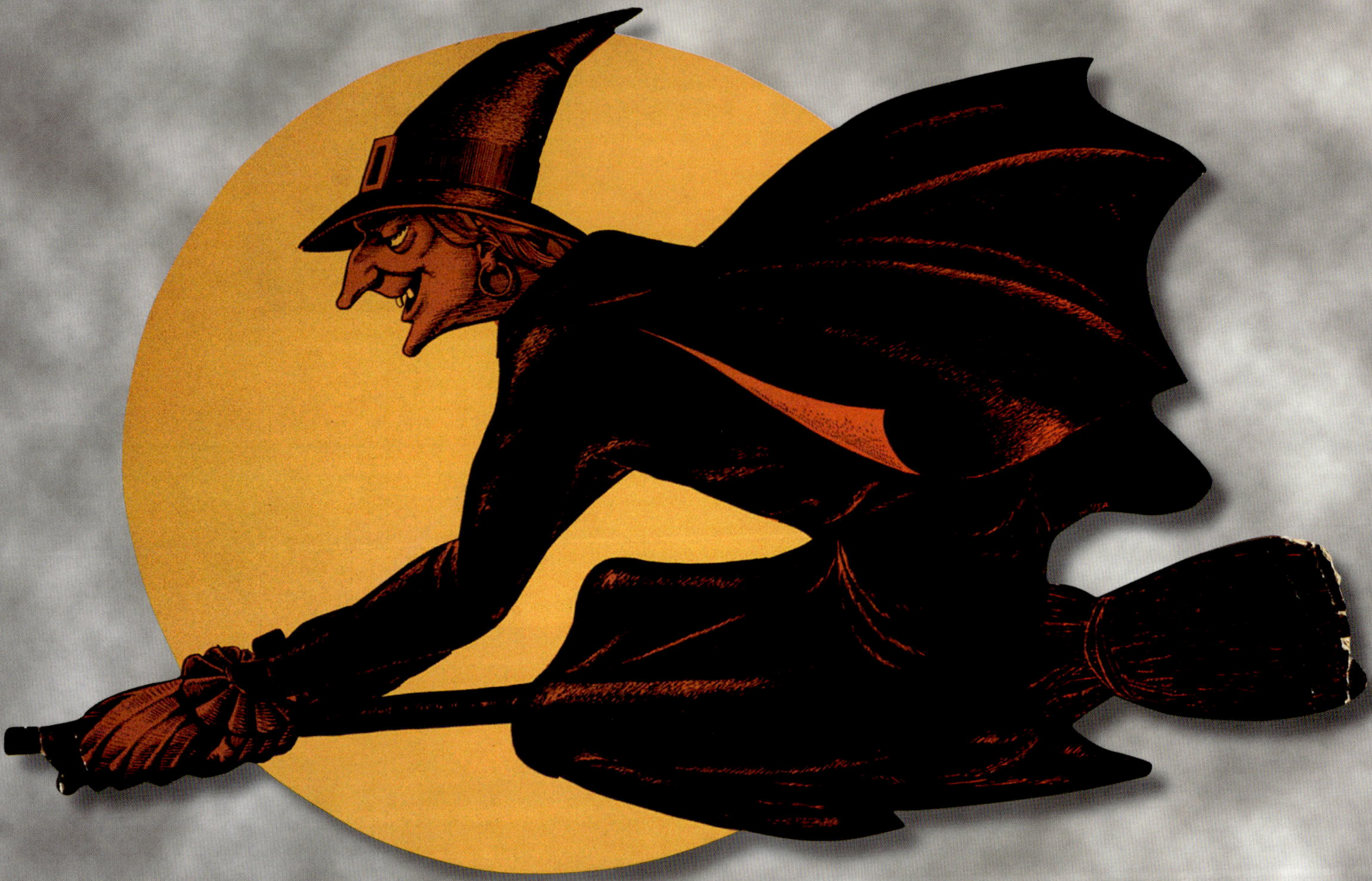

WITCH CUTOUT
Initial Release: 1964
Production Run: 1964 – 1968
A party favorite for Halloween decorating. A flying Witch in striking three-color design, silhouetted on a bright yellow moon. Printed on quality stock and die-cut to shape. Size 13" x 19".
Value: $55 each

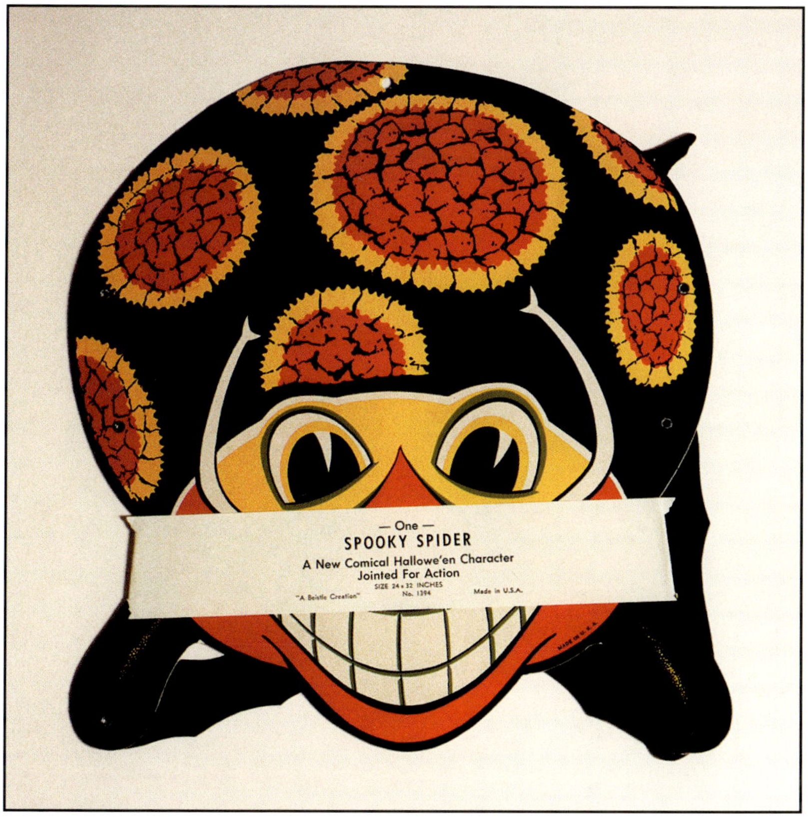

SPOOKY SPIDER
Initial Release: 1964
Production Run: 1964 – 1968
A new jointed Halloween figure to excite the imagination and delight the pranksters. Fully jointed legs are eyeleted to body. Brightly printed in four colors on quality stock and die-cut to shape. Size approximately 24" x 32".
*Two views shown of this piece: one with the spider's legs extended and the other with spider enclosed in its paper strip wrapper.
Value: $45 – $50 each

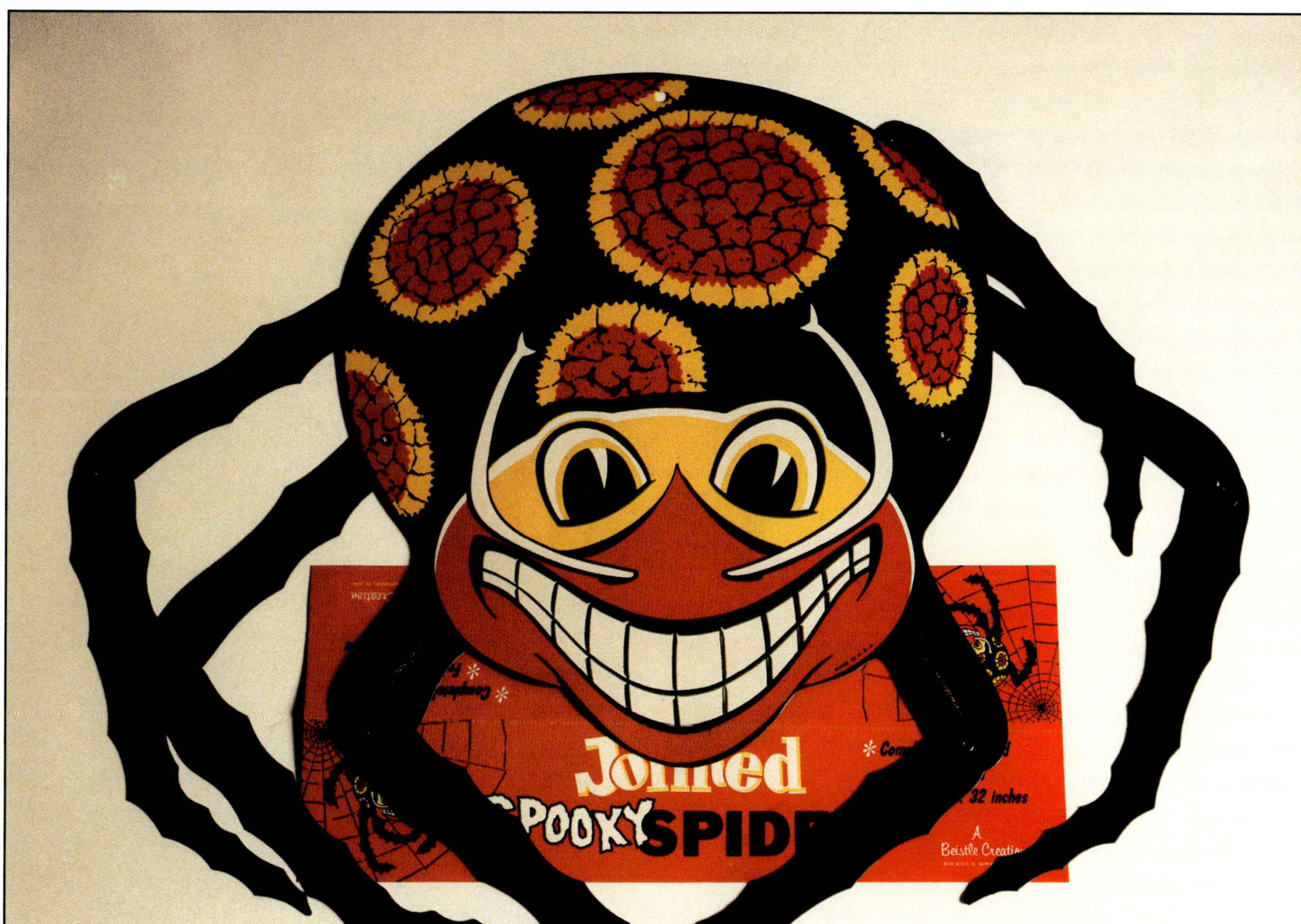

WITCH HAZEL
Initial Release: 1960
Production Run:
One year only: 1960
This "chubby" witch with her "be-deviled" cat will lend a gay and comical note to party decorating. Printed in three colors on heavy cardboard. Witch and cat are silhouetted on a bright yellow moon. Size 19" x 27".
Value: $65

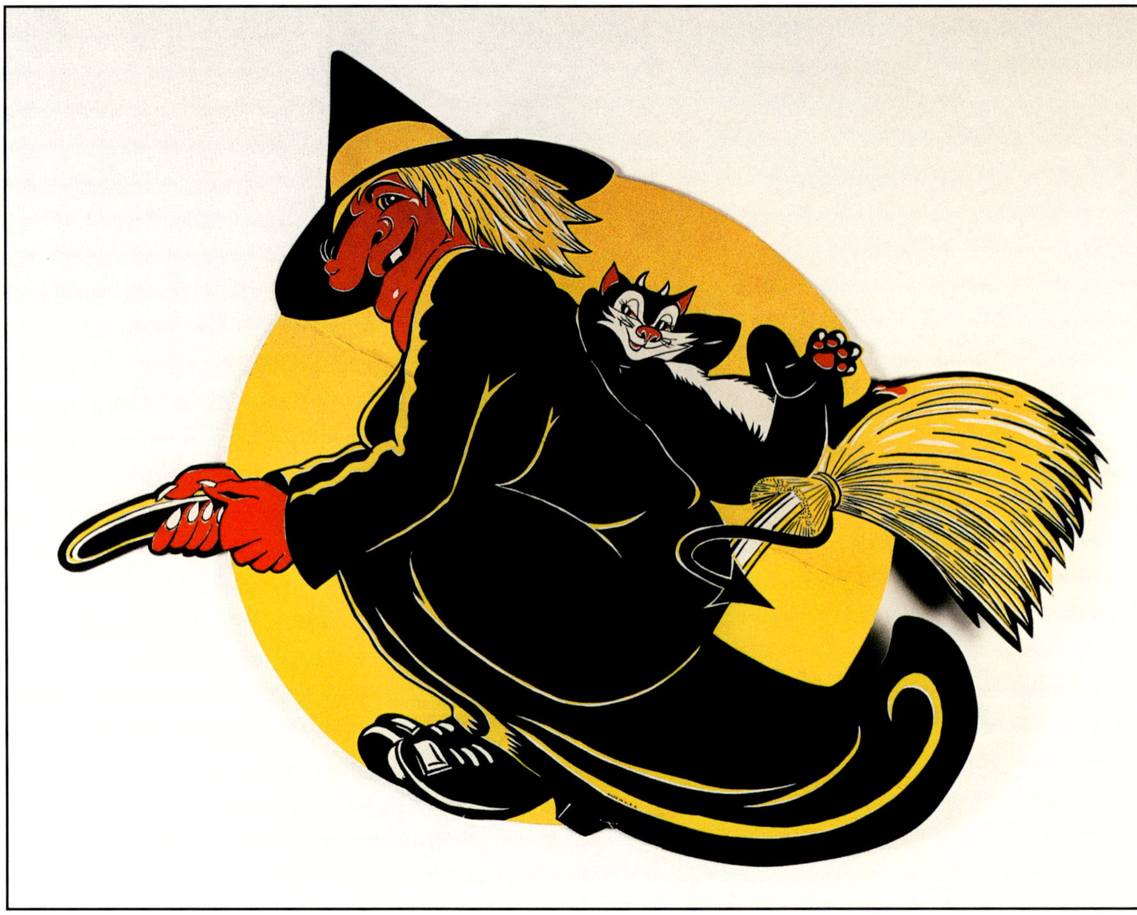

OWL AND CROW DECORATION
Initial Release: 1961
Production Run: See author's note (*) below
A popular addition to your line of Halloween party decorations. These amusing Halloween figures are expertly designed with expanding arms and wings of golden-yellow tissue. Owl and crow gaily printed in four colors on quality stock and die-cut to shape. Size 21" x 25". Packed folded flat. Two designs.
*The production run on the Crow lasted only until 1964, whereas the Owl's popularity lasted until 1968. I have to admit, I didn't realize that the bird-like die cut was supposed to be a crow until I came upon the description in the Beistle sales catalogues.
Value: $85 (for the Crow only)
Value: $65 (for the Owl only)

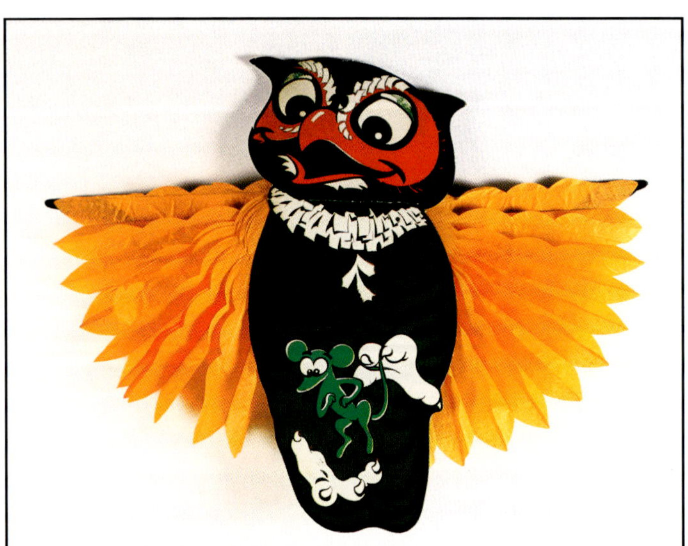

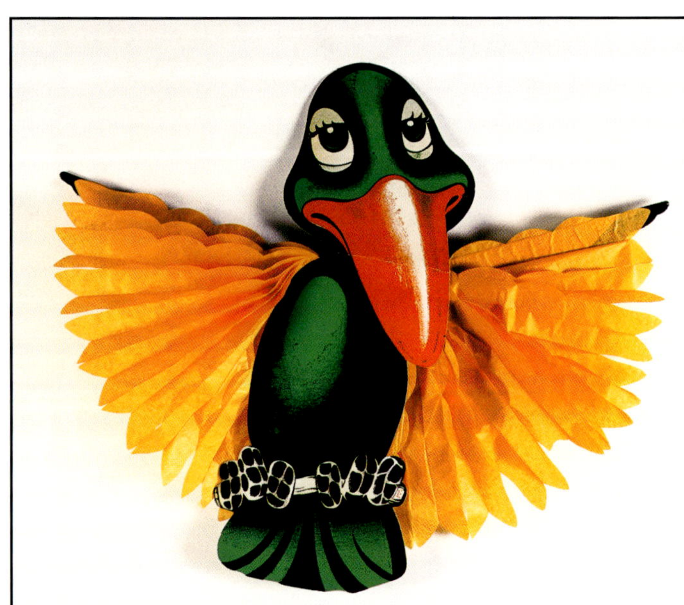

PIRATE GOBLIN
Initial Release: 1967
Production Run: 1967 – 1970
A jolly pirate to delight the youngsters. Fully jointed arms and legs are expertly eyeleted to the body. Printed in a vivid four-color design and die-cut to shape. Size 24" x 32". One design. Each packed in a clear poly bag with header.
*This one's for you, Jared!
Value: $65

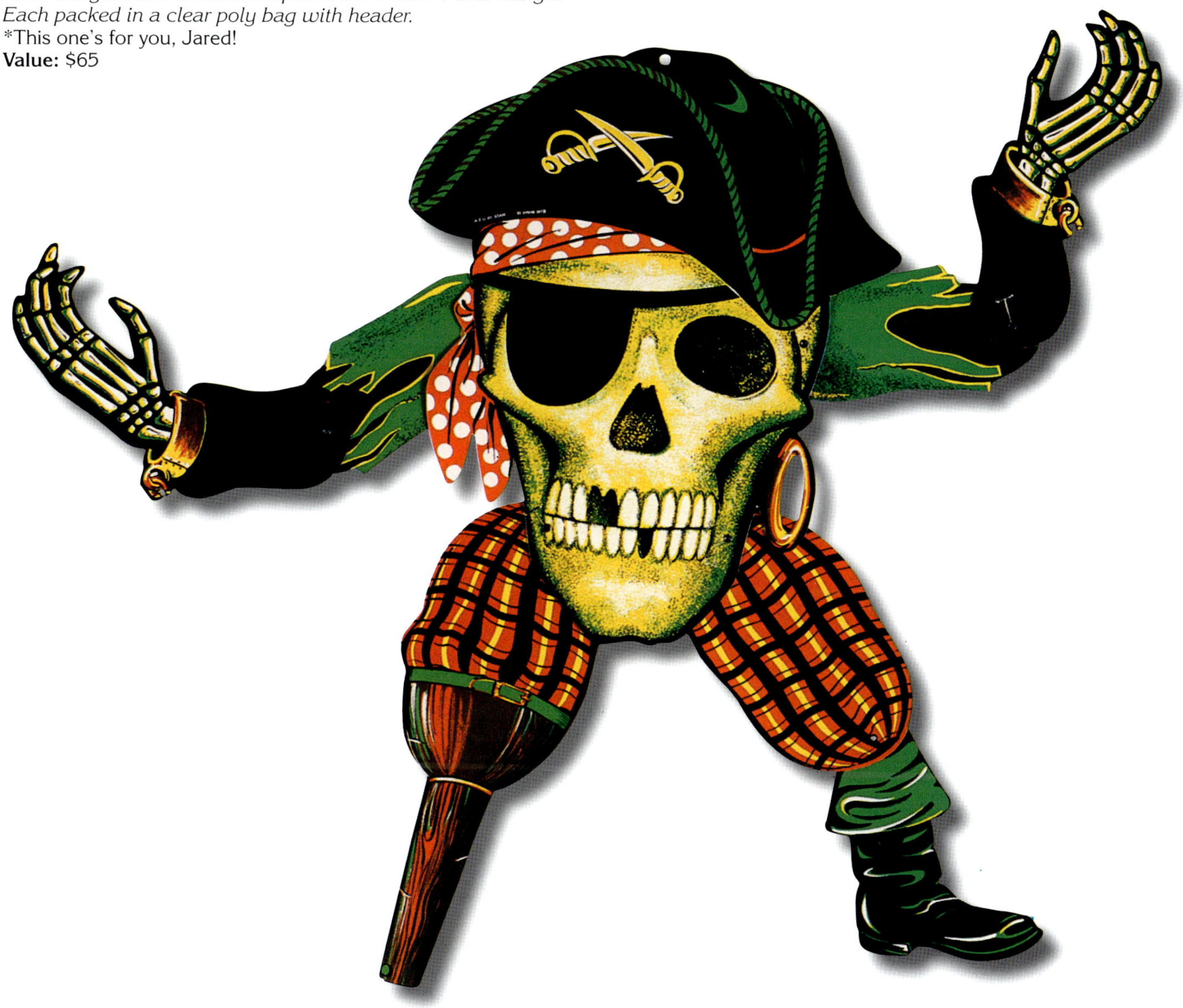

STANDING WITCH
Initial Release: 1955
Production Run: 1955 – 1956
A large witch cleverly designed to fold flat and open with a full round skirt to form the standing easel. Made of fine heavy stock, printed orange and black and die-cut to shape. Stands 23.25" high. One design. Always a Halloween favorite.
*What a great piece! An unusual and stunning centerpiece if there ever was one. The piece in black and white is actually a test-run model used as a preliminary sample to check out any faults in the design prior to adding color. These types of pieces are very, very rare and accordingly, have a greater value.
*What an archival find! Here's another interpretation of this witch: this artist's model features jointed arms and she has lost her hissing cat. This example was never marketed.
Value: $200

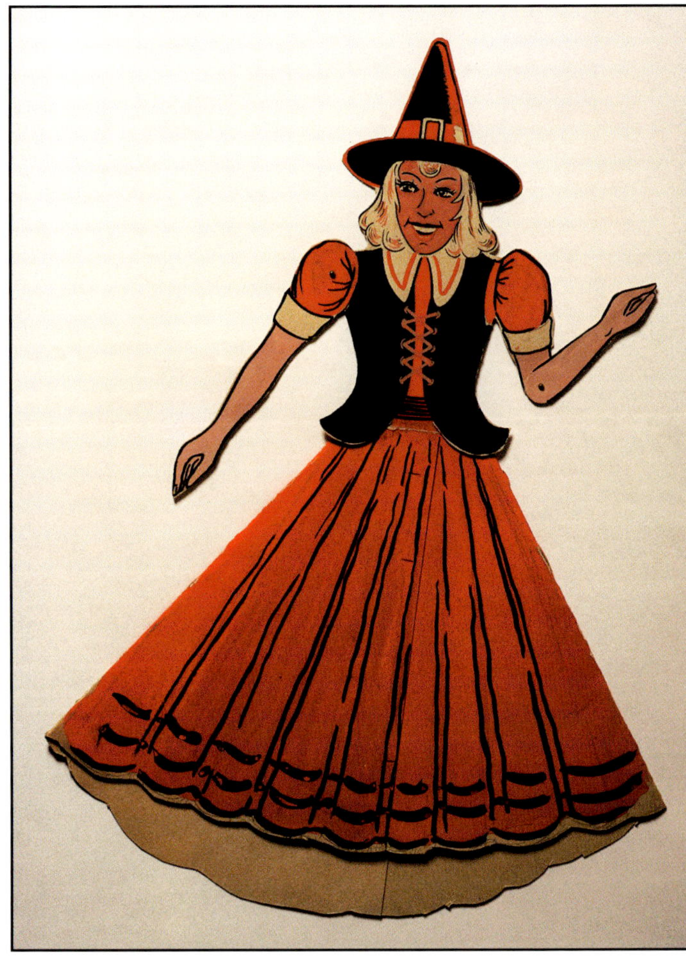

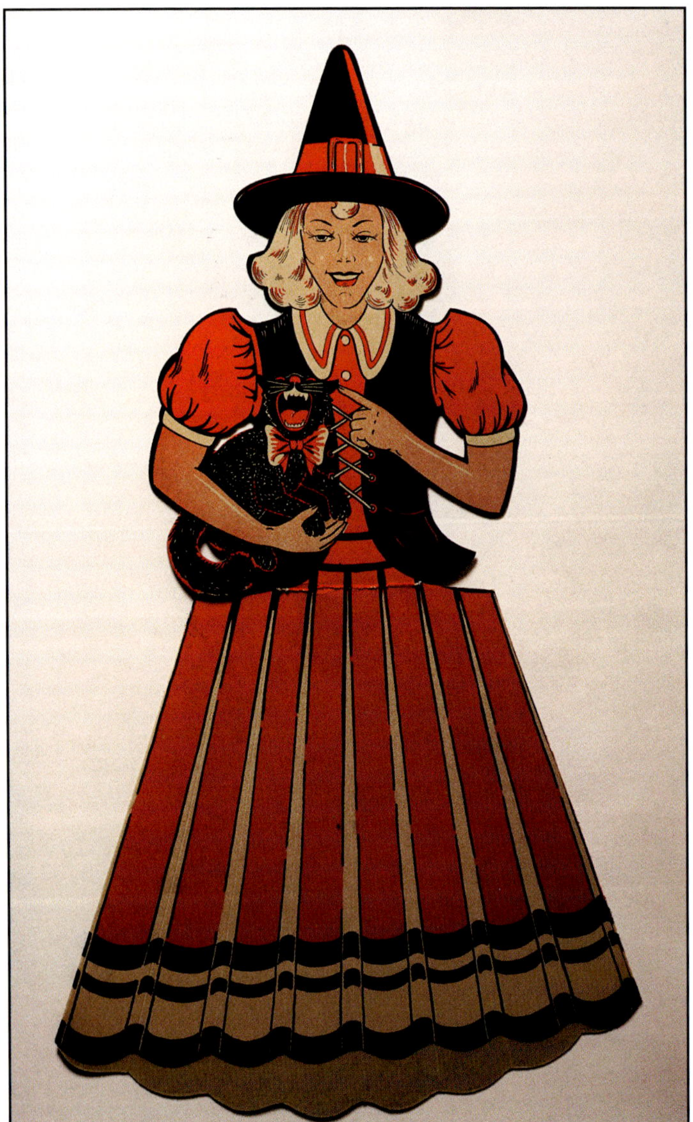

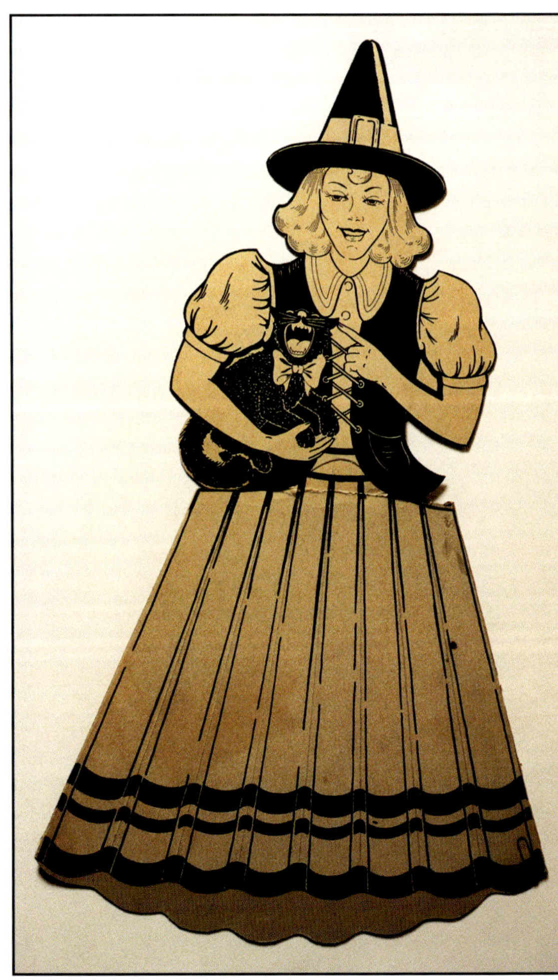

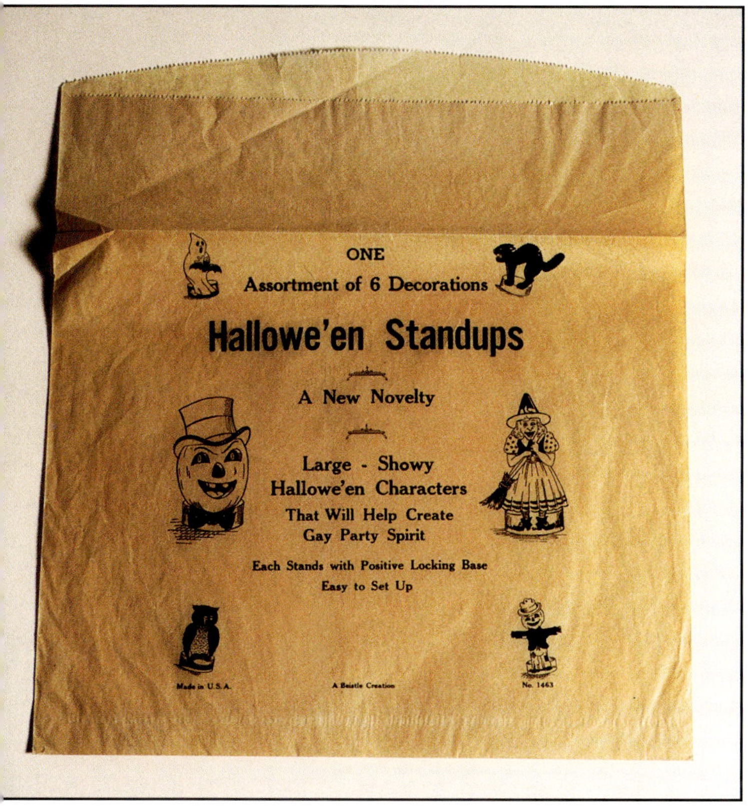

HALLOWEEN STANDUPS
Initial Release: 1955
Production Run: 1955 – 1965
Add to the party spirit by trimming the tables with these unusual party favors. Six designs printed in three colors on quality stock and die-cut to shape. All figures have a locking base for standing. Average size 5" x 9.5" with a 3" circular base. One assortment of six designs packaged in a printed glassine bag.
*Shown with the original glassine envelope/bag. Showing all 6 original designs.
Value: $150 for the set including glassine bag

(Continued on following page)

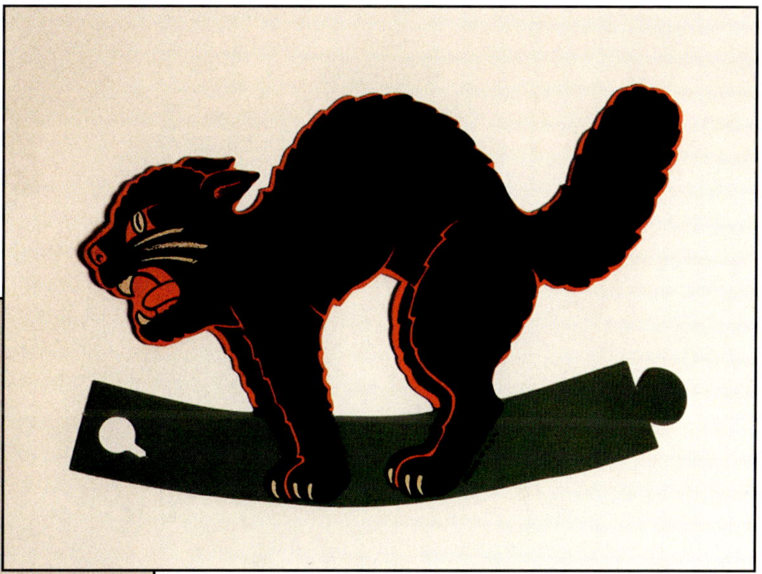

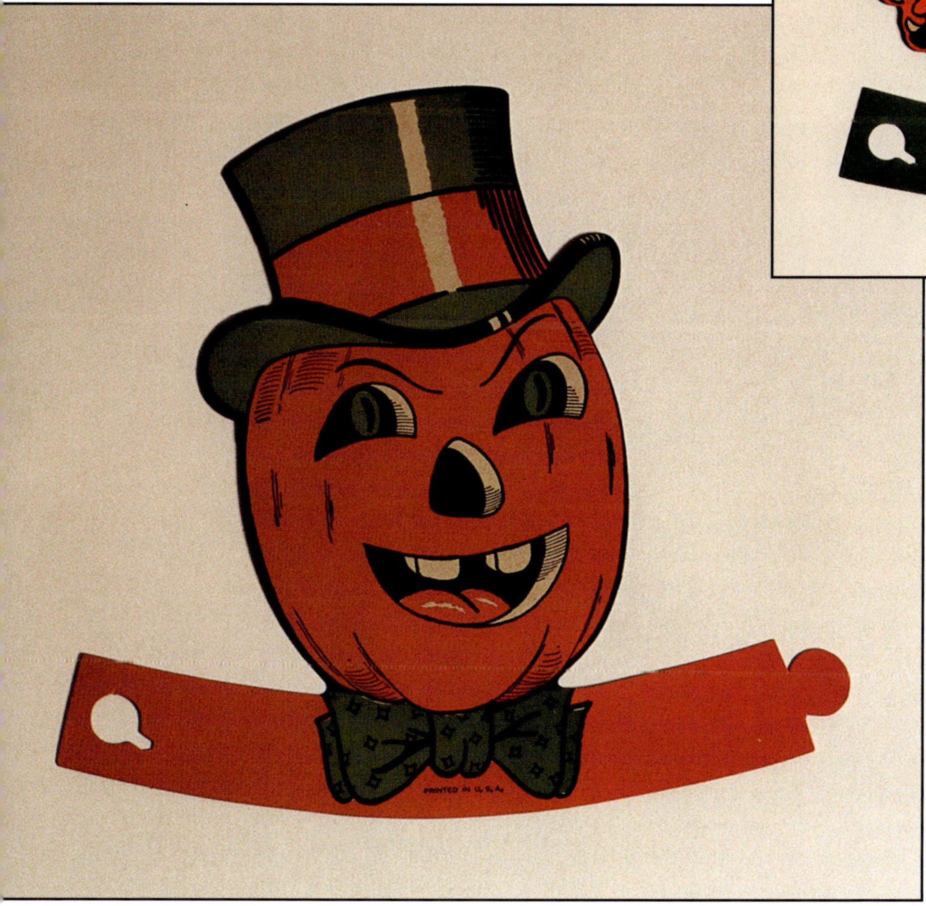

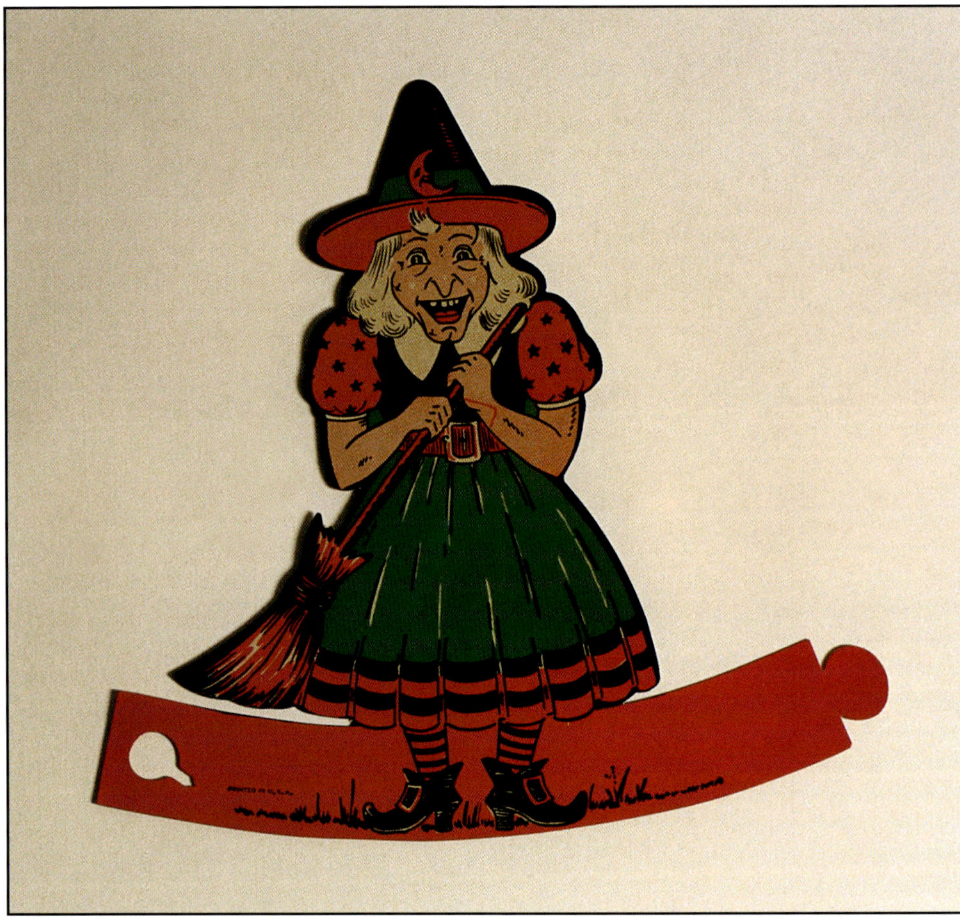

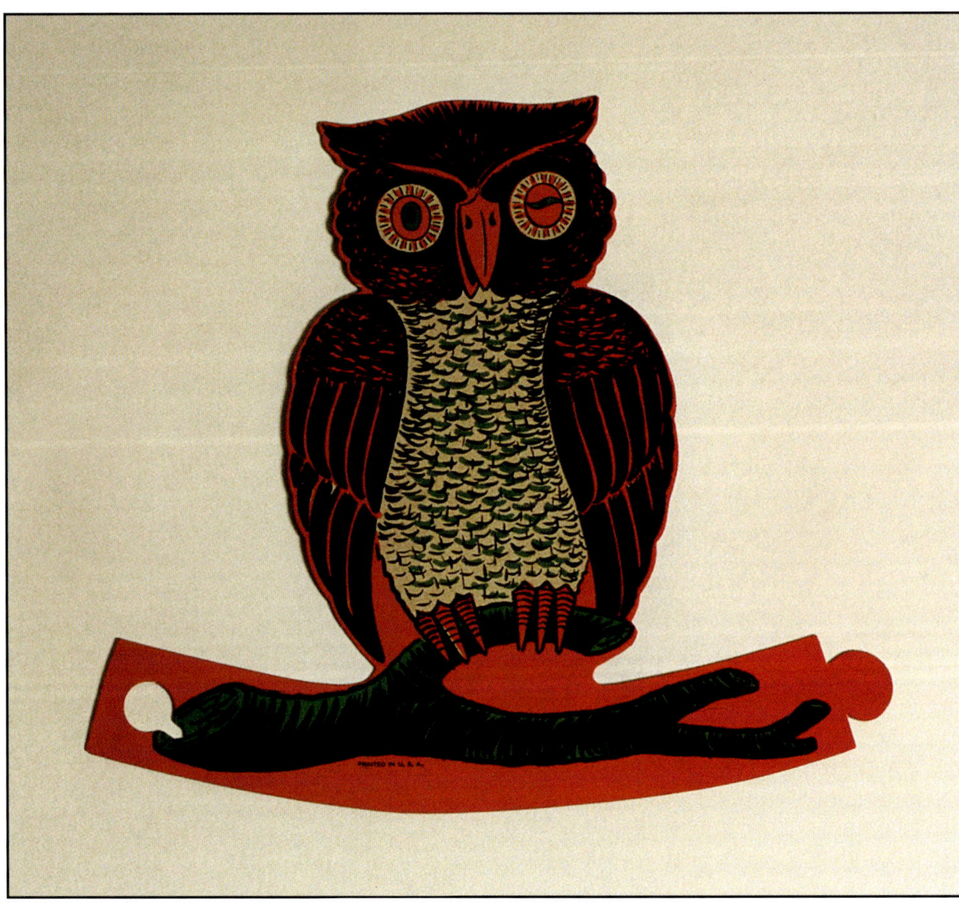

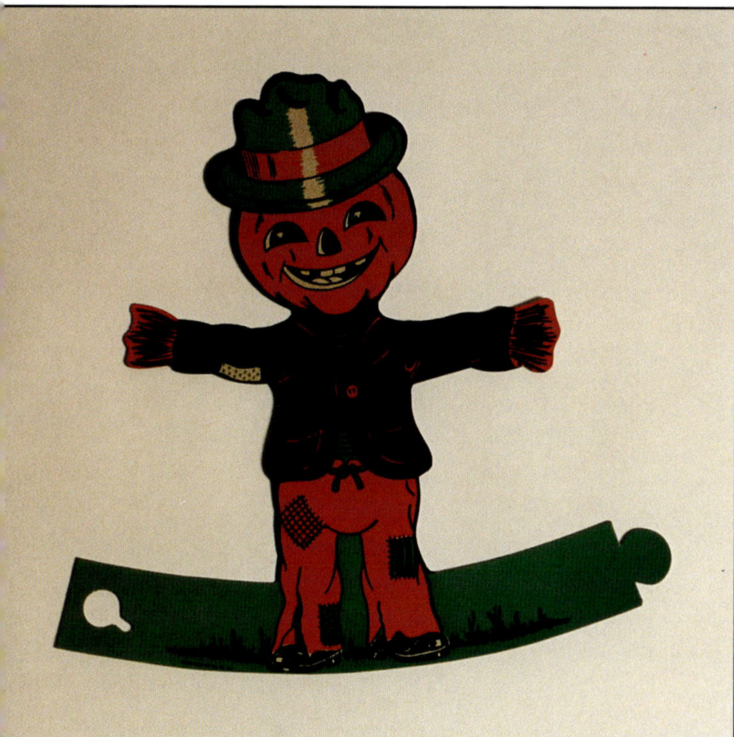

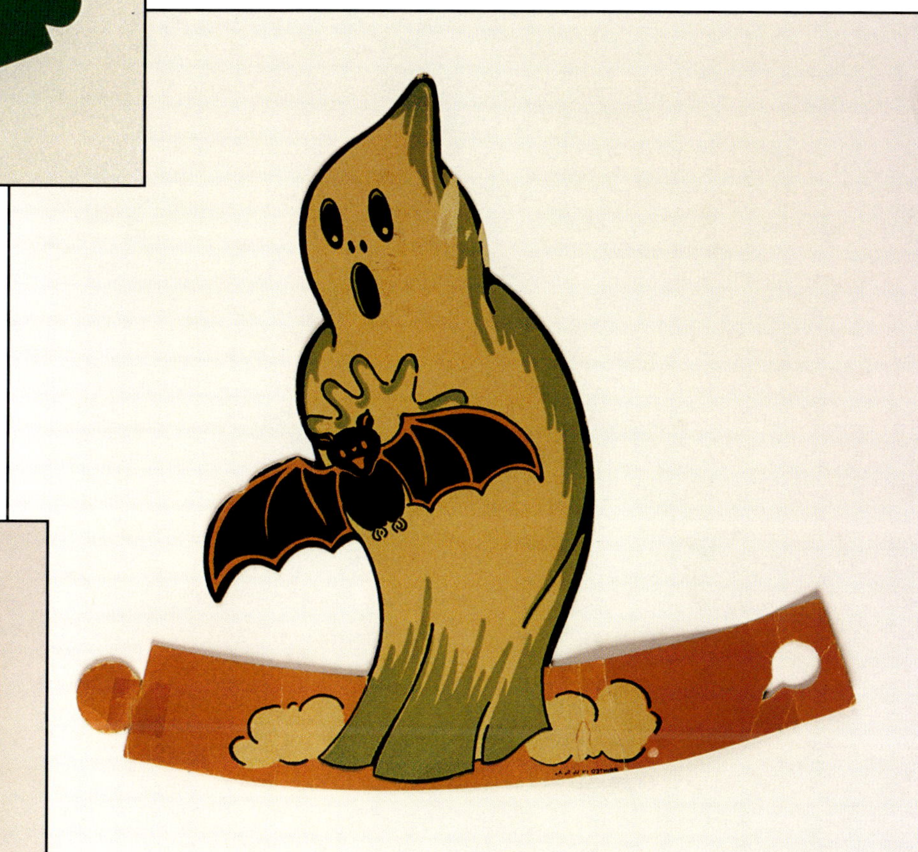

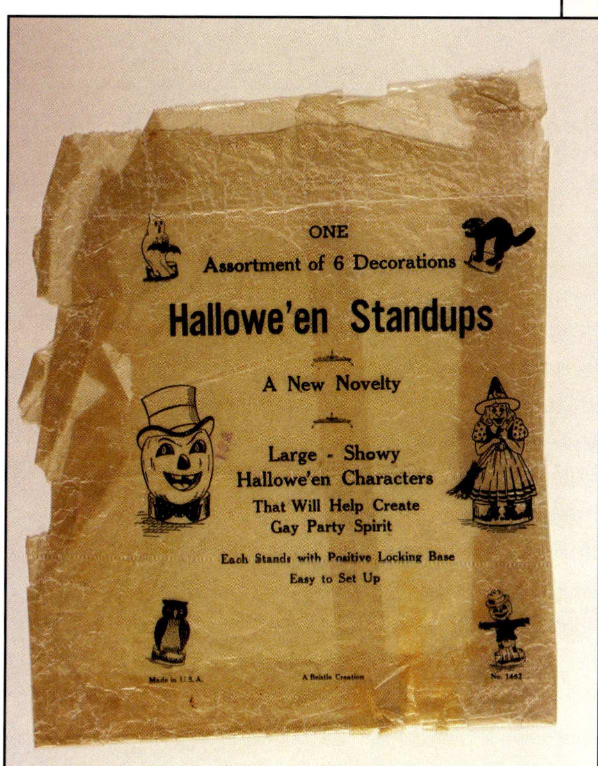
ONE
Assortment of 6 Decorations
Hallowe'en Standups
A New Novelty
Large - Showy
Hallowe'en Characters
That Will Help Create
Gay Party Spirit
Each Stands with Positive Locking Base
Easy to Set Up
Made in U.S.A.
A Beistle Creation

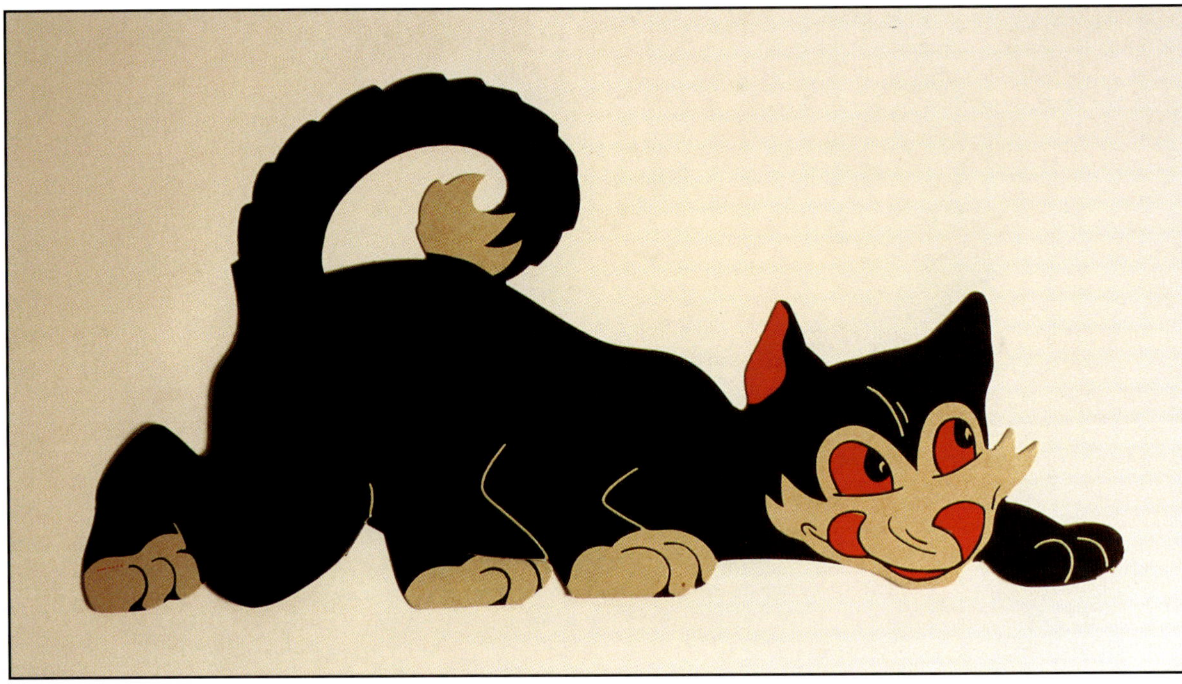

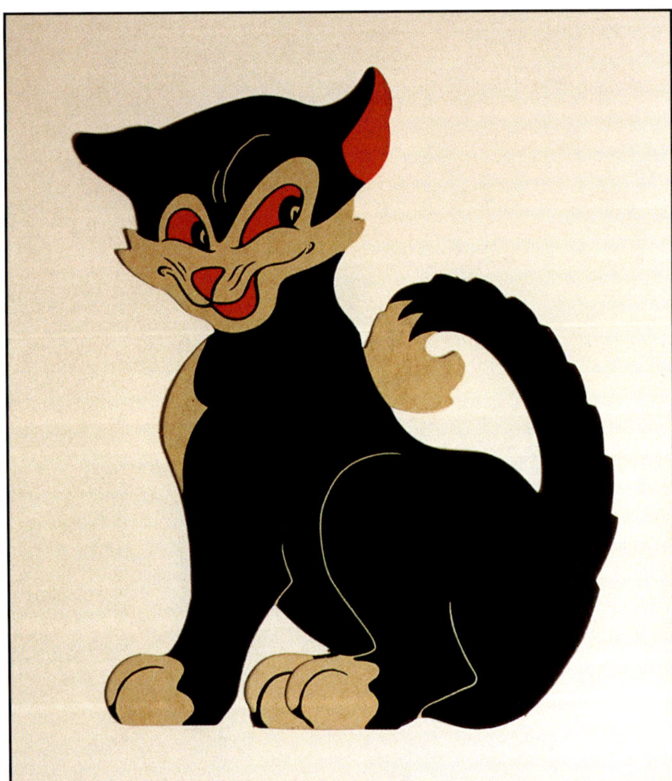

LARGE NOVELTY CATS
Initial Release: 1948
Production Run:
1948 – 1969
These frisky black cats stand upright. Six designs printed one side in orange and black on heavy cardboard. Average size 11" x 13".
*The coloring changed to a vibrant fluorescent three-color design as well as their size (9" x 12") in 1970.
Value: $35 each

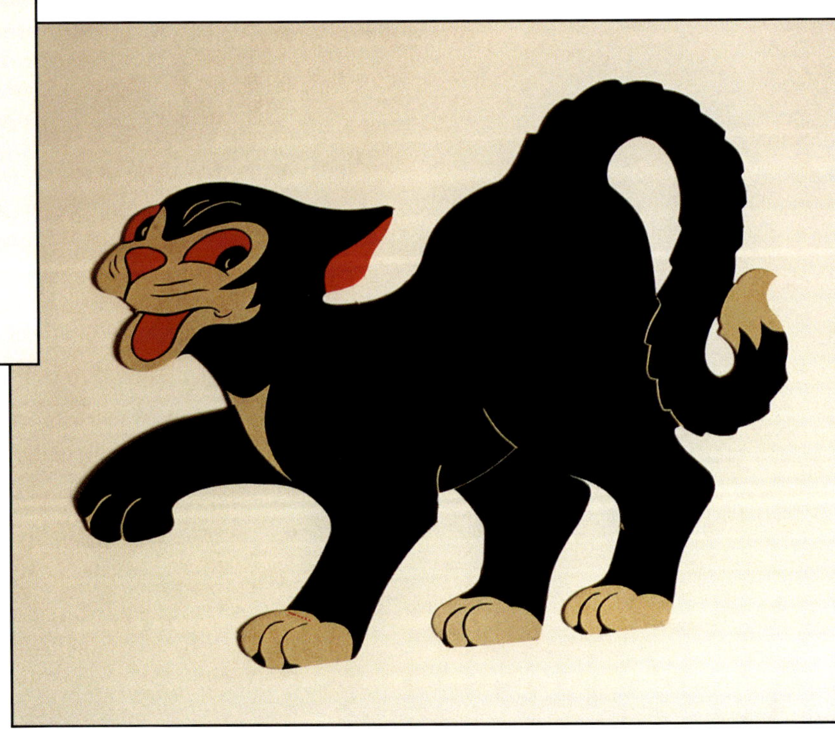

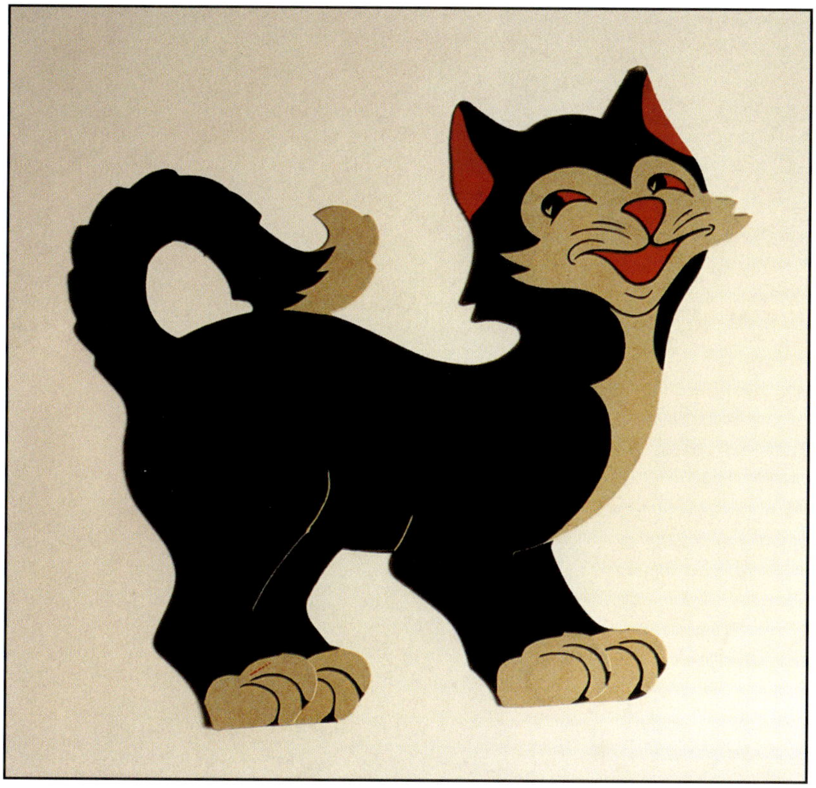

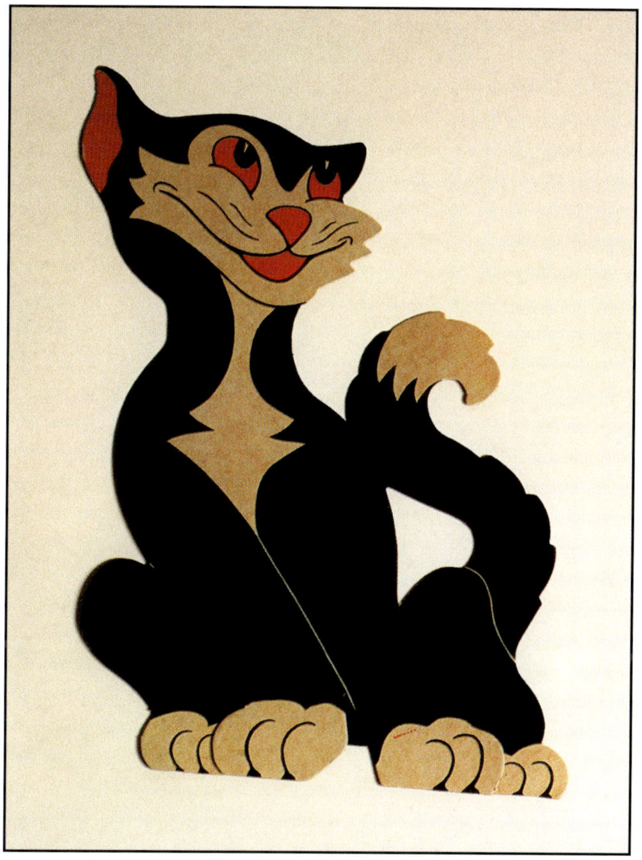

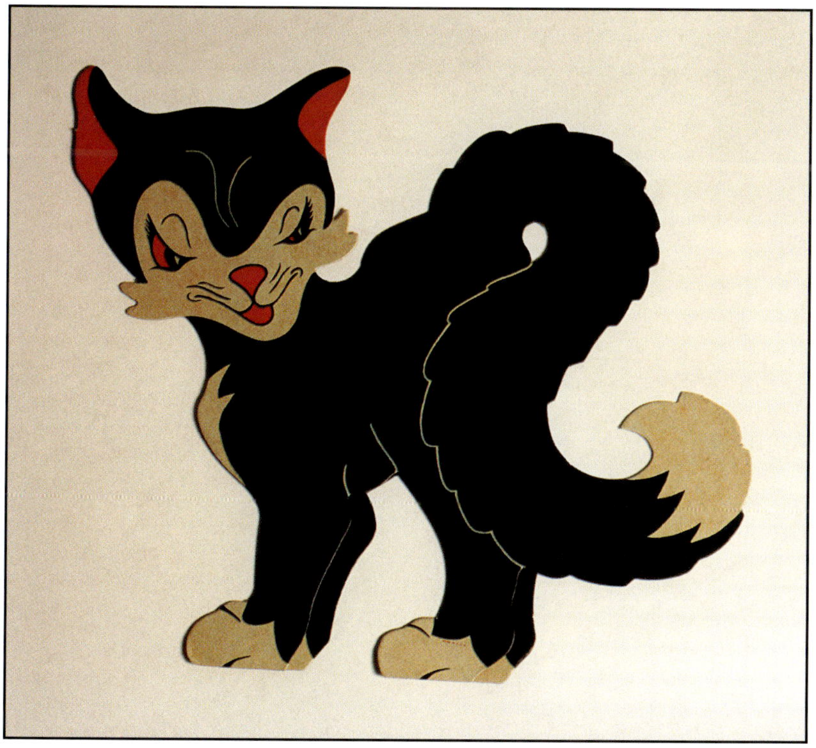

LARGE EMBOSSED HALLOWEEN CUTOUT DECORATIONS
Initial Release: 1941
Production Run: 1941 – 1970
Designed especially for the discriminating buyer who is looking for the best in embossed decorations. This particular set of five designs has three figures 8.5" x 24" and two figures 13" x 14.5". Three-color printing, deeply embossed on cardboard. Packed one dozen assorted to box. For use in Homes, Stores, Theatres, Hotels, Taverns and Taprooms.
*I was quite surprised to find how early these pieces were first introduced to the public. I started trick-or-treating in the mid-1950s and remember quite vividly these Halloween icons decorating our neighbor's windows.
*In 1971 Beistle updated this set's look from a three-color design to a brightly printed one in four colors. Also, this was the introduction of the Owl with both eyes open.
*The "updated" set was still enjoying a healthy sales run up to 1985, which is my cutoff date for this book. For whatever reason, the Owl lost its popularity and was discontinued in 1980.
Value: $35 – $55 range

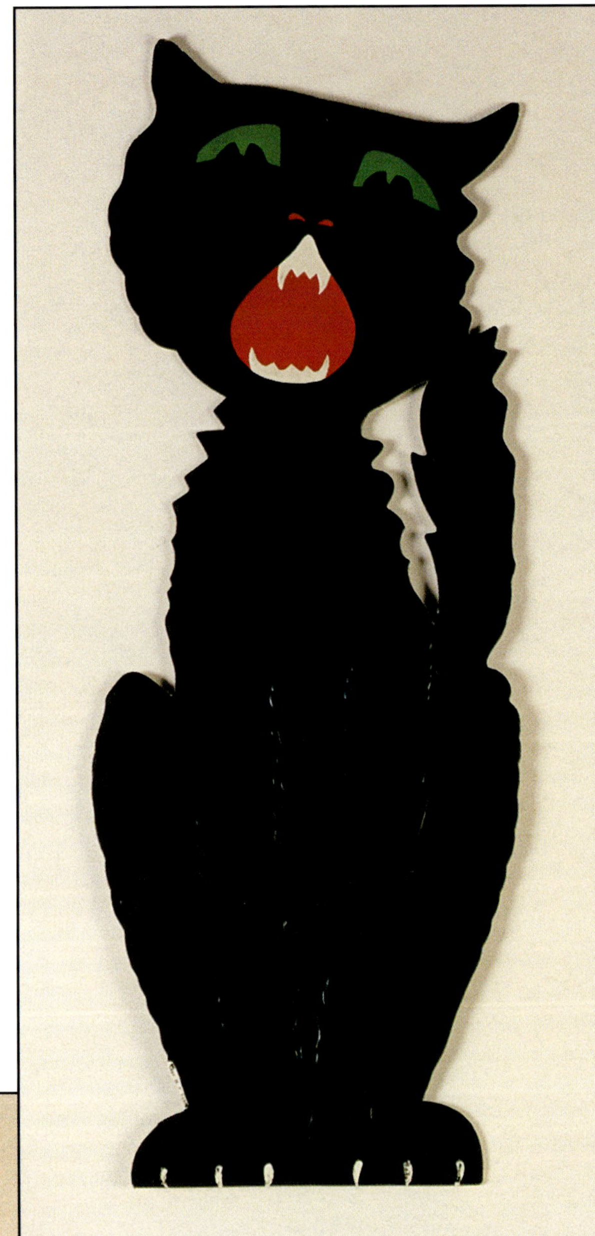

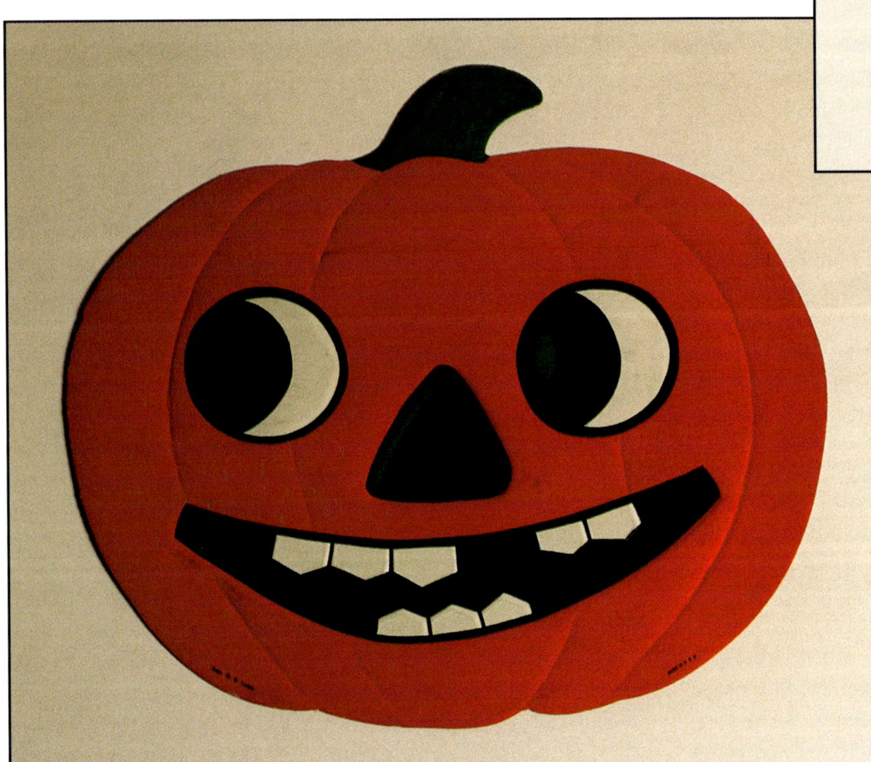

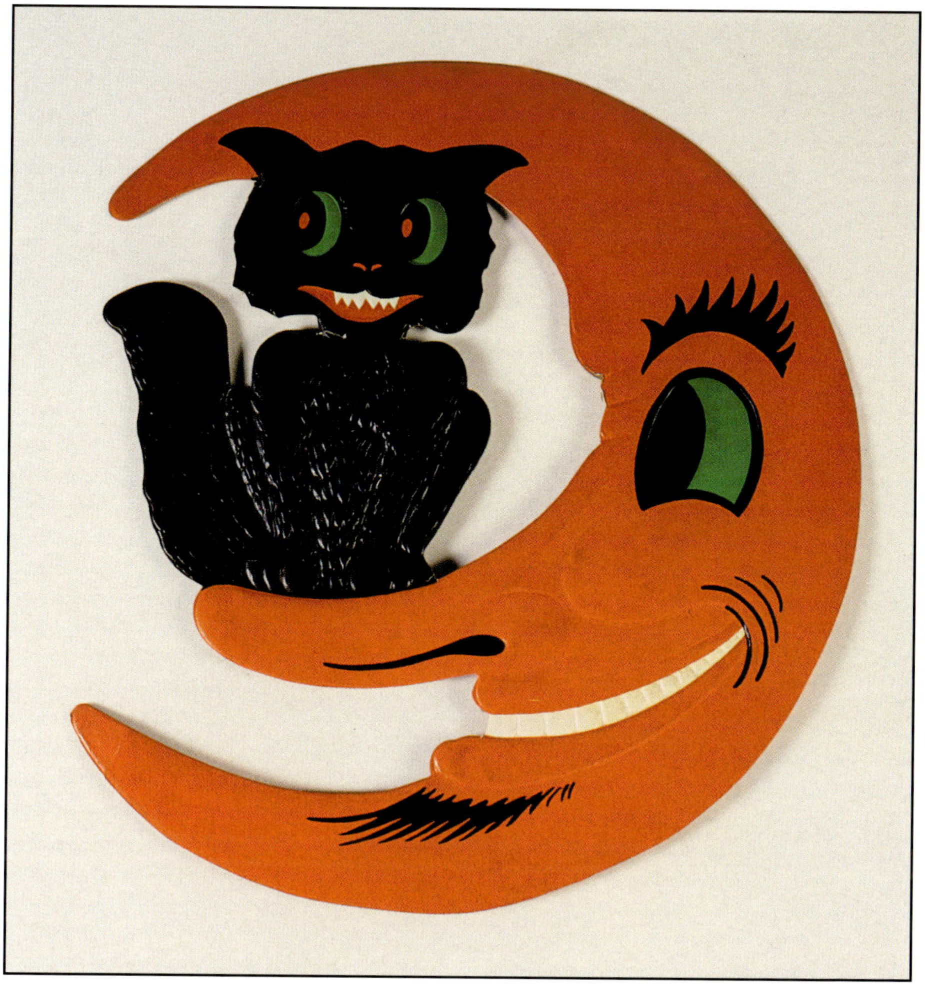

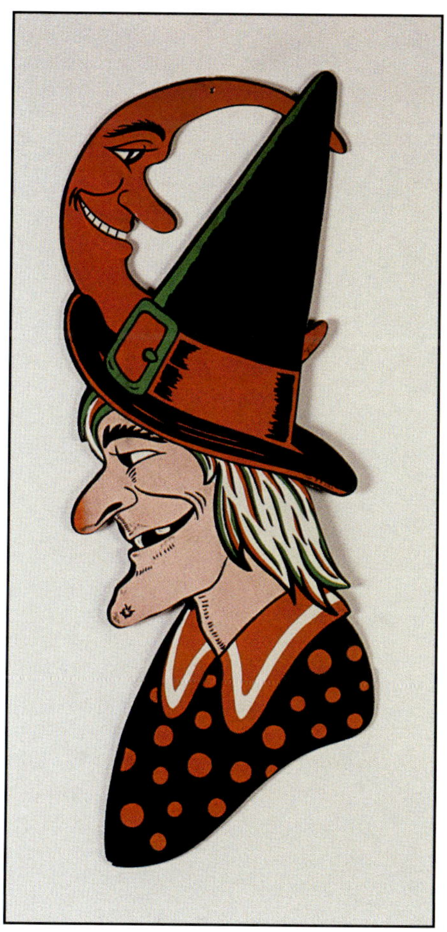

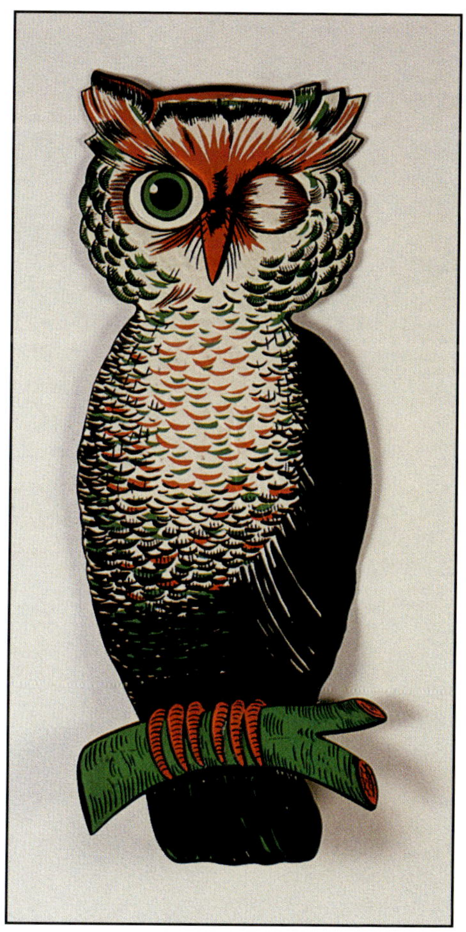

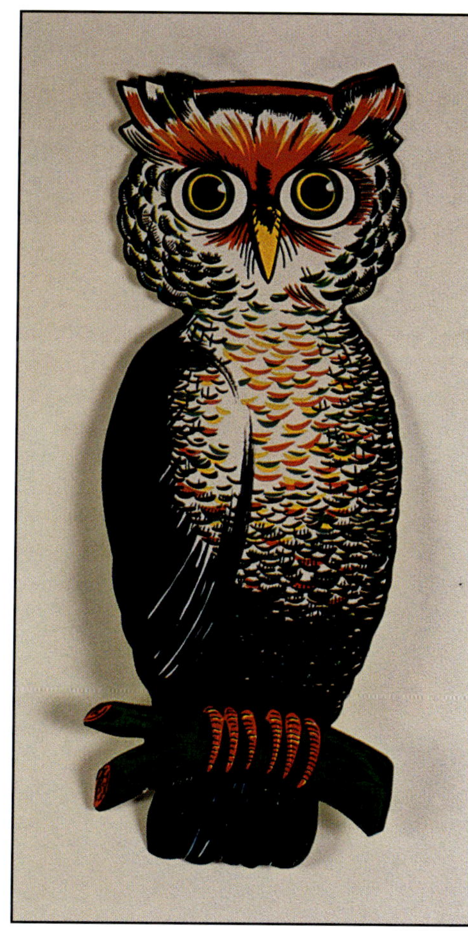

CLOWN DANCER
Initial Release: 1940
Production Run: 1940 – 1947
Printed orange and black head, hands, body and feet on cardboard with orange and black folding honeycomb tissue arms and legs.
*Dancer shown with its paper wrapper to the right.
Value: $35

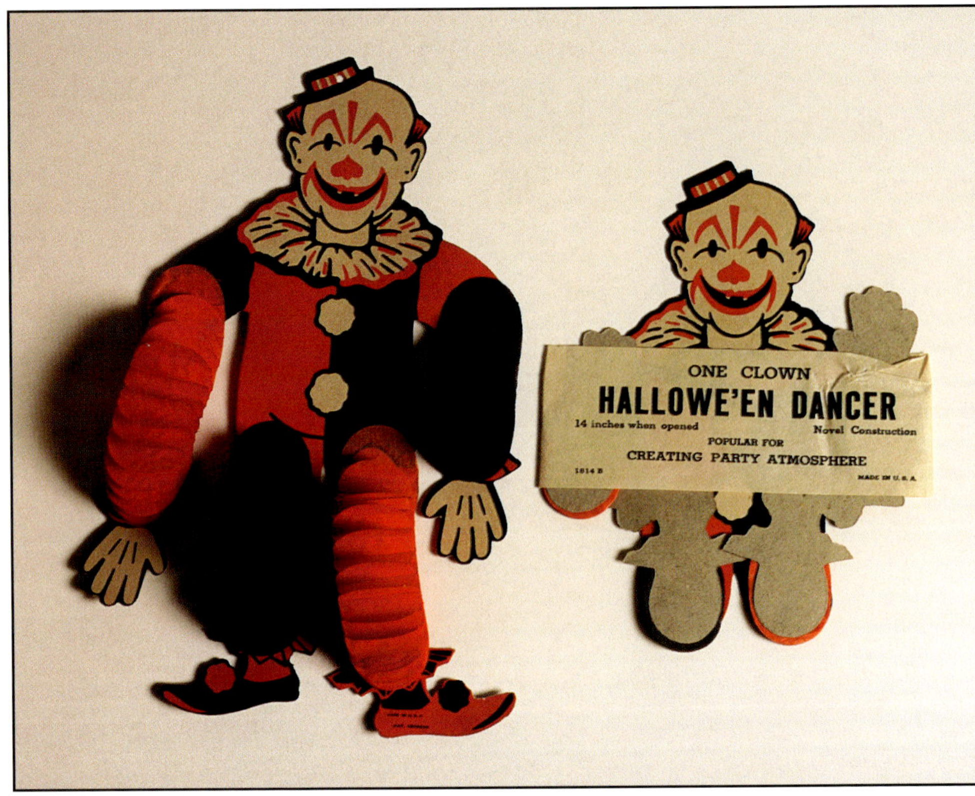

EMBOSSED CUTOUTS
Initial Release: 1952
Production Run: 1952 – 1966
Excitingly new and attractively priced are these outstanding Halloween figures. Printed in three colors, orange, green and black, on high quality embossing board. Deeply embossed and die-cut to shape. Four designs. Approximately 6.5" x 18" in size.
*A rare behind-the-scenes look at two views of this set of die-cuts after the printing process but before their shapes have been cut out.
Value: $55 – $75 each

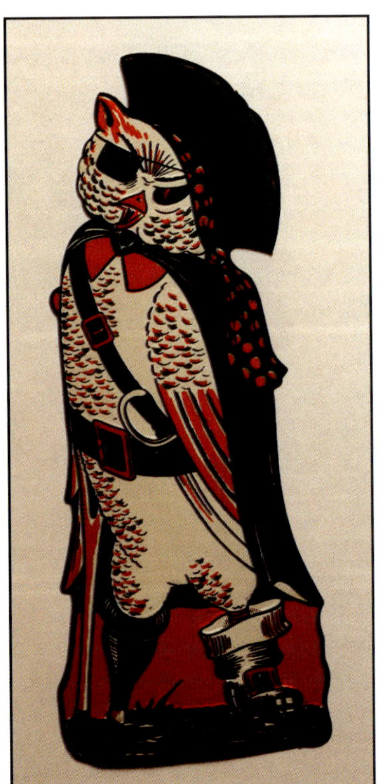
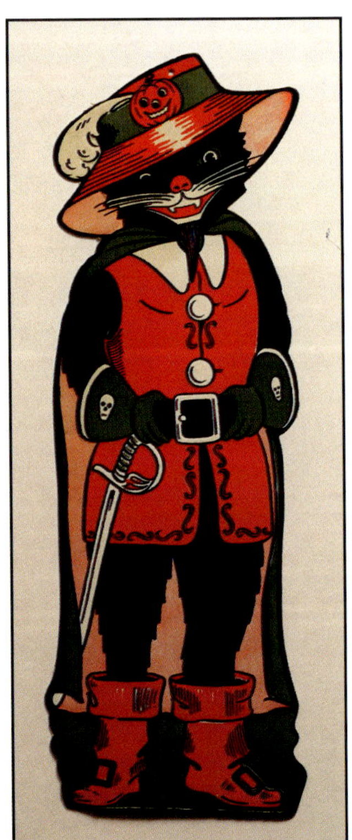
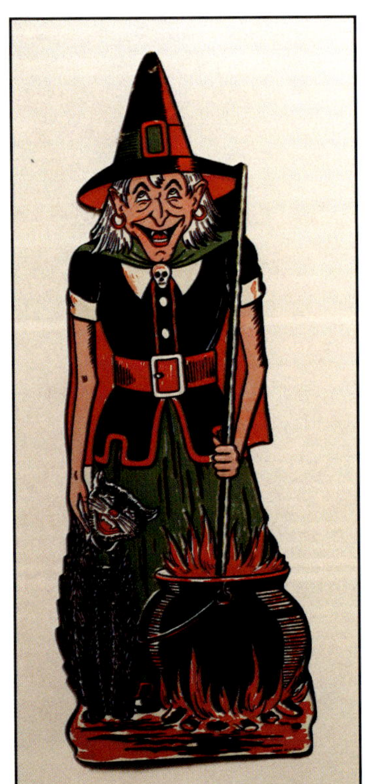
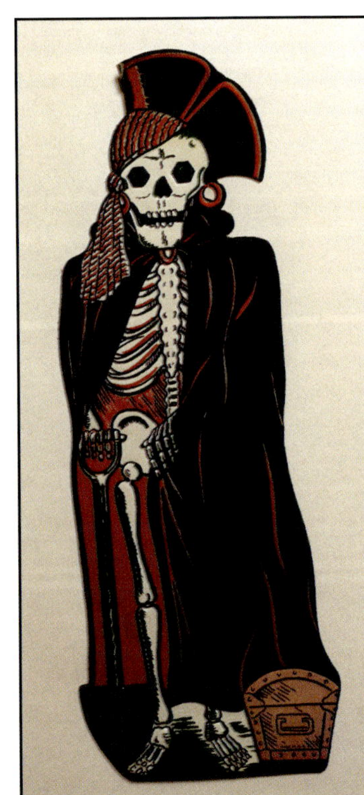

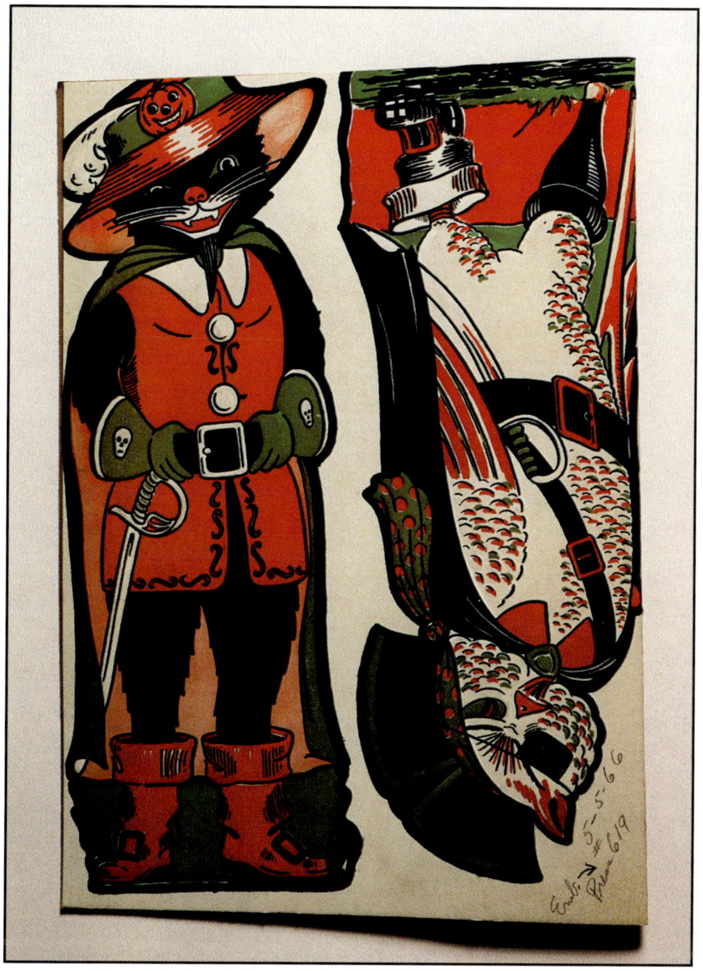

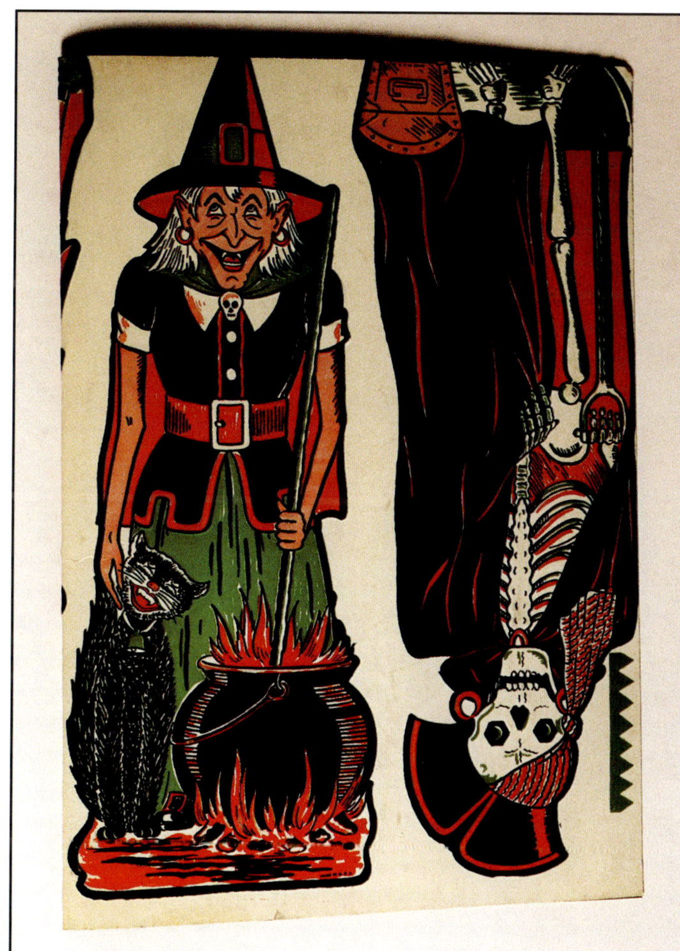

HALLOWEEN CENTERPIECE
Initial Release: 1955
Production Run: One year only: 1955
Printed in two colors orange and black on heavy stock and die-cut to shape, these appropriate Halloween scenes are formed into a closed hexagon-shaped centerpiece, that's not only decorative but useful. When placed on the table, the open center may be filled with candies, fruits or nuts. Size 6" wide, 10" long, and 9" high. Two designs.
*As sometimes happens, I could only find the one example in the Beistle archives. The two accompanying photos show both the front and back of this treat bowl.
Value: $125 each

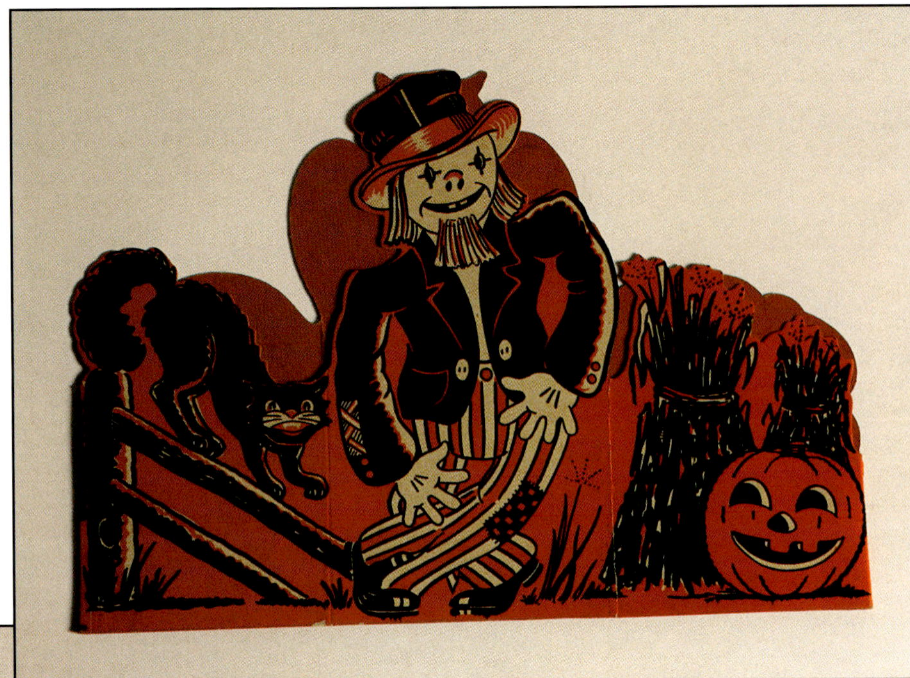

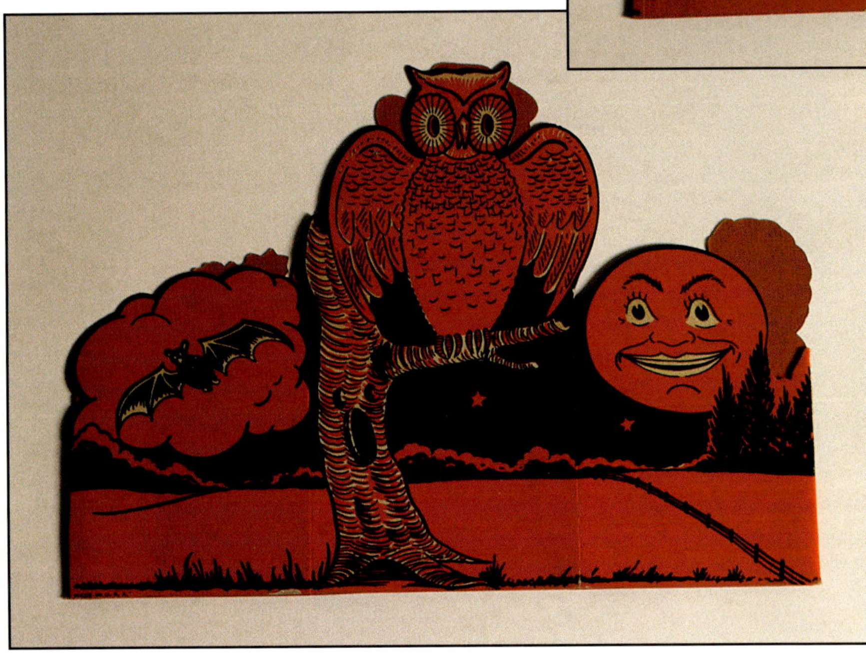

WITCH ON BROOM
Initial Release: 1952
Production Run: 1952 – 1966
Silhouette witch die-cut from stiff black paper mounted on a 12" broom stick with a 5" orange and black fringed crepe paper broom. Effective as a hanging or wall decoration. Size 10" x 12".
*Note the annotations made on the artist's model including where to place the embossed Beistle mark along with their customary "Made in USA."
Value: $15

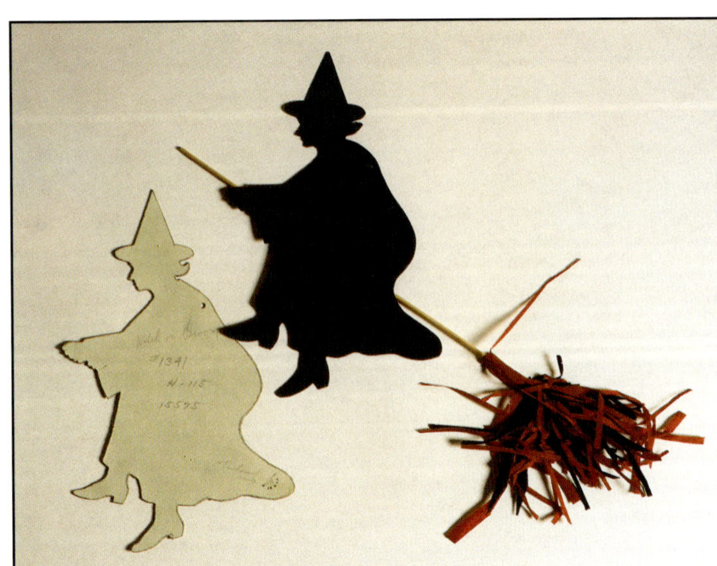

CREEPY ALICE
Initial Release: 1957
Production Run: 1957 – 1968
This gruesome witch face lends the right atmosphere to Halloween decorating. Printed one side, orange and black, on quality white stock with finely fringed orange and black crepe hair on either side of face. An ideal hanging decoration for wall or window. Size 18.25" x 14.5". One design.
*You can count this one in as another Halloween icon from the Baby Boomer era. Check out the updated version of 1969 – not only are the features modernized but the spelling of her name is given a new twist (Creepy Alyce).
Value: $65

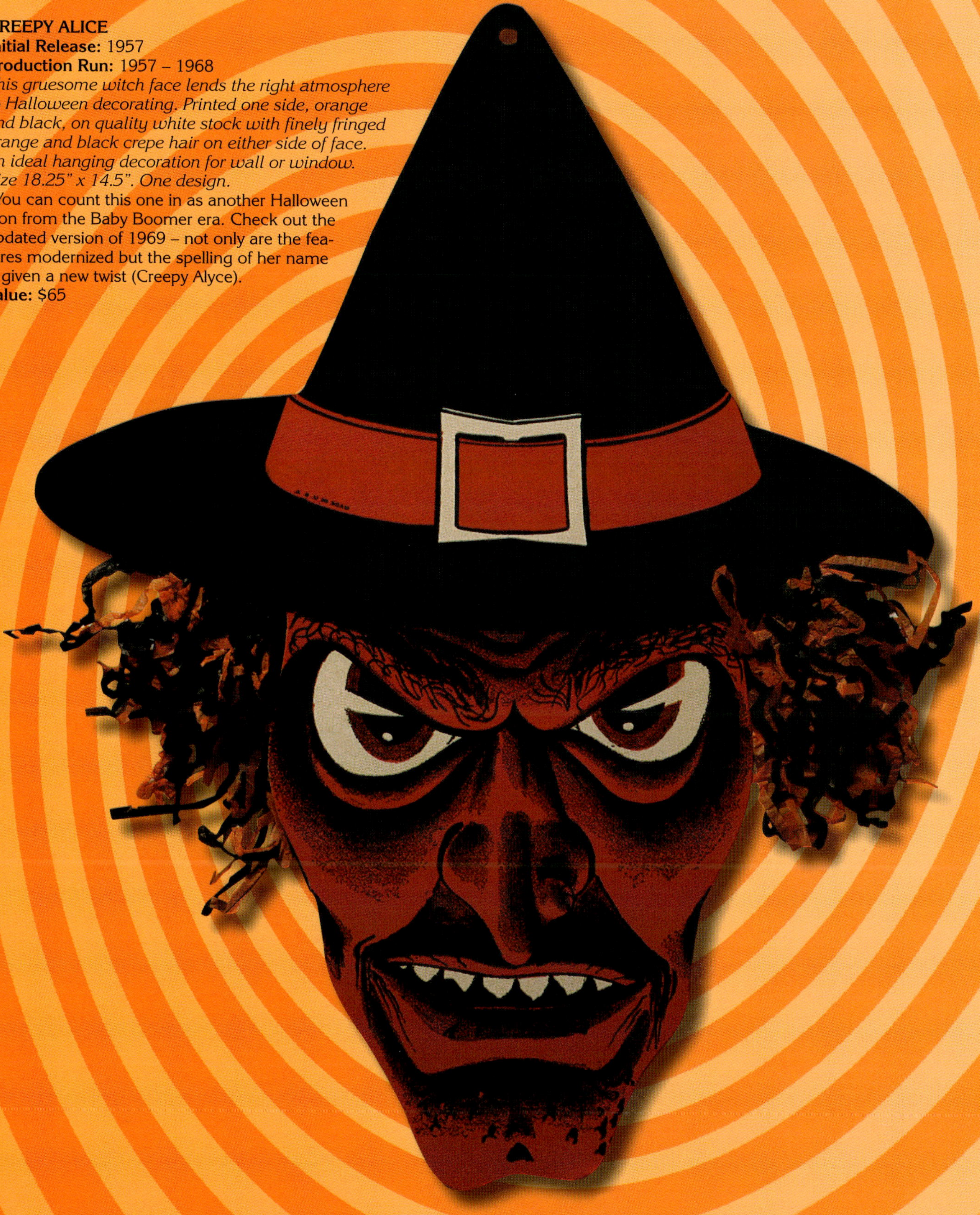

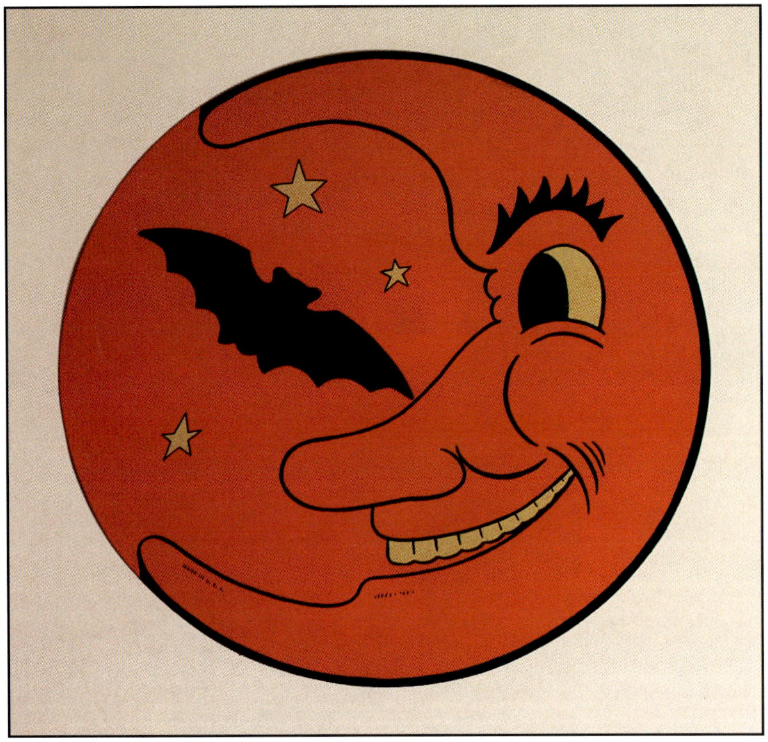

REALISTIC HALLOWEEN CUTOUTS
Initial Release: 1955
Production Run: 1955 – 1958
Halloween characters projected on appropriate background create a dimensional effect which makes these new wall decorations real in appearance. The characters are cleverly attached to the background and designed to move freely so that the slightest vibration will set them in motion. Size 12" x 12". Packed equally assorted four designs.
Value: $35 – $55 range

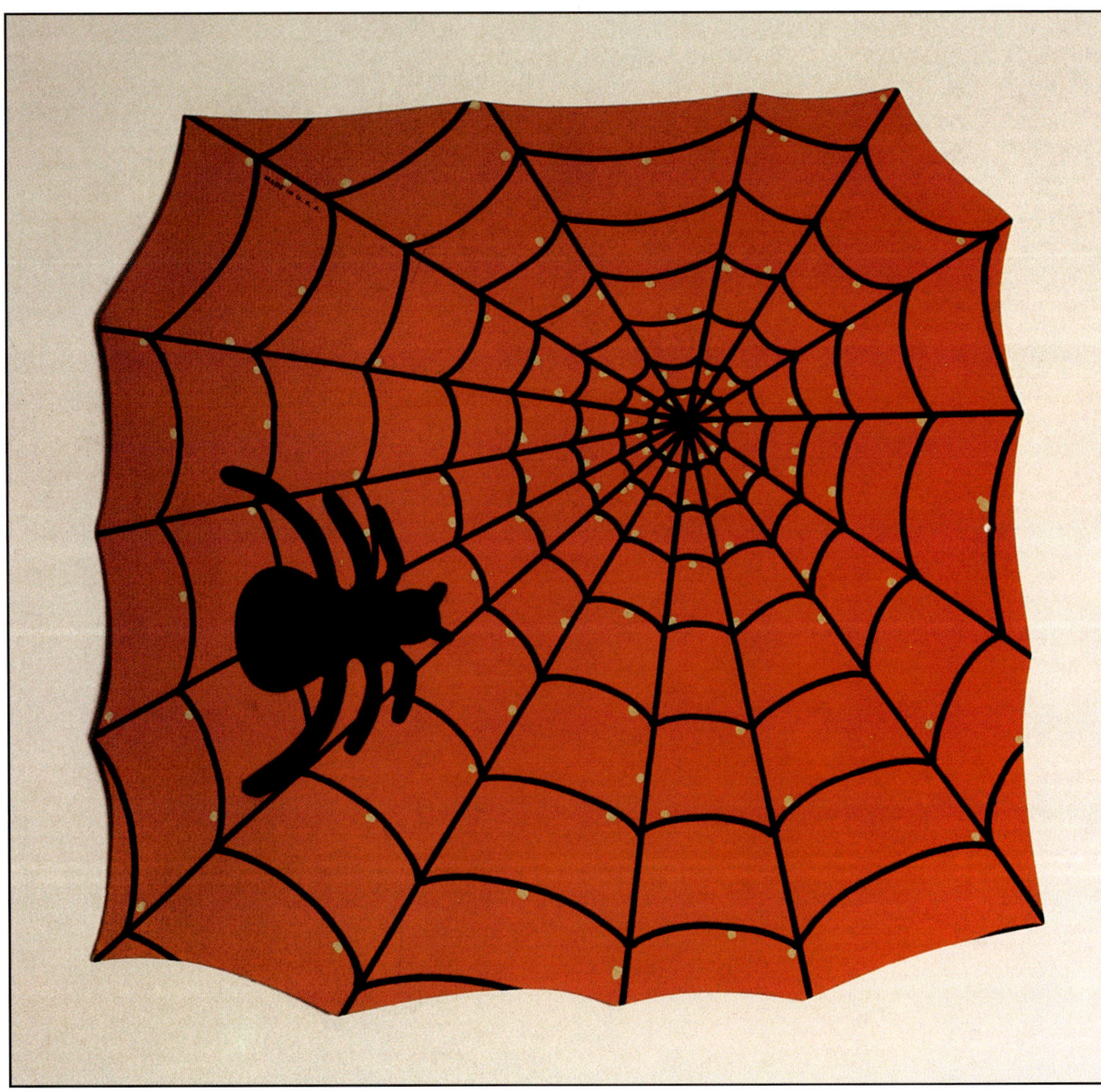

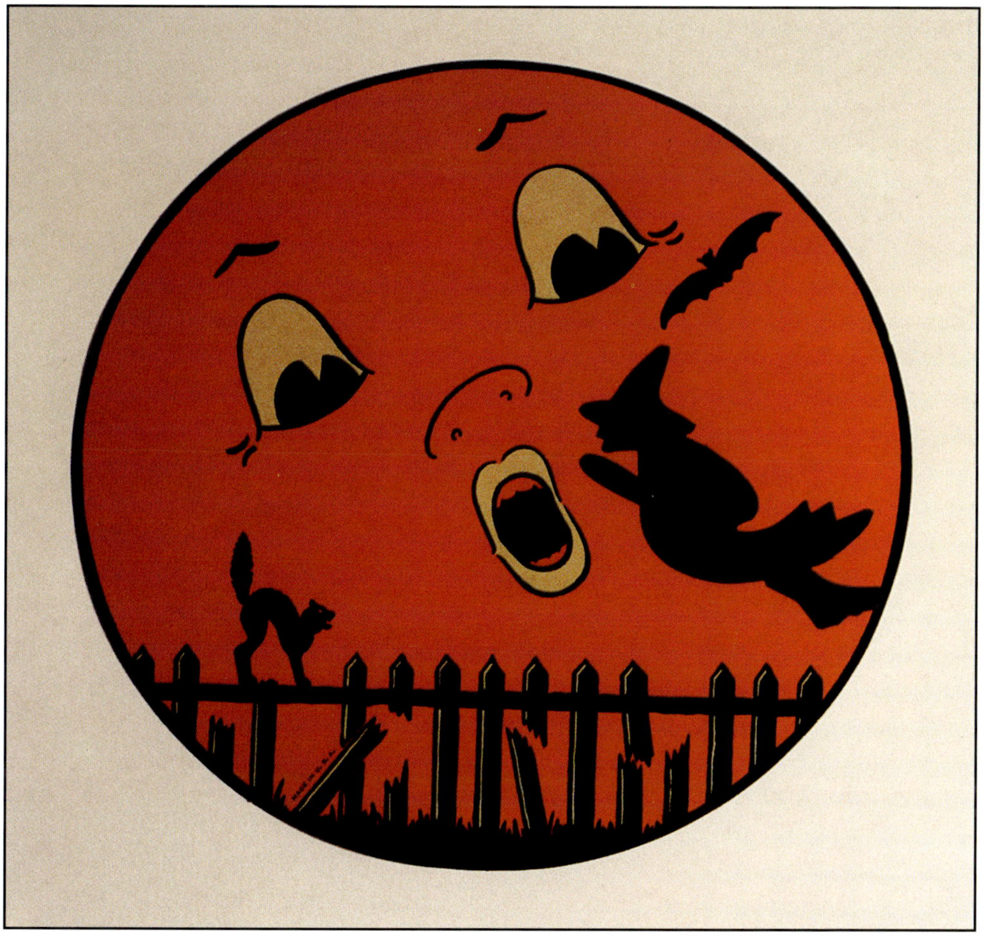

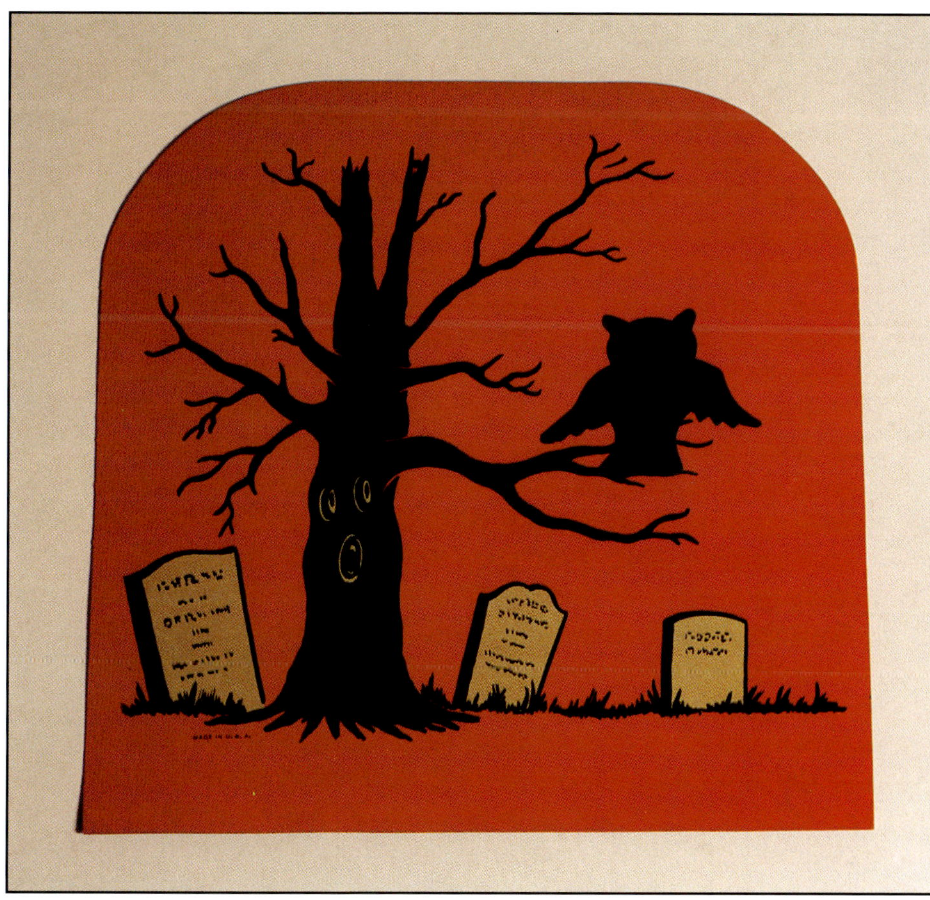

LARGE EMBOSSED CUTOUTS
Initial Release: 1952
Production Run: 1952 – 1963
A deluxe set of embossed plaques. This comical "Sad Witch" and happy "Jack-O-Lantern" will please the buyer looking for large wall decorations. Two designs printed in three bright contrasting colors on fine quality embossing board. Size 12" x 18".
Value: $45 – $65 range

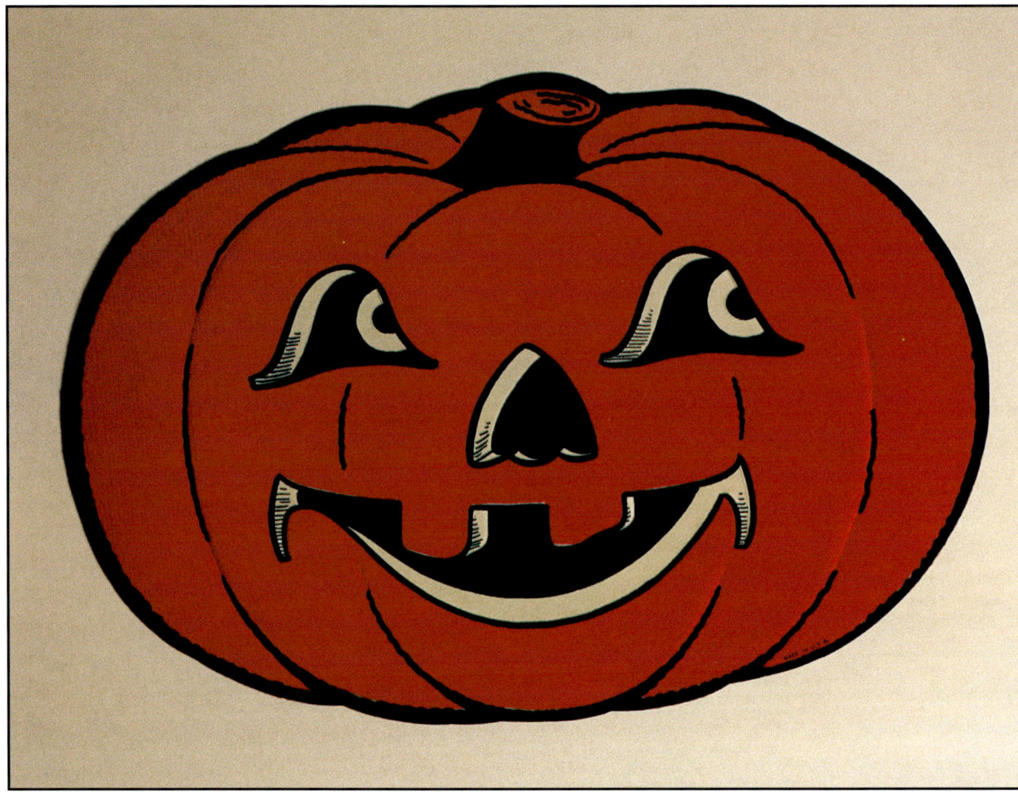

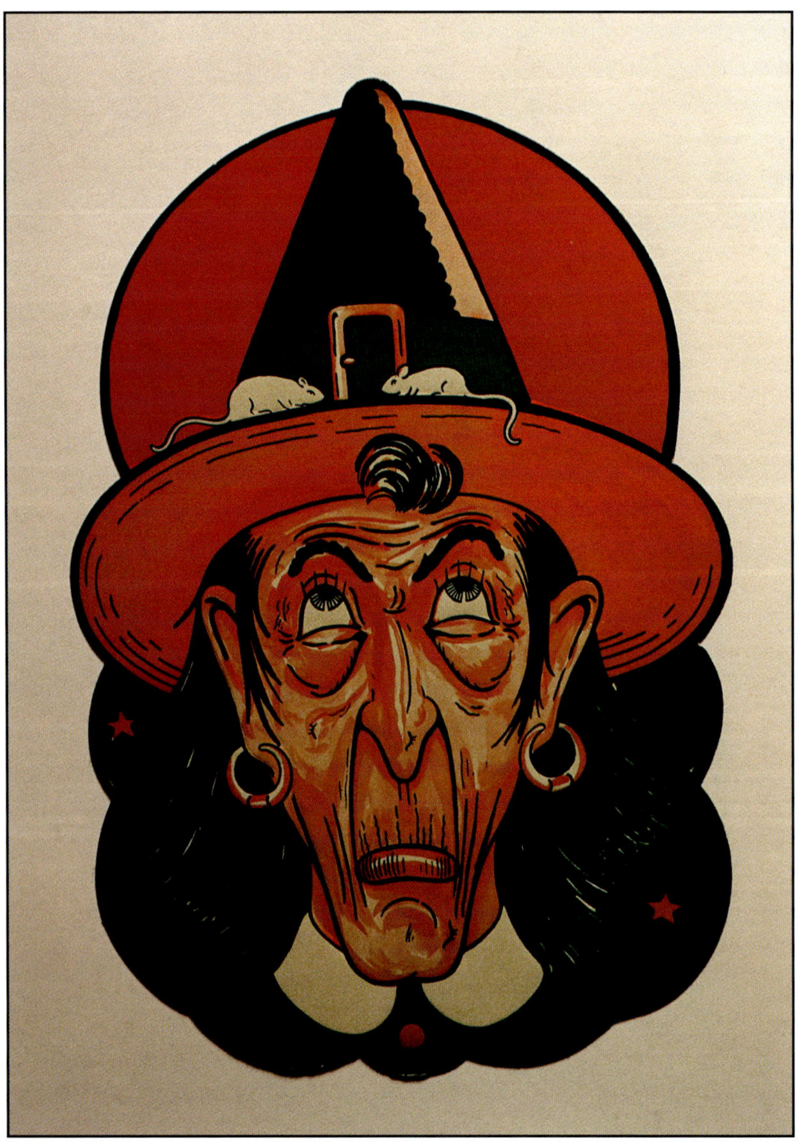

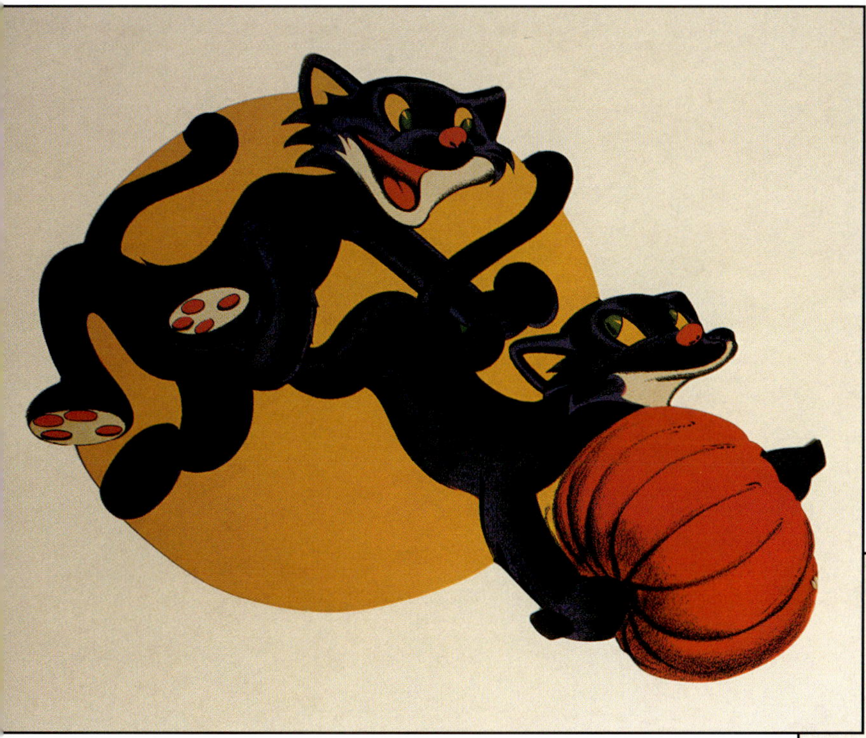

HALLOWEEN PLAQUES
Initial Release: 1960
Production Run: 1960 – 1962
A popular new assortment of colorful Halloween plaques priced for volume sales. Printed in gay, bright six-color design on quality stock and die-cut to shape. Packaged three designs in a polyurethane bag with printed top. Size 11" x 15.5".
Value: $45 – $55 range

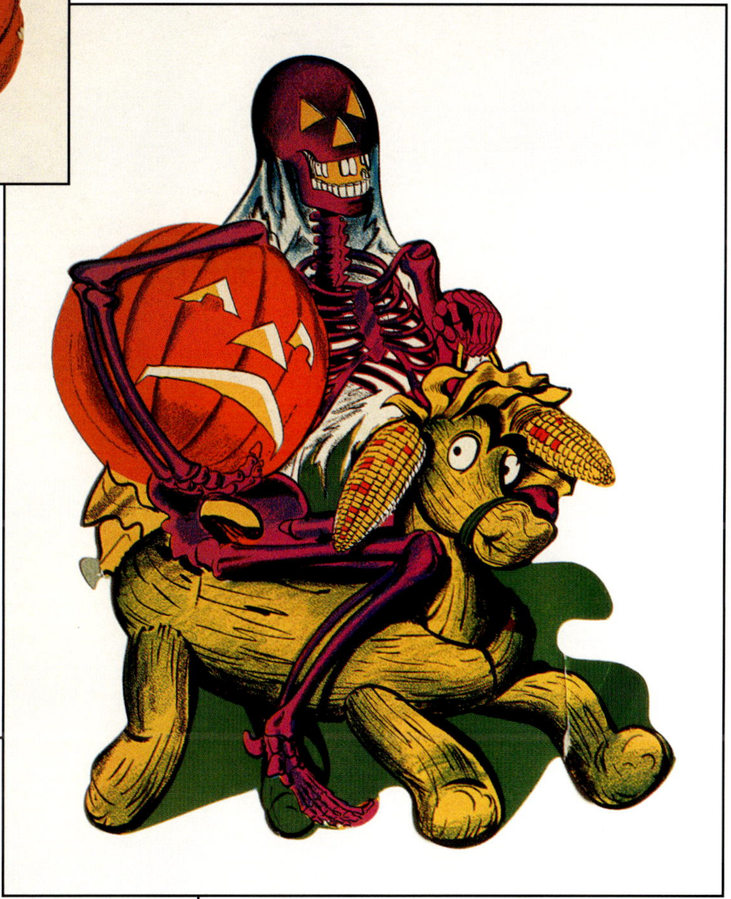

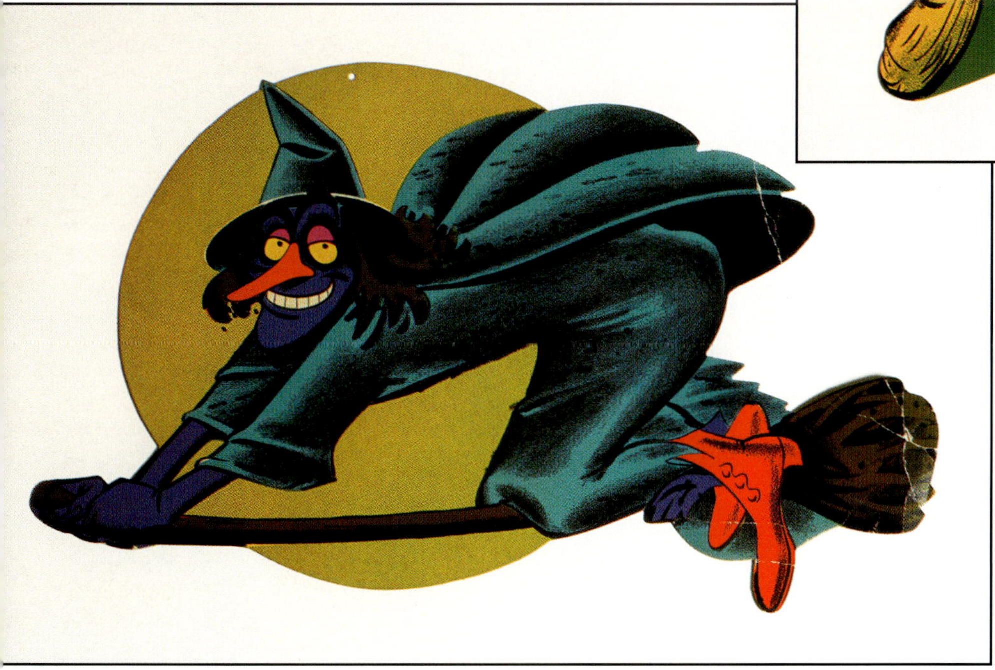

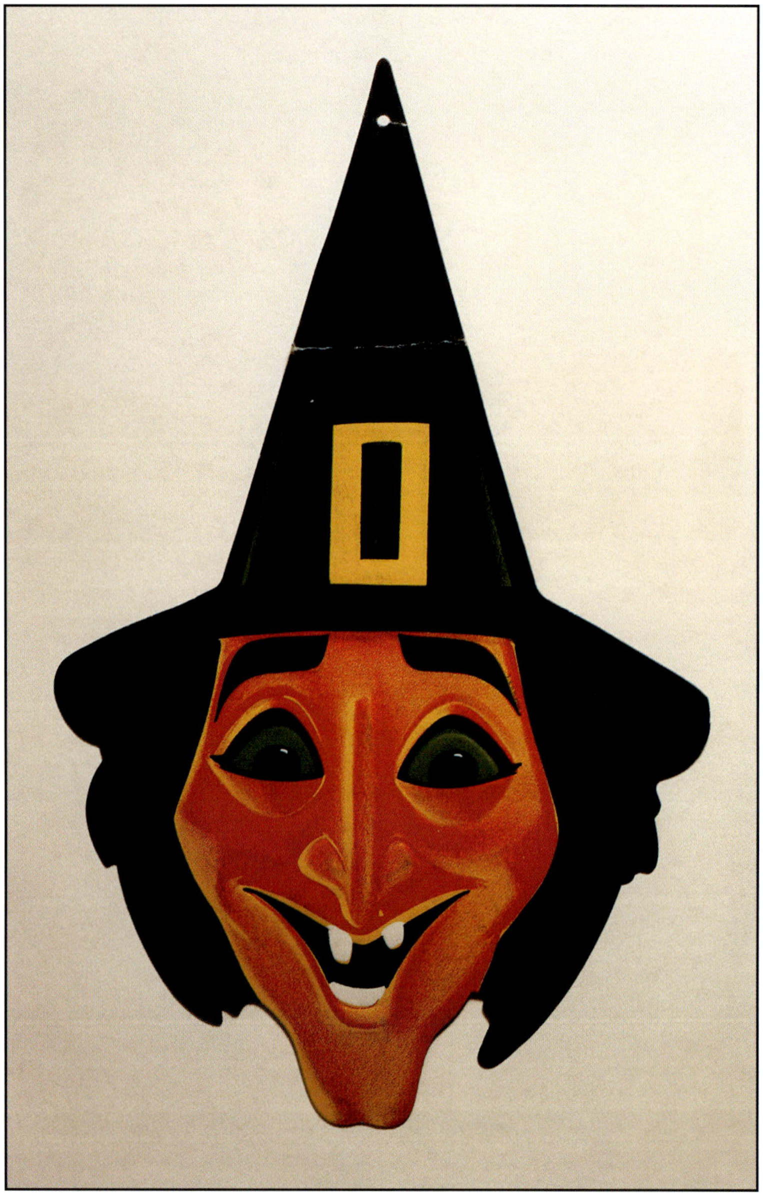

LARGE EMBOSSED CUTOUTS
Initial Release: 1964
Production Run: 1964 – 1972
A new deluxe set of embossed plaques. Four designs printed in three bright colors, deeply embossed and die-cut to shape. Quality decorations that add lively zeal to seasonal festivities. Approximately 12" x 18" in size.
Value: $25 – $40 range

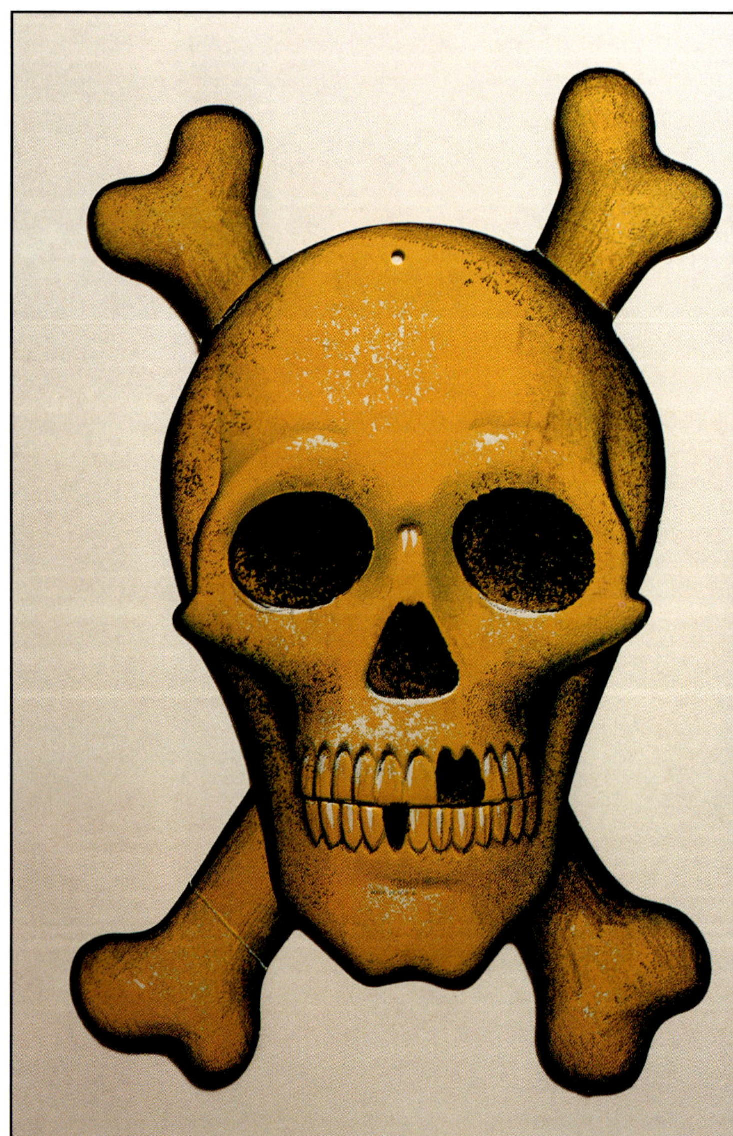

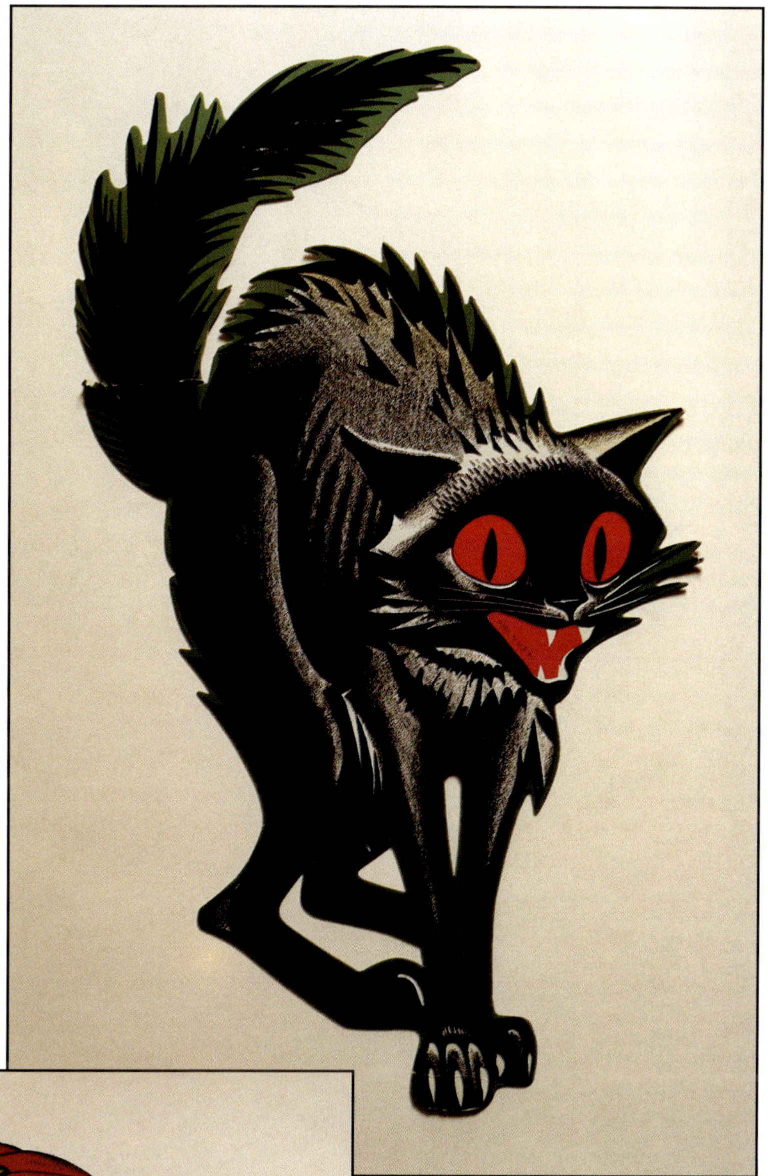

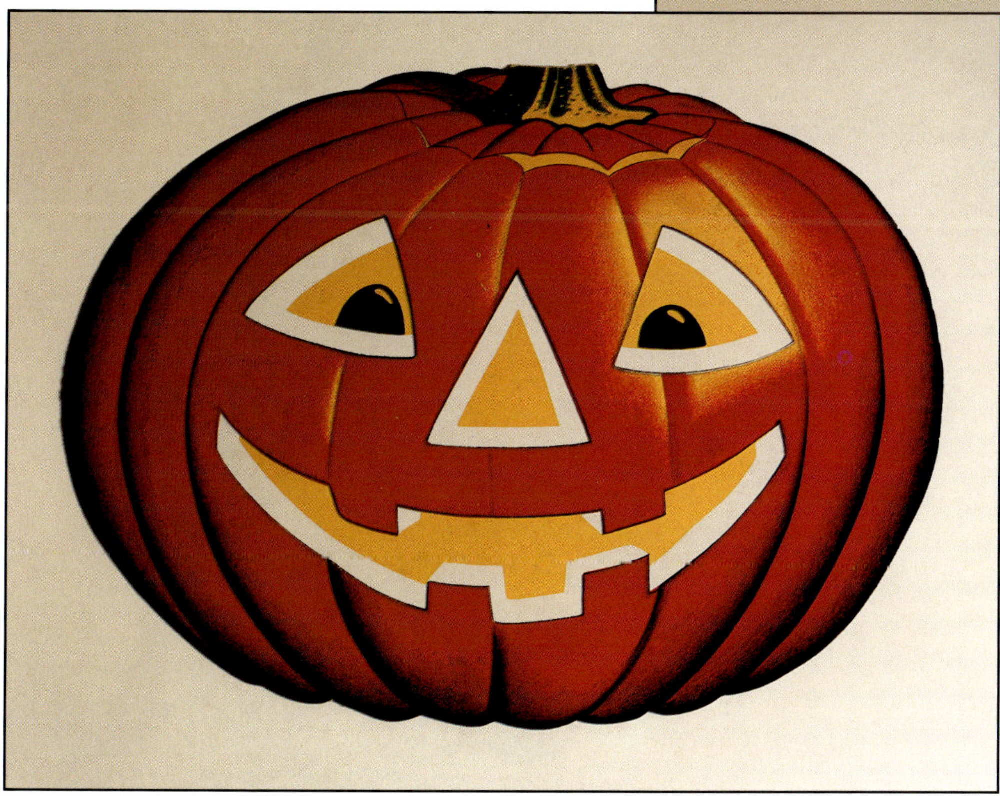

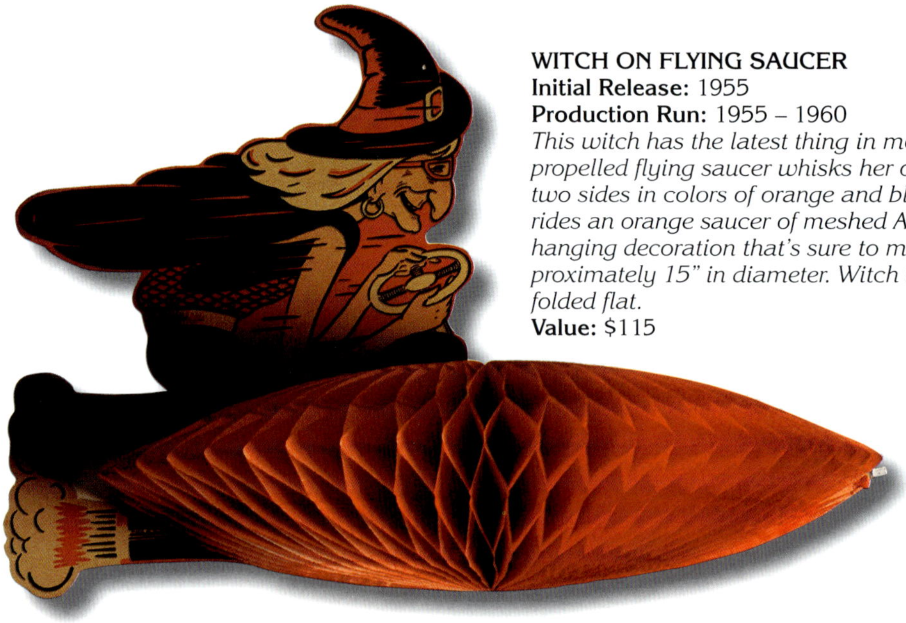

WITCH ON FLYING SAUCER
Initial Release: 1955
Production Run: 1955 – 1960
This witch has the latest thing in modern transportation, as a jet propelled flying saucer whisks her on her merry way. Printed on two sides in colors of orange and black, this Halloween witch rides an orange saucer of meshed Art-Tissue. A new and exciting hanging decoration that's sure to make a big hit. Saucer approximately 15" in diameter. Witch 9" x 11". One design. Packed folded flat.
Value: $115

WITCH ON SAUCER
Initial Release: 1961
Production Run: 1961 – 1966
A popular-priced Halloween Centerpiece or hanging decoration. Printed in colors of orange and black with saucer-shaped base of bright golden yellow meshed Art-Tissue. Saucer 15" in diameter. Witch cutout 9" x 11". One design. Packed folded flat.
*I happen to prefer this "updated" version of the 1955 model. The former gives the feeling of stiffness while the abovementioned die-cut exudes more of a feeling of fluidity of movement. Again, I need to mention the attention to detail that is Beistle's forte. Note how when the die cut is folded flat (for storage), the area that will only be seen when it is unopened is completely decorated as a flying saucer.
Value: $145

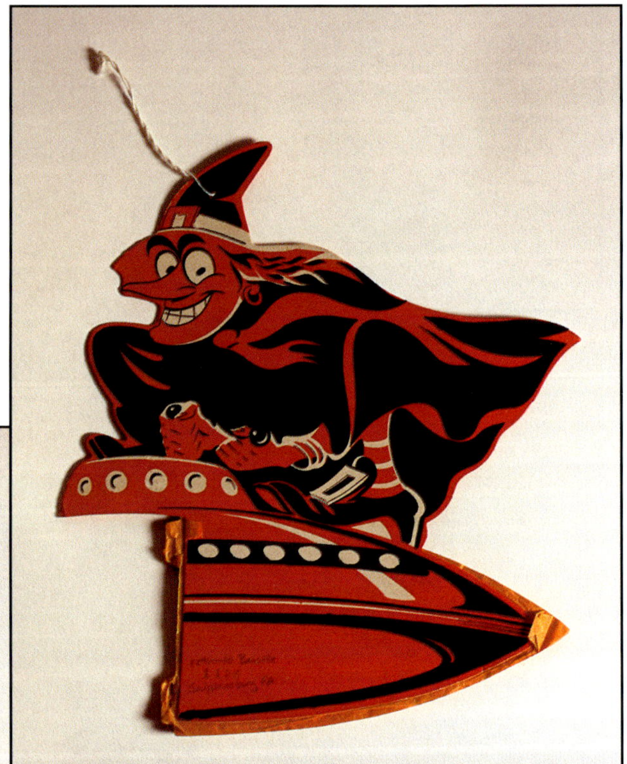

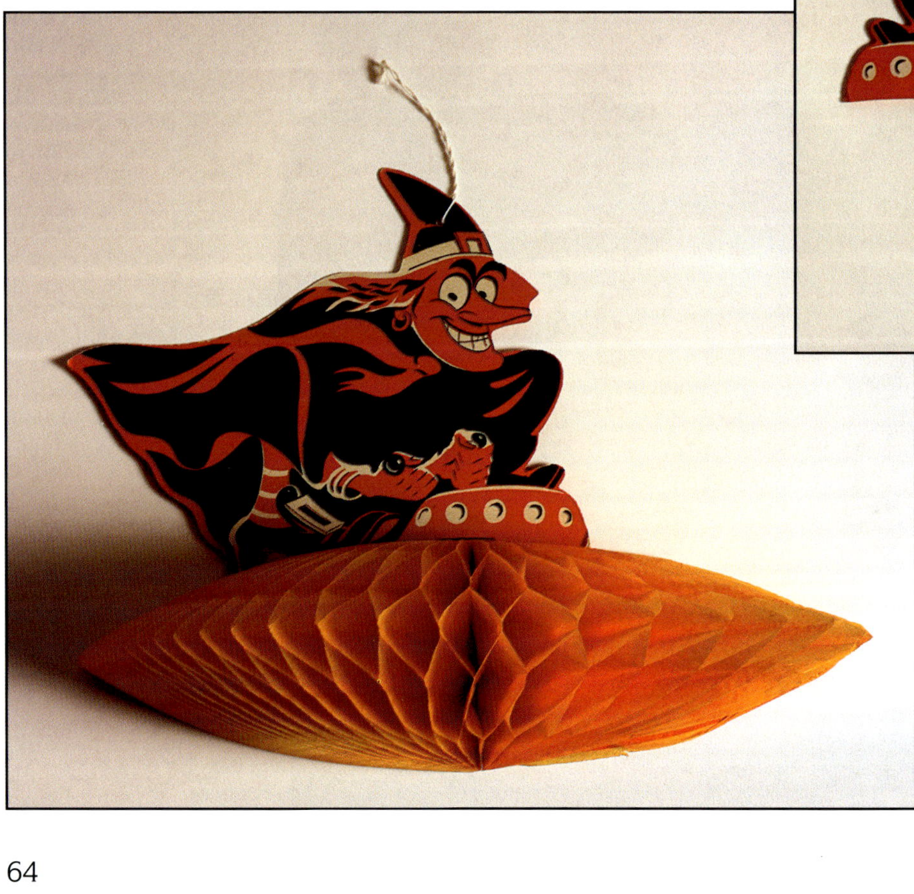

SCARECROW CENTERPIECE

Initial Release: 1960
Production Run: 1960 – 1970
A new popular priced Halloween centerpiece. Comical scarecrow printed both sides in three colors. Yellow cornshock and orange pumpkin of meshed Art-Tissue open full-round to complete centerpiece and form a standing base. Size 10" x 12". One design. Packs folded flat.
*In 1964, the Beistle Company offered this centerpiece packaged in a printed poly bag with header.
Value: $45

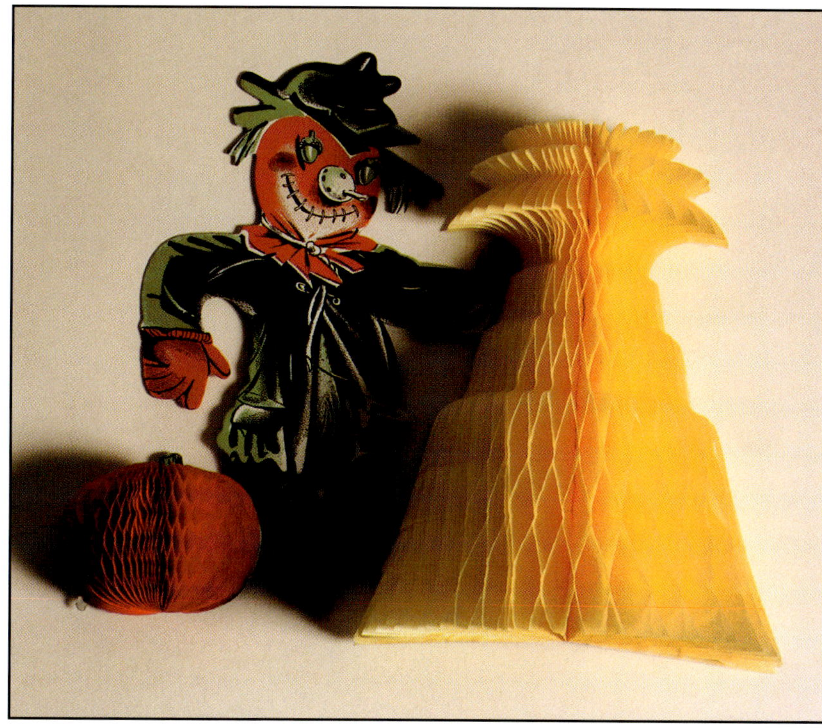

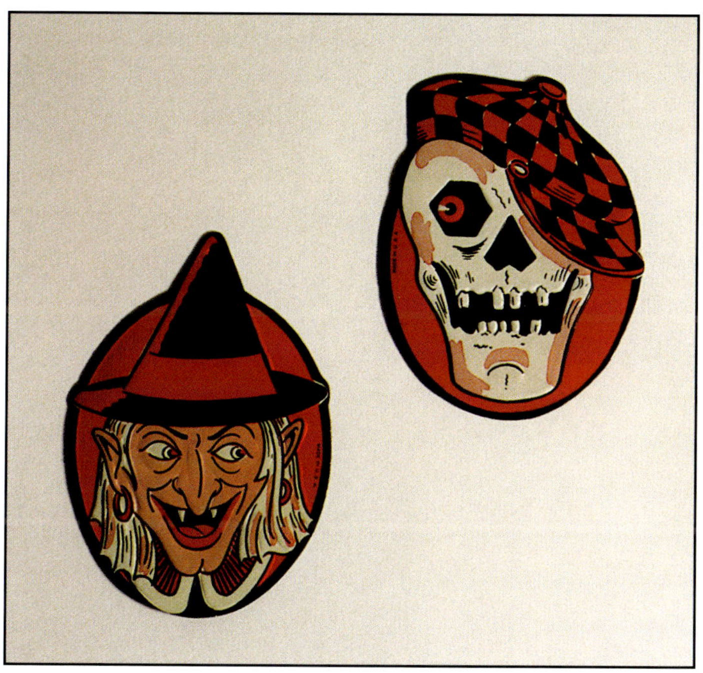

EMBOSSED CUTOUTS

Initial Release: 1952
Production Run: 1952 – 1955
A gay assortment of eight designs; an embossed specialty, printed in rich colors, orange and black on high grade embossing board. A lively party decoration for trimming walls and windows. Size 4.5" x 6".
*Another behind-the-scenes view: a set of eight Halloween decorations before they are die cut alongside the way they were packaged. Also observe the notations on the packaged set where it is written that as of 5/06/55, these pieces were deemed obsolete and were subsequently discontinued as of 1956.
Value: $375 for the set of eight

(Continued on following 2 pages)

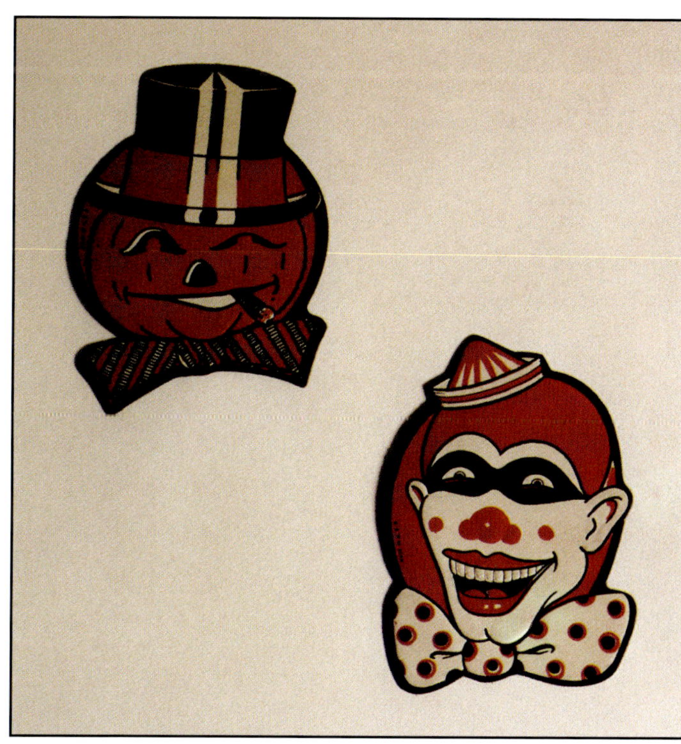

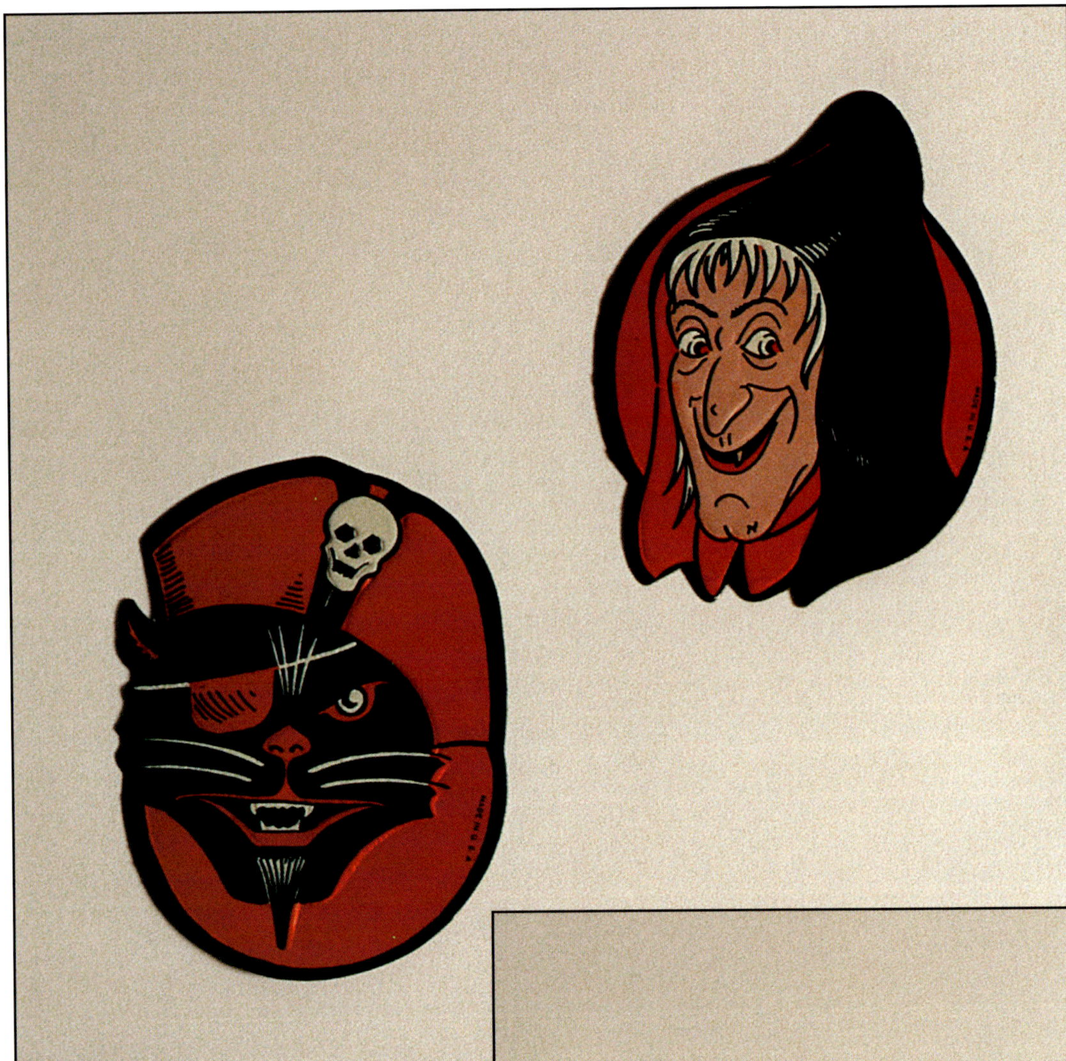

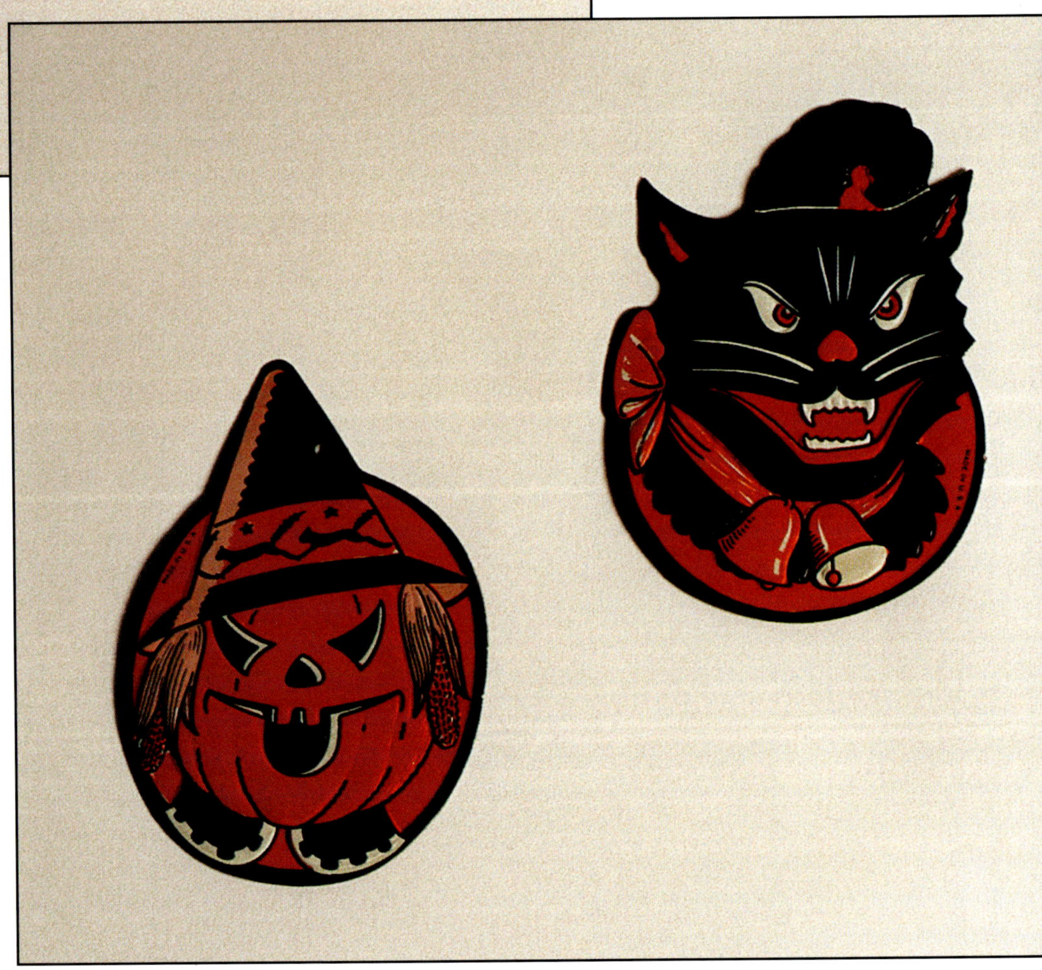

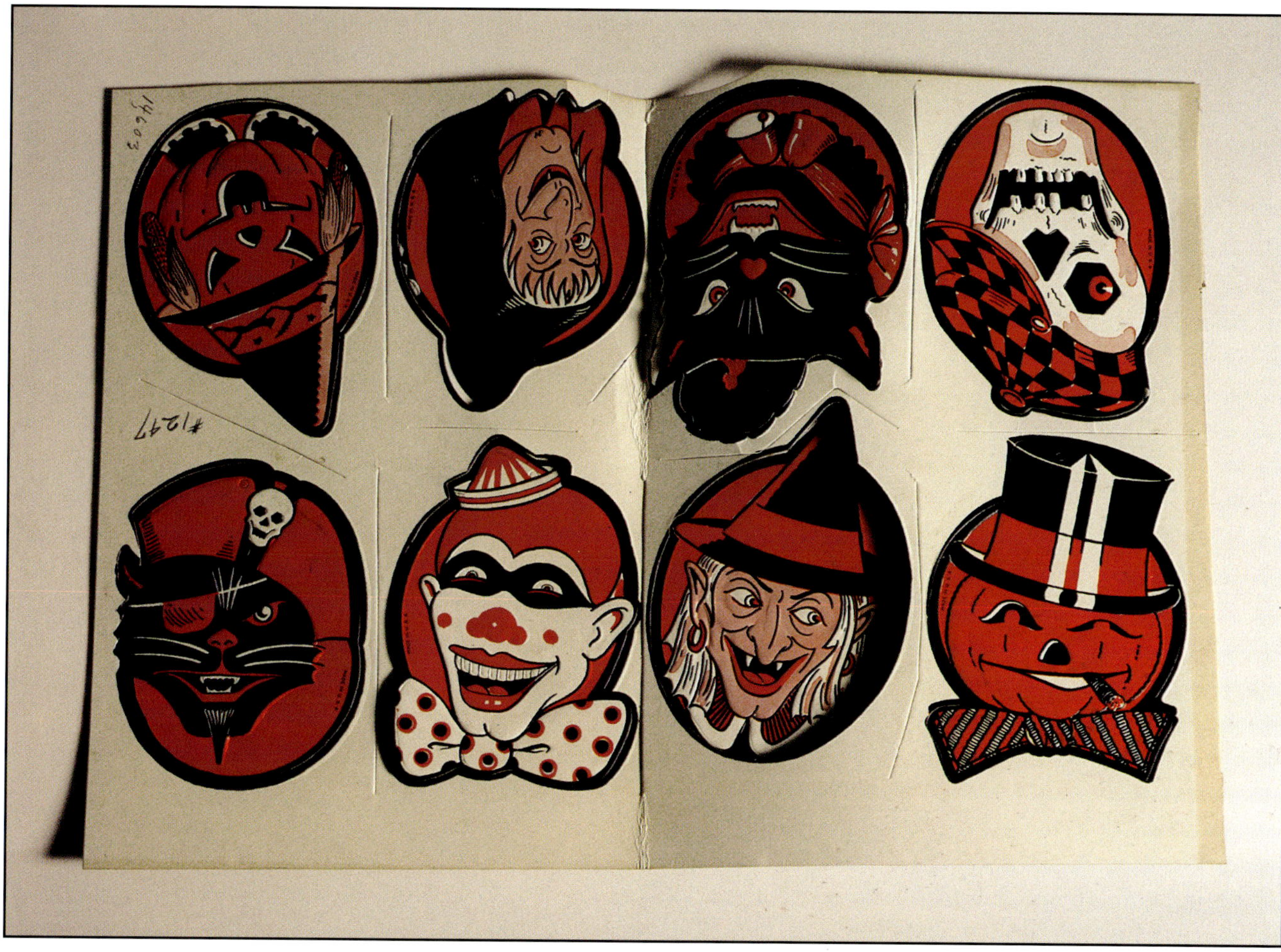
14603
#1247

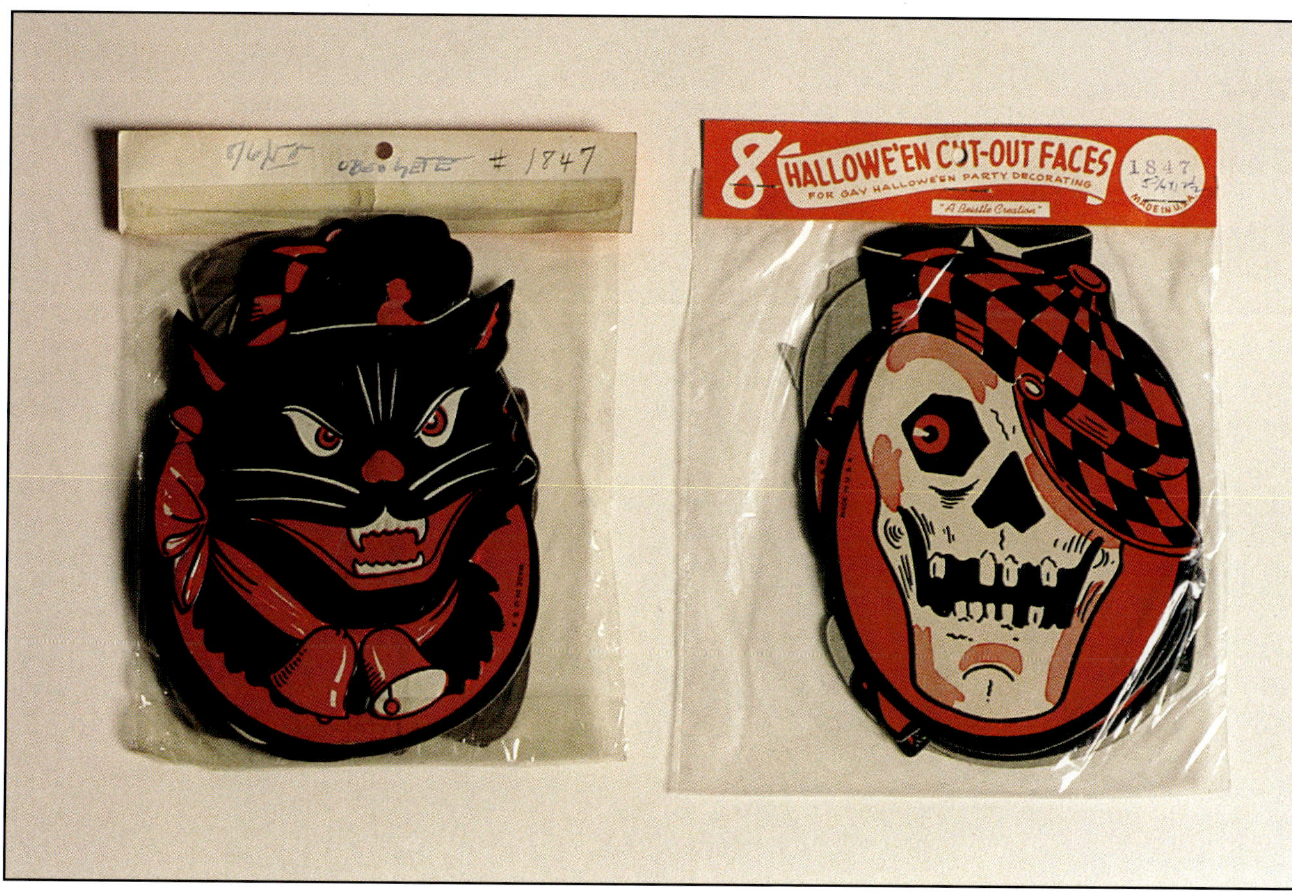
OBSOLETE # 1847
8 HALLOWE'EN CUT-OUT FACES
FOR GAY HALLOWE'EN PARTY DECORATING
"A Beistle Creation"
1847
MADE IN U.S.A.

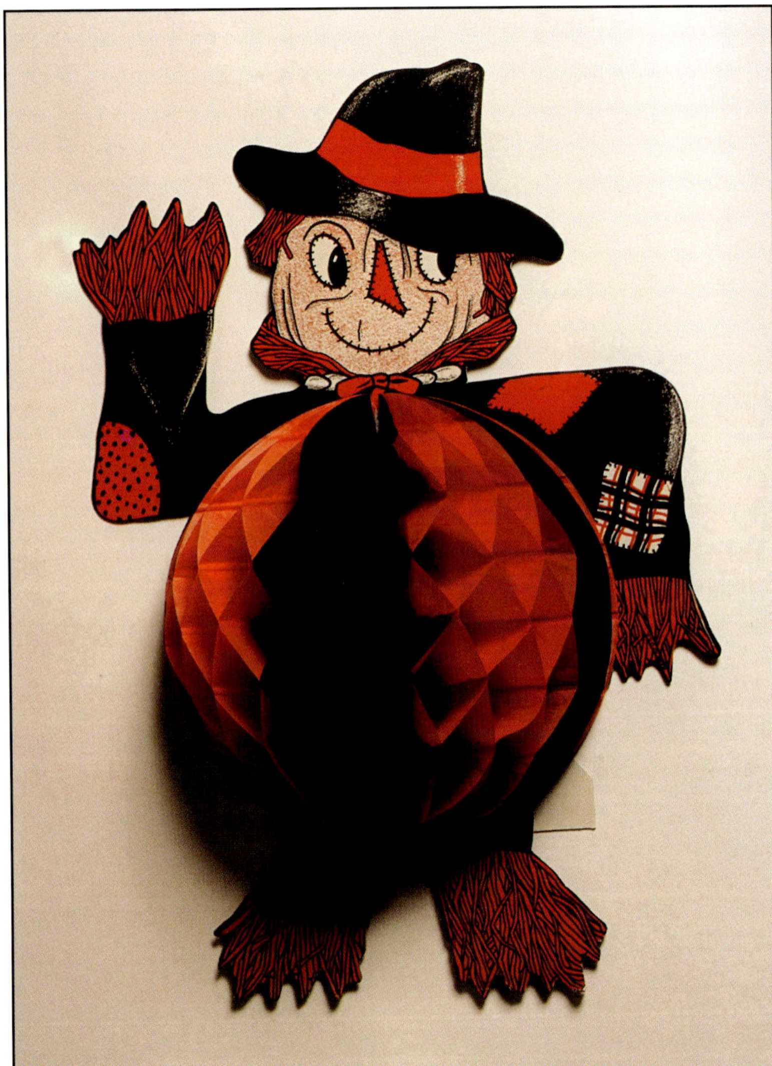

SCARECROW AND OWL
Initial Release: 1960
Production Run: 1960 – 1965
A new novelty decoration. Halloween characters printed in orange and black with Art-Tissue bodies. Folded flat, they open half-round with self-locking easel to form a "roly-poly" scarecrow and owl. Size 13" x 14". Two designs.
Value: $45 each

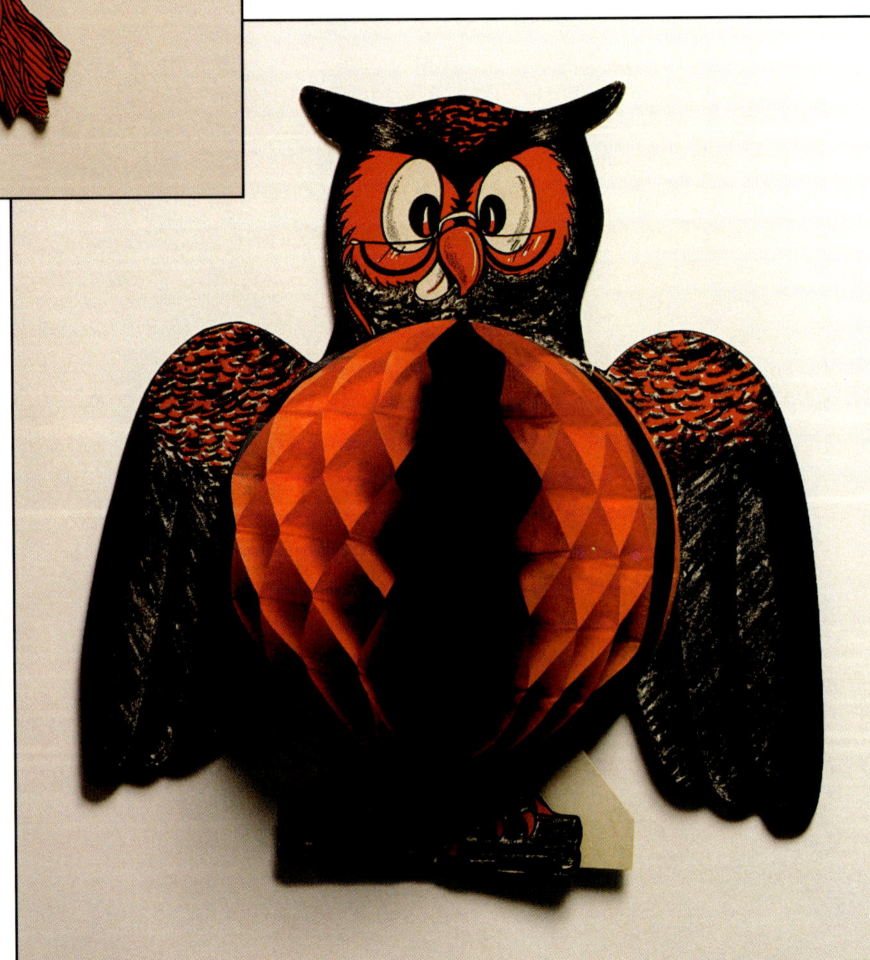

EMBOSSED SKULL WITH TRANSPARENCY
Initial Release: 1951
Production Run: 1951 – 1967
When placed before a light of any kind the red glassine behind the cutout eyes and nose of this embossed skull produces an eerie effect. Embossed on fine cardboard. Size 8.25" x 9.25".
*A view of the back of the die-cut showing the tissue paper inserts.
Value: $35

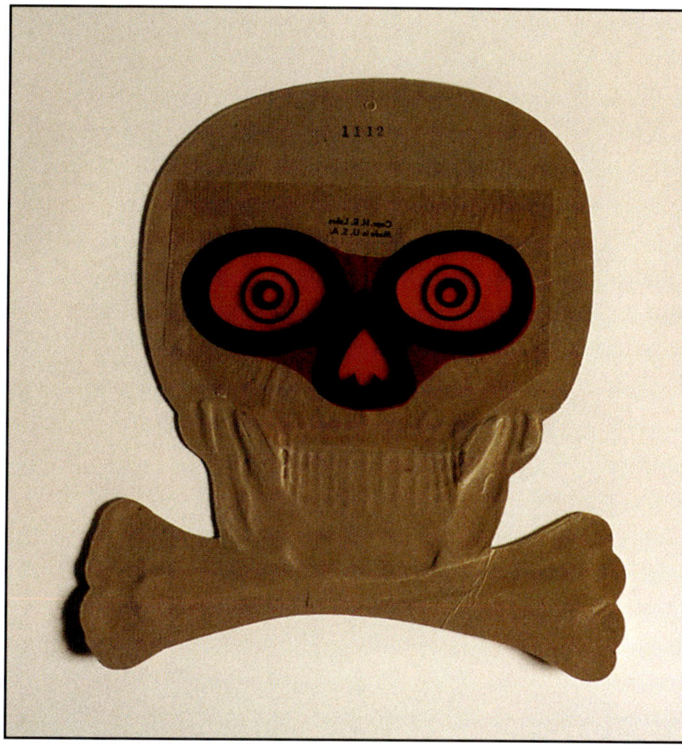

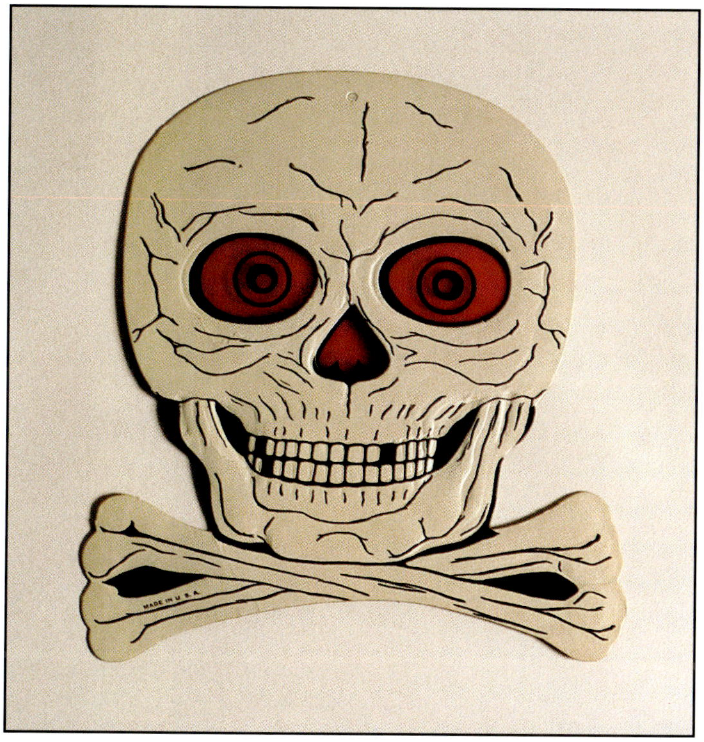

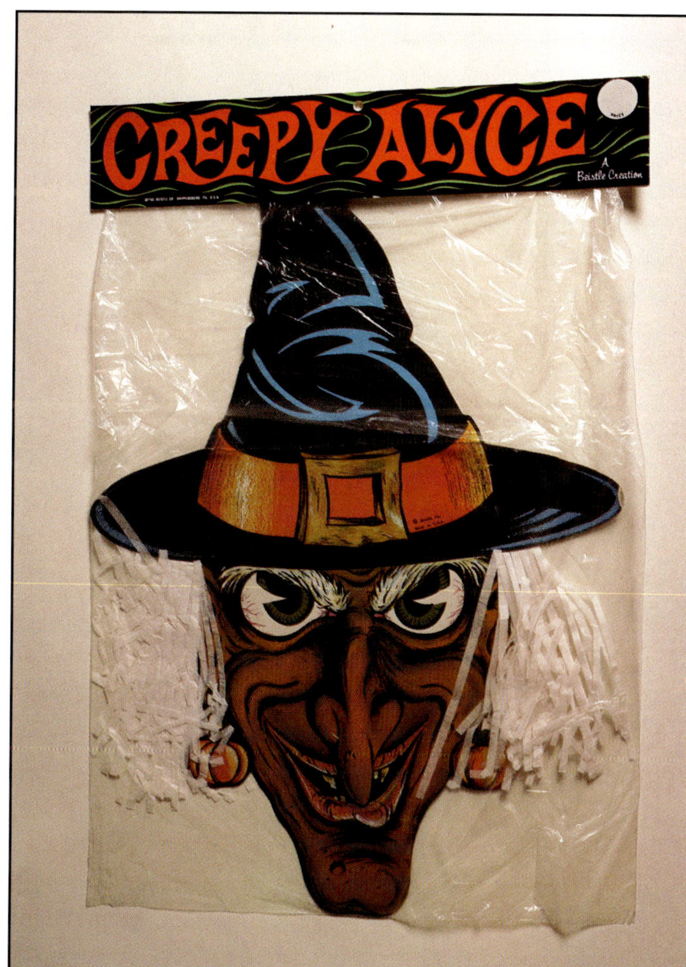

CREEPY ALYCE
Initial Release: 1969
Production Run: 1969 – 1974
A party favorite for Halloween decorating. This haunting face is printed in four-color design with finely fringed white tissue hair attached. Size 13.5" x 19.5". One design.
*This die-cut could be purchased with or without a clear poly bag with a printed header.
Value: $30

12-INCH HALL-O-ETTES
Initial Release: 1957
Production Run: One year only: 1957
A new idea in colorful Halloween decorations. 4" x 6" orange and black Halloween cutout highlighted with a 12" bright yellow Art-Tissue sunburst. An attractive hanging, window or wall decoration. Packed equally assorted. 8 designs.
*Showing three of the eight designs.
Value: $55 each

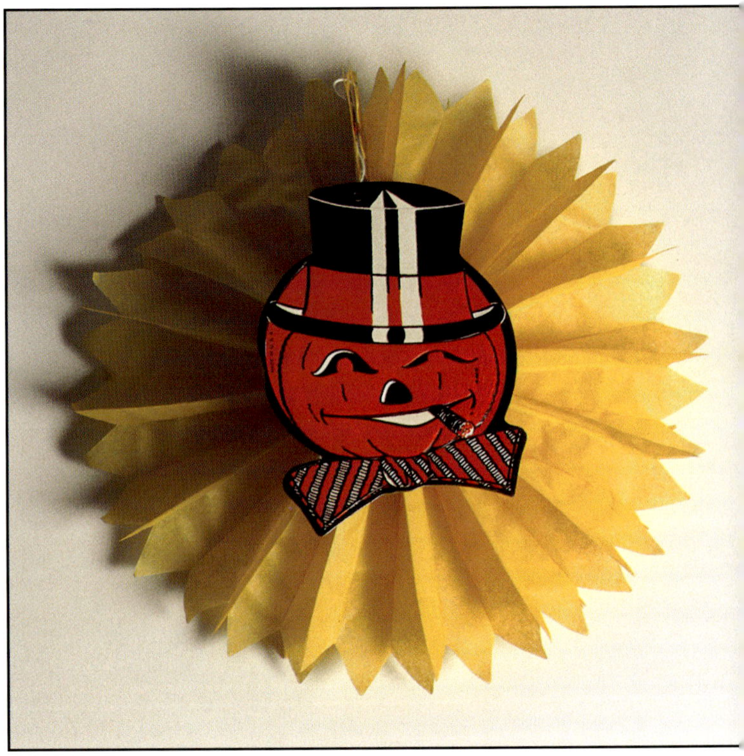

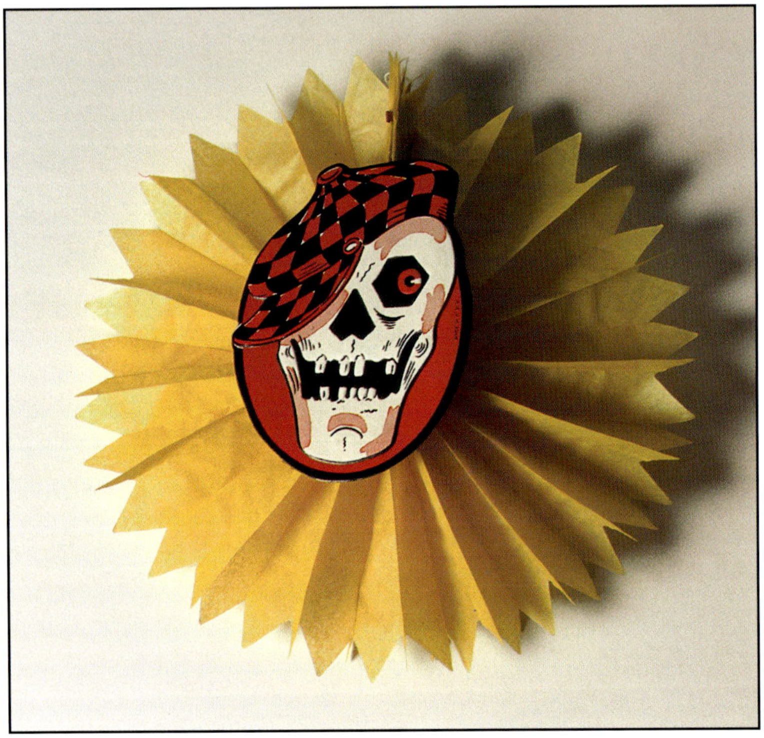

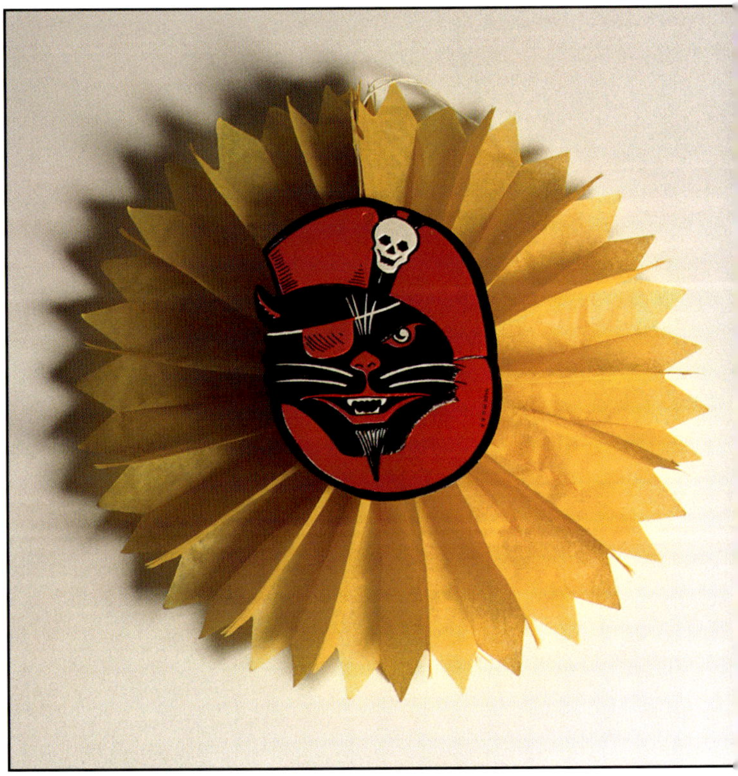

LARGE HALLOWEEN CUTOUTS
Initial Release: 1957
Production Run: 1957 – 1962
Four popular Halloween characters printed in three colors on fine stock. Die-cut to shape these attractive designs make a lively window or wall decoration. Two figures approximately 26" x 10.5" and two approximately 14.5" x 14.5".
Value: $20 – $35 range

(Continued on following page)

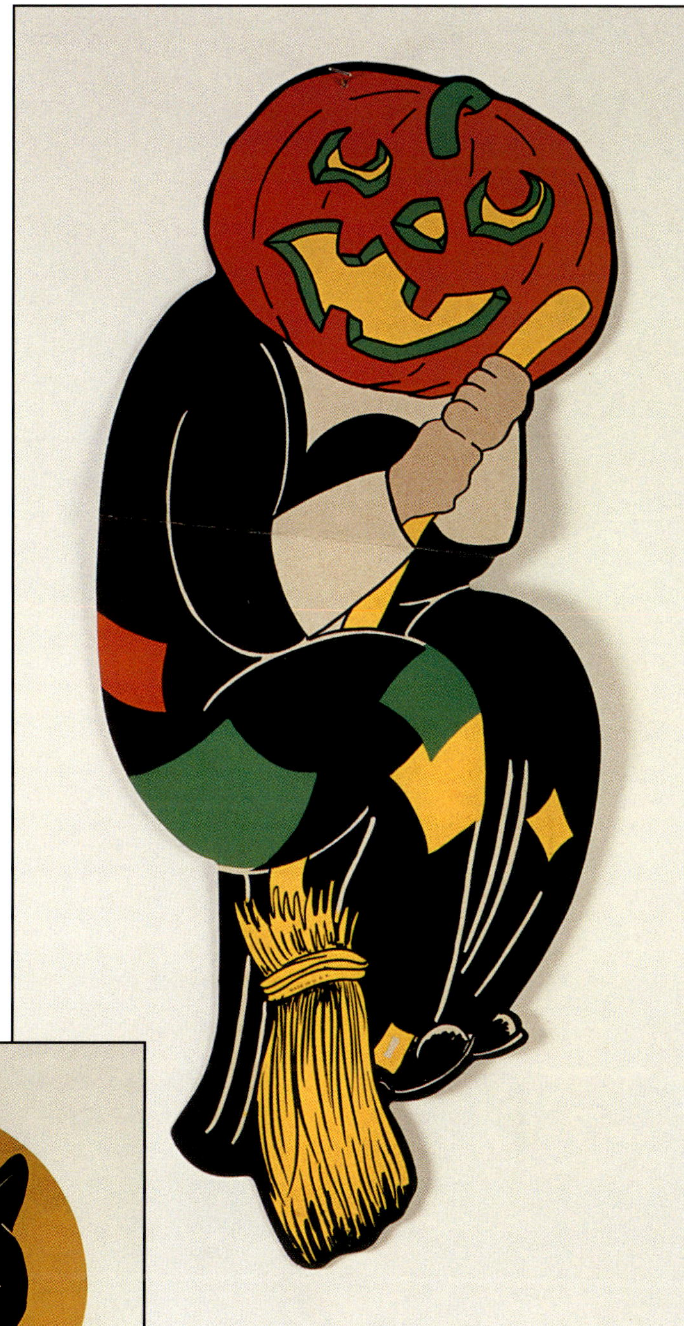

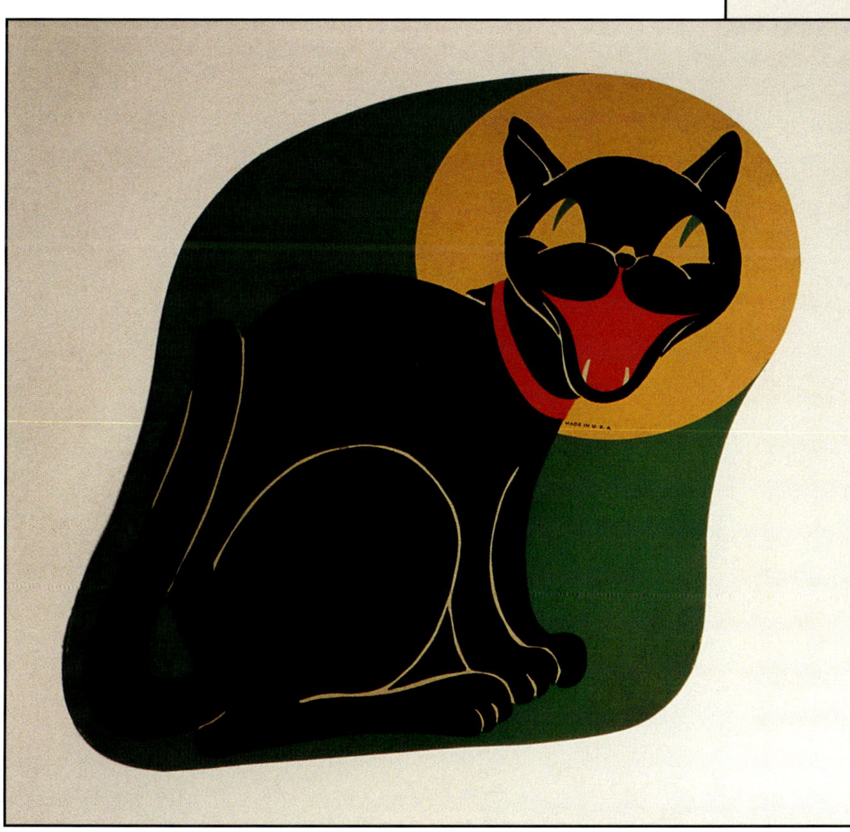

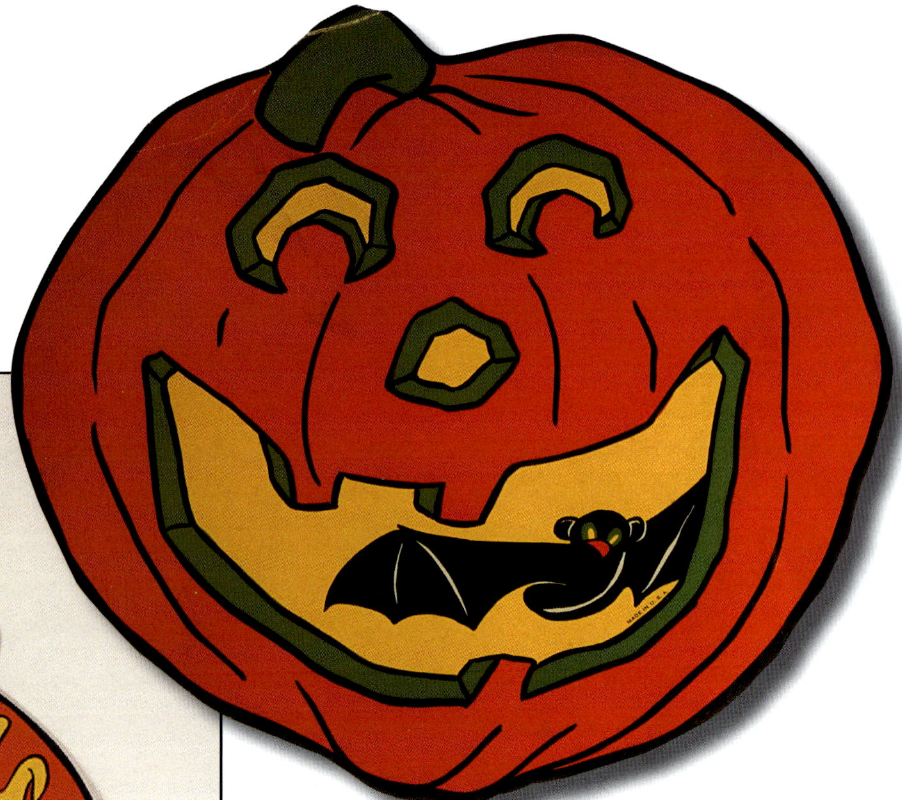

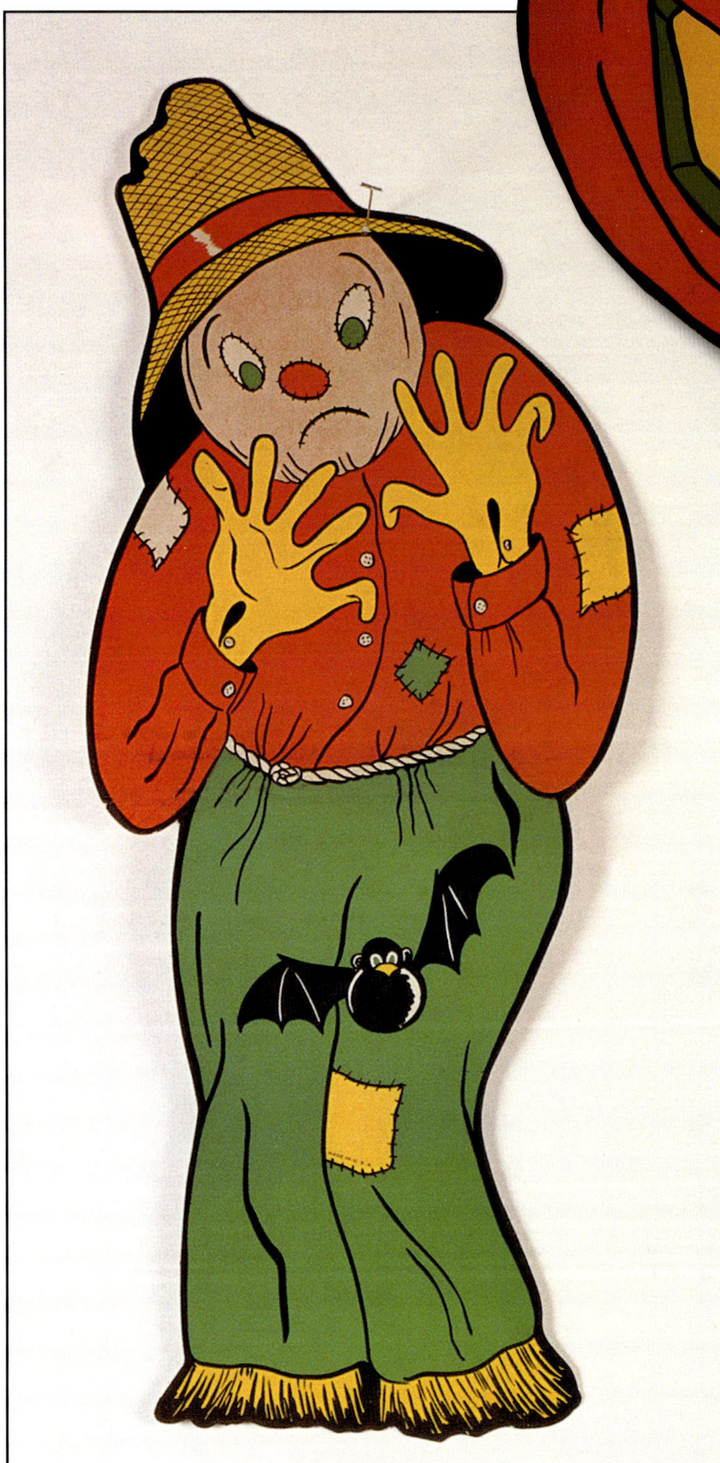

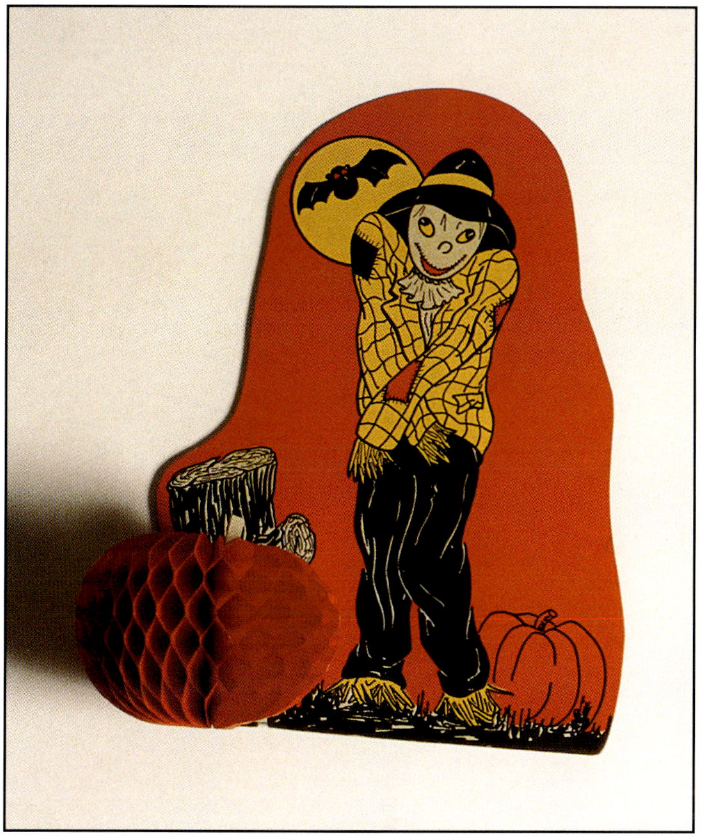

REALISTIC HALLOWEEN CUTOUTS
Initial Release: 1957
Production Run: 1957 – 1958
These attractive Halloween cutouts will lend a gay note to party decorating. Novel die-cut Art-Tissue parts open full round to complete and add realistic dimensions to appropriate Halloween scenes. Background designs are colorfully printed one side on fine white stock. May be used as a standing table and window decoration or wall plaque. Three designs equally assorted. Size 9" x 6.25". Folds flat for packing.
Value: $35 each

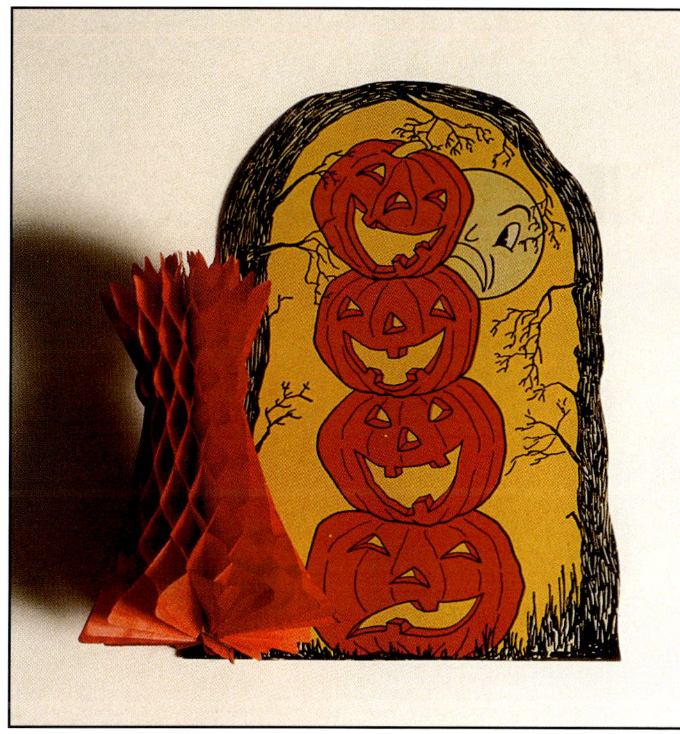

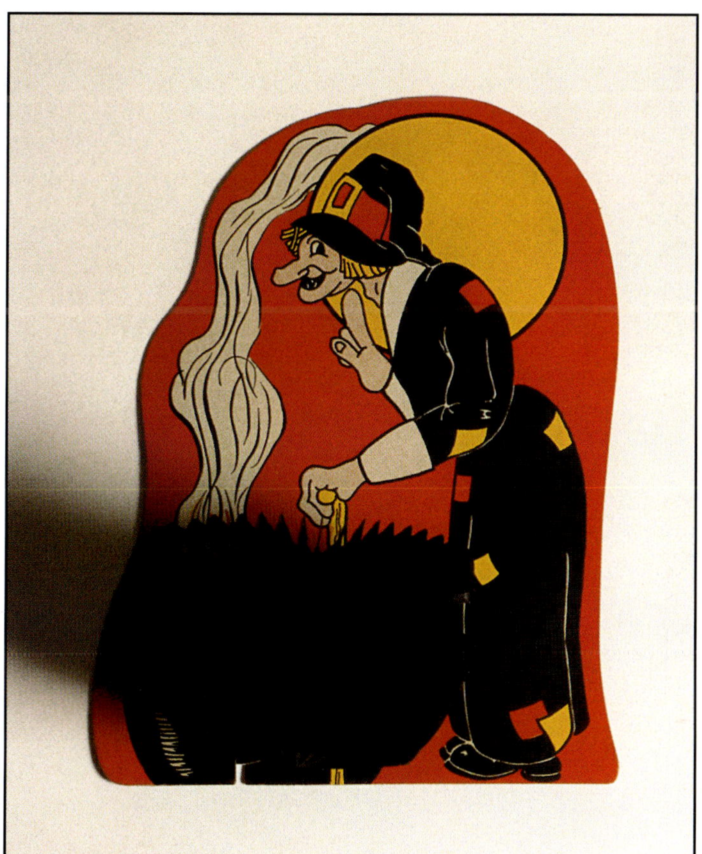

EMBOSSED SKULL WITH CAT
Initial Release: 1957
Production Run: One year only: 1957
This new and delightful Halloween decoration is a real Halloween thriller. Cleverly designed so that eyes move from side to side as cat swings freely from skull and crossbones. Die-cut from heavy stock and printed and embossed as illustrated. Size 9" x 19". Packed one in a cellophane bag with printed heat sealed top.
Value: $175

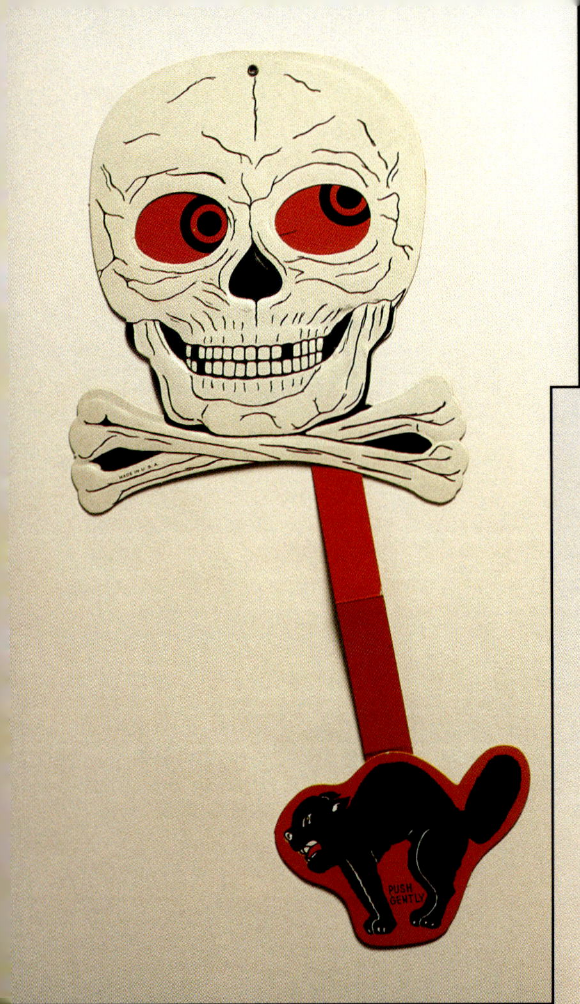

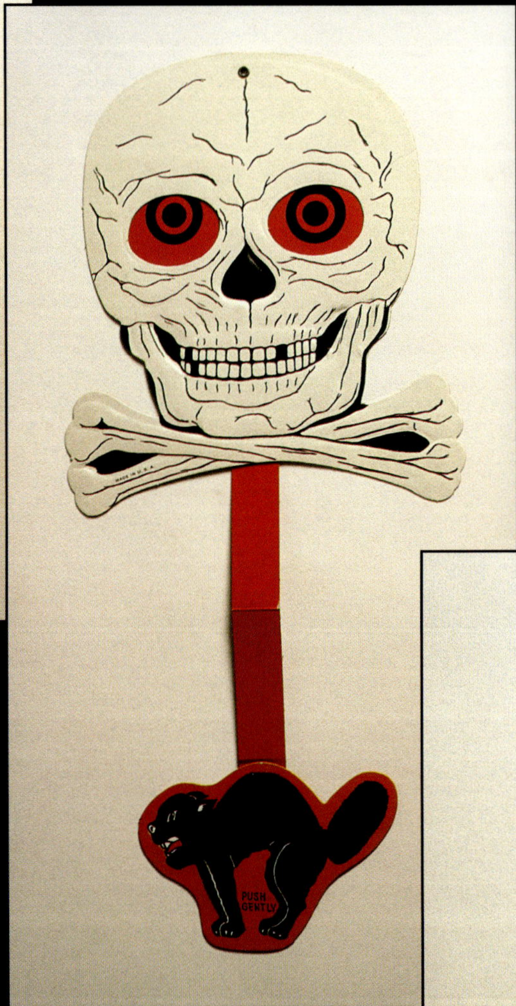

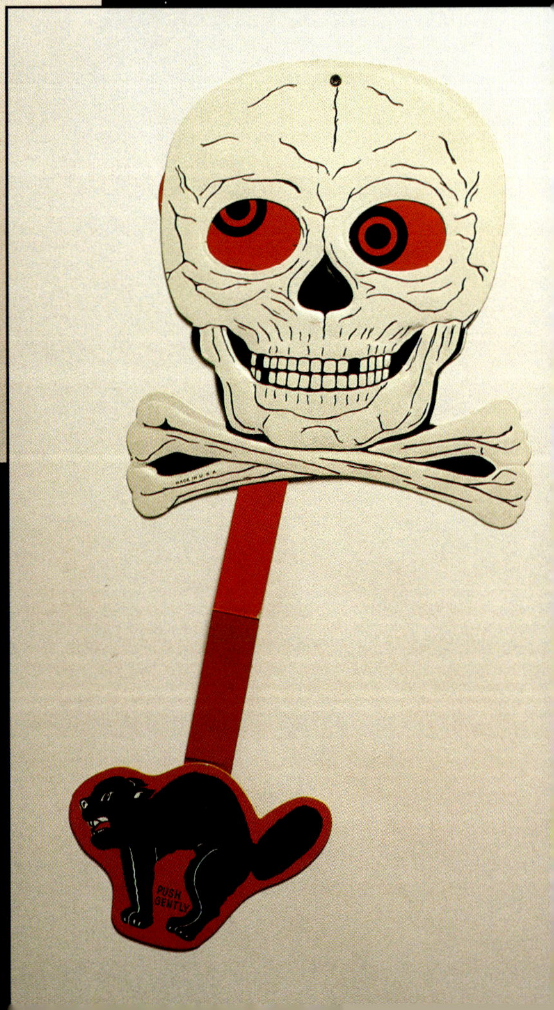

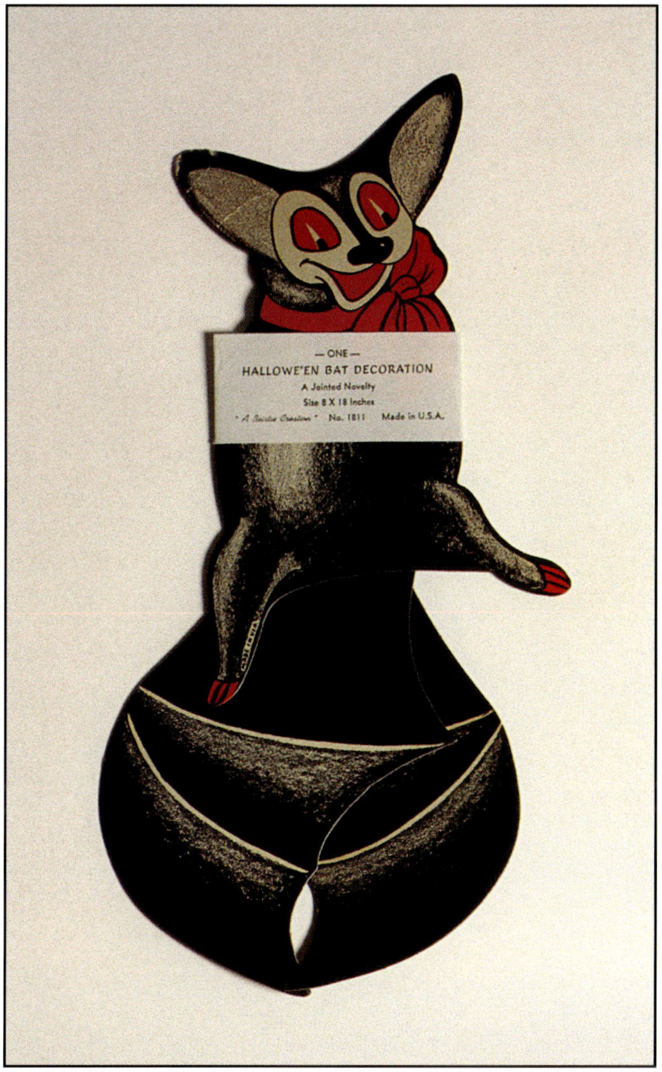

JOINTED BAT
Initial Release: 1960
Production Run: 1960 – 1965
A new comical Halloween character that will add gay atmosphere to party decorating. Wings eyeleted to body lend variety of realistic poses. Printed orange and black and die-cut to shape. Size 9" x 17.5". One design.
*The Stock Number on this bat was #1810. You had the option of buying the piece with a printed band (used as a sales aid) which changed the Stock Number to #1811.
Value: $35

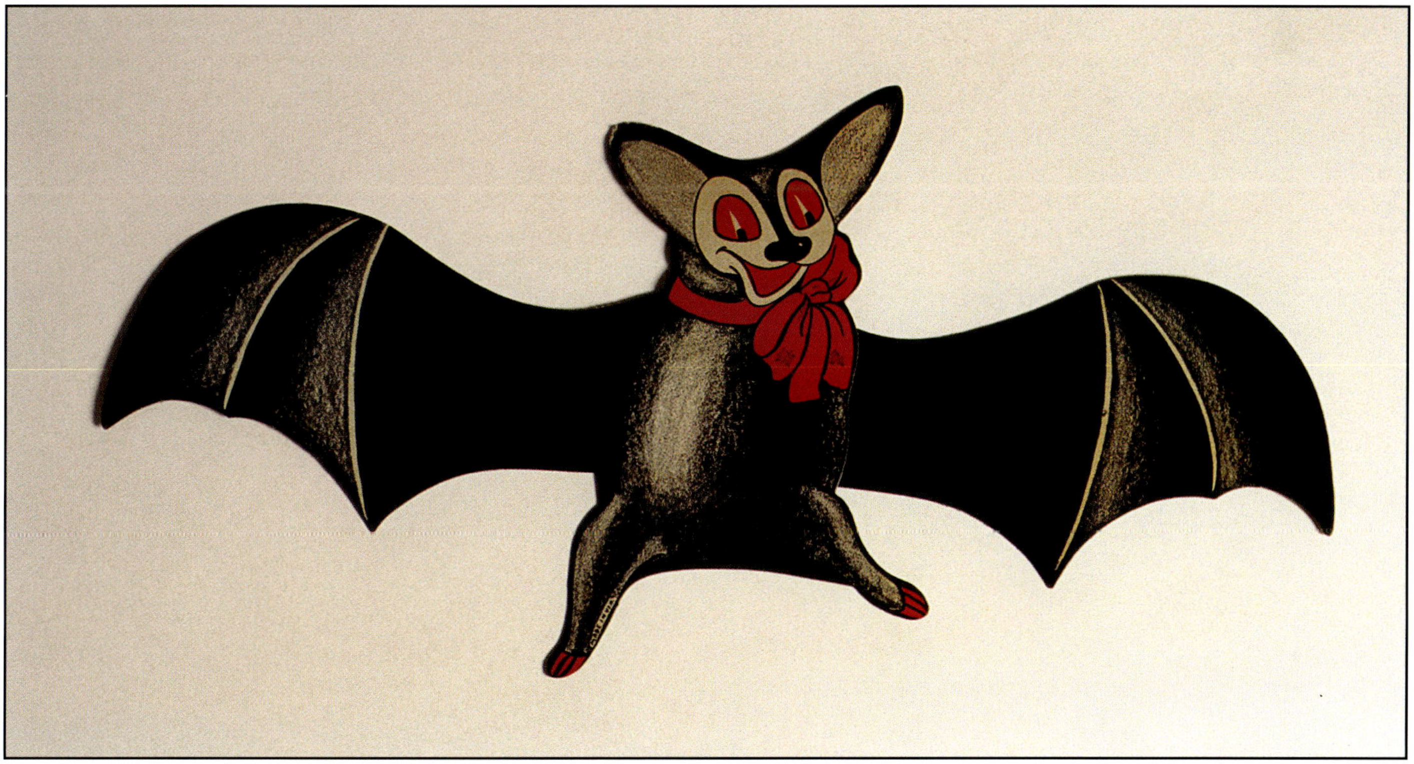

JOINTED SCRATCH CAT
Initial Release: 1960
Production Run: 1960 – 1967
Large sized scratch cat printed in black with orange trim on cardboard, and die-cut to shape. Head and tail eyeleted for use in a variety of poses. Equal assortment, rights and lefts. Size 14" x 15".
*The above cat was sold under Stock Number 1123. Stock Number #1124 gave the buyer the option of purchasing this piece with a printed band (used as a sales aid).
Value: $20 each

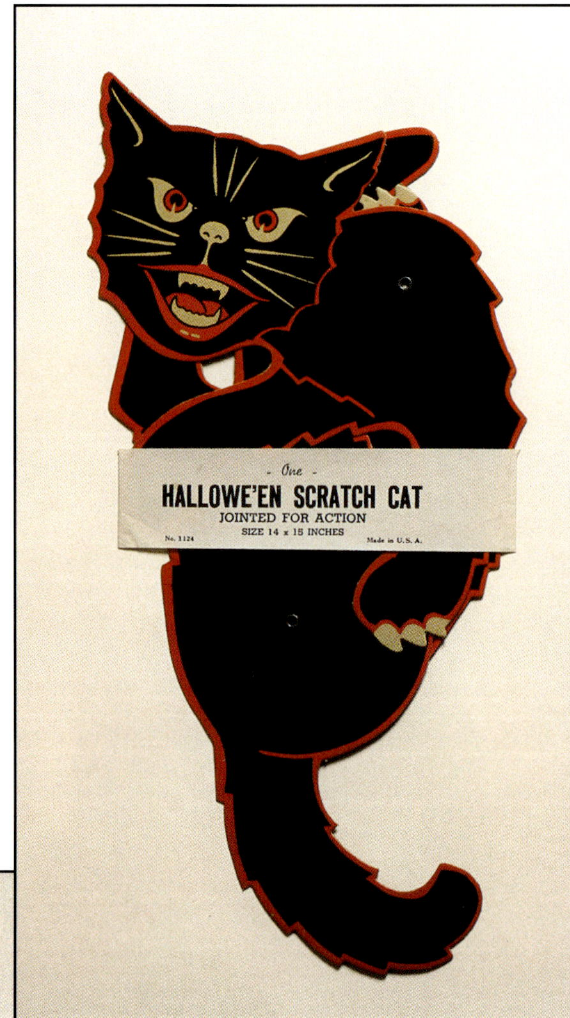

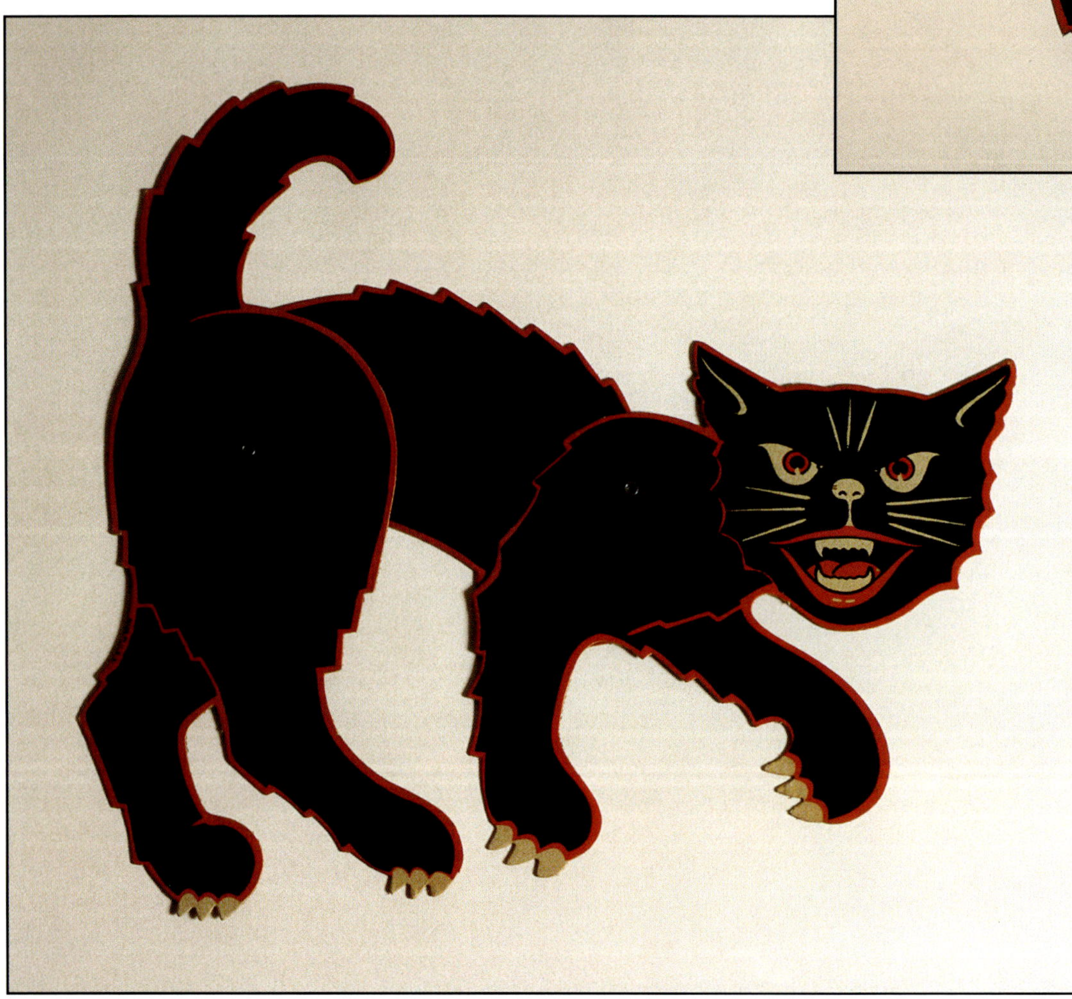

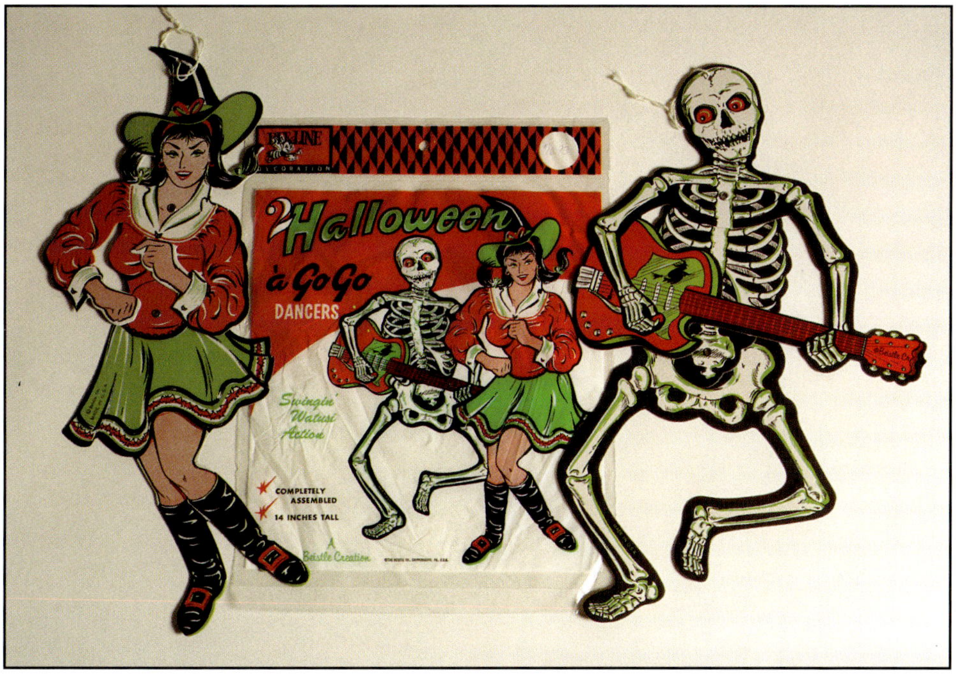

GO GO DANCERS

Initial Release: 1966
Production Run: 1966 – 1968

These amusing dancers will provide lots of fun and laughs, and are sure to be a teen-age party favorite. Printed in a three-color design, die-cut and expertly eyeleted to wiggle and dance with a flick of your finger. Size approximately 6" x 14". Packed 2 designs in a printed poly bag with header.

*An update from the original Beistle twosome of 1955 with a lean towards a more modern look. The Witch looks like she could have starred on the "Hullabaloo" TV show.

*A look at these Halloween characters fresh off the press waiting to be die cut. I happen to love the "before" and "after" look.

Value: $25 – $30 range

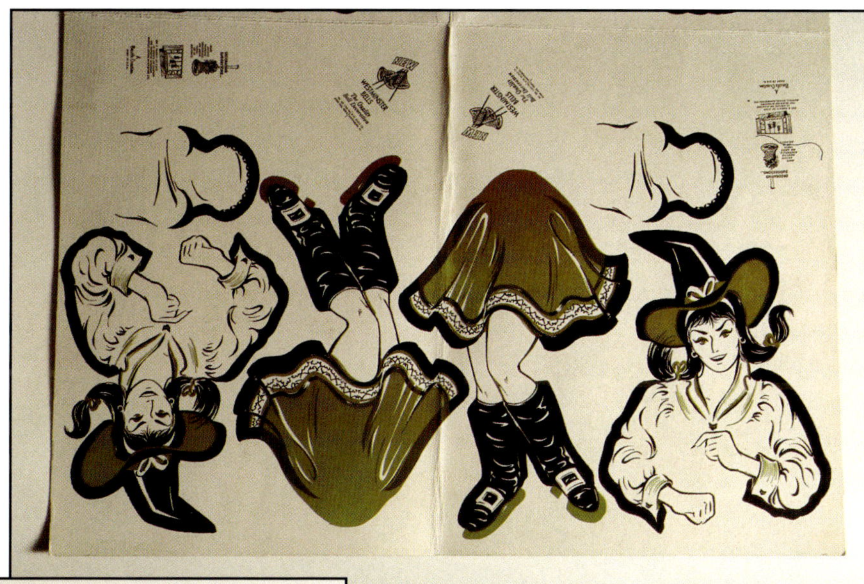

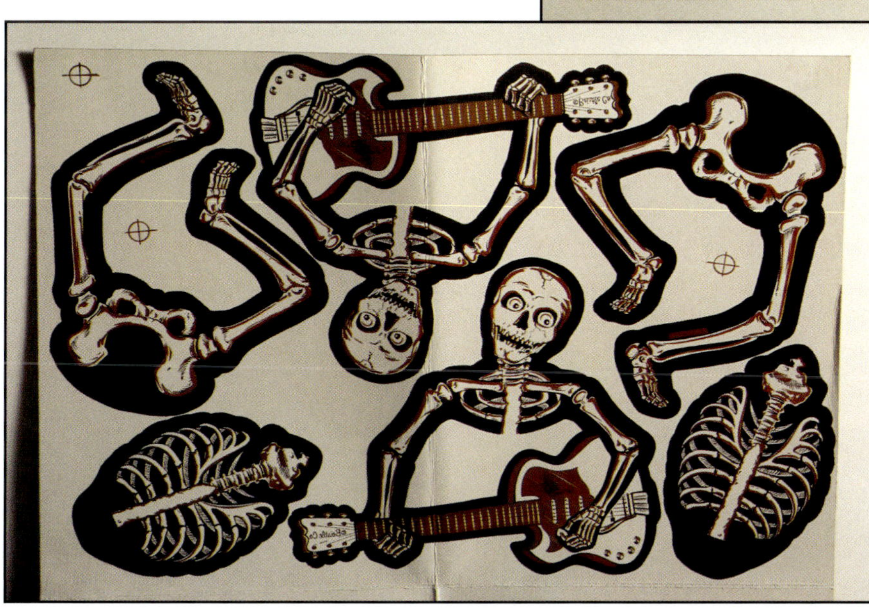

SCARECROW DANCER
Initial Release: 1960
Production Run: 1960 – 1970
A dancing scarecrow with head, body, hands and feet printed orange, yellow and black. Arms and legs of orange and black Art-Tissue. Complete with printed directions on back. Packed flat. One design.
*This decoration brings back a lot of Baby Boomer memories for me.
Value: $35

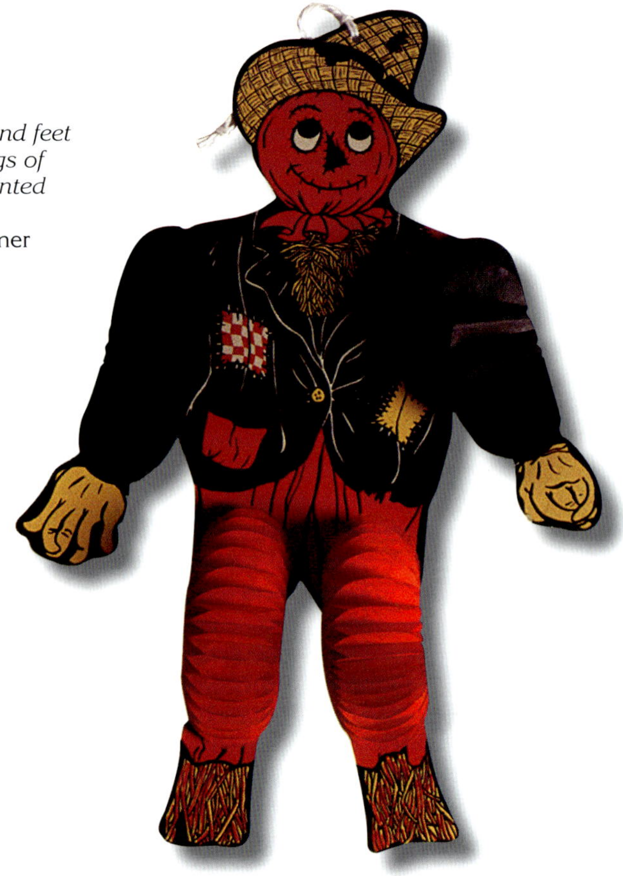

SKELETON DANCER
Initial Release: 1952
Production Run: 1952 – 1956 (see author's notes)
New style. This action toy's a party favorite of kids and adults alike. A dancing skeleton with printed head, hands and feet. Body, arms and legs of white Art-Tissue. Packed flat. One design.
*In 1957, Mr. Bones takes on a new look: his honeycomb tissue paper torso transforms into a die-cut cardboard one in a lovely skeletal detail. Also, the facial features of the skull have a more realistic look to them.
*In 1964, the Beistle Company decided to package both the Scarecrow Dancer and the Skeleton Dancer together. Size was 5" x 18". Packed two designs in a printed poly bag with header. Completely assembled with printed directions on the die-cut's back.
Value: $45 each (for early skeleton)
Value: $35 each (for later skeleton)

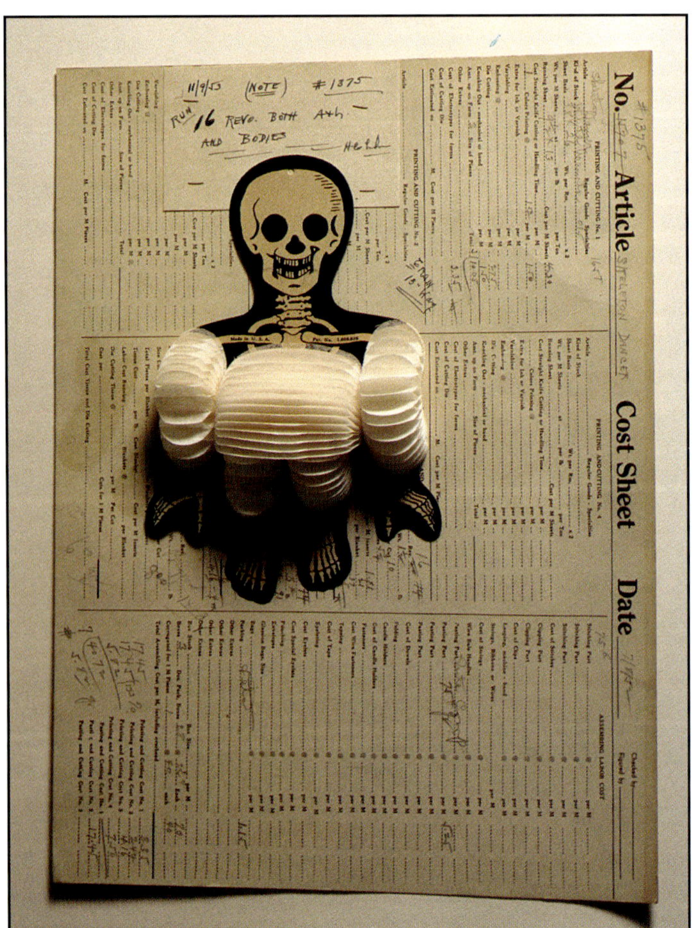

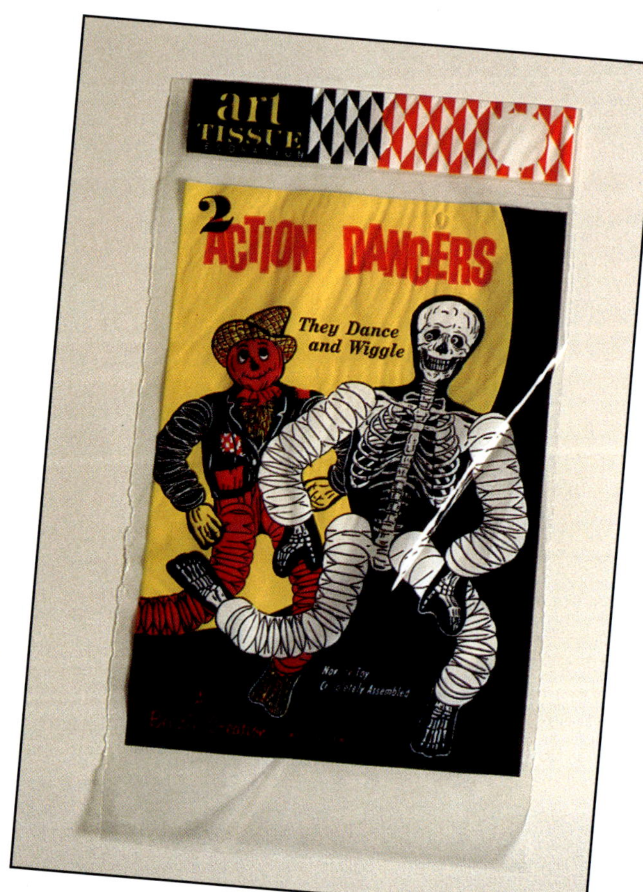

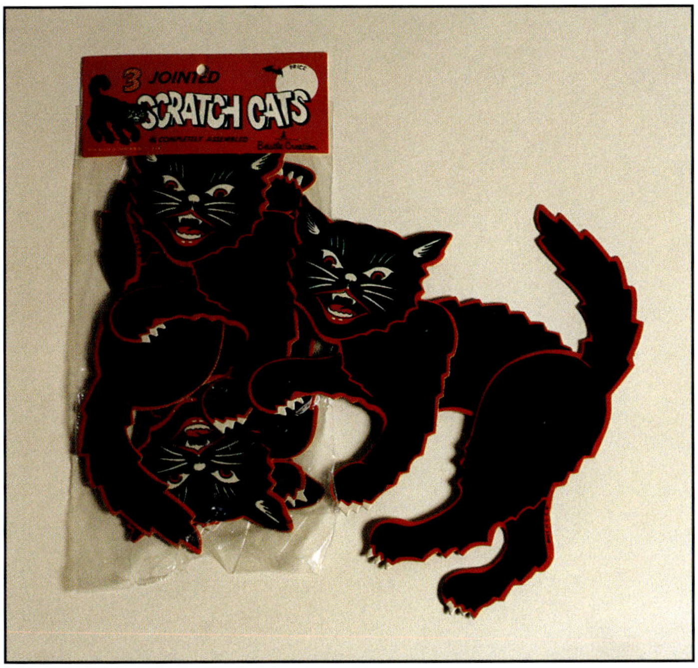

JOINTED SCRATCH CATS
Initial Release: 1967
Production Run: 1967 – 1968
Novelty cardboard cats printed orange and black design and die-cut to shape. Head and tail eyeleted for use in a variety of poses. Size 7" x 8". Three pieces per package in a clear poly bag with header.
Value: $18 per cat

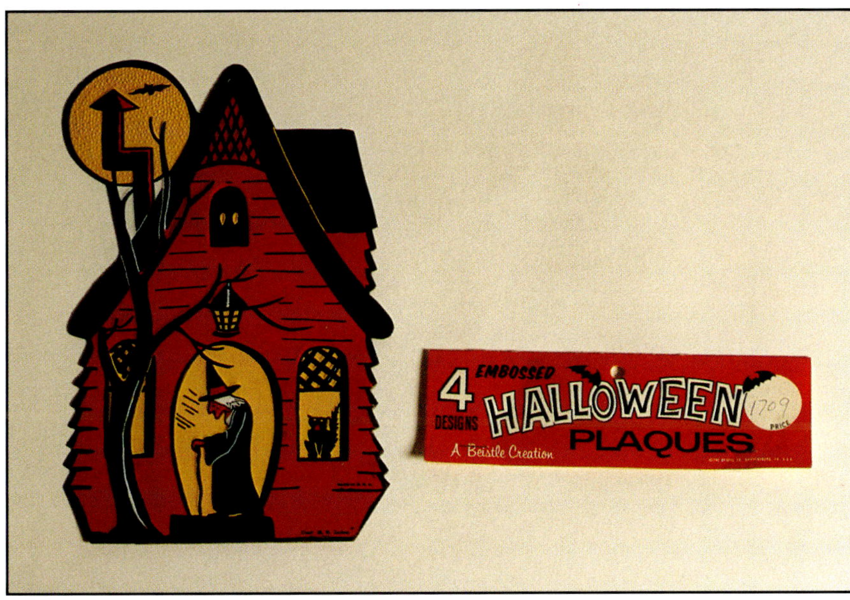

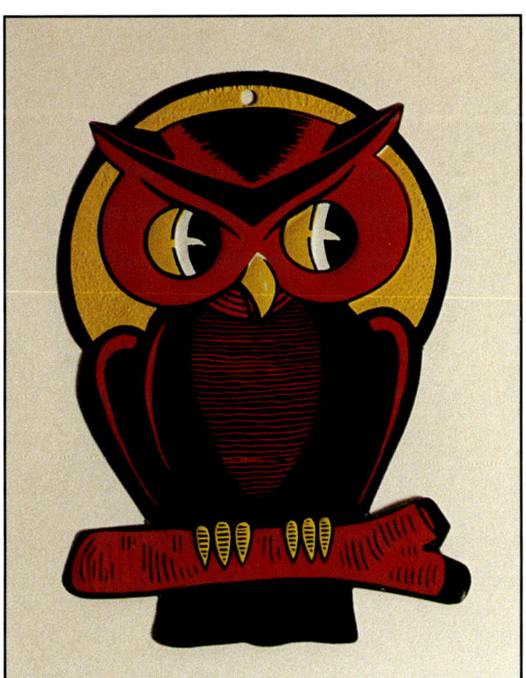

EMBOSSED CUTOUTS
Initial Release: 1967 *(see author's notes)
Production Run: 1967 – 1985+
A swanky set of embossed cardboard Halloween cutouts. Printed in a bright three-color design and die-cut to shape. Average size 6.5" x 9.5". Packed assorted four designs in a clear poly bag with header.
*This set made its official debut in 1941 under Stock Number 1109 and was sold to wholesalers four dozen to a box. In 1967, Beistle decided to take these eight figures, break them up into two sets of four, and package them in a clear poly bag. The eight die-cuts had their look updated in 1971 with the addition of another color to their palette: green. Compare the four-color modernized versions to their senior cousins.
*Since 1941, this eight-piece set was called "Embossed Halloween Plaques" until the year 1967 when Beistle decided not only to update their look but their name besides. They changed it to "Embossed Cutouts." These sets were sold under Stock Number 1709. Subsequently, the four-color sets were sold under Stock Number 0709.
*The popularity of these die-cuts is astounding! I believe that these pieces are still in production to this day but the cutoff year for my book is 1985.
Value: $25 – $35 range (3-color die-cut)
Value: $15 – $20 range (4-color die-cut)

(Continued on following 2 pages)

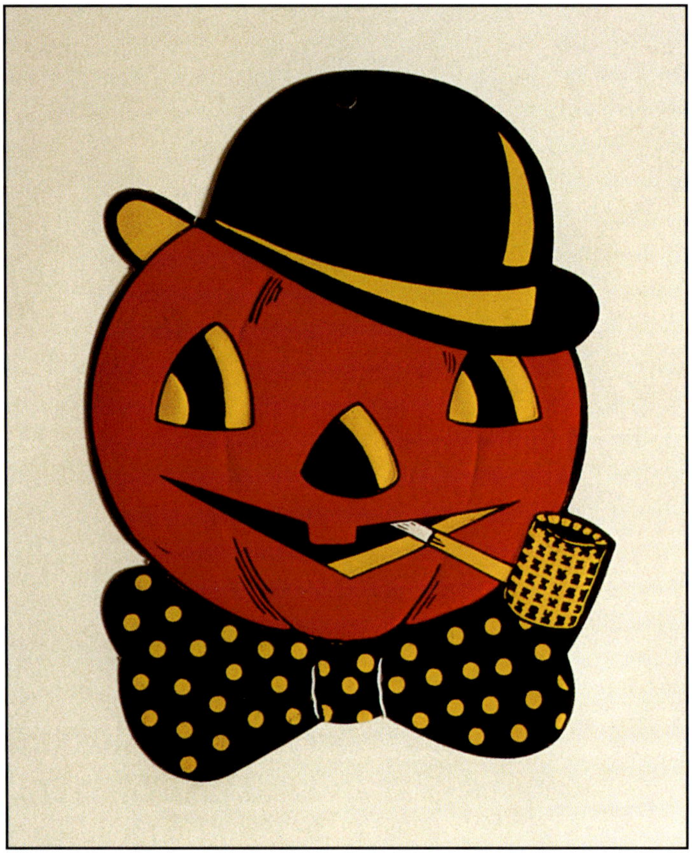

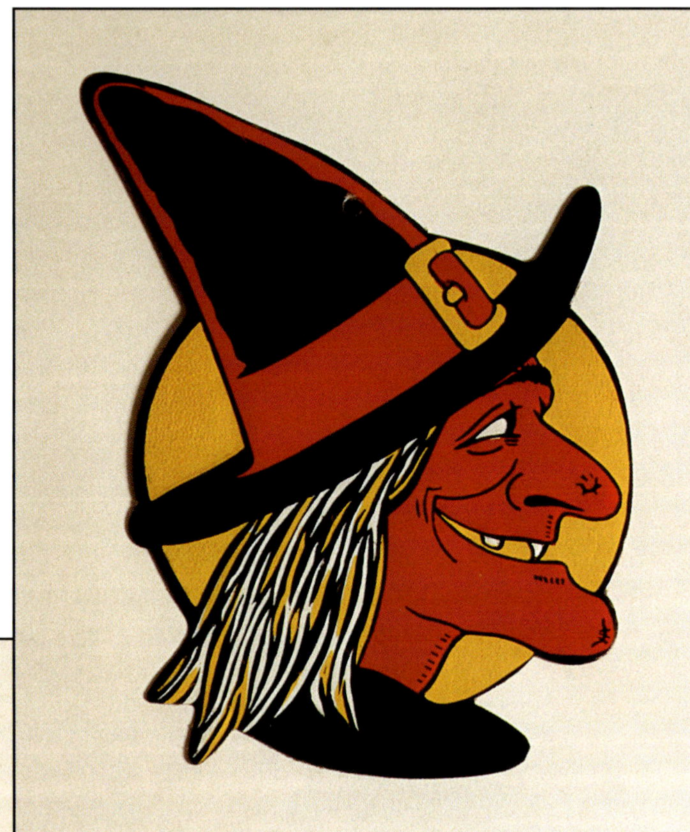

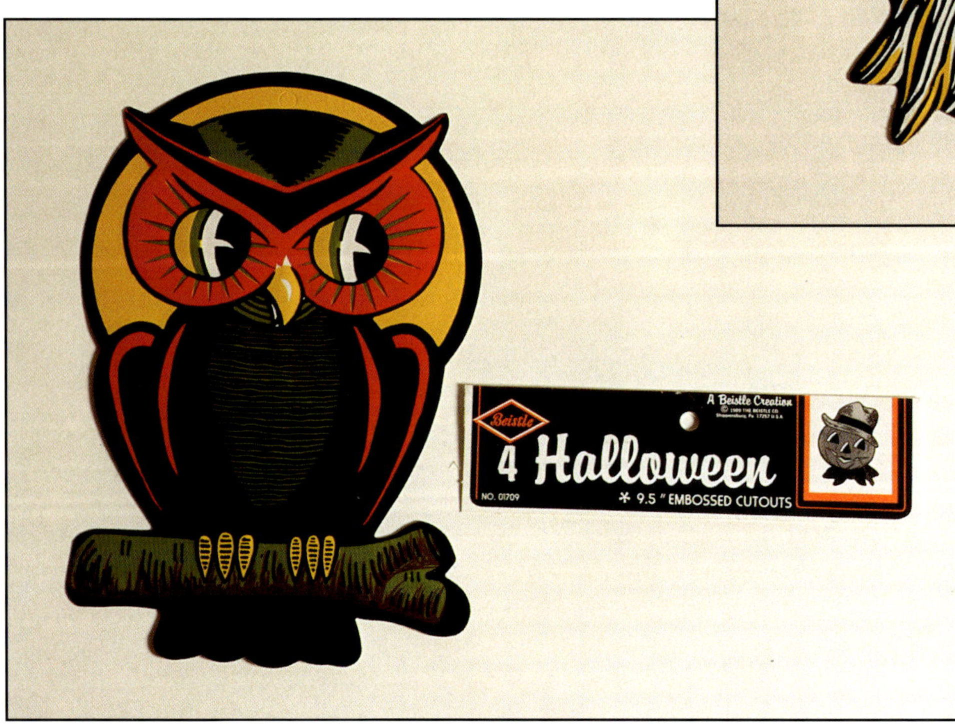
A Beistle Creation
Beistle
4 Halloween
NO. 01709
* 9.5" EMBOSSED CUTOUTS

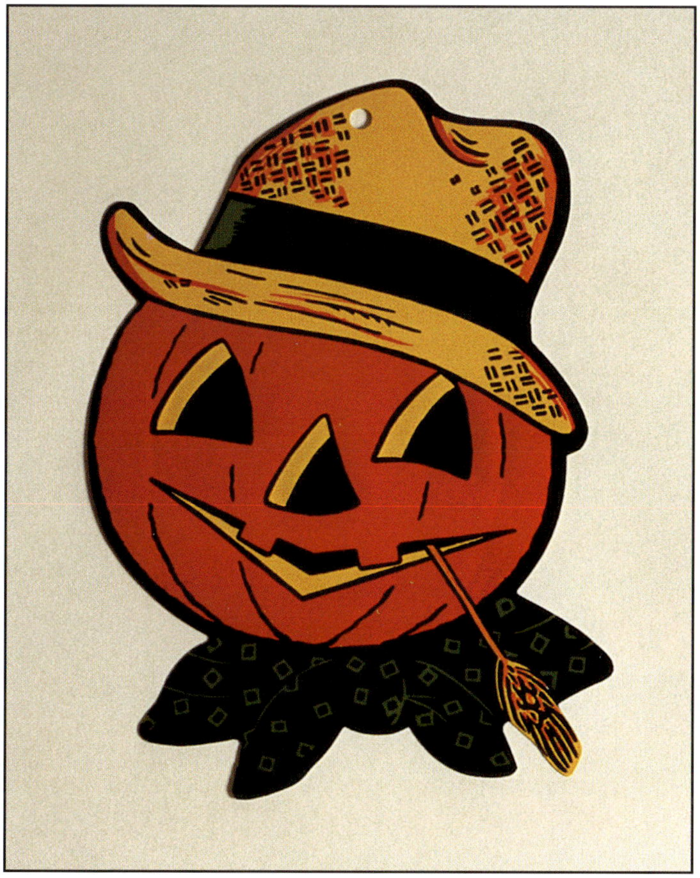

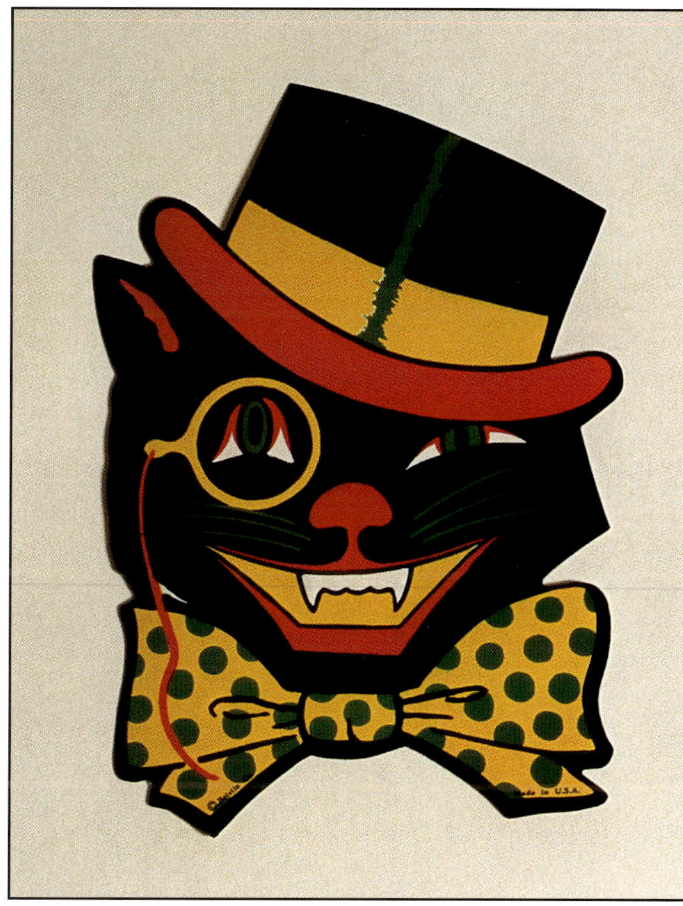

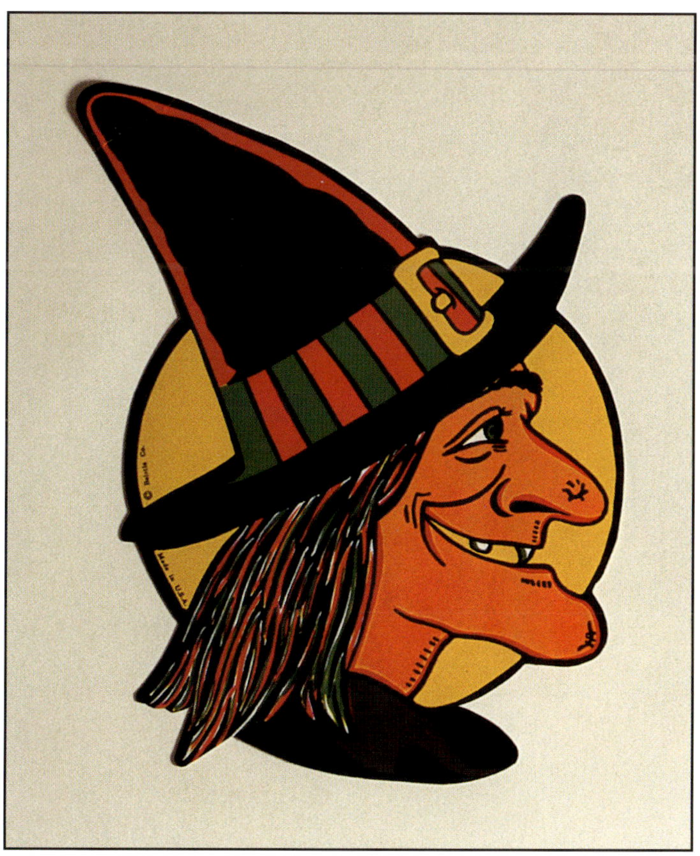

EMBOSSED CAT AND PUMPKIN HEADS
Initial Release: 1949
Production Run: 1949 – 1965
Amazingly inexpensive for such fine quality embossed cardboard cutouts. Four different designs in orange, black and green. Average size 8.5" x 12.5".
*These decorations stir up memories for the Baby Boomers. A great set of iconic Halloween adornments.
*Note the variation in color on the Jack-O-Lanterns to the left and the black cats on the far right. The pieces with the lighter shades of color are the earlier pieces; the darker die-cuts are later updated versions.
*In 1966, Beistle changed the selection of this set to one frowning Jack-O-Lantern, one black cat with the side-long glance, and two smiling Jack-O-Lanterns.
Value: $35 – $45 range for each

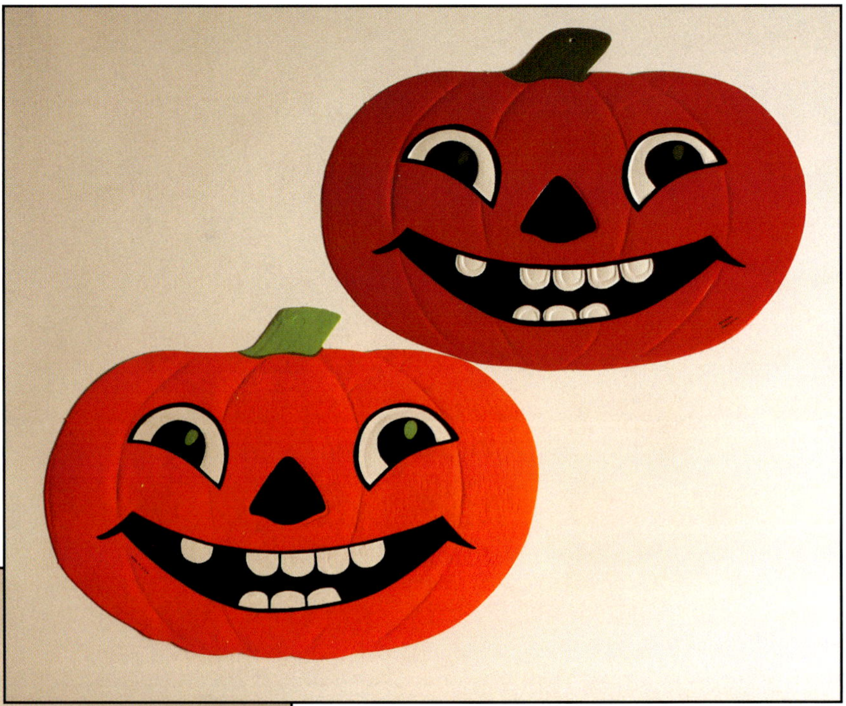

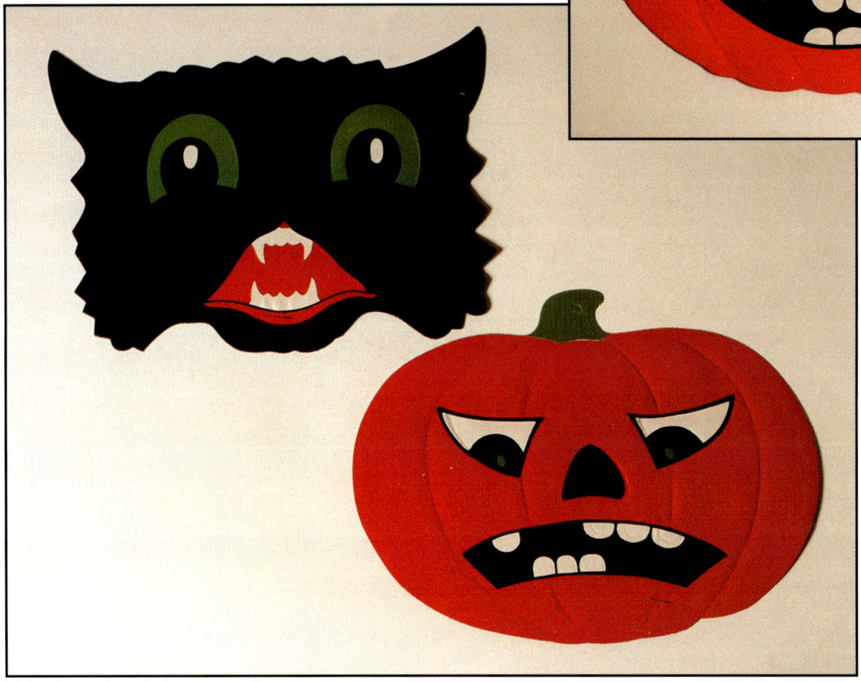

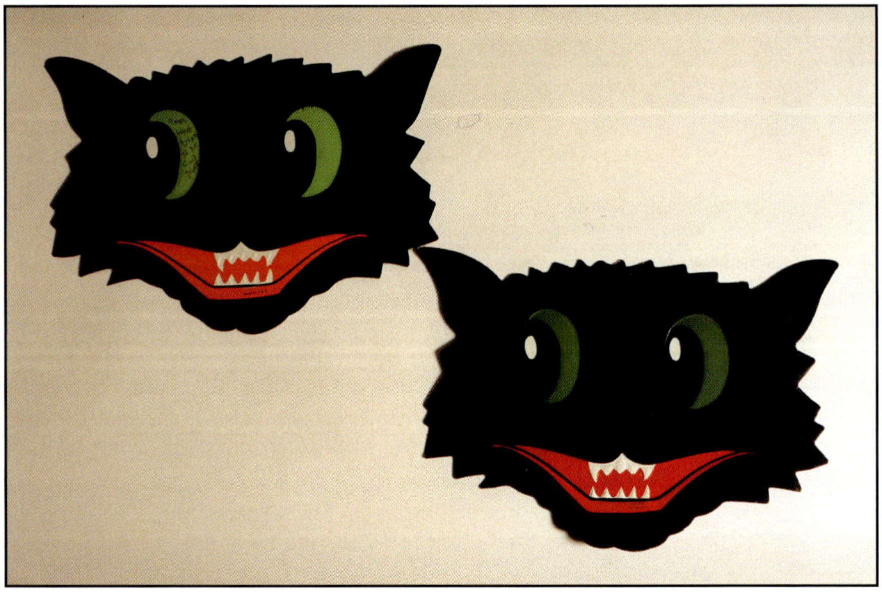

BLACK SCRATCH CAT
Initial Release: 1948
Production Run: 1948 – 1949
A novel decoration. Movable head and tail sections eyeleted to body. Printed one side on heavy card-board. Size 14" x 15" with string loop.
Value: $35

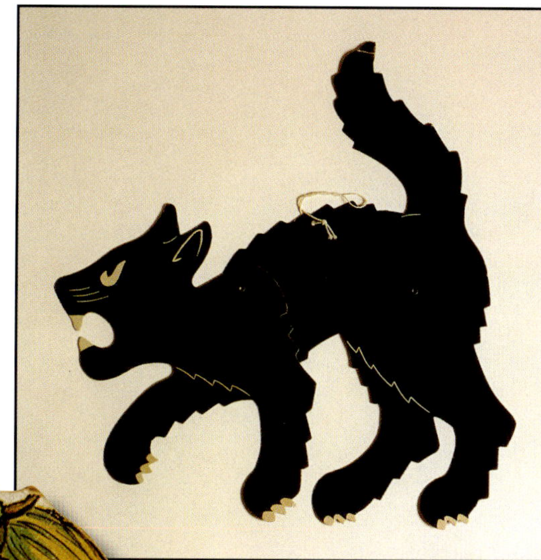

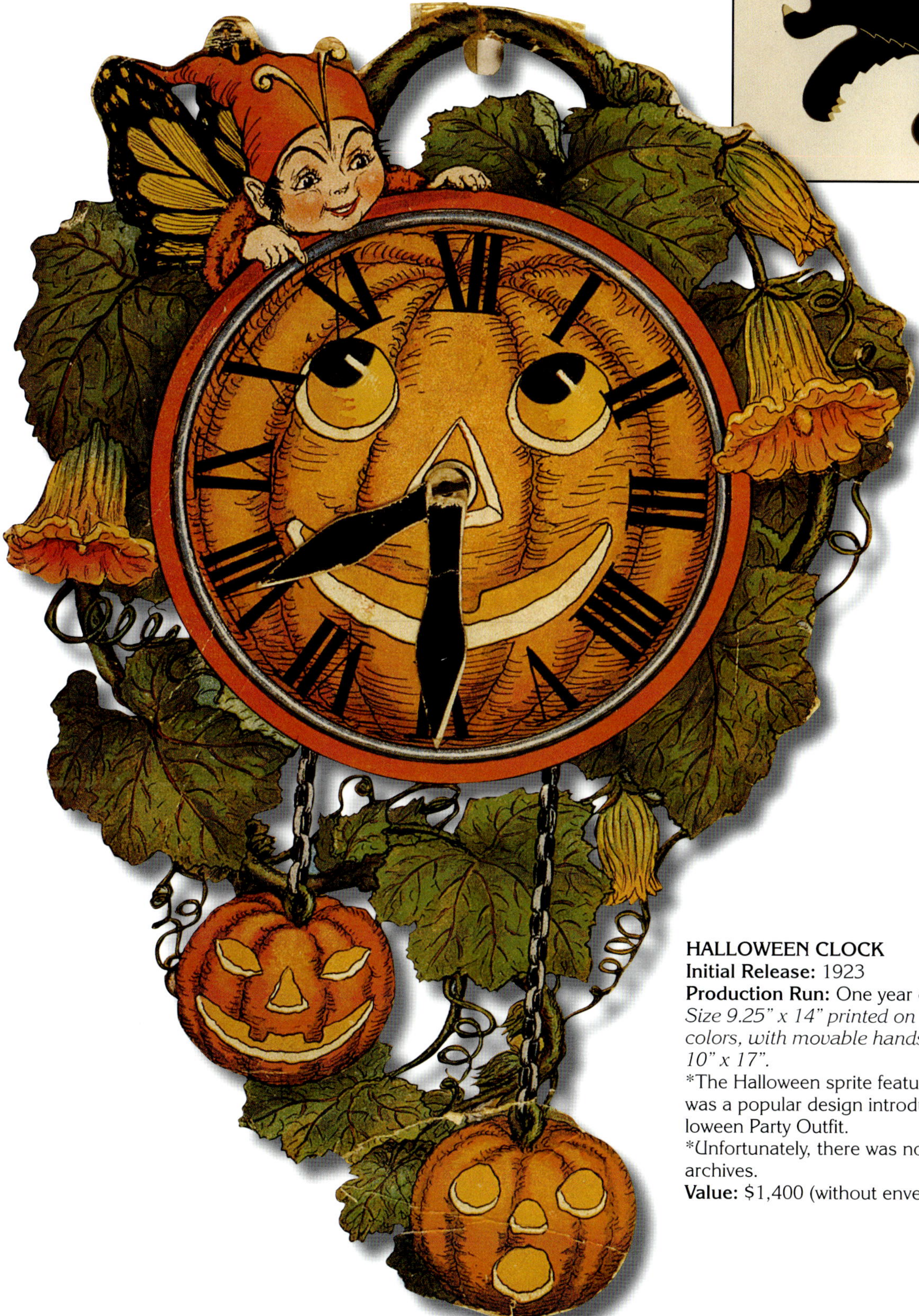

HALLOWEEN CLOCK
Initial Release: 1923
Production Run: One year only: 1923
Size 9.25" x 14" printed on heavy cardboard in 4 colors, with movable hands, each in printed envelope 10" x 17".
*The Halloween sprite featured at the top of the clock was a popular design introduced with the Beistle Halloween Party Outfit.
*Unfortunately, there was no envelope in the Beistle archives.
Value: $1,400 (without envelope)

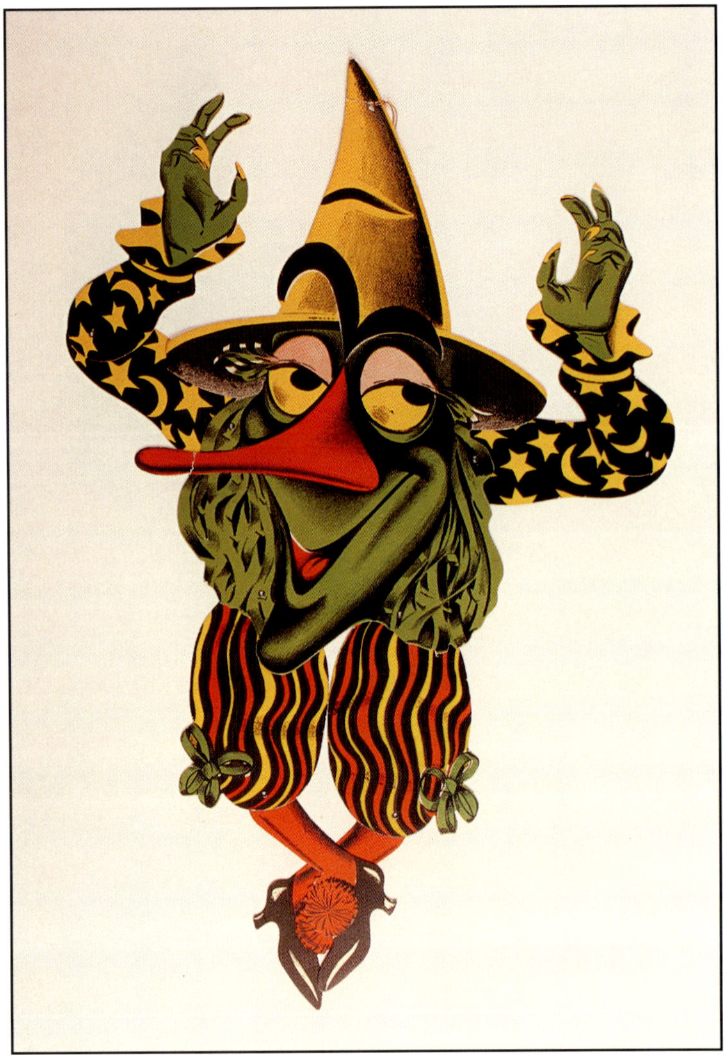

WITCH GOBLIN
Initial Release: 1960
Production Run: 1960 – 1969
This amusing Witch Goblin is sure to be a party favorite for Halloween decorating. Fully movable arms and legs are eyeleted to body. Gaily printed in four colors on quality stock and die-cut to shape. Size as illustrated approximately 24" x 32". One design.
*In 1970, Beistle "modernized" the appearance of this Witch which completely changed her look.
Value: $65

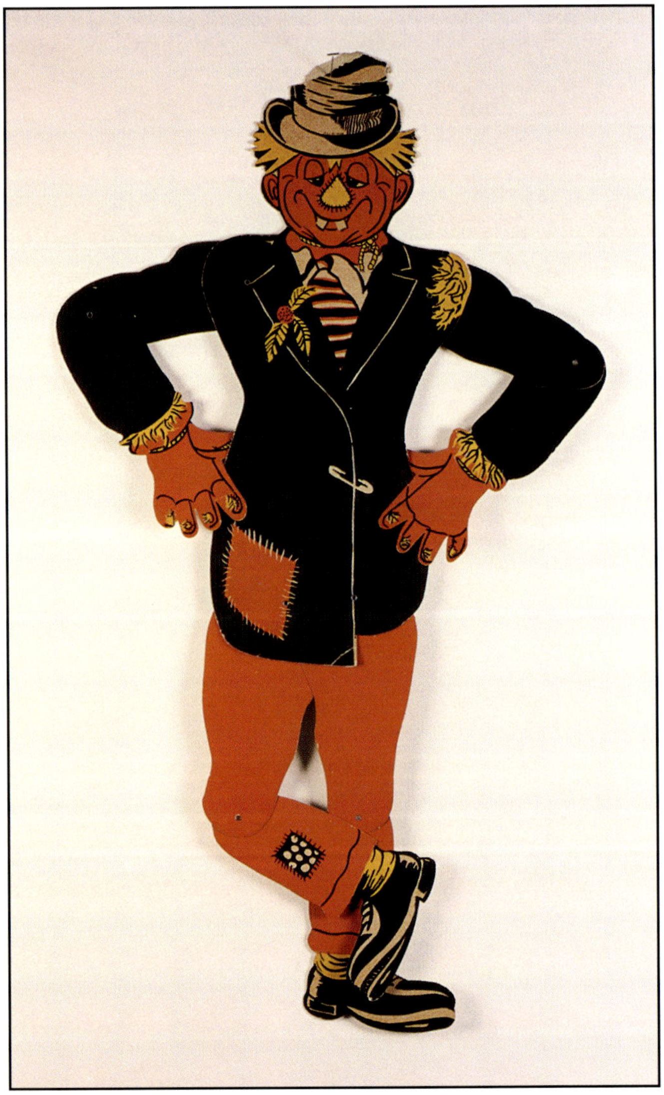

JOINTED SCARECROW
Initial Release: 1960
Production Run: 1960 – 1962
This comical scarecrow will lend a gay note to your Halloween decorating. Fully jointed arms and legs eyeleted to body. Printed one side, three colors, on heavy white stock and die-cut to shape. Size 36" tall. One design.
Value: $65

JACK-O-LANTERN GOBLIN
Initial Release: 1960
Production Run: 1960 – 1970
A Jolly Jack-O-Lantern Goblin that will add gay party spirit to Halloween decorating. Fully movable arms and legs are eyeleted to body. Gaily printed in four colors on quality stock and die-cut to shape. Size as illustrated approximately 24" x 32". One design.
*Another great Baby Boomer Halloween memory. I remember our neighbors always decorating their front door in the fall with this jaunty JOL.
*In 1971, Beistle "modernized" the look of this character which totally changed its look.
Value: $85

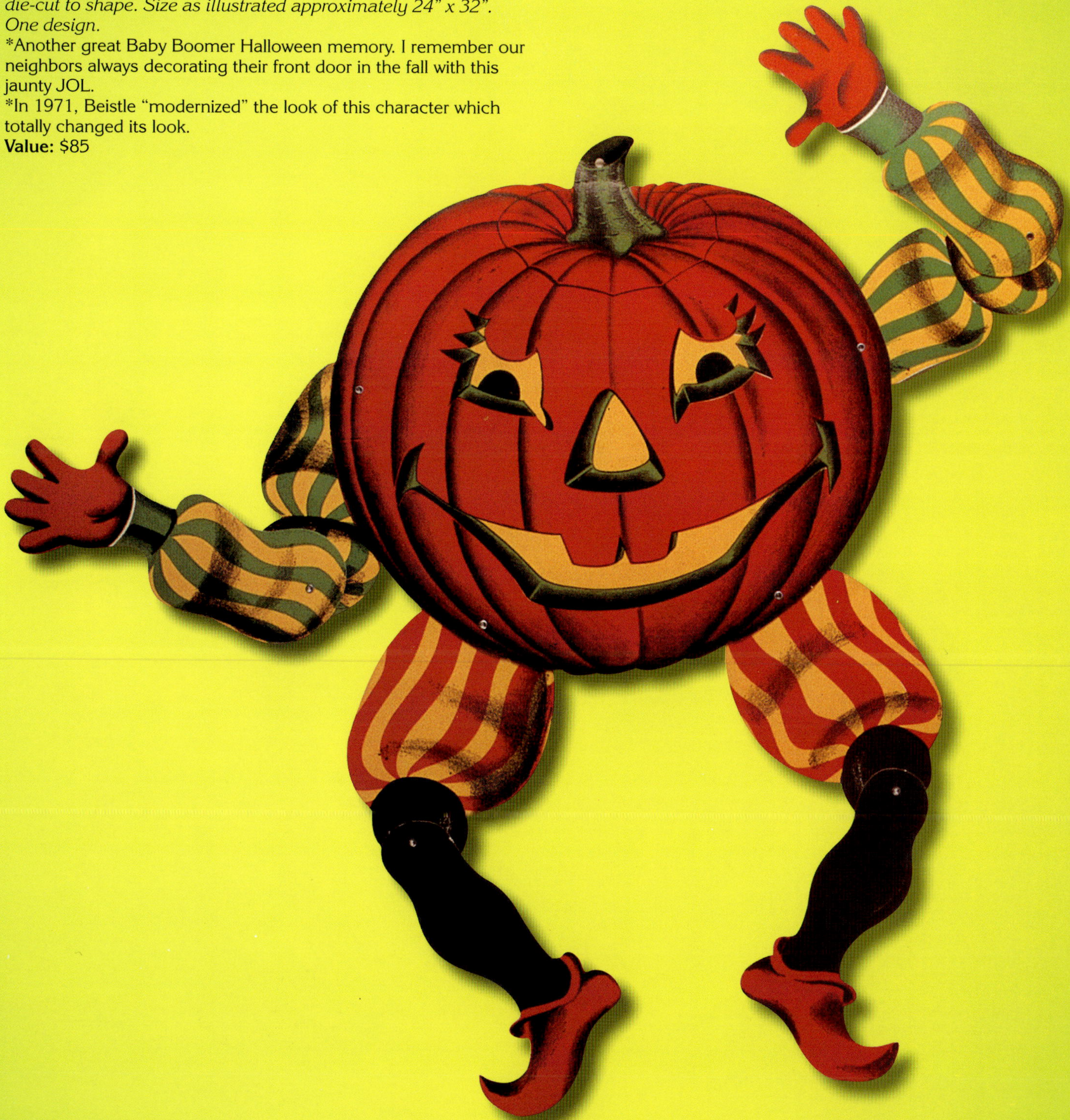

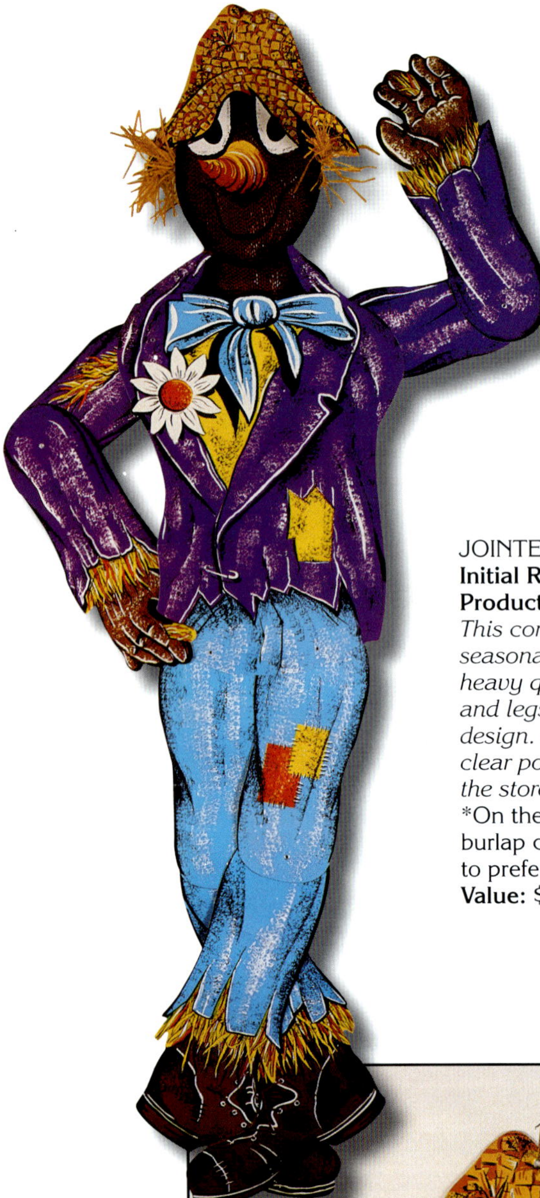

JOINTED SCARECROW
Initial Release: 1964
Production Run: 1964 – 1980
This comical Halloween Scarecrow will lend a gay note to seasonal decorating. Gaily printed in a four-color design on heavy quality stock and die-cut to shape. Fully movable arms and legs are expertly eyeleted to body. Size 15" x 55" tall. One design. Each Scarecrow completely assembled is packed in a clear poly bag with printed header for rack or counter sale in the stores.
*On the photo at right is an artist's model of the scarecrow's burlap covered face in a much lighter shade of brown. I happen to prefer this one – it looks more "lifelike" if you will.
Value: $65

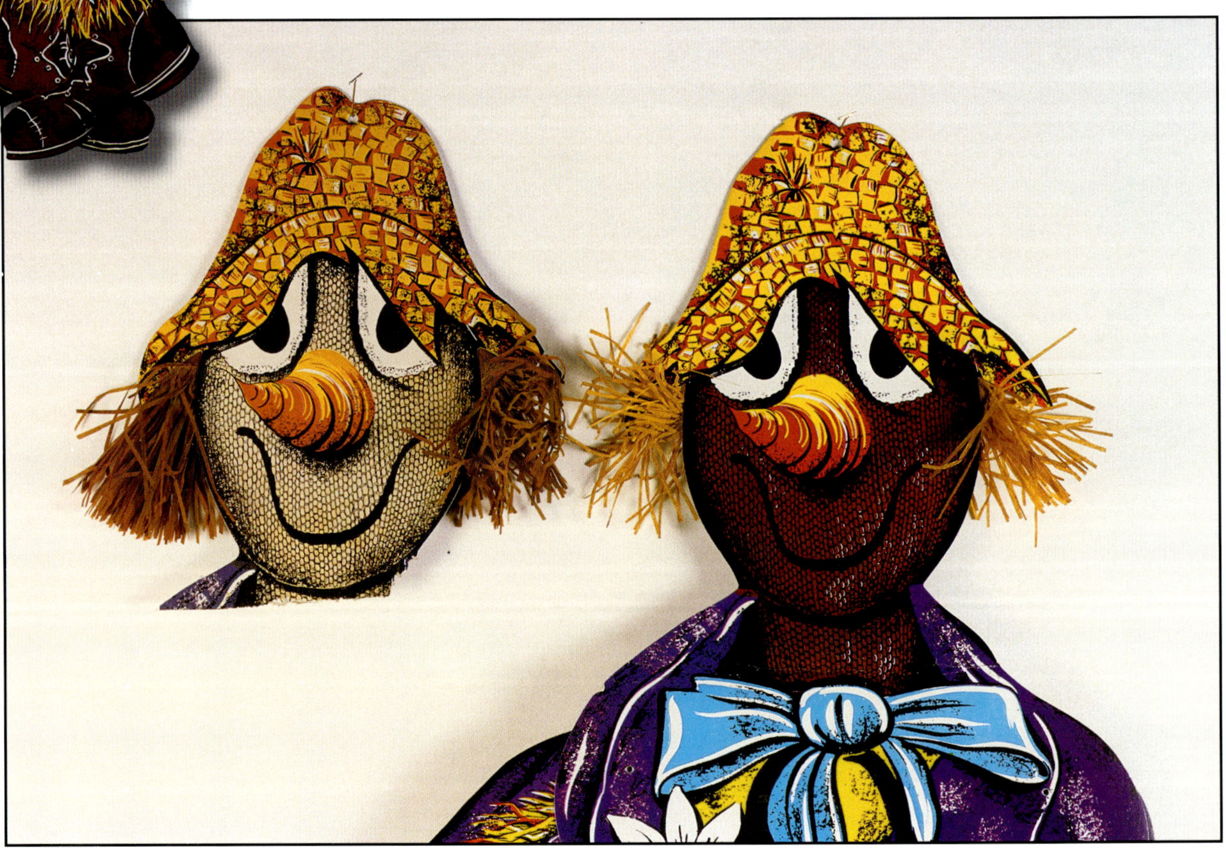

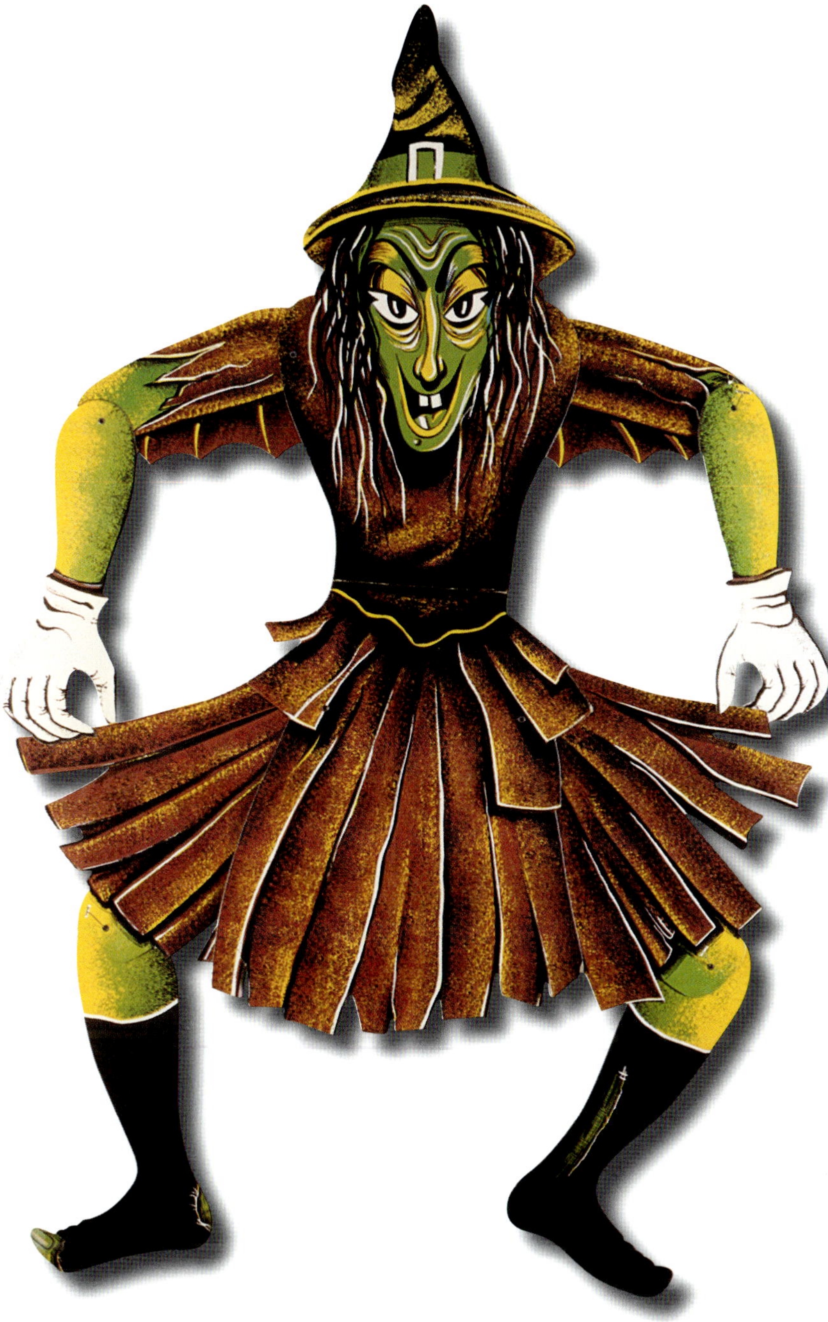

JOINTED WITCH
Initial Release: 1966
Production Run: 1966 – 1968
This enchanting Halloween witch will add thrills and chills to any party decorating scheme. Printed in a bright four-color design on heavy quality stock and die-cut to shape. Fully jointed arms and legs expertly eyeleted to body. Size 24" x 40". One design. Completely assembled and packed in a clear poly bag with header.
*Below is an example of the header attached to the clear poly bag.
Value: $65

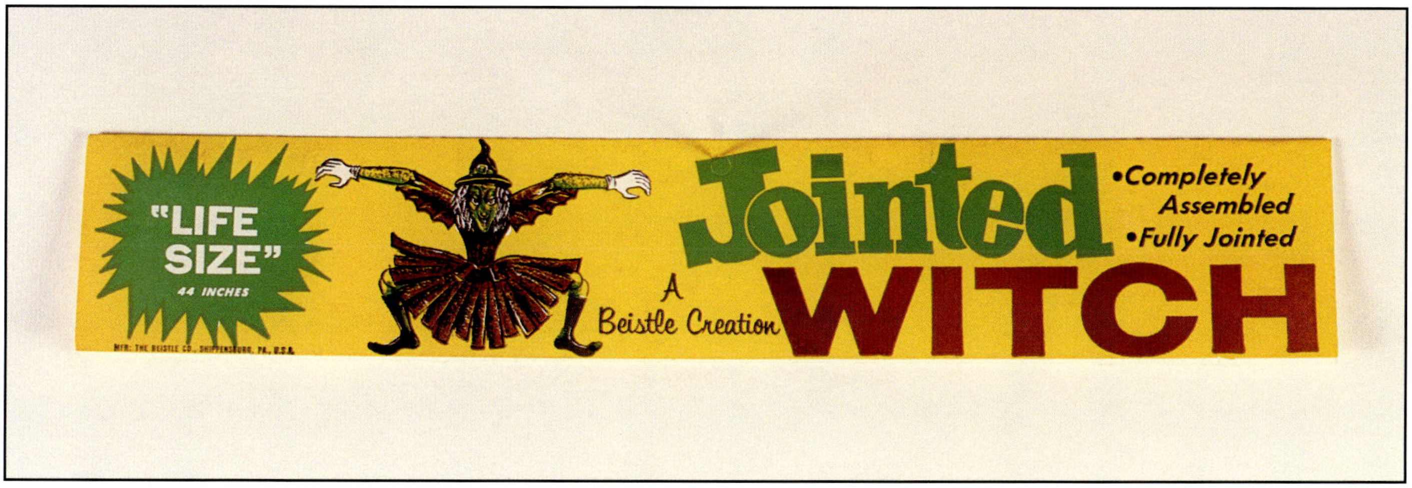

HALLOWEEN FAVOR-ETTES
Initial Release: 1966
Production Run: 1966 – 1968
Create Halloween Party atmosphere with these unusual table favors. Six designs printed in three colors and die-cut to shape. Cleverly designed with locking bases for standing. Average size 4" x 8" with a 3" circular base. Six designs packed in a printed poly bag with header.
*Showing the six designs with the front and back view of the printed poly bag. Take note of the artist's drawing for the front of the package. Included is the artist's rendition of the bat flying over the cemetery.
Value: $165 (which includes the printed poly bag)

(Continued on following 3 pages)

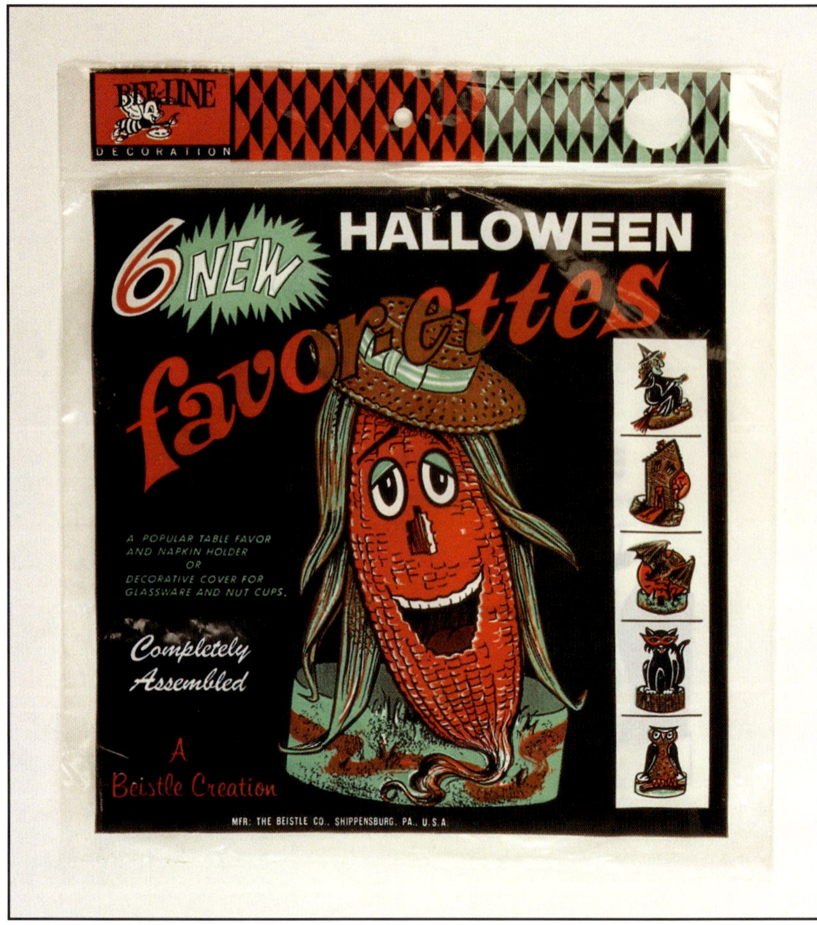

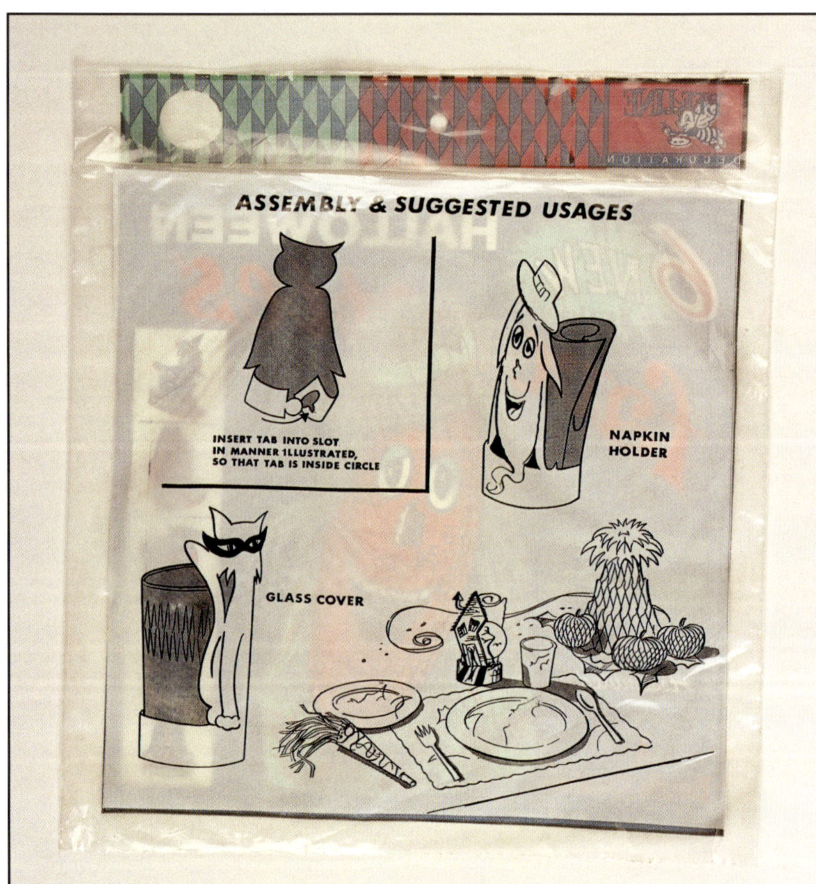

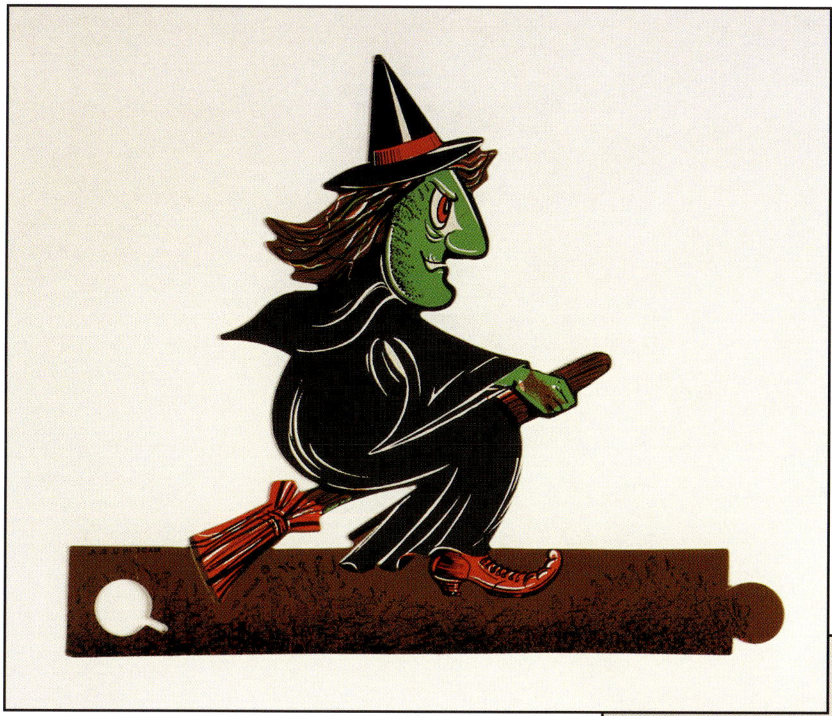

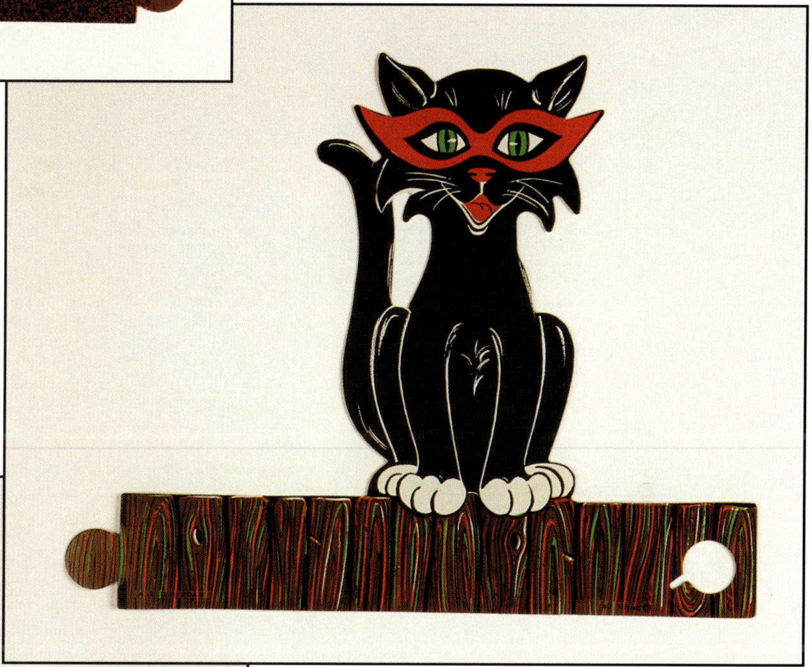

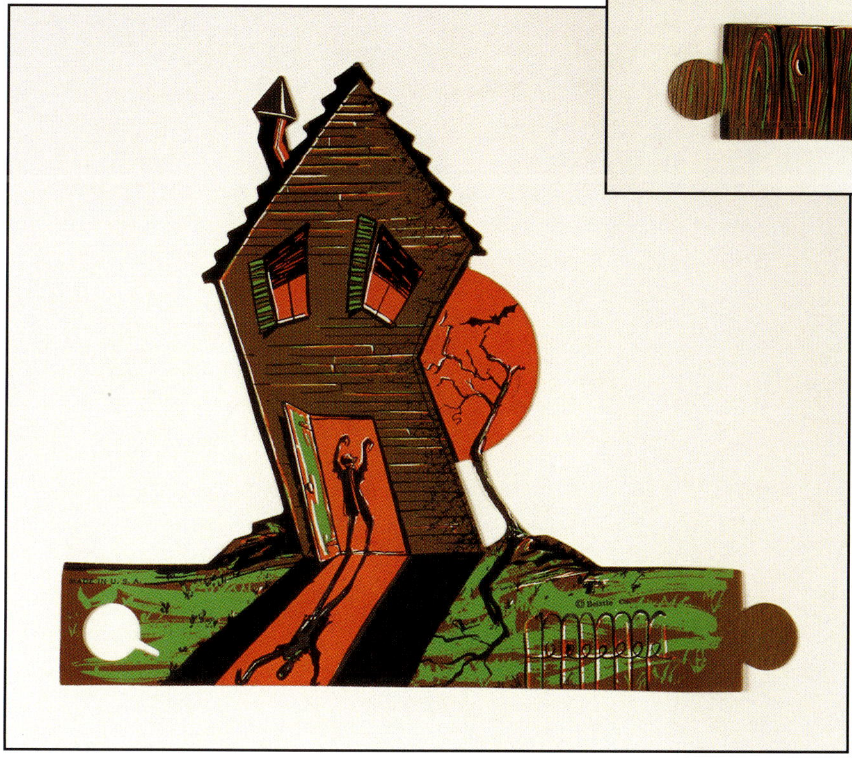
MADE IN U.S.A.
© Beistle

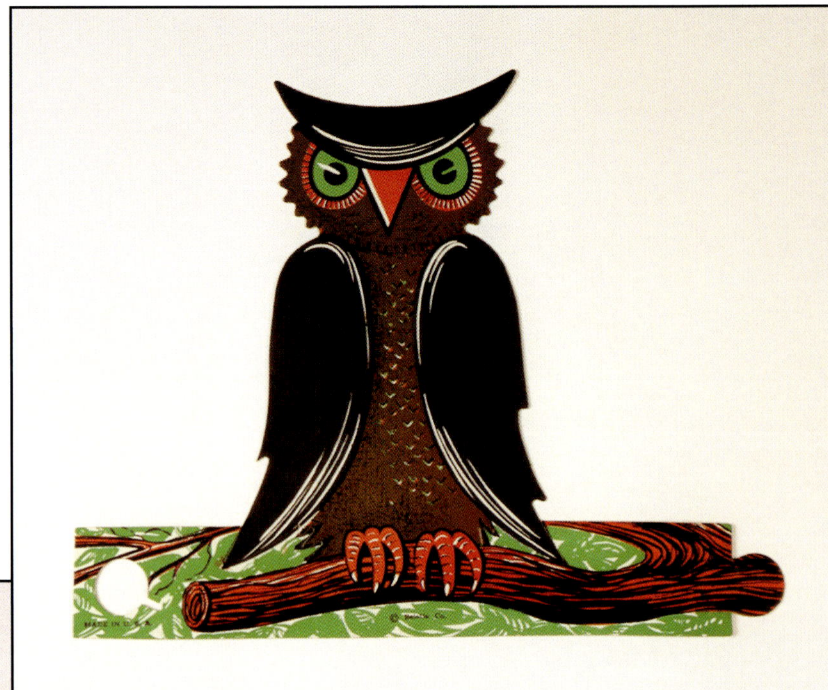

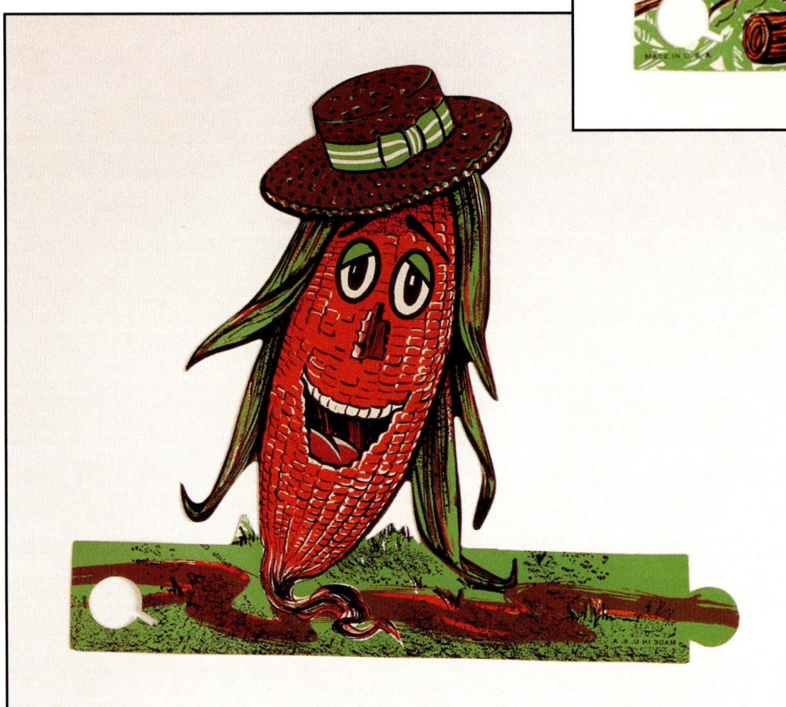

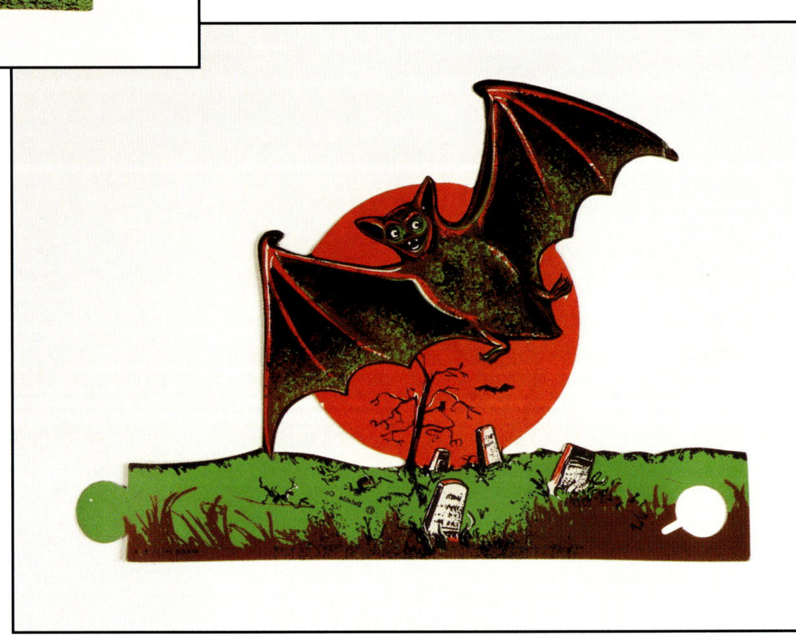

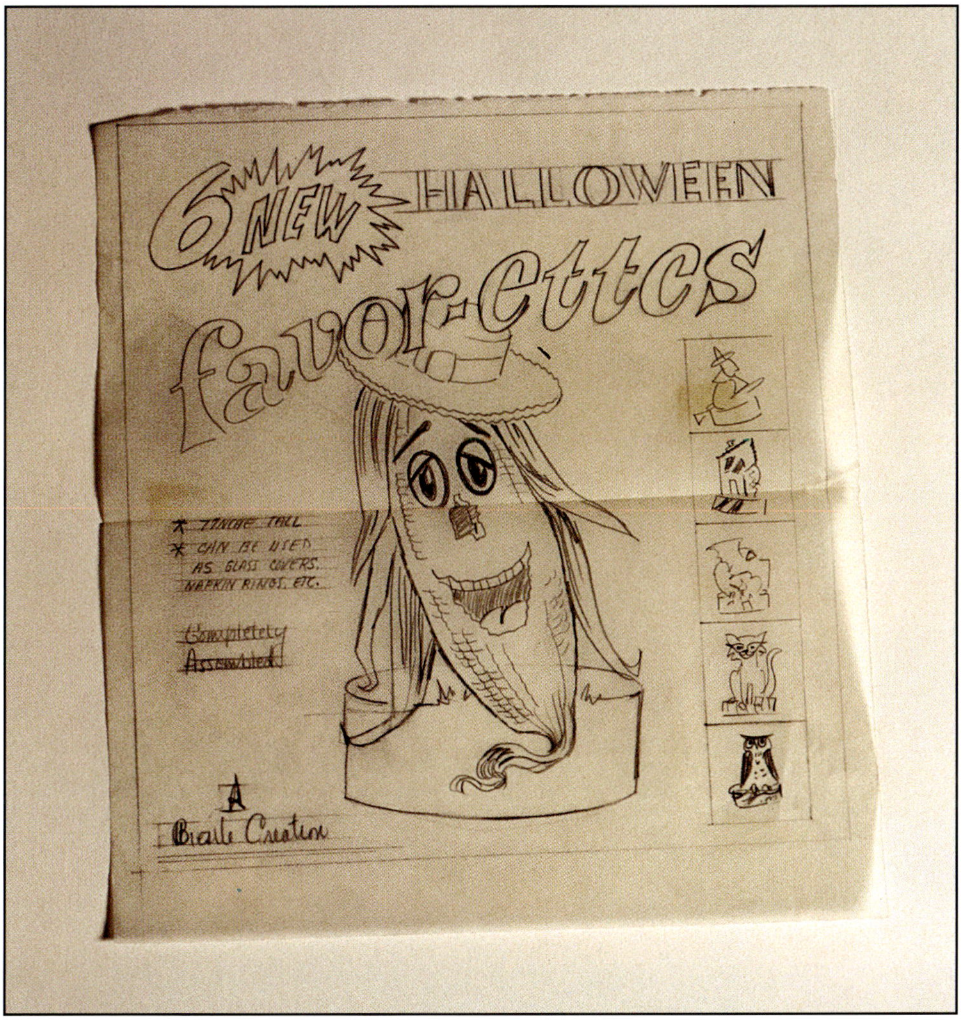
6 NEW HALLOWEEN
favor-ettes
* CAN BE USED AS GLASS COVERS. NAPKIN RINGS, ETC.

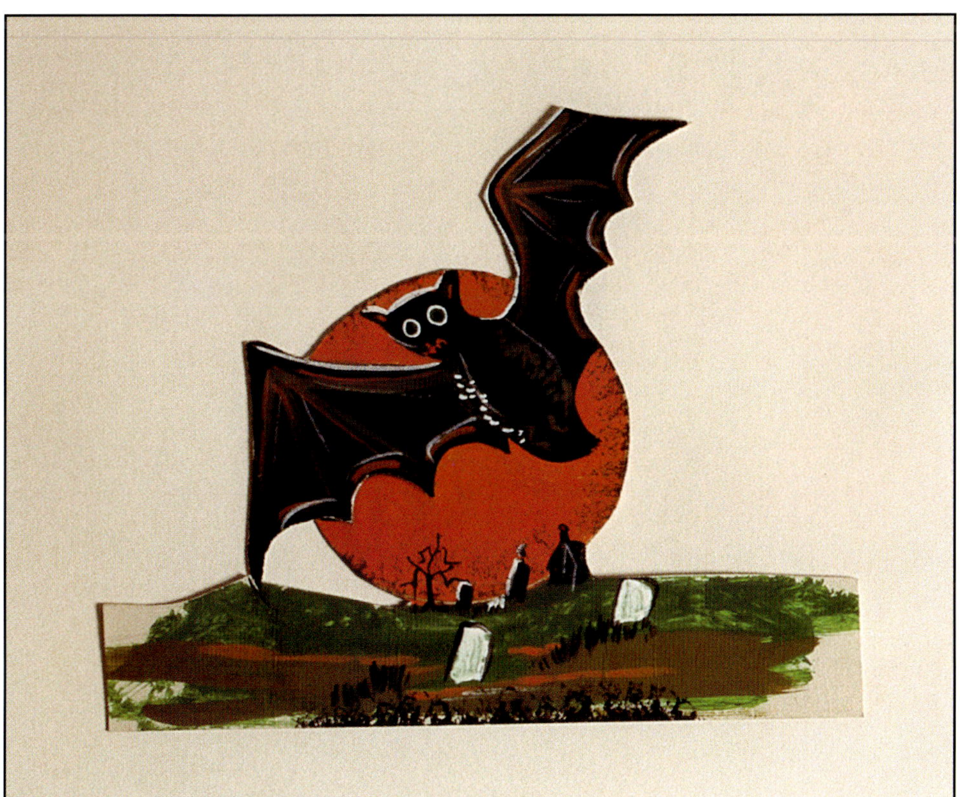

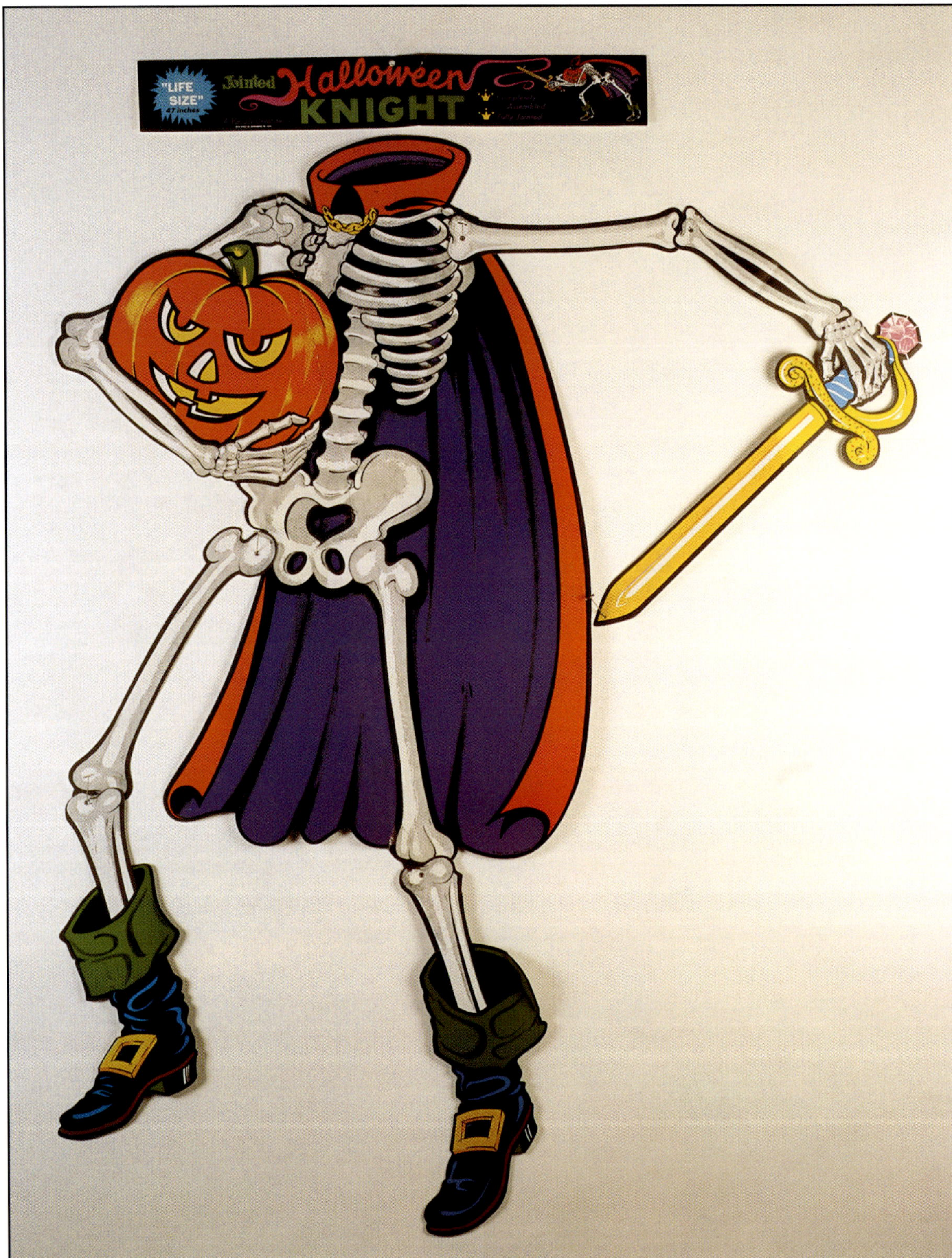

HALLOWEEN KNIGHT
Initial Release: 1969
Production Run: 1969 – 1970
A startling new Halloween character that's sure to delight party decorators. This swashbuckling Knight with his bright cloak, gleaming sword and Jack-O-Lantern head tucked neatly under one arm is printed in a bold four-color design. Die-cut to shape with parts expertly eyeleted to permit free movement in a variety of positions. 47" tall. One design. Completely assembled and packed in a clear poly bag with header.
*Die-cut shown with its poly bag header. This one's for you, Daniel!
Value: $75

MISS PUMPKIN HEAD (a.k.a. **HALLOWEEN DANCING ELF** and/or **PUMPKIN DOLL**)
Initial Release: 1923
Production Run: 1923 – 1932
*It always comes as a delightful surprise when I discover a Beistle piece that has a healthy production run and in its course will have subtle variations to its design. I happened across the piece on the left on my most recent visit to the Beistle archives. Notice how the model on the right appears to be wearing culottes while the cutie on the left looks to be sporting a lettuce-leaf skirt. Also, there is a huge difference in coloring – both vivid just the same.
*This one's for you, Elizabeth!

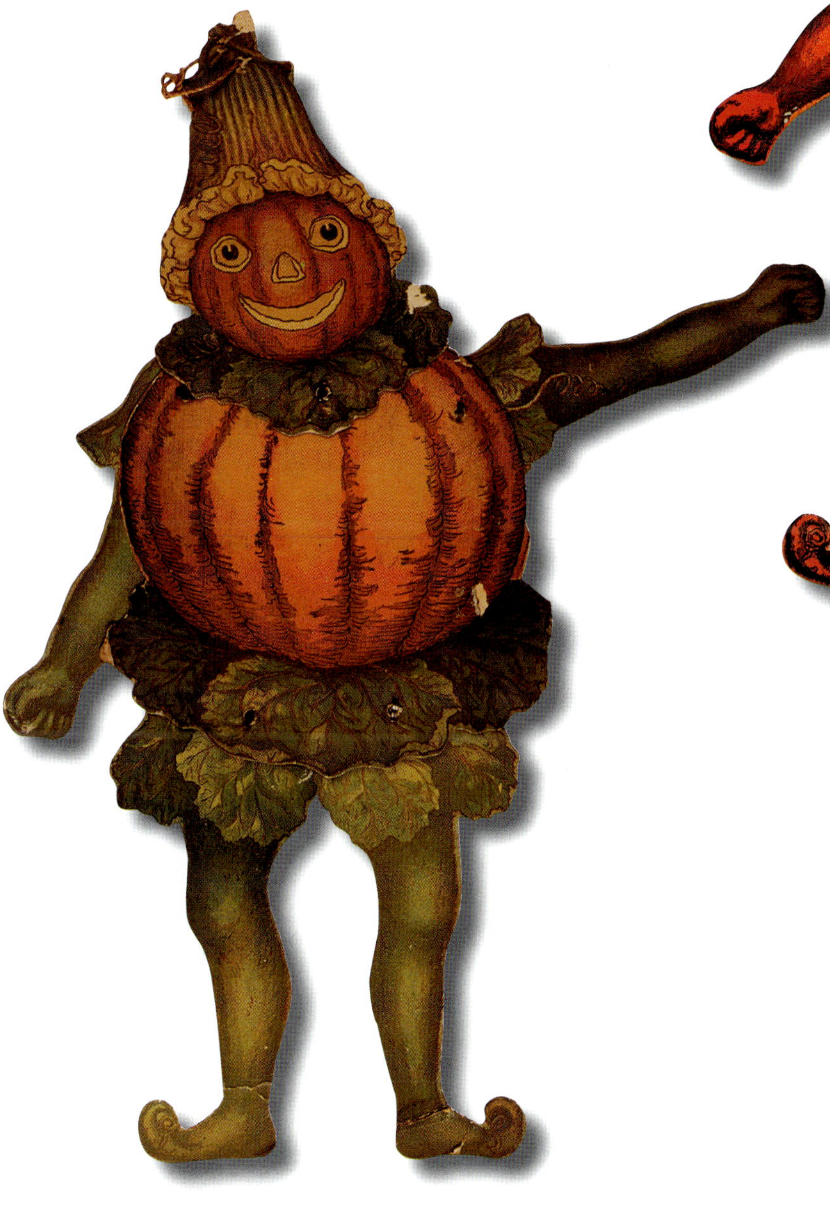

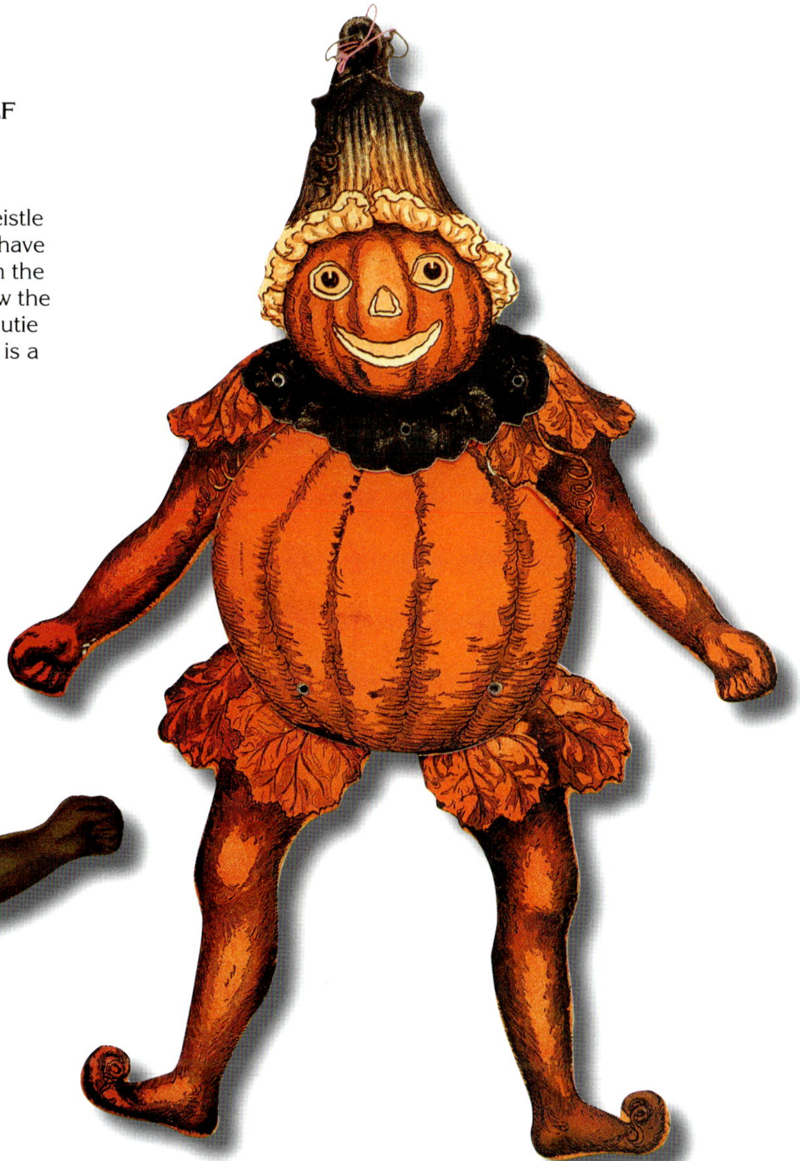

FLUORESCENT CUTOUTS
Initial Release: 1970
Production Run: 1970 – 1977
A delightful new set of Halloween cutouts. Four designs in vivid fluorescent three-color print. Size 9' x 11". Packed four pieces in a crystal-clear poly shrink-pack with printed header.
Value: $65 for the set

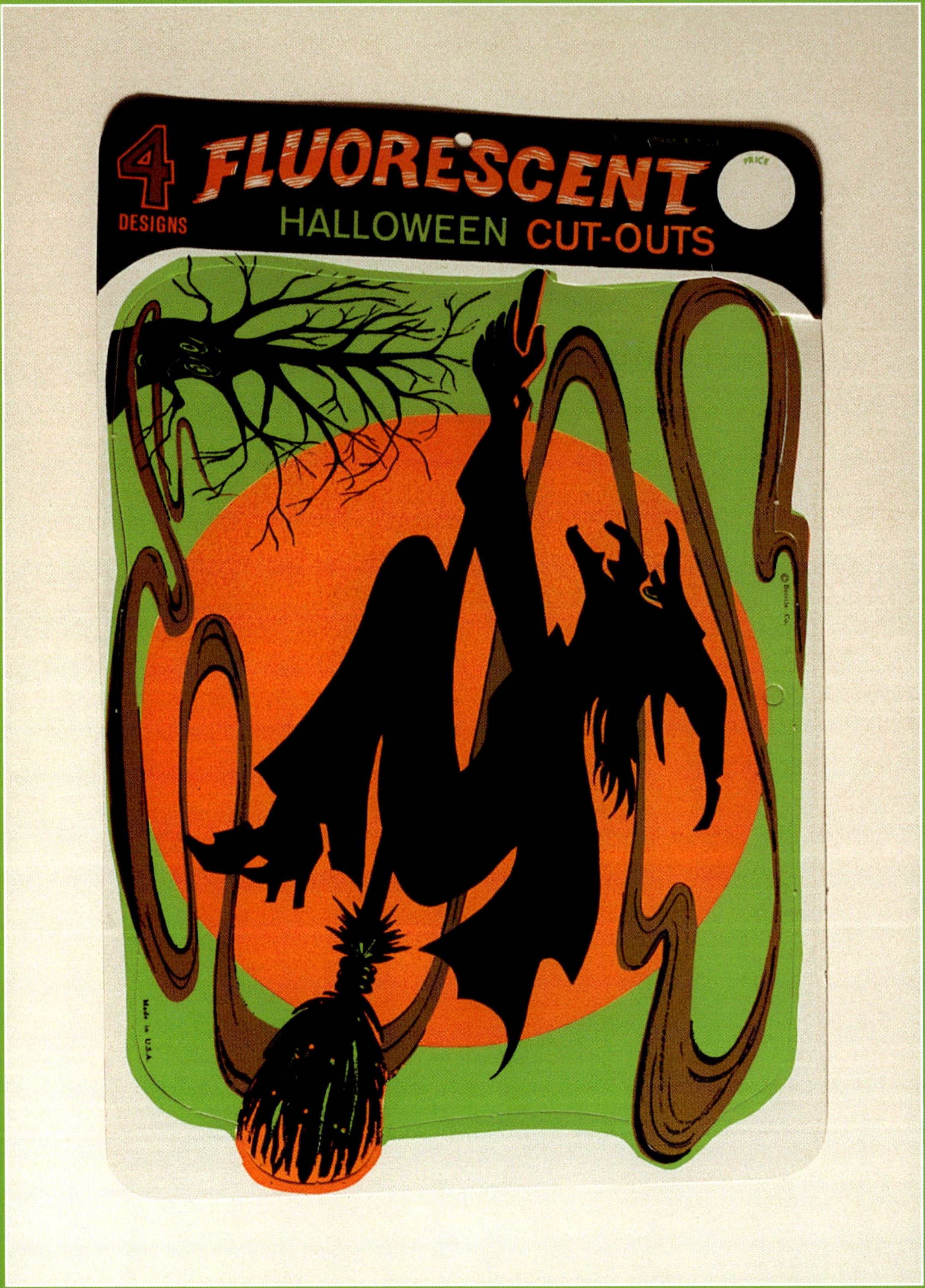

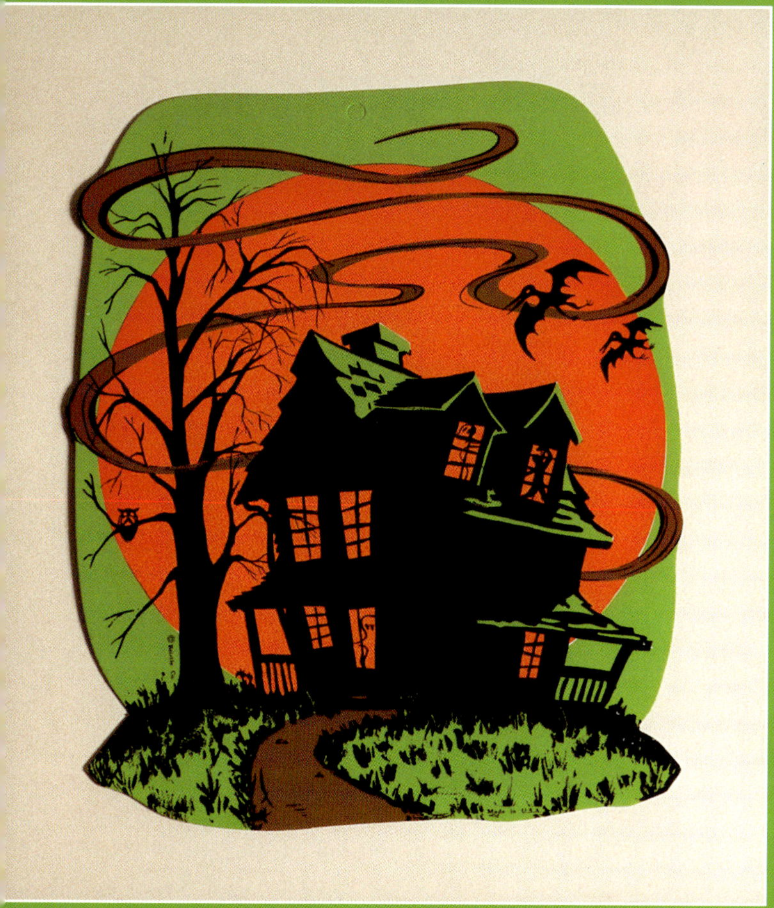

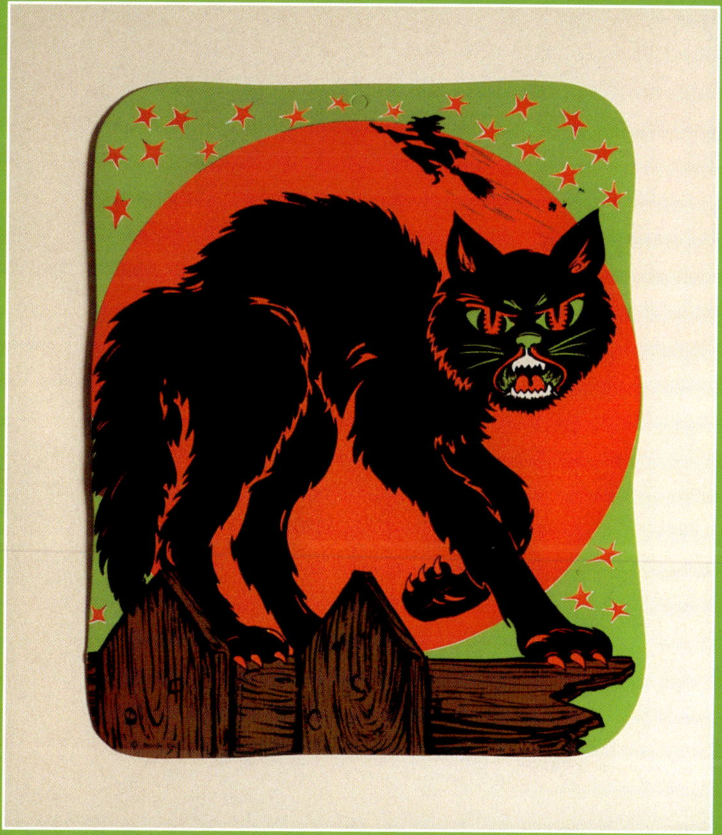

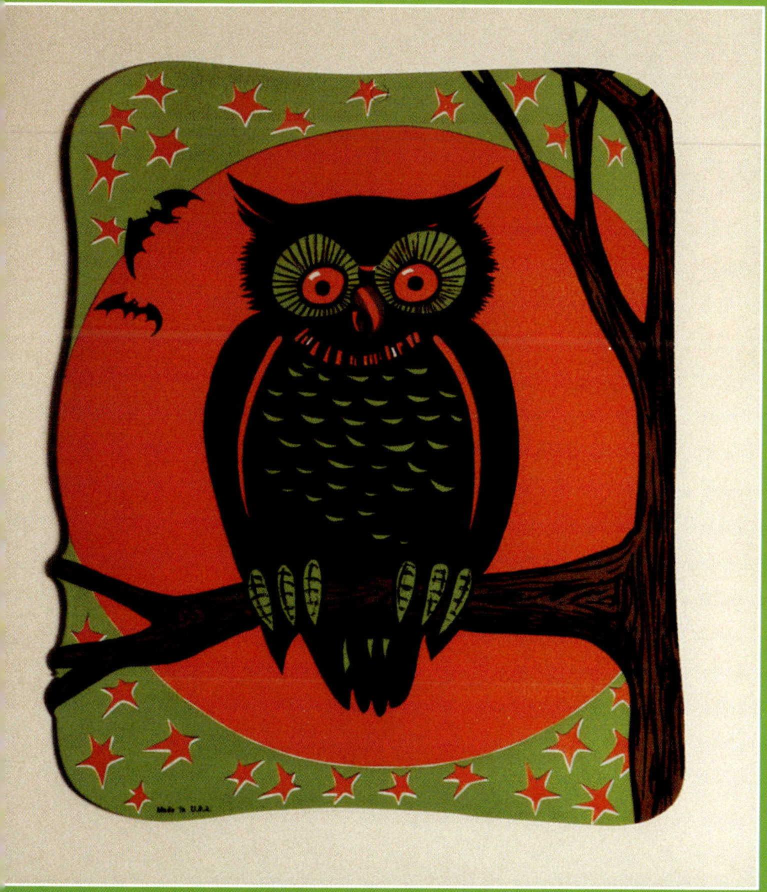

HALLOWEEN CUTOUTS
Initial Release: 1976
Production Run: 1976 – 1980
A favorite for party decorating. Printed in vivid fluorescent four-color Halloween designs and die-cut to shape. Packed assorted four designs.
*In 1981, these die-cuts were sold in either a 12" size or 22" size. They were packaged in assorted four designs and/or bulk packaging. Also, this is the year that they dropped the Owl and Moon.
Value: $12 – $25 range

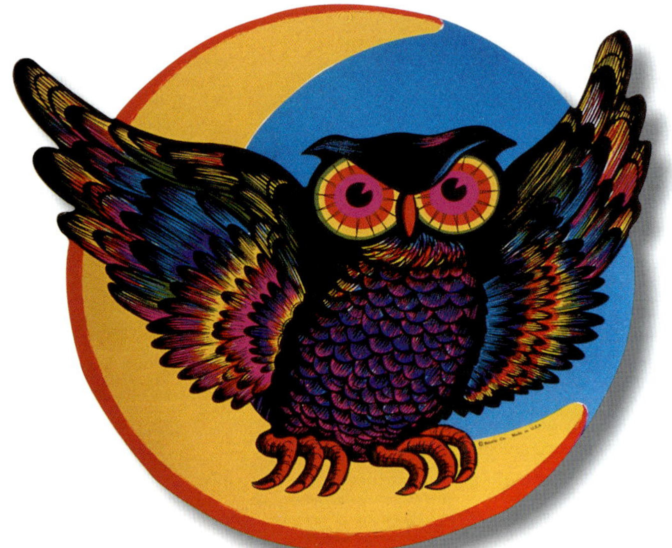

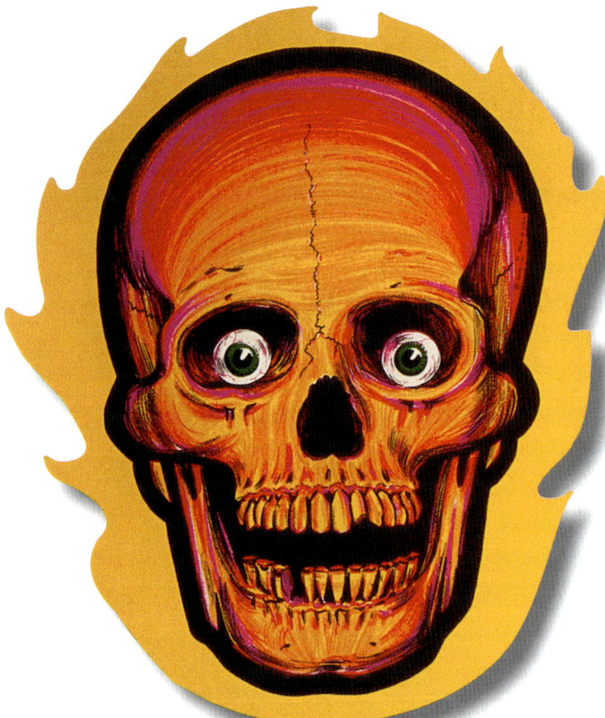

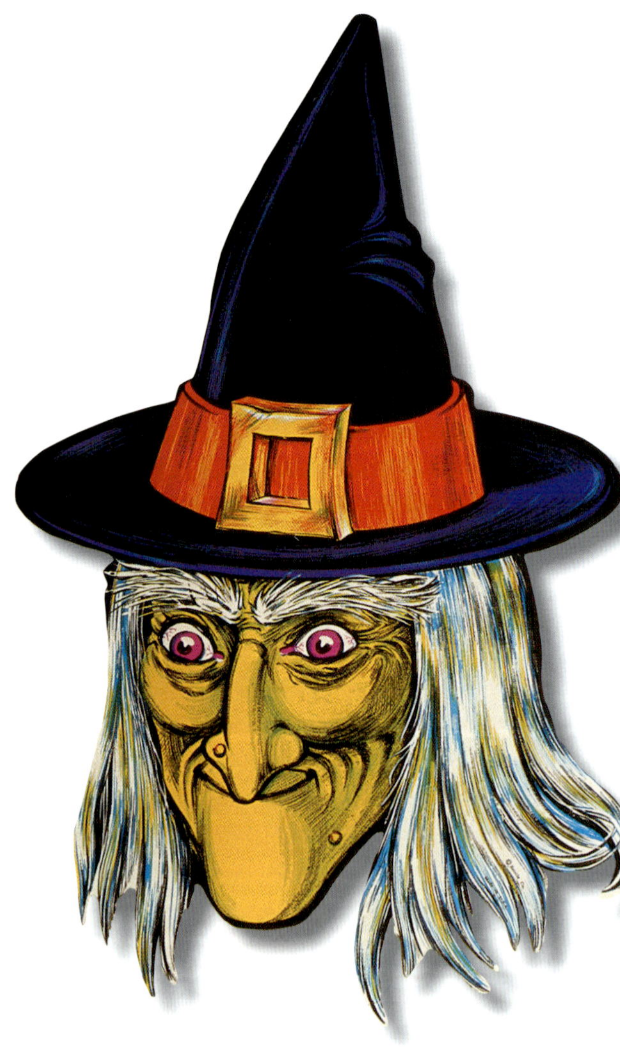

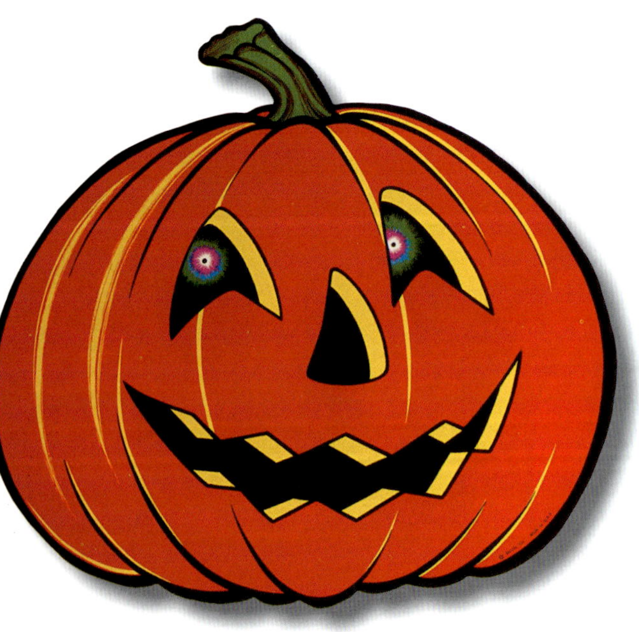

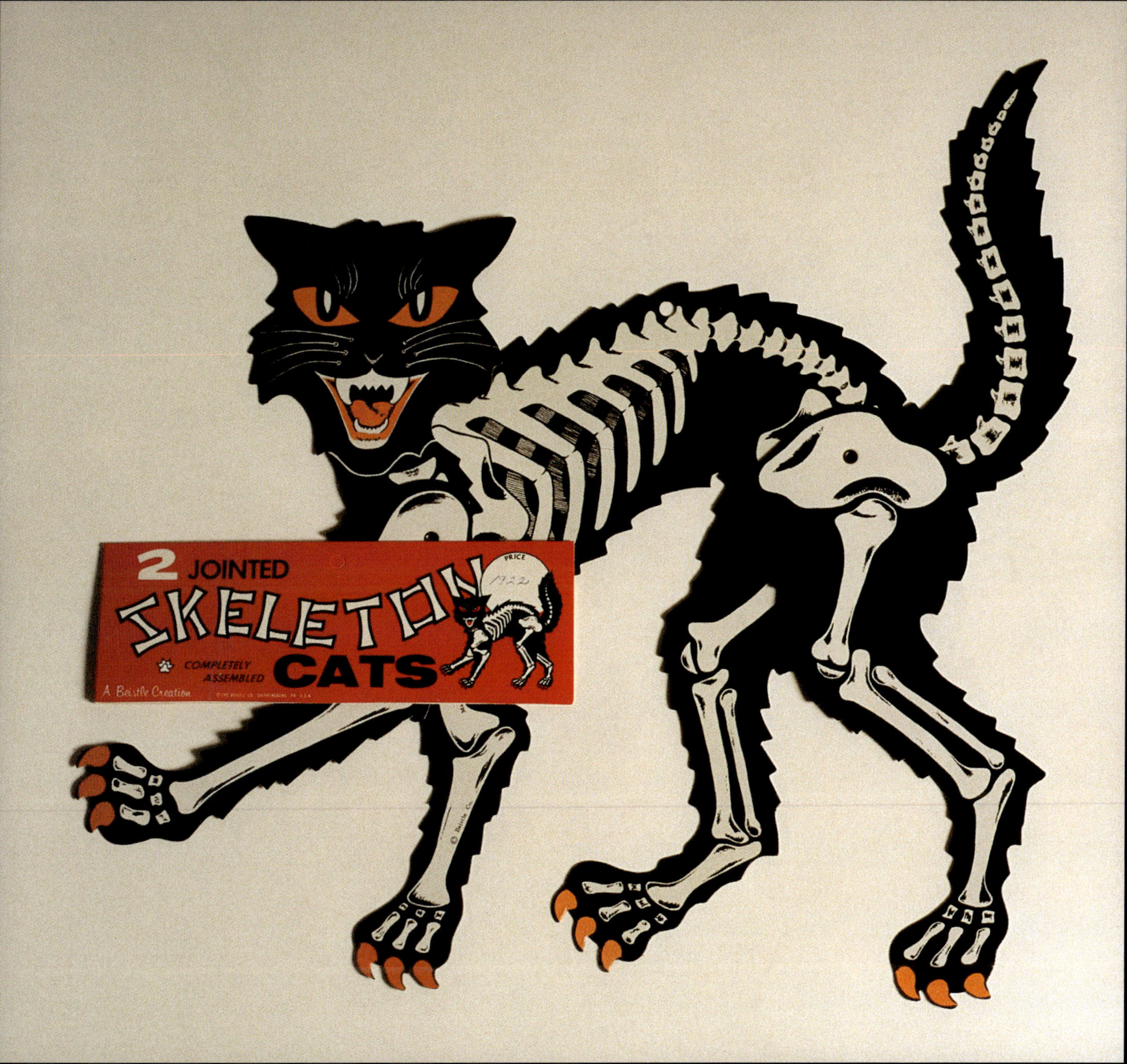

SKELETON CAT
Initial Release: 1970
Production Run: One year only: 1970*
This terrified cat embraces the eerie Halloween spirit. Printed in a two-color design and die-cut to shape with head, tail and legs eyeleted to body. Size 14' x 16". Two designs, one facing left, one right. Packed assorted two pieces in a clear poly bag with header.
*This style cat was sold only one year. In 1971, Beistle "updated" its look by making the cat totally skeletal and with a more demonic look.
*Die-cut shown with its header.
Value: $45

JACK-O-LANTERN FACES
Initial Release: 1961
Production Run: One year only: 1961
These jolly Jack-O-Lantern faces will lend a gay note to party decorating. Printed in three colors on shiny white light weight stock. Packed six pieces in a clear polyurethane bag with heat sealed printed top. Size 7.5" x 9.5". Two each of three designs equally assorted to bag.
*The three designs are shown here.
Value: $18 – $22 range

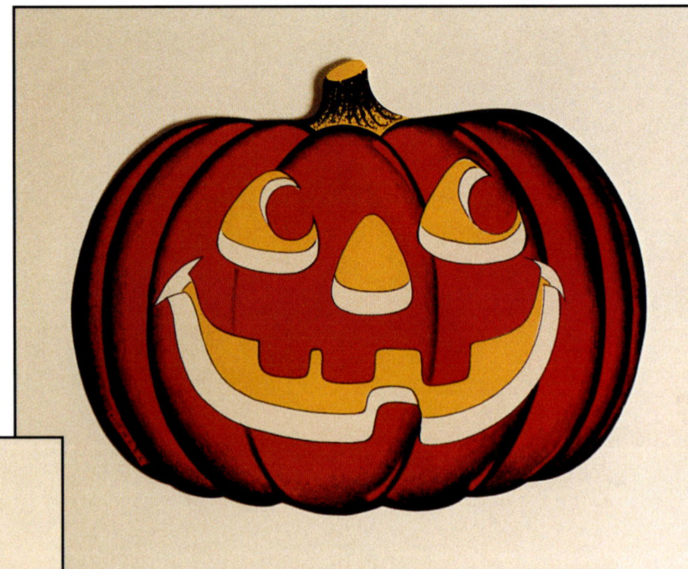

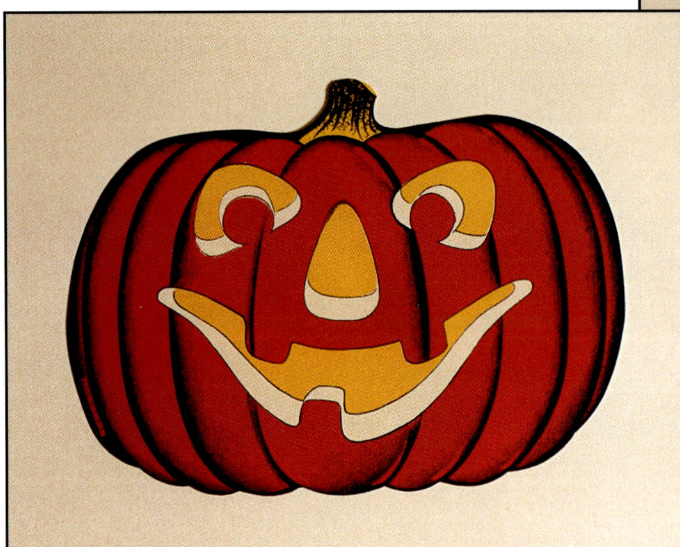

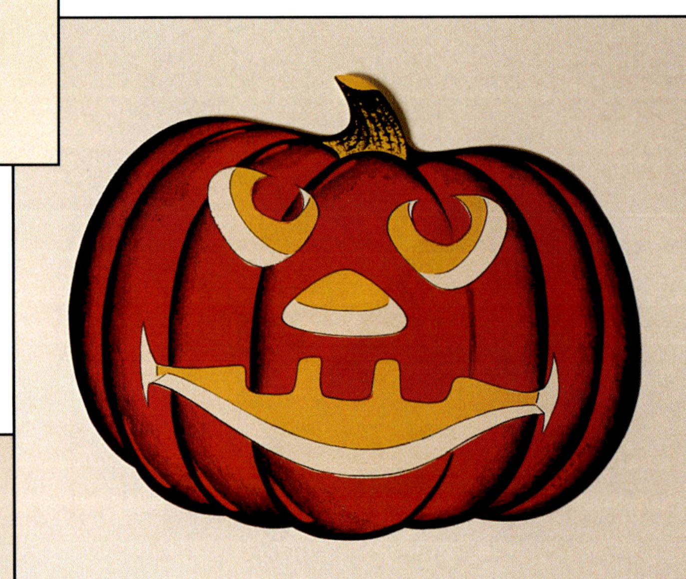

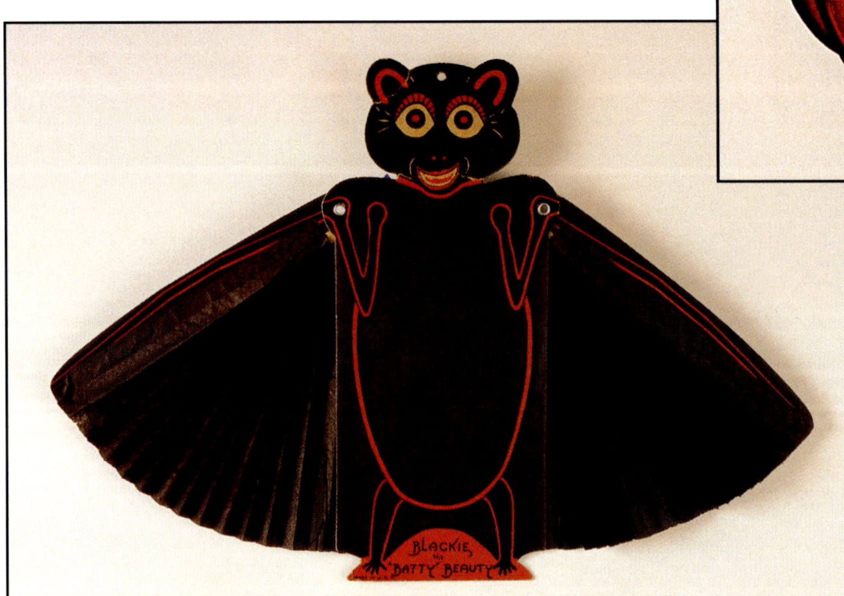

BLACKIE THE BATTY BEAUTY
Initial Release: 1952
Production Run: 1952 – 1956
This comical Halloween character may be used either hanging or standing. Children delight at expanding wings of black Art-Tissue, eyeleted to body. Printed orange and black on heavy stock and die-cut to shape. Size 9" x 15", opened. One design. Packed folded flat.
Value: $45

CHAPTER 3
Party Games

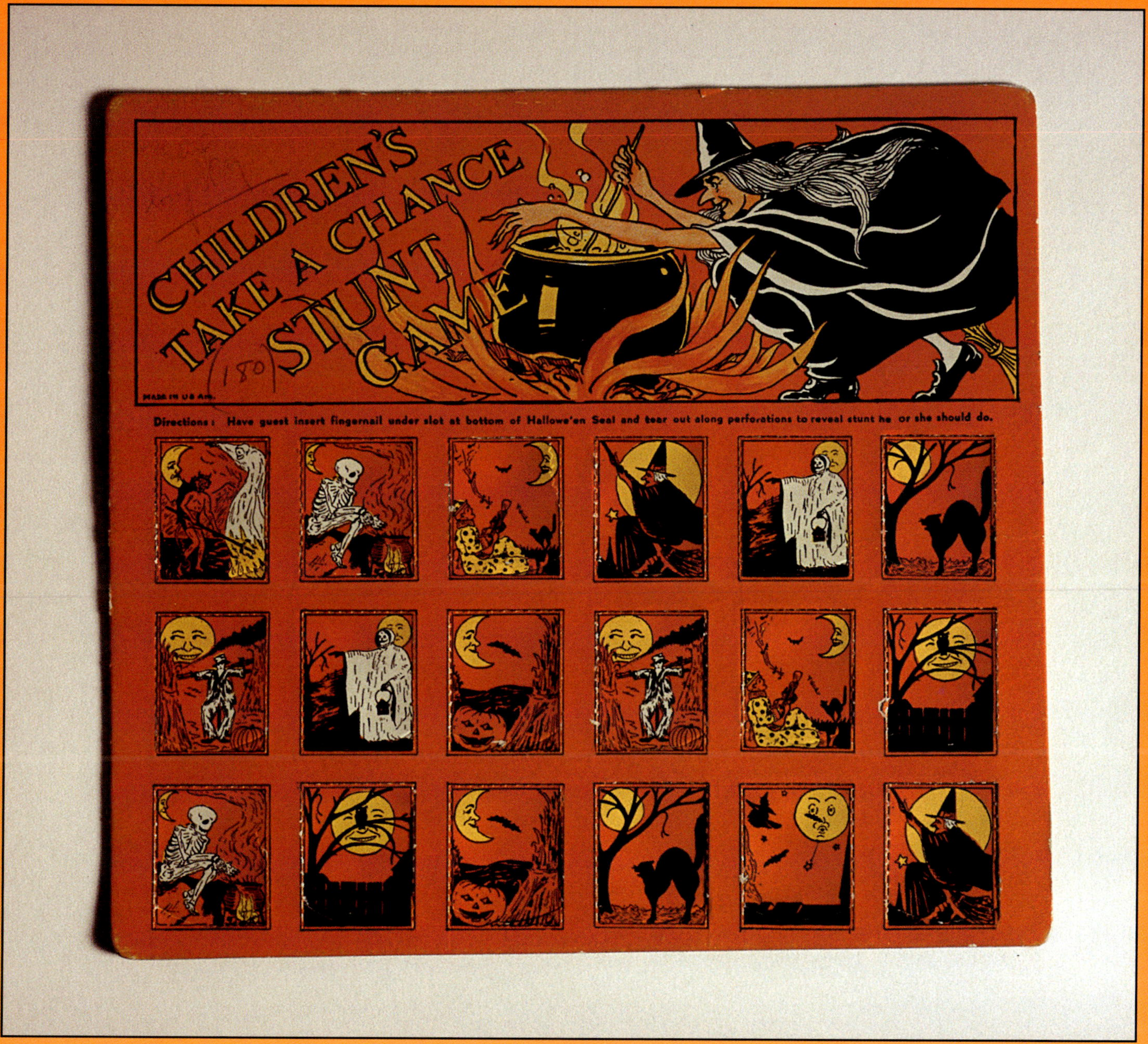

HALLOWEEN STAMP STUNT GAME
Initial Release: 1934
Production Run: 1934 – 1942
One design, size 8.5" x 9", printed in Halloween colors and varnished on cardboard. With perforated stamps to remove, revealing stunts.
*Also known as the "Children's Take-A-Chance Stunt Game."
Value: $125

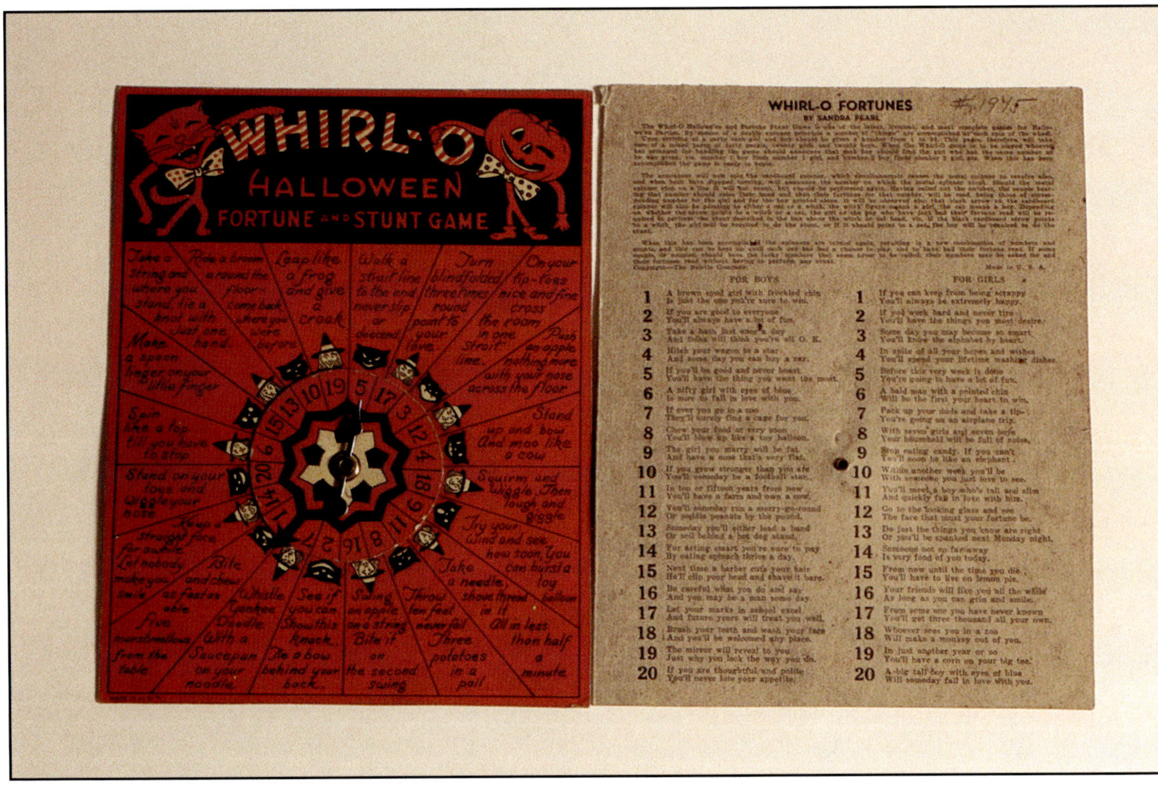

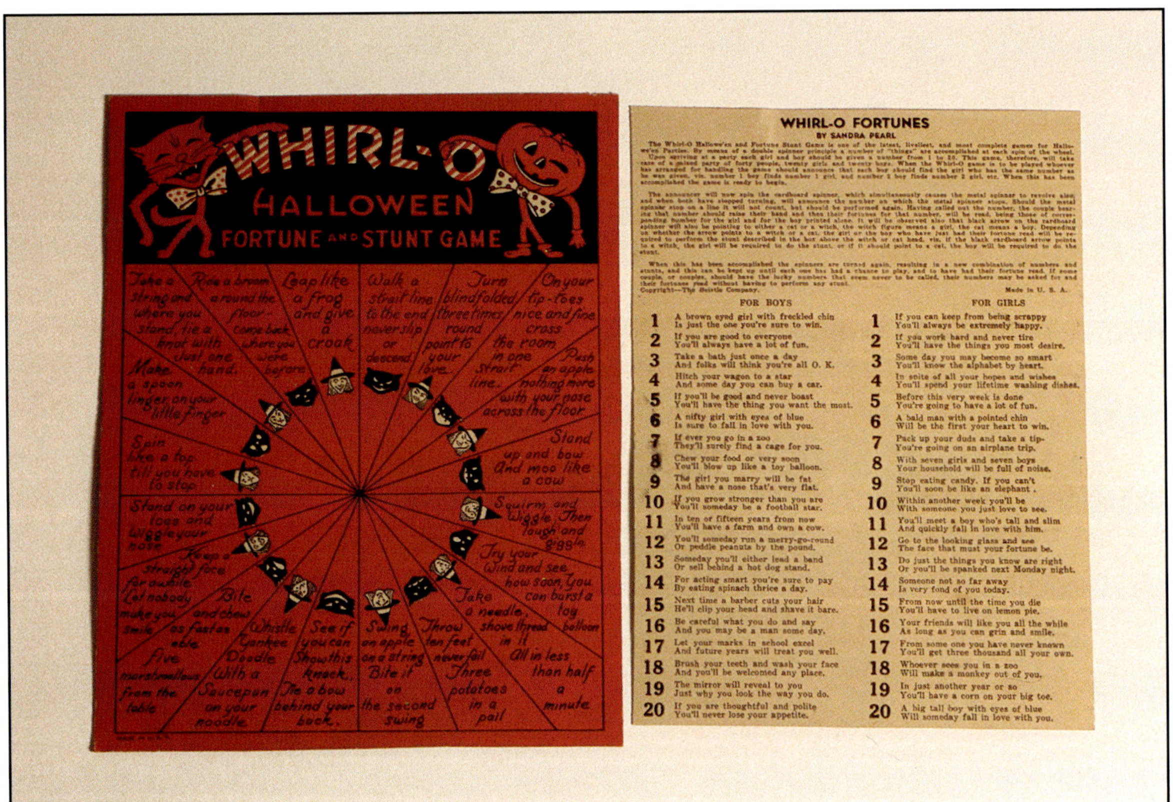

WHIRL-O-GAME
Initial Release: 1949
Production Run: 1949 – 1964
An entertaining two-in-one fortune and stunt game, printed orange and black on heavy cardboard. Metal spinner points to 20 different stunts and numbers. Number reveals fortune on back for both boys and girls.
*The top photo illustrates both the front and back of the game; below, a rarely seen artist's prototype.
Value: $95

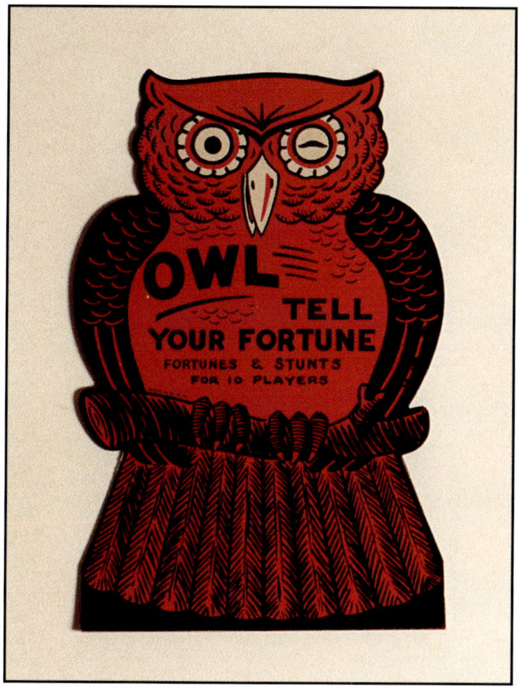

OWL TELL YOUR FORTUNE GAME

Initial Release: 1955
Production Run: 1955 – 1961
This wise old owl conceals ten exciting stunts and fortunes that are sure to add to the party fun and make it a gay Halloween for everyone. Printed in two colors on fine stock and die-cut to shape. Tail feathers are die-cut so that they may be removed and each feather will reveal a stunt and fortune. Size 6" x 9". One design.
Value: $85

JACK-O-LANTERN STUNT AND FORTUNE GAME

Initial Release: 1955
Production Run: 1955 – 1964
Sixteen lively stunts and exciting fortunes concealed in a printed and perforated cardboard Jack-O-Lantern. Is sure to add to the gaiety of any Halloween party. Size 6.25" x 9.25". One design. Directions included.
*The photo at right shows the front of the game surrounded by a number of extra game pieces revealing various stunts and fortunes. I wonder who came up with the stunt, "Give a sales talk"? The photo below reveals the back of the game.
Value: $100

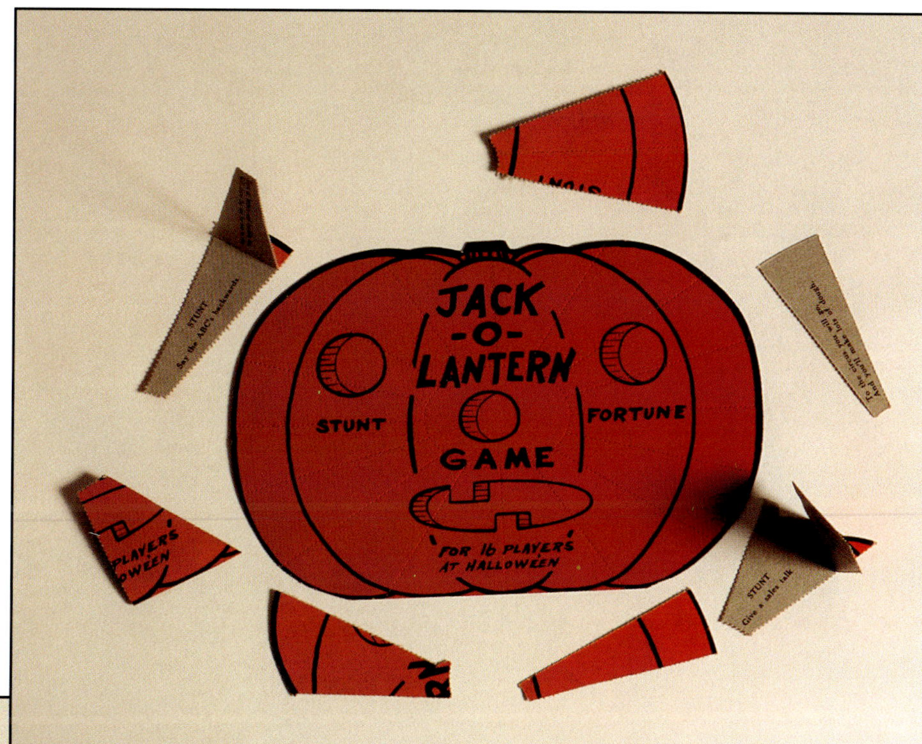

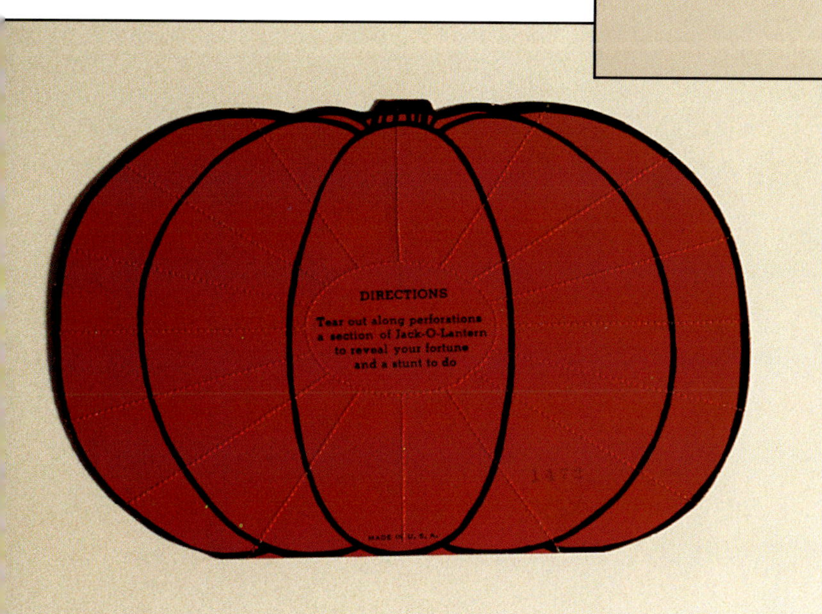

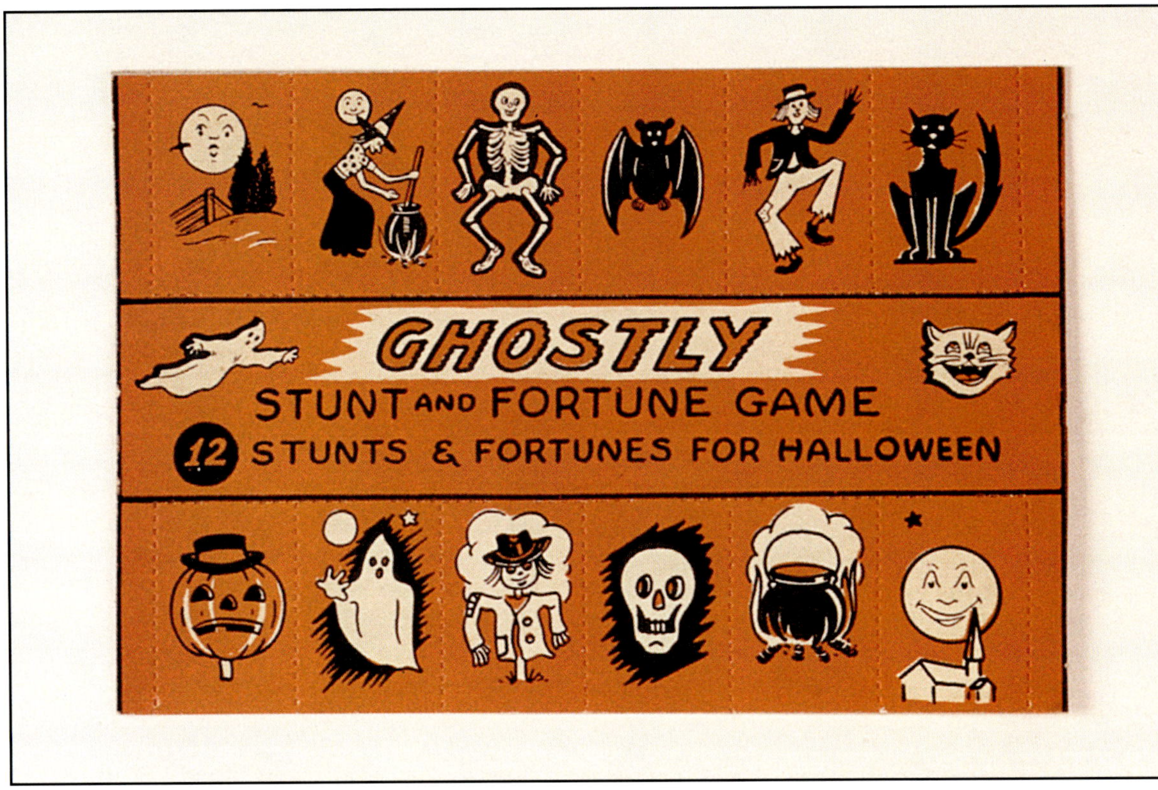

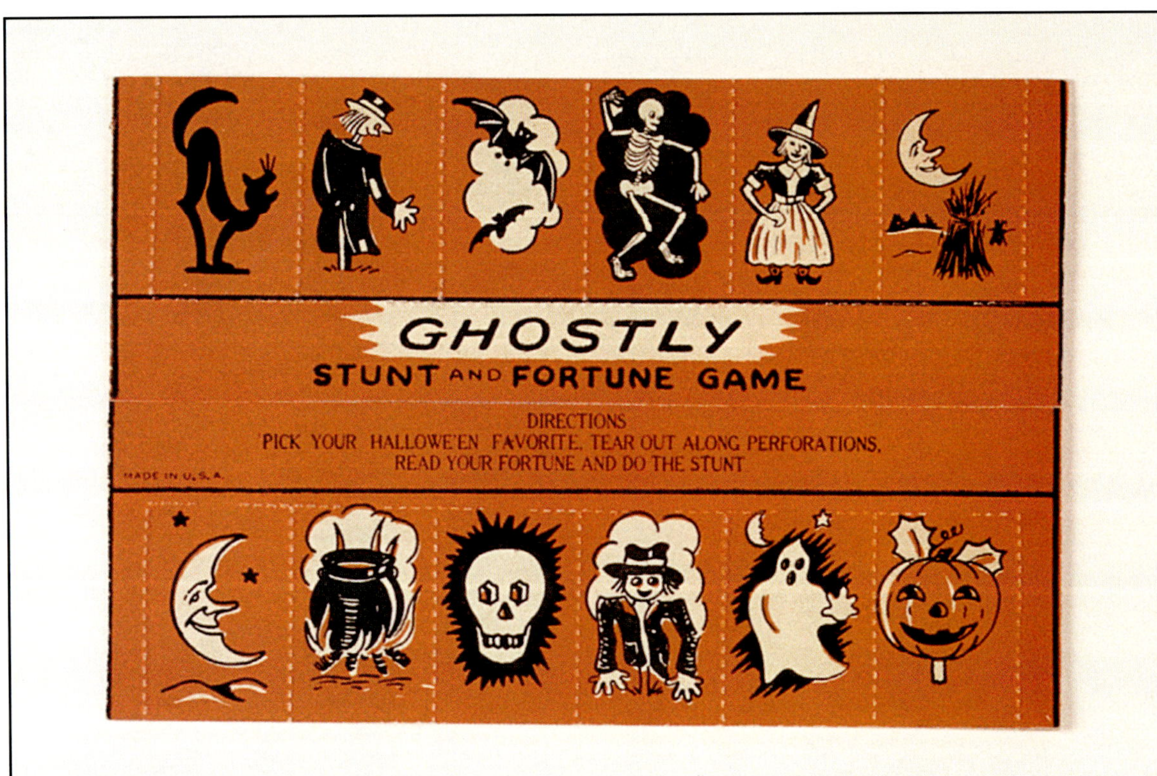

GHOSTLY STUNT AND FORTUNE GAME
Initial Release: 1955
Production Run: 1955 – 1958
A popular priced Halloween game that will interest all groups and enliven any party. Twelve stunts and fortunes concealed in a perforated card. Printed in orange and black. Size 4.25" x 6.25". One design. Instructions included.
*Showing both the front and back of the game. Notice how the front decorations differ from the ones on the back.
Value: $75

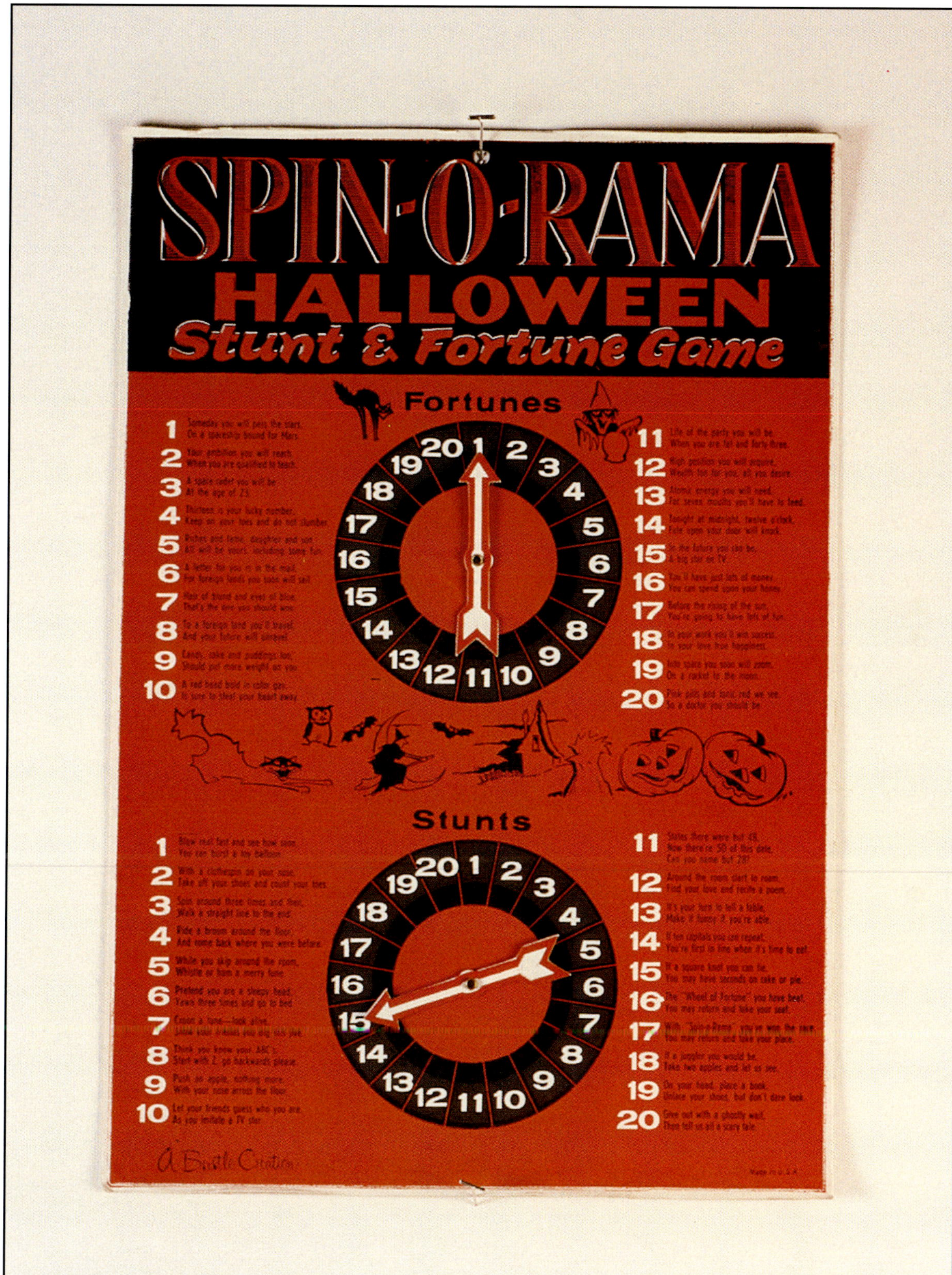

SPIN-O-RAMA GAME
Initial Release: 1961
Production Run: 1961 – 1965
Your Halloween party is sure to be a "Real Success" with the help of this popular "Jumbo" Spinner Game. This new exciting two-in-one Stunt and Fortune Game will provide an entertaining evening for both boys and girls and is adaptable to any number of players. Printed in colors of orange and black on heavy durable cardboard stock. Size 12.25" x 18.25".
Value: $110

CHAPTER 4
Party Hats and Masks

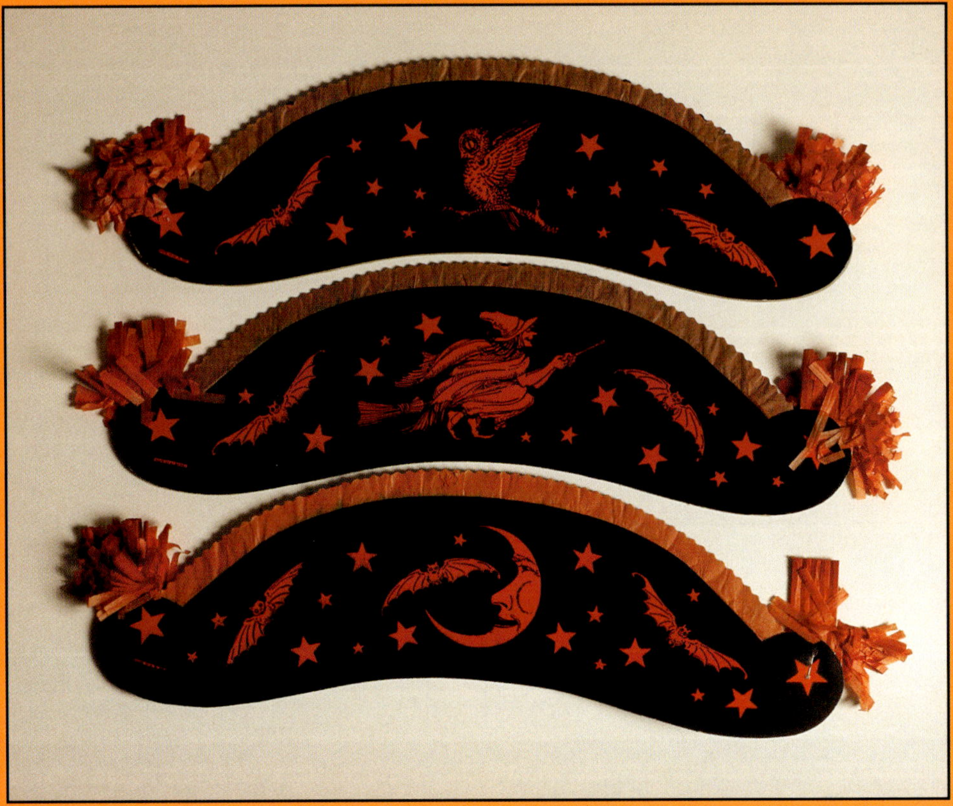

NAPOLEAN HAT
Initial Release: 1936
Production Run: One year only: 1936
Printed on cardboard with honeycomb tissue crown and tissue plumes. 4 designs.
*The four designs shown here: three in orange and black and one in black and white. The ones in orange and black have the tissue plumes.
Value: $45 each

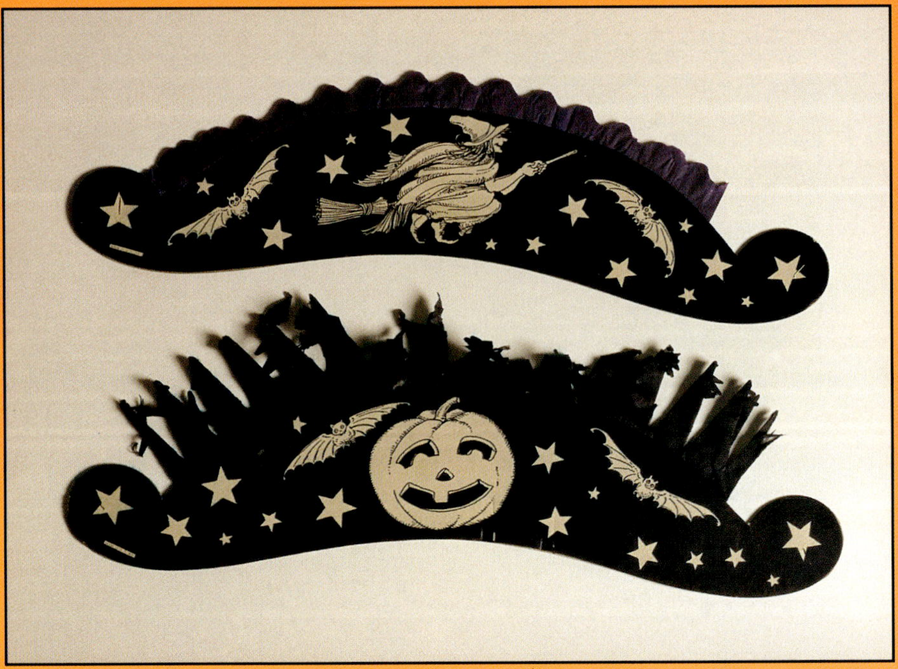

MASKS
Initial Release: 1936
Production Run: 1936 – 1939
Die-cut and printed on cardboard in natural colors – elastic head support. Size 8" x 9". 15 designs.
*Eleven of the 15 designs shown here. Notice the artist's model with notes displayed alongside the completed design.
Value: $20 each

(Continued on following 5 pages)

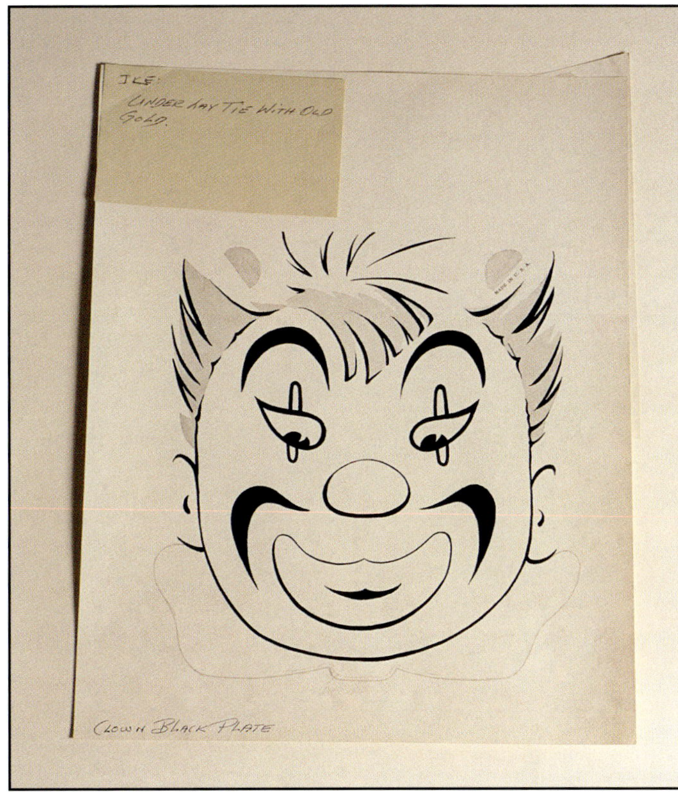

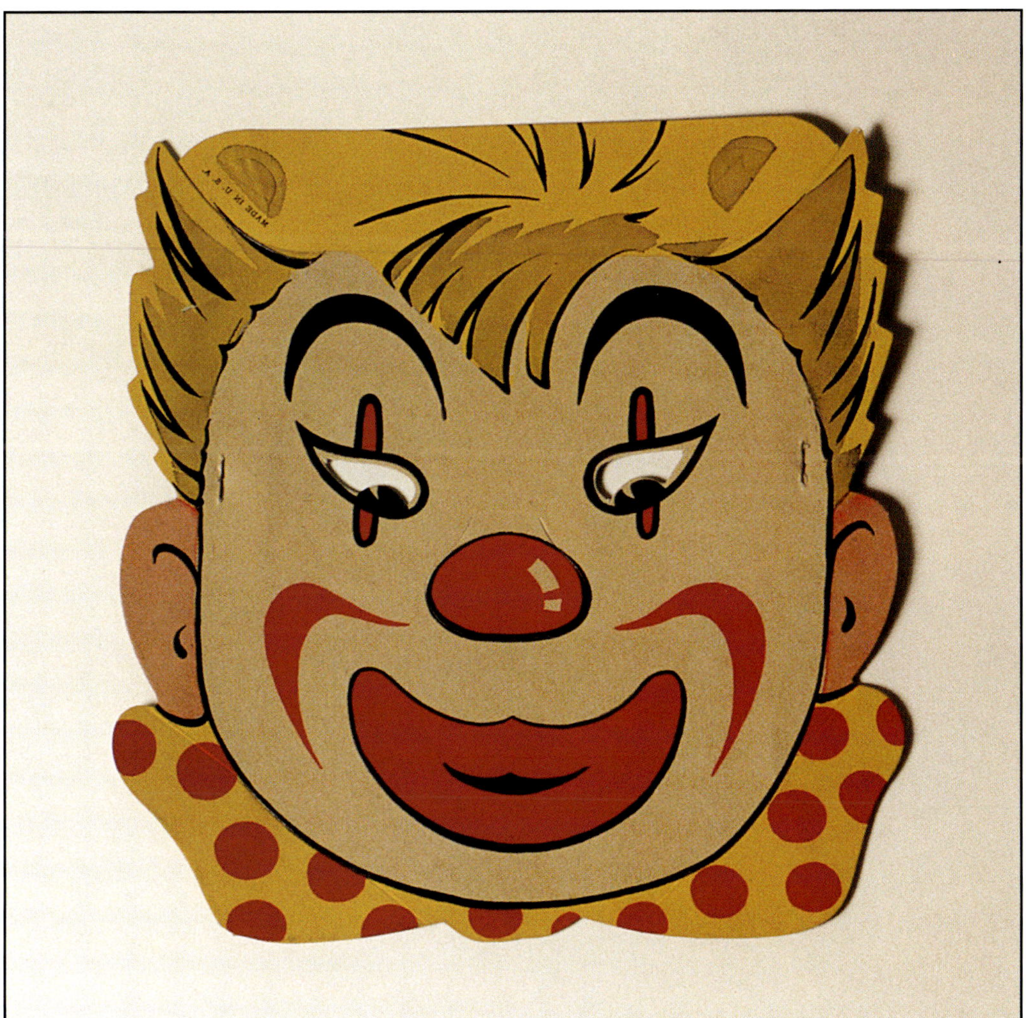

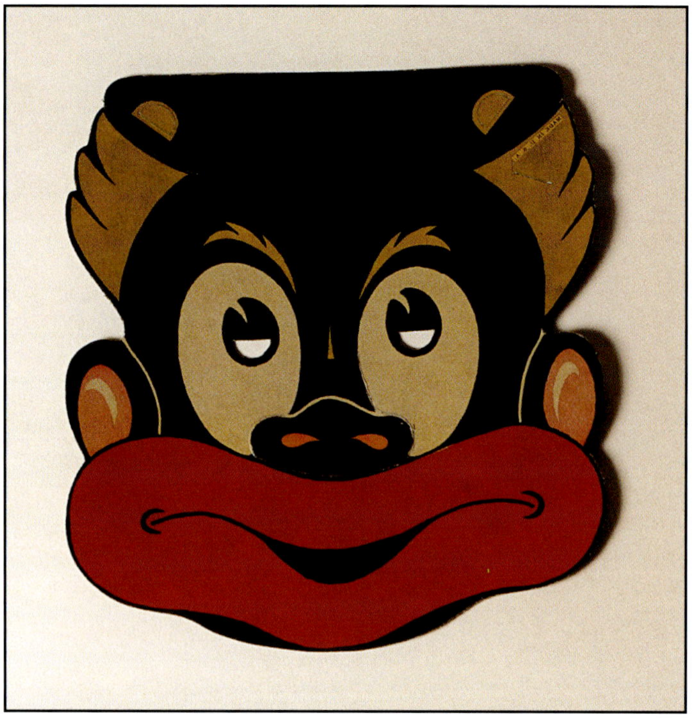

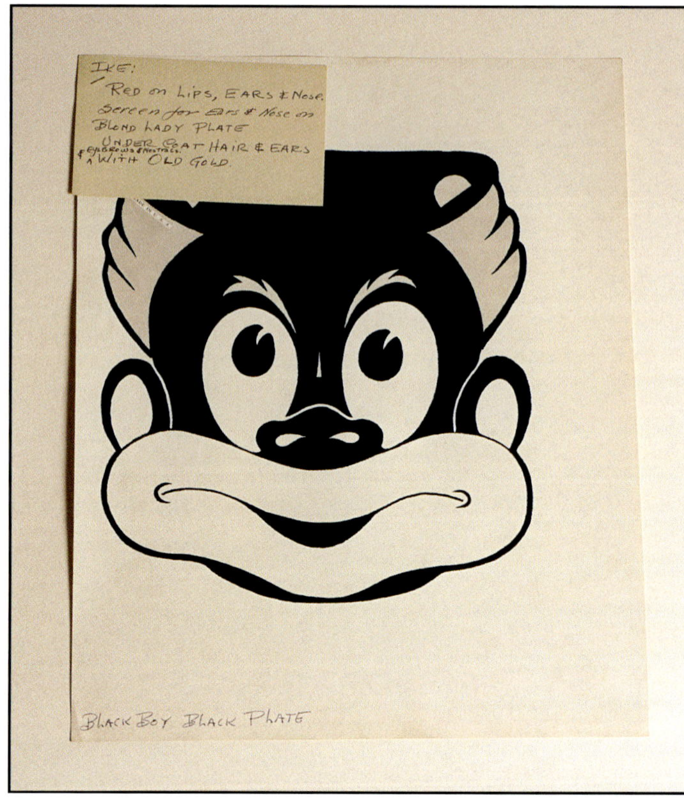
IKE:
RED on LIPS, EARS & NOSE.
Screen for Ears & Nose on
BLOND LADY PLATE
UNDER COAT HAIR & EARS
& EYEBROWS & NOSTRILS
WITH OLD GOLD.
BLACK BOY BLACK PLATE

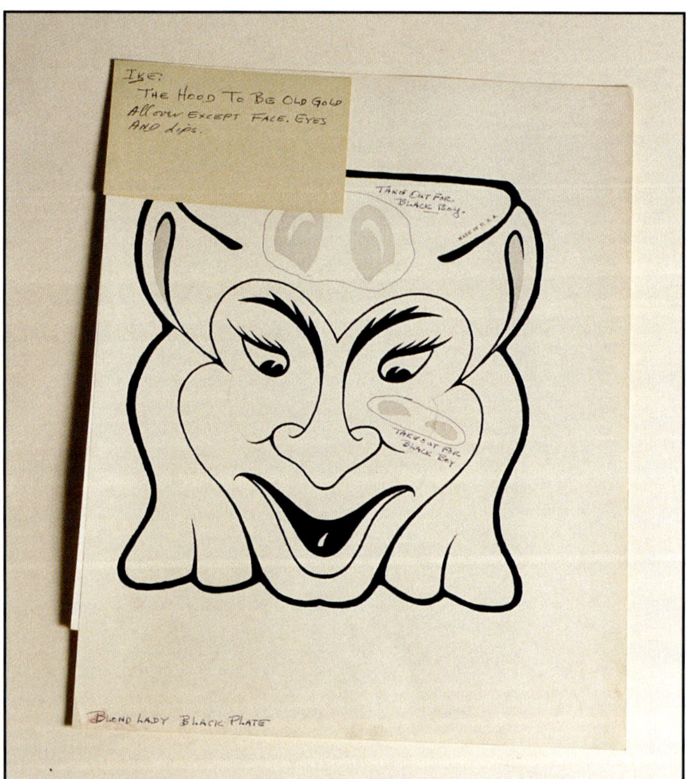
IKE:
THE HOOD TO BE OLD GOLD
All over EXCEPT FACE, EYES
AND Lips.
TAKE OUT FOR
BLACK BOY.
TAKE OUT FOR
BLACK BOY
BLOND LADY BLACK PLATE

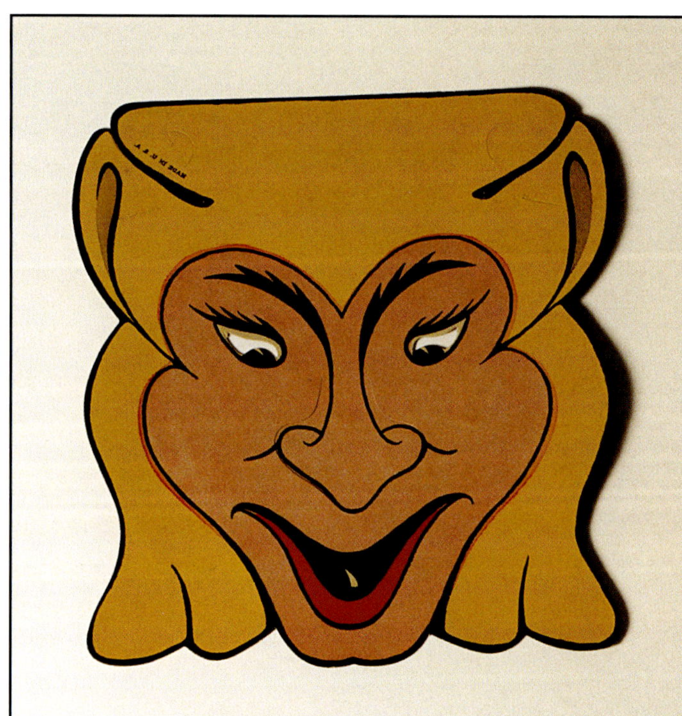

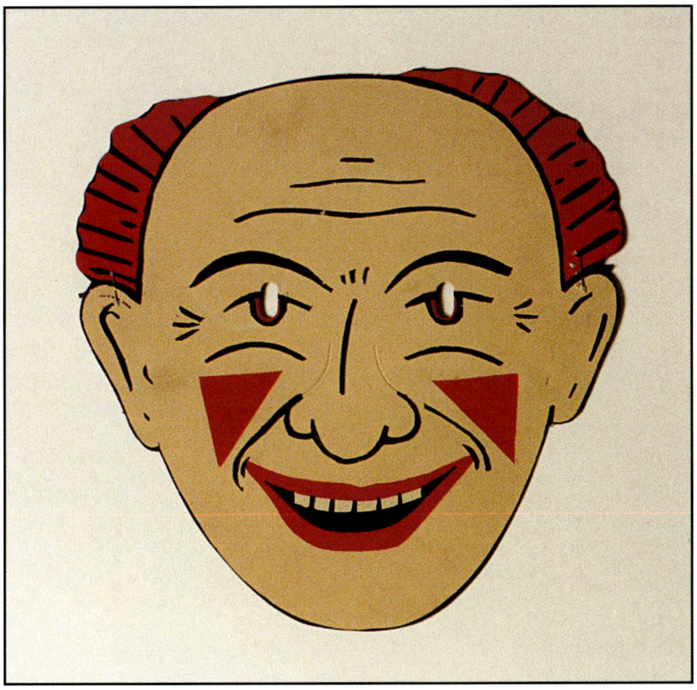

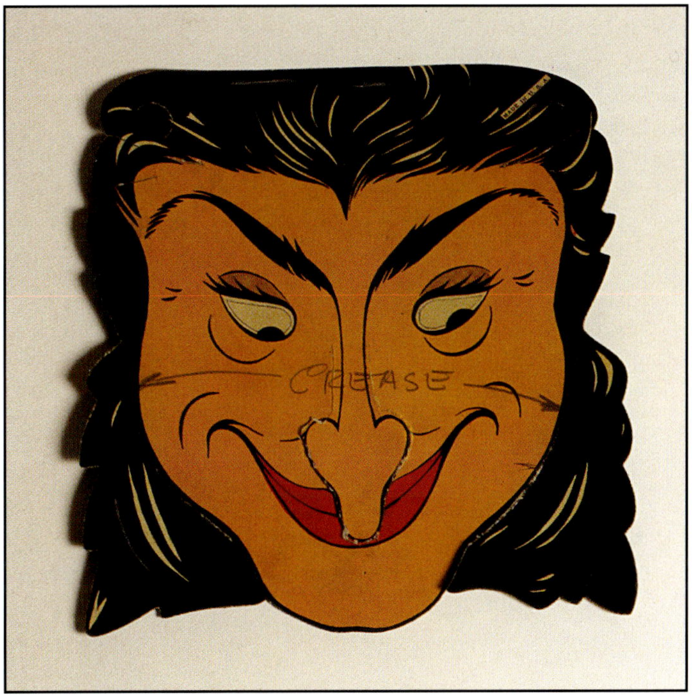
CREASE

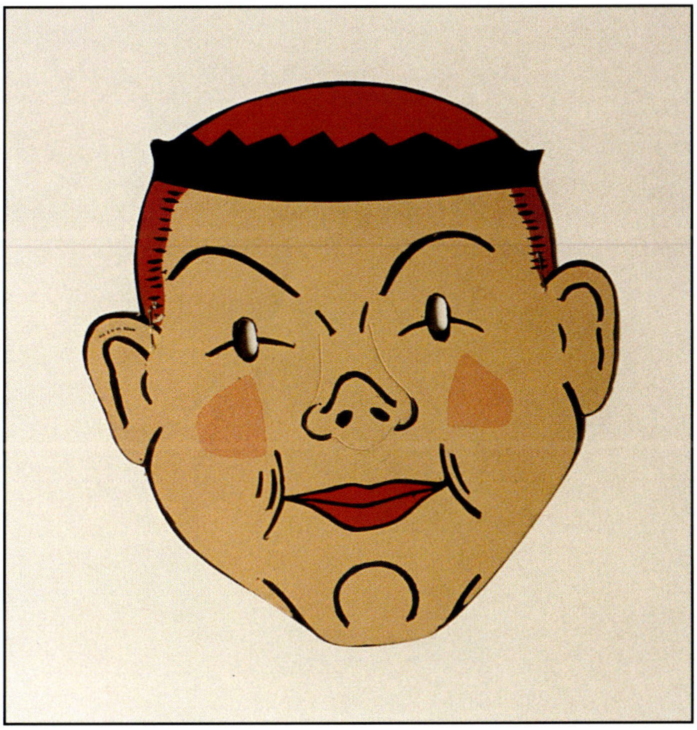

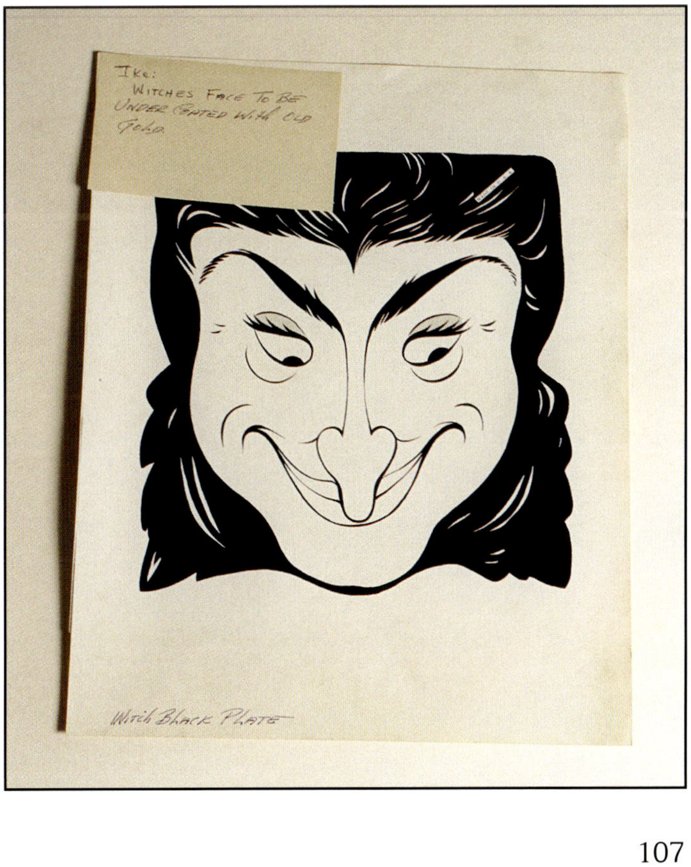
Ike:
Witches Face To Be
Under Coated With Old
Gold.
Witch Black Plate

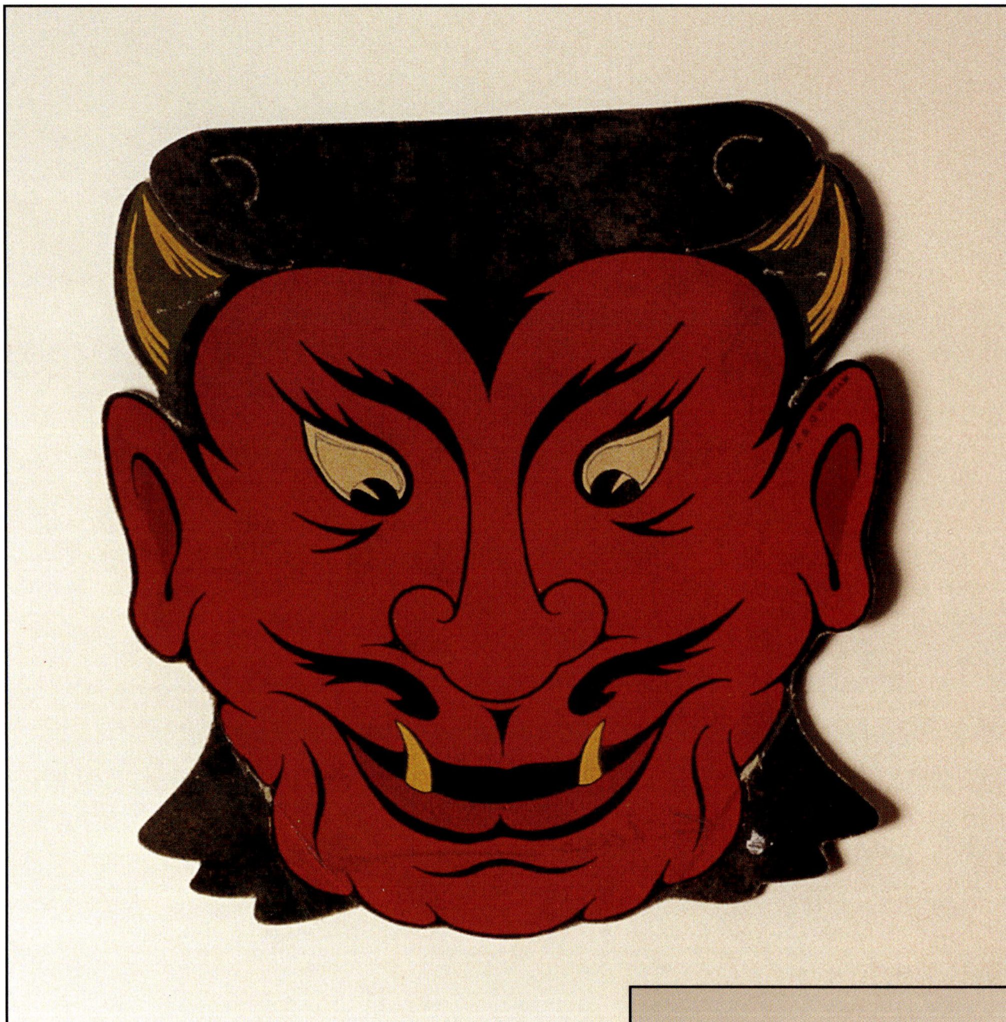

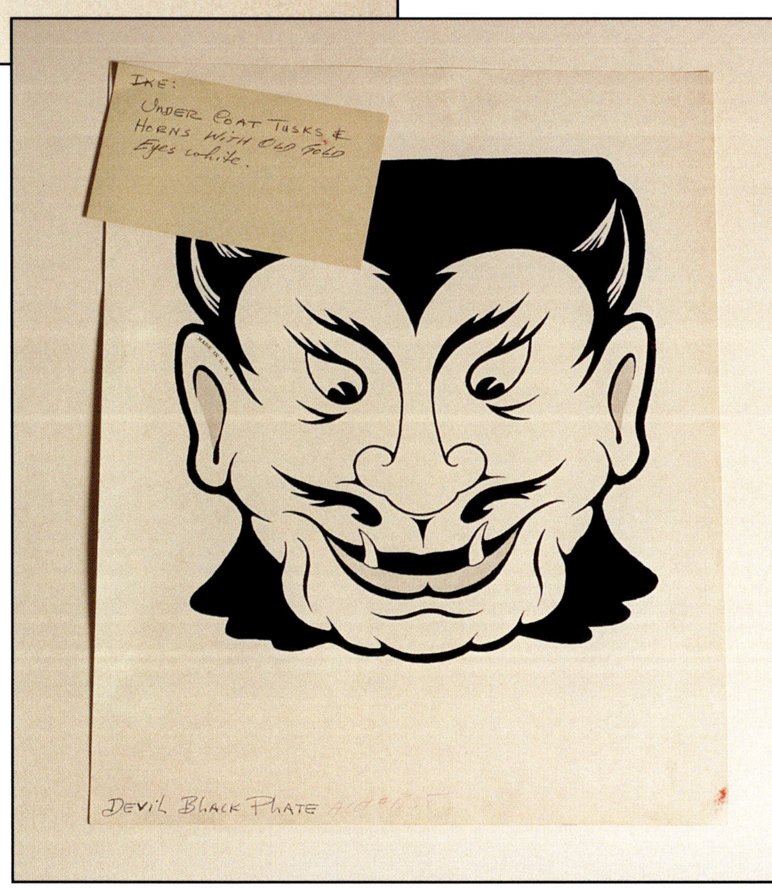
IKE:
UNDER COAT TUSKS &
HORNS WITH OLD GOLD
Eyes white.
DEVIL BLACK PLATE

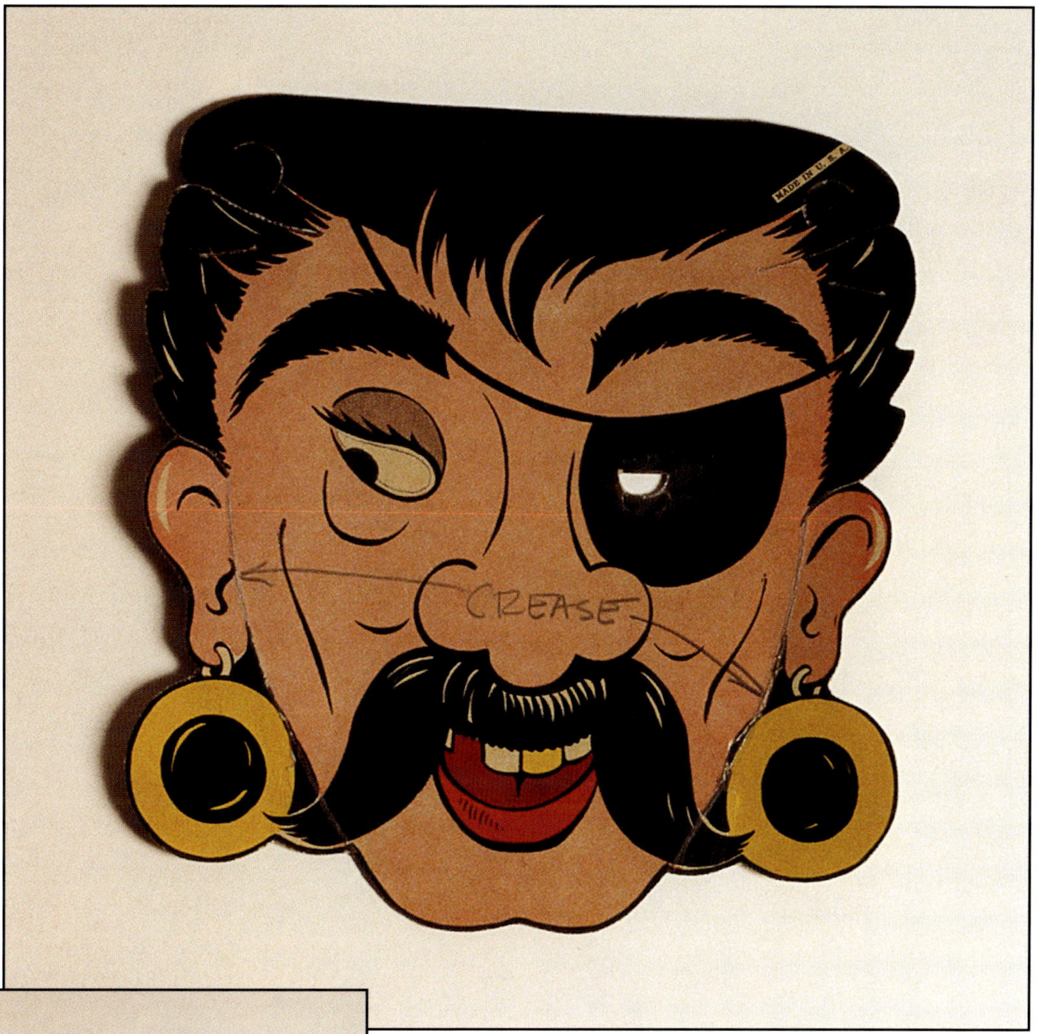
MADE IN U.S.A.
CREASE

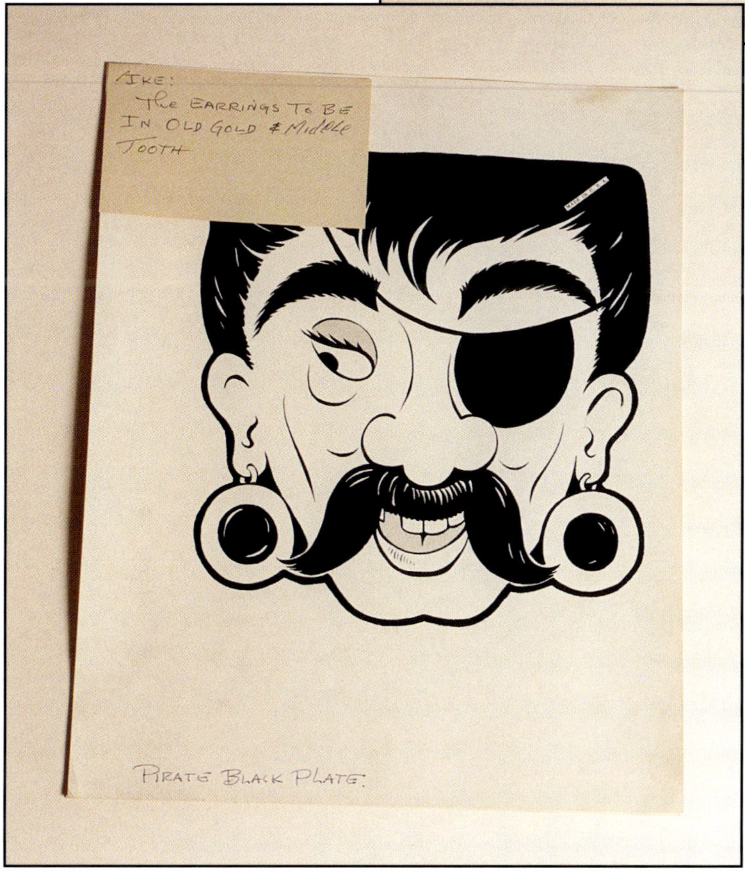
IKE:
The EARRINGS TO BE
IN OLD GOLD & Middle
TOOTH
PIRATE BLACK PLATE.

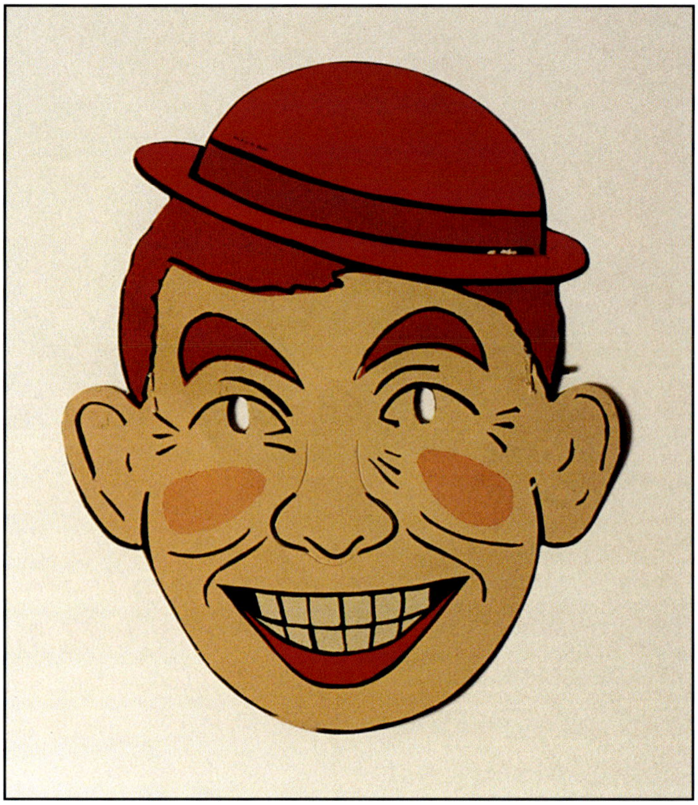

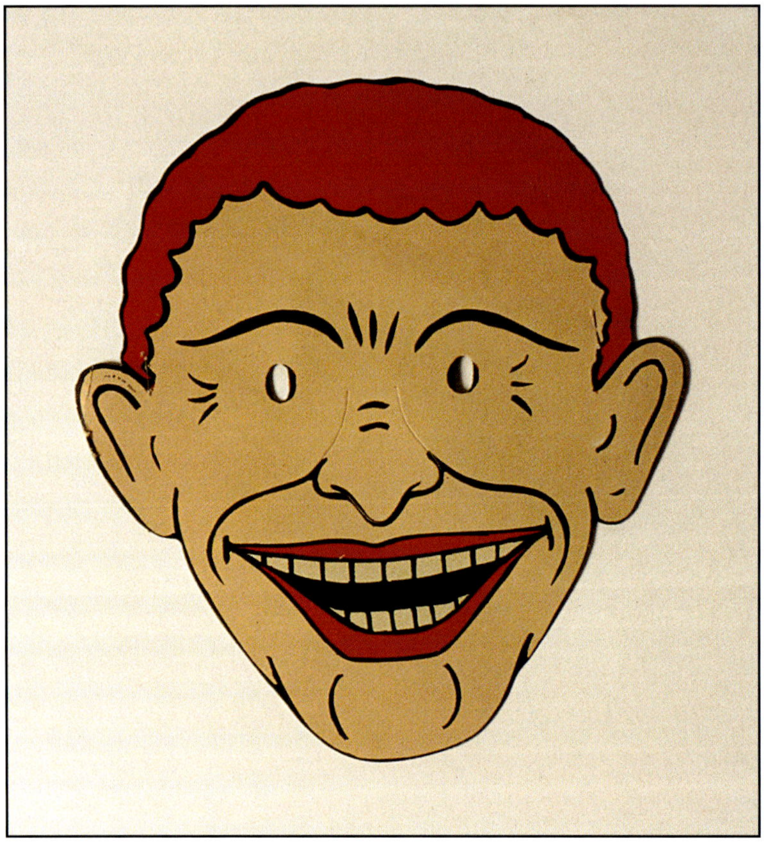

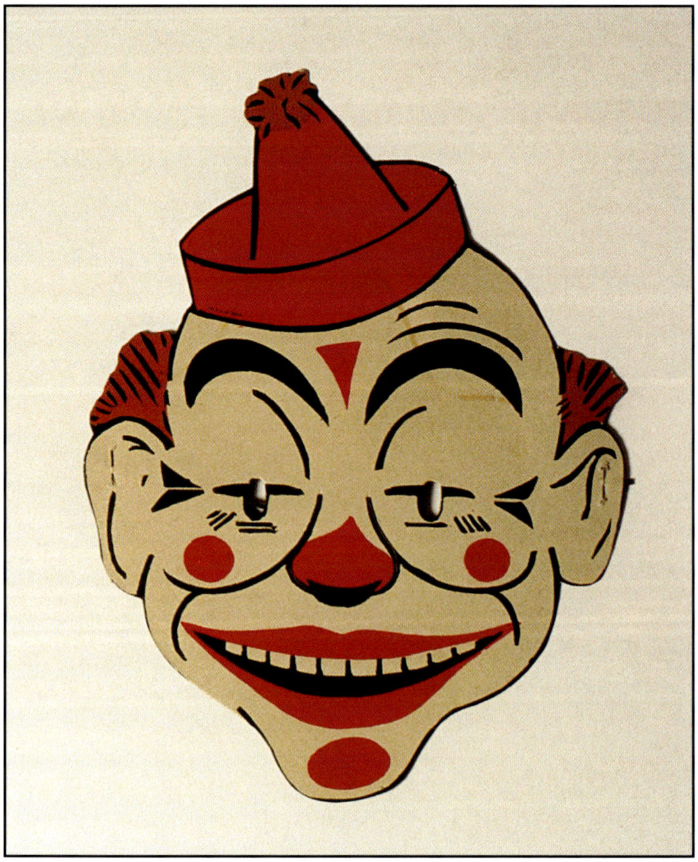

HAT MASKS
Initial Release: 1936
Production Run: 1936 – 1938
Comic faces printed in natural color on cardboard with tissue crown. 12 designs.
*Showing four examples.
Value: $25 each

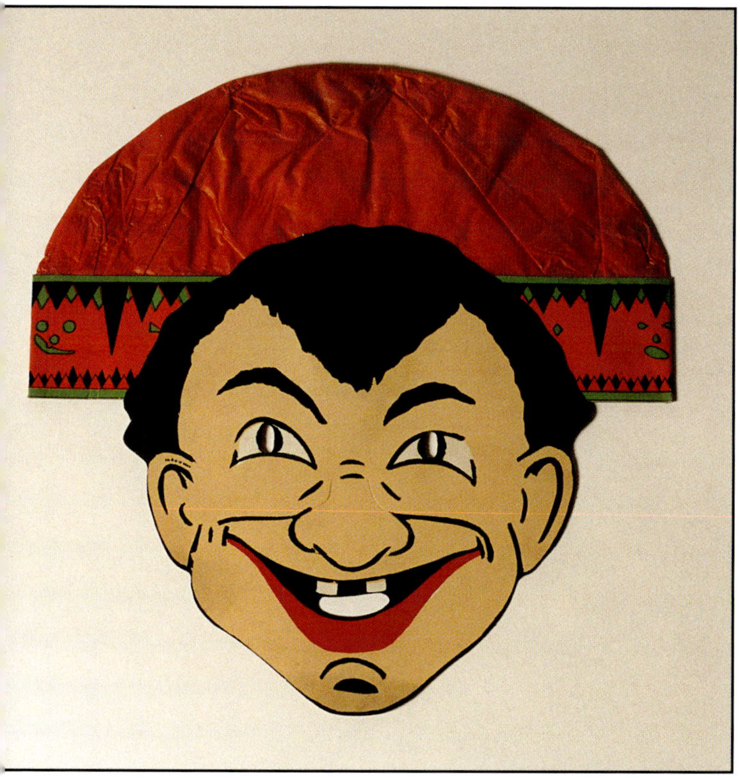

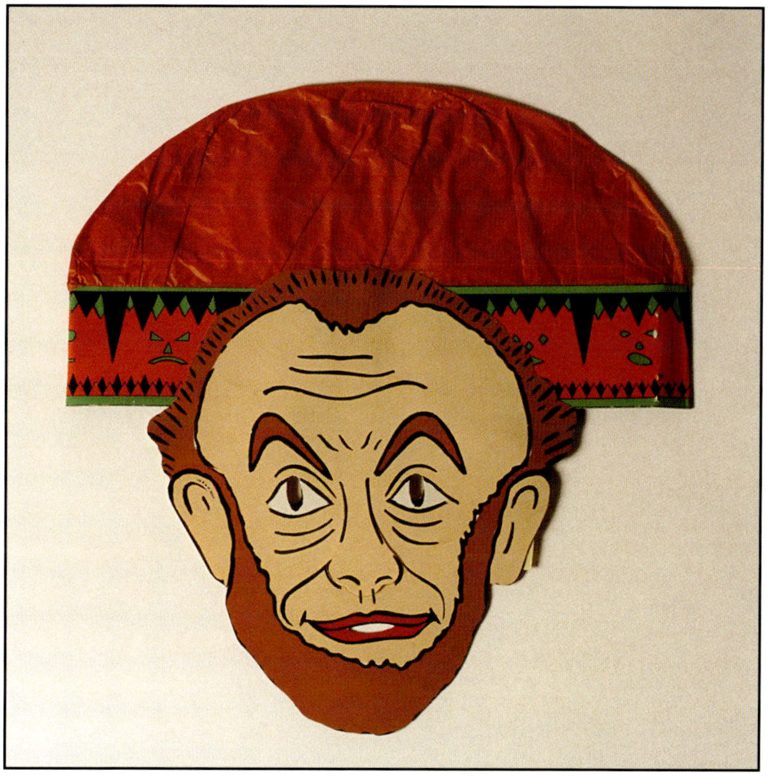

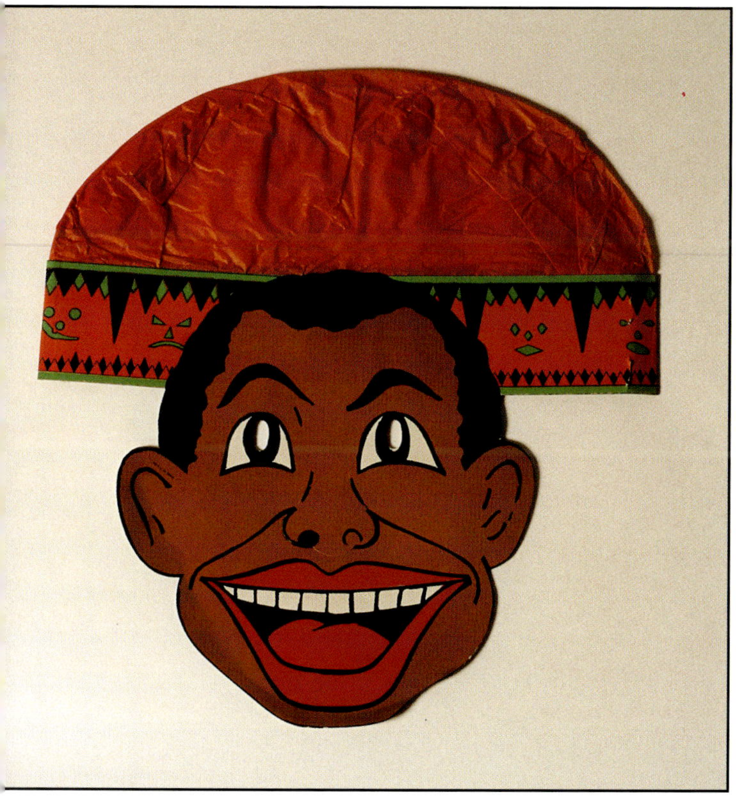

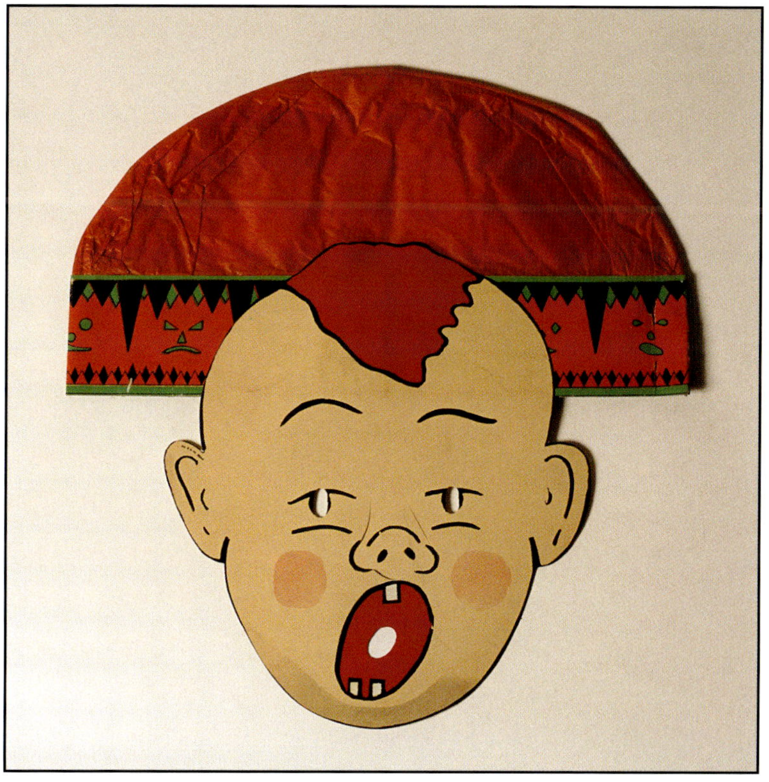

HEAD DRESS MASK
Initial Release: 1936
Production Run: 1936 – 1939
Printed cardboard black or orange crepe trim.
Elastic cord head support. 7 designs.
*Showing five of the seven designs.
Value: $25 each

ALPINE HAT
Initial Release: 1938
Production Run: One year only: 1938
There's a trim jauntiness to this printed paper hat with printed cardboard band, meshed tissue crown and decorated with feather and cut-out characters.
*All four designs are included here which were first introduced in 1929 in a set of four Halloween Roly-Polys.
Value: $45 each

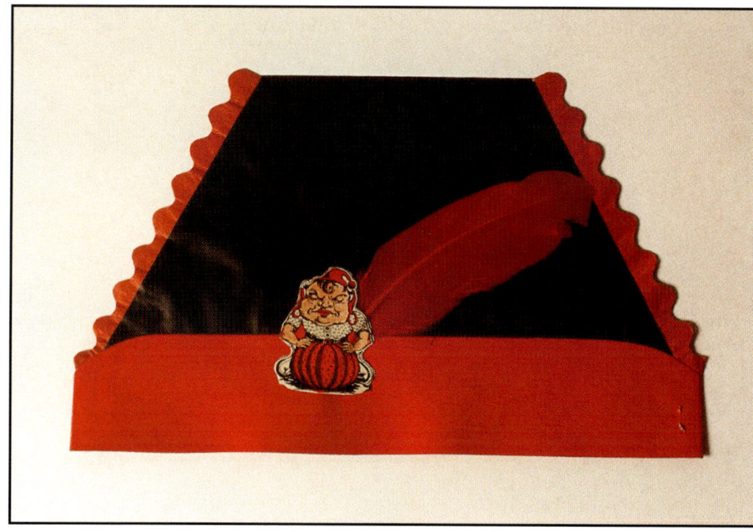

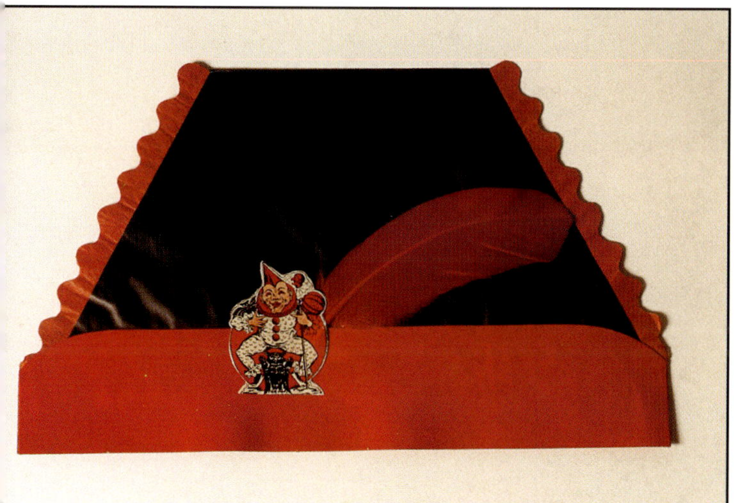

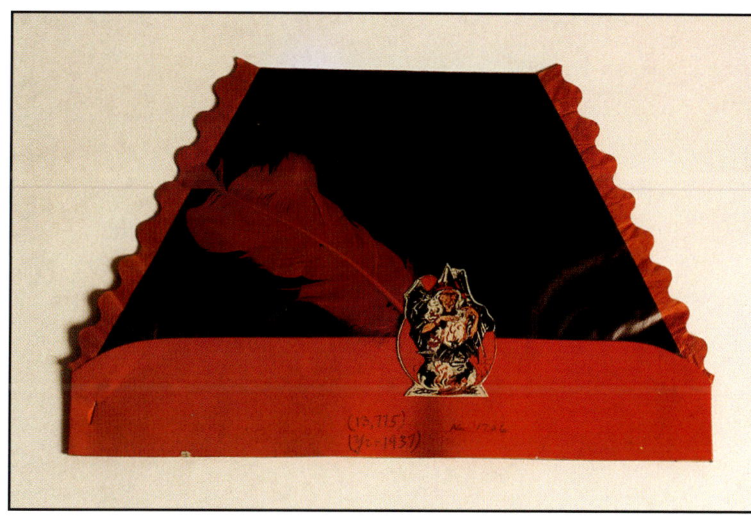

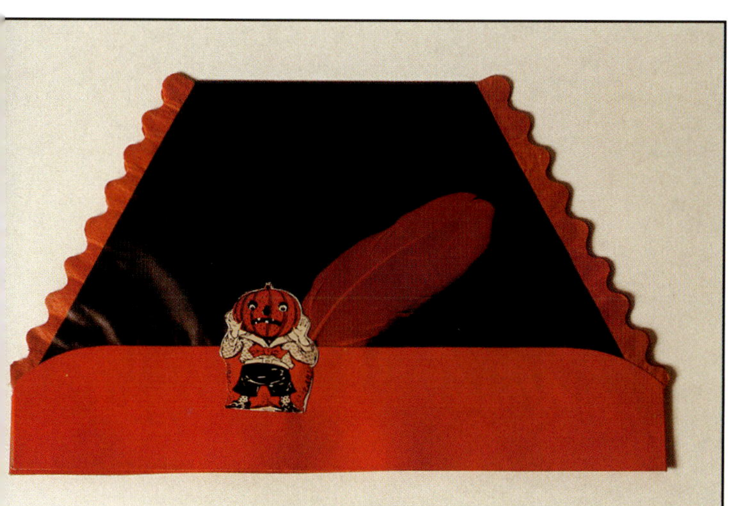

FRINGED CREPE HAT
Initial Release: 1938
Production Run: 1938 – 1940
Glamour and witchery portrayed in these beautiful new fringe crepe hats with 2.25" printed band. Assorted shapes and printed decorations. 6 designs.
*Three designs showcased here.
Value: $20 each

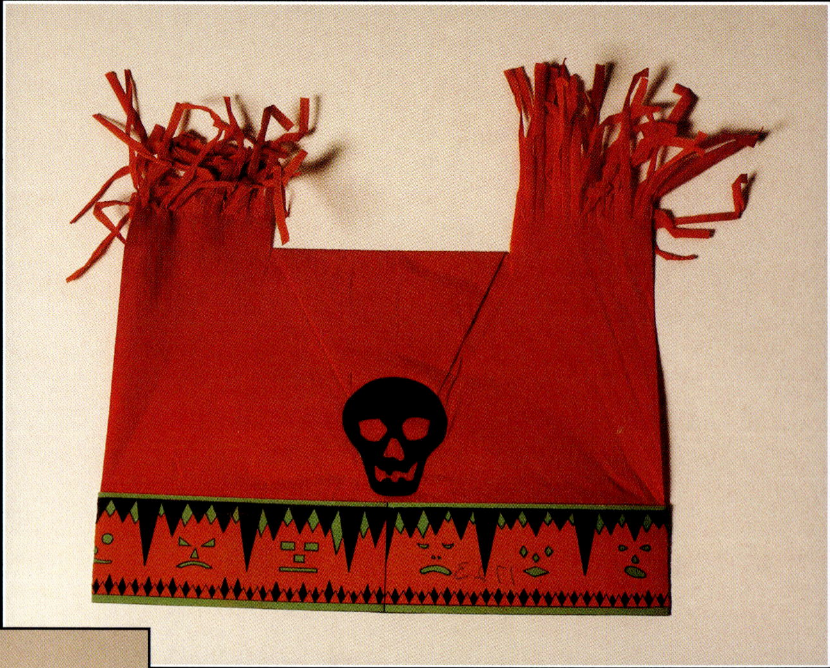

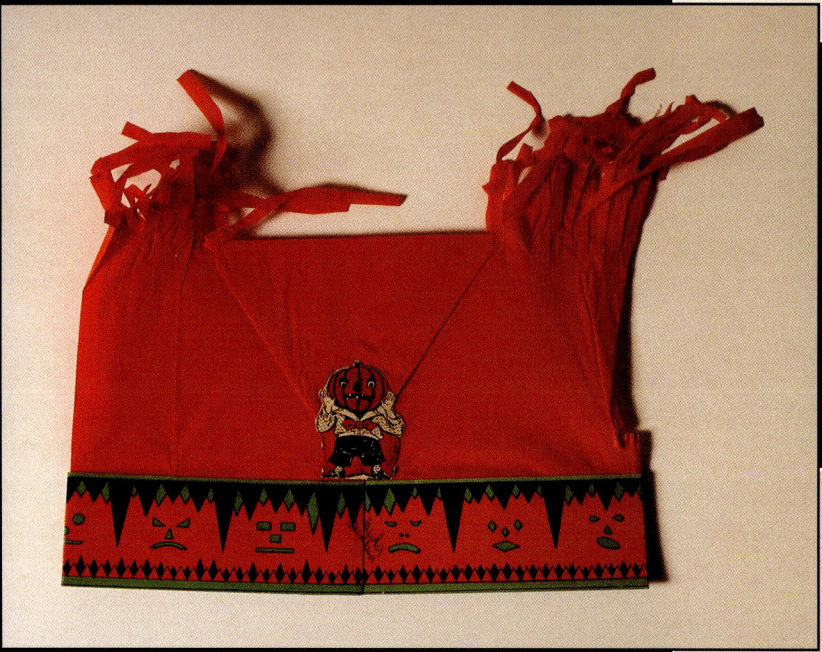

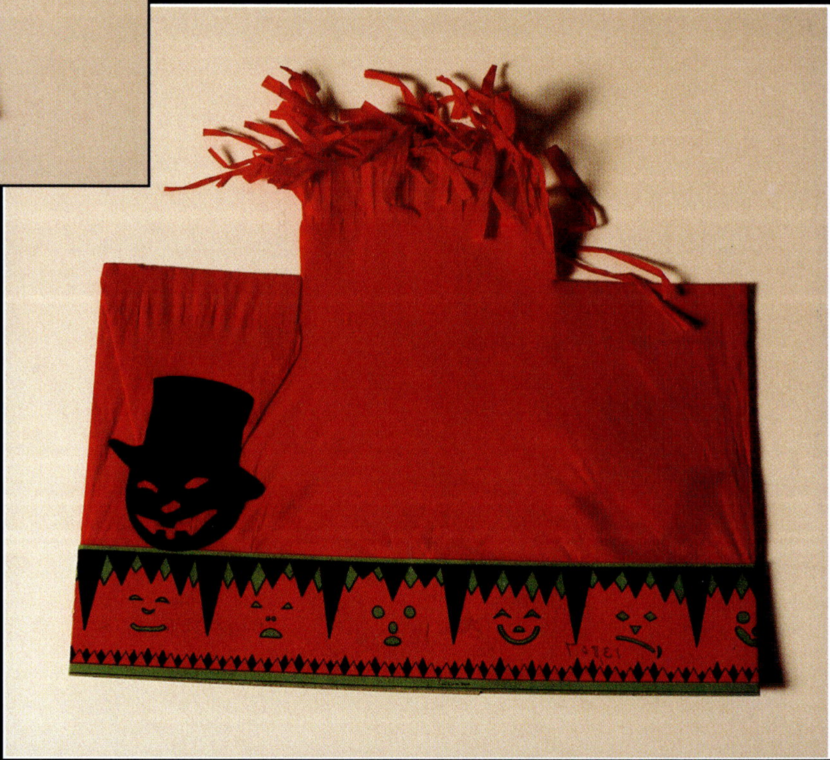

FANCY CREPE HATS

Initial Release: 1941
Production Run: One year only: 1941
Here's a colorful assortment of Halloween Party Hats. Four orange and two black crepe designs. Fancy double band of orange and black crepe around the bottom. Sweat band. Machine sewed. Color printed decorations. Size 9.5" x 11.5".
Value: $35 each

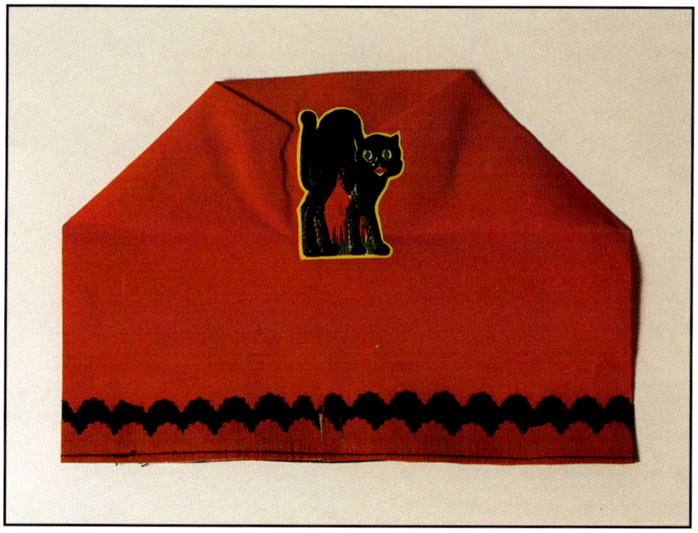

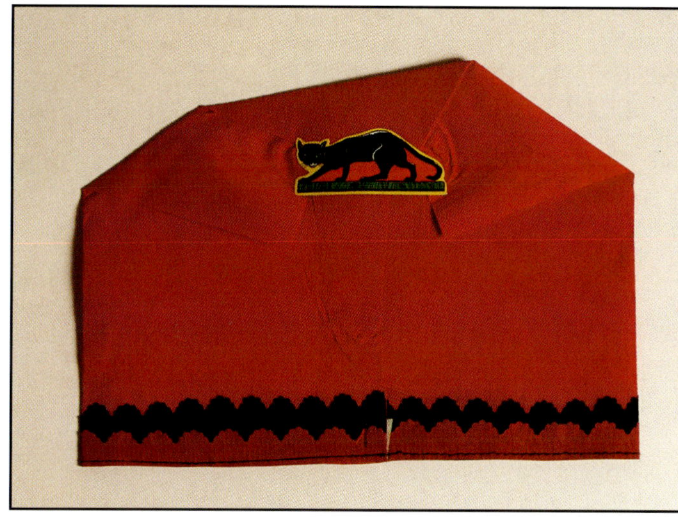

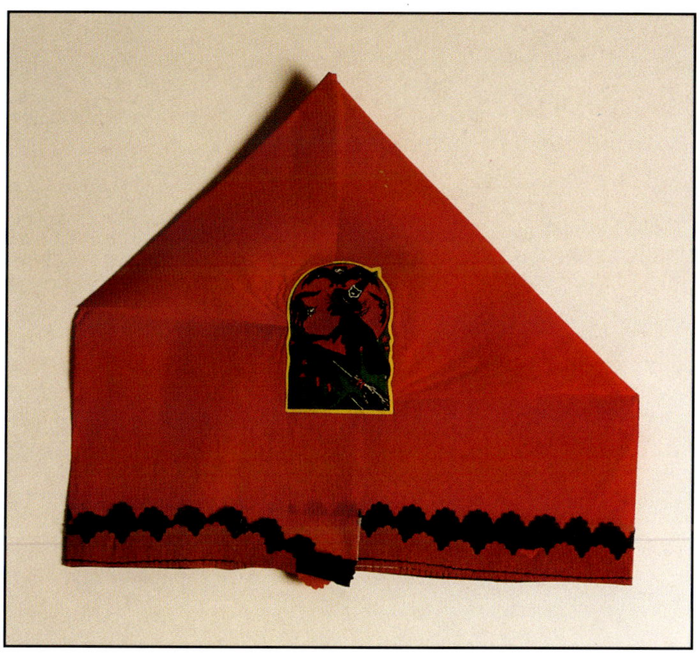

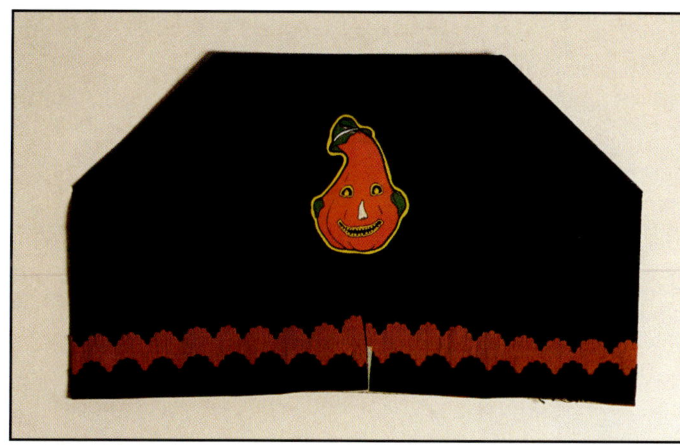

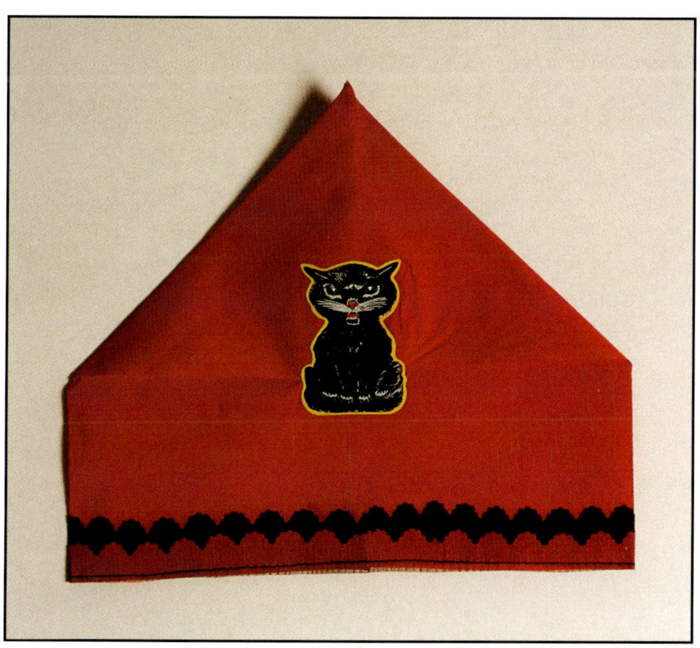

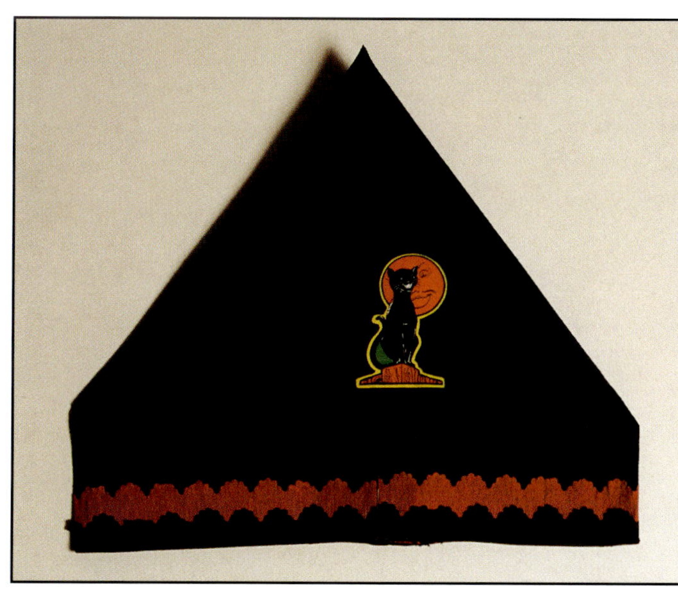

HALLOWEEN HATS

Initial Release: 1939 Business Builder

Set of six hats that lend color to a smart advertisement. An attractive assortment of 6 interesting designs. Will put pep into any late October or early November event.

*I believe these were marketing samples and the idea never took off.

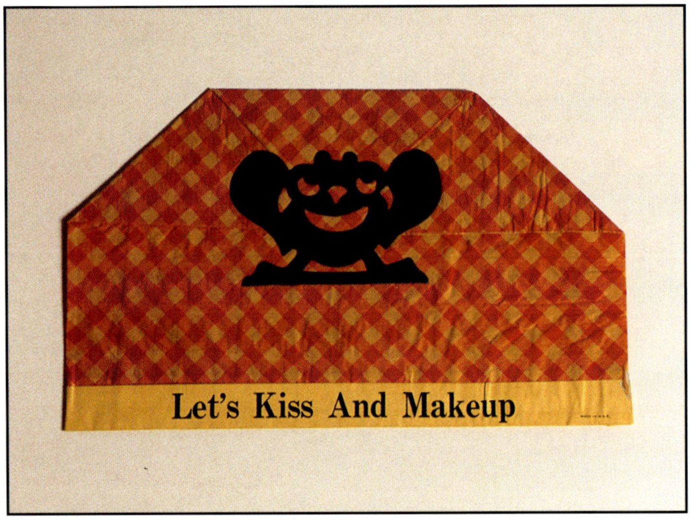

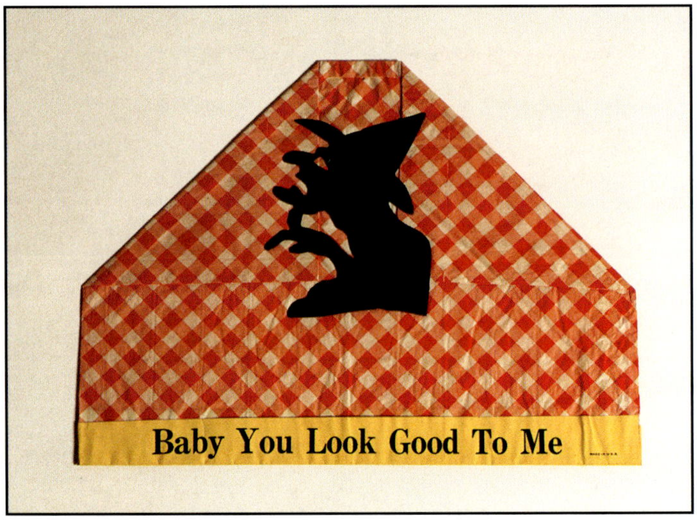

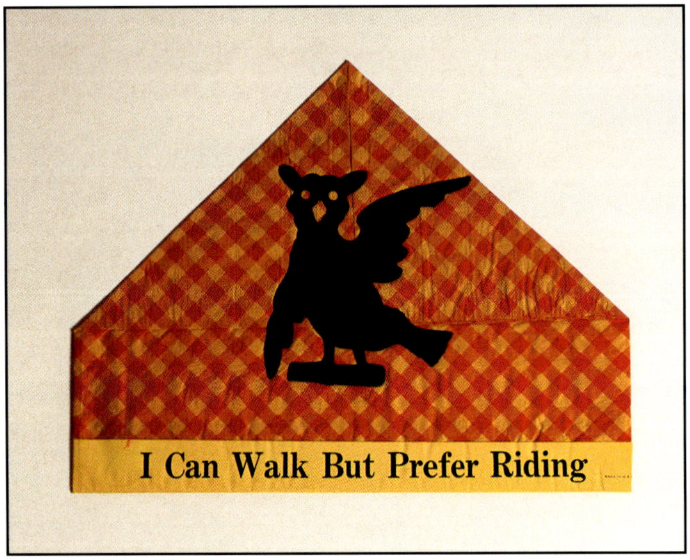

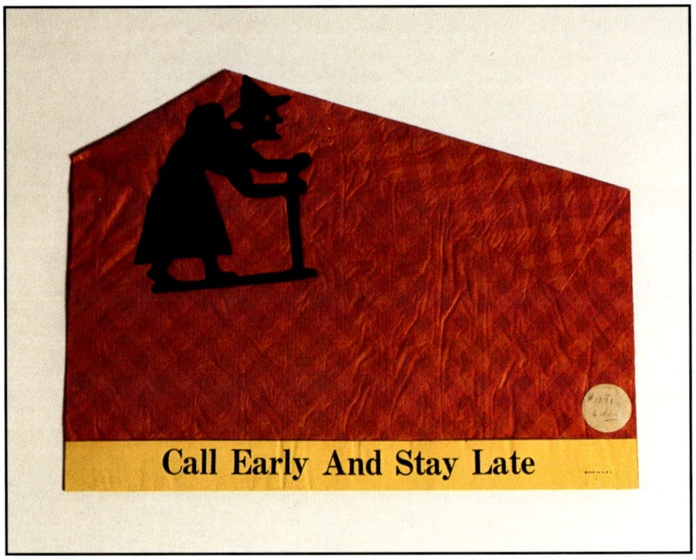

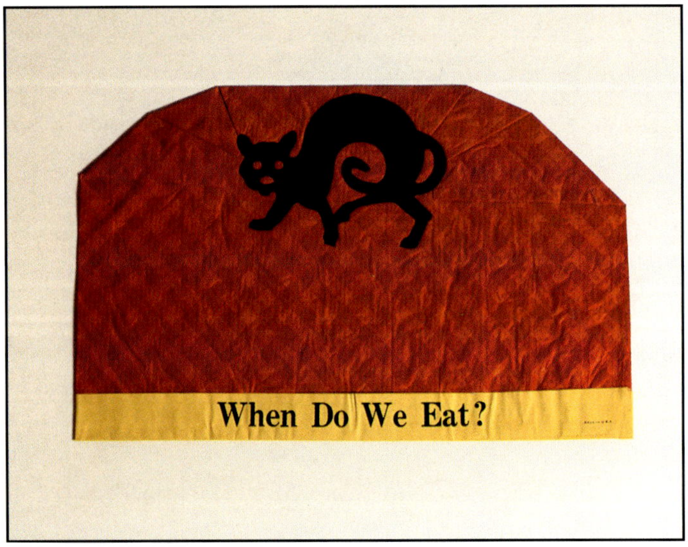

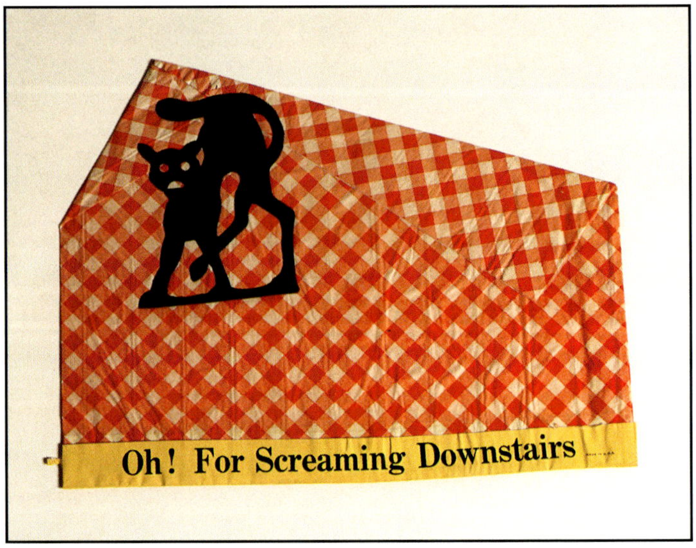

NOVELTY HAT MASK
Initial Release: 1948
Production Run: 1948 – 1962
Something new. This half-mask designed with added feature of a small miniature hat cutout printed as part of the mask. Printed in orange and black and die-cut from heavy cardboard. Complete with elastic.
*As you can see from the one photo, companies such as Canada Dry used these masks as a give-away with the purchase of their product.
*It looks as if there were a choice of two different eyeholes: one for an adult, the other for a child.
Value: $15 each

(Continued on following page)

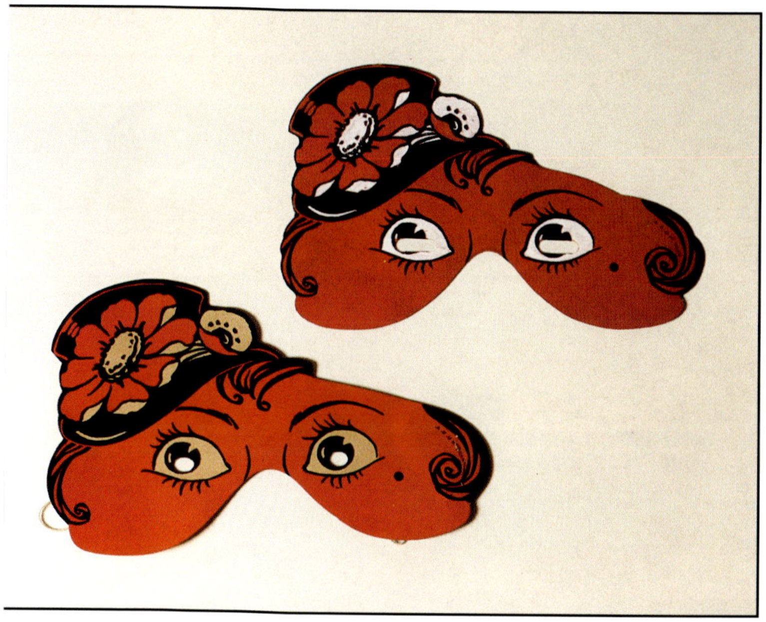

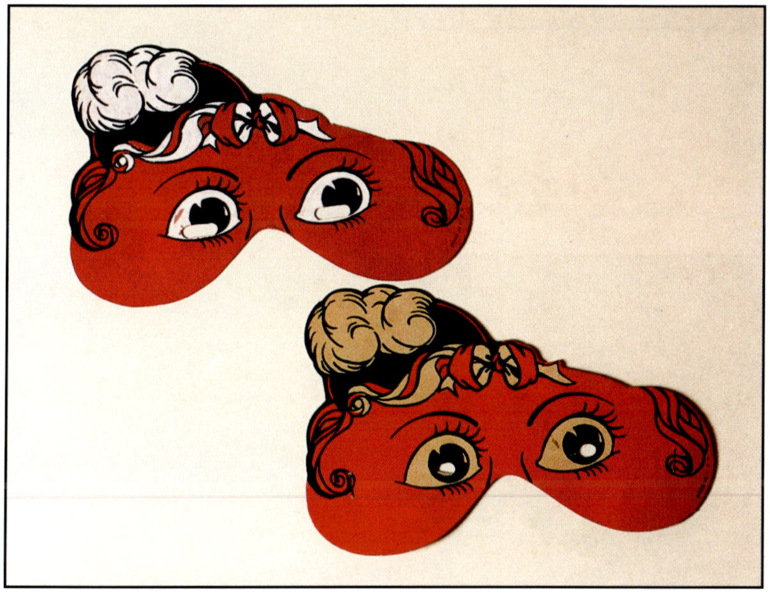

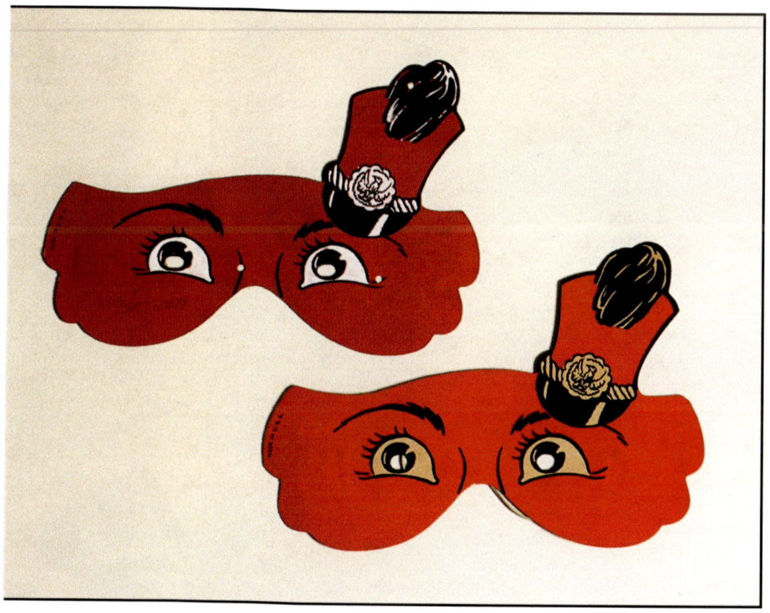

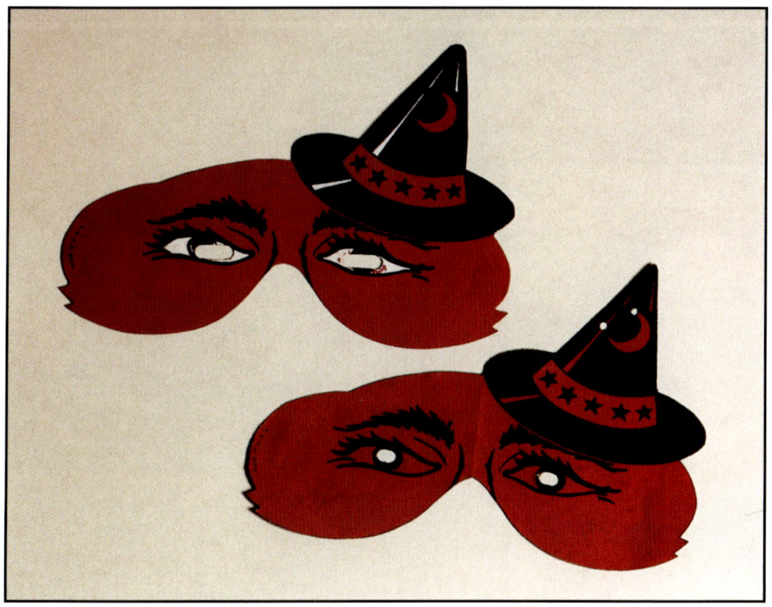

CREPE HAT
Initial Release: 1940
Production Run: One year only: 1940
Clever creations of fringed crepe paper folded and machine sewed to a one-inch cardboard band of black patent leather finished paper. Die-cut orange and black decorations add to effectiveness of the hat. 6 designs.
*Three designs are shown here; do you recognize them? They are three of the four Big Silhouettes set first released by Beistle in 1936. I love these bold horror pictures; they convey perfectly the feeling of the Halloween season.
Value: $45 each

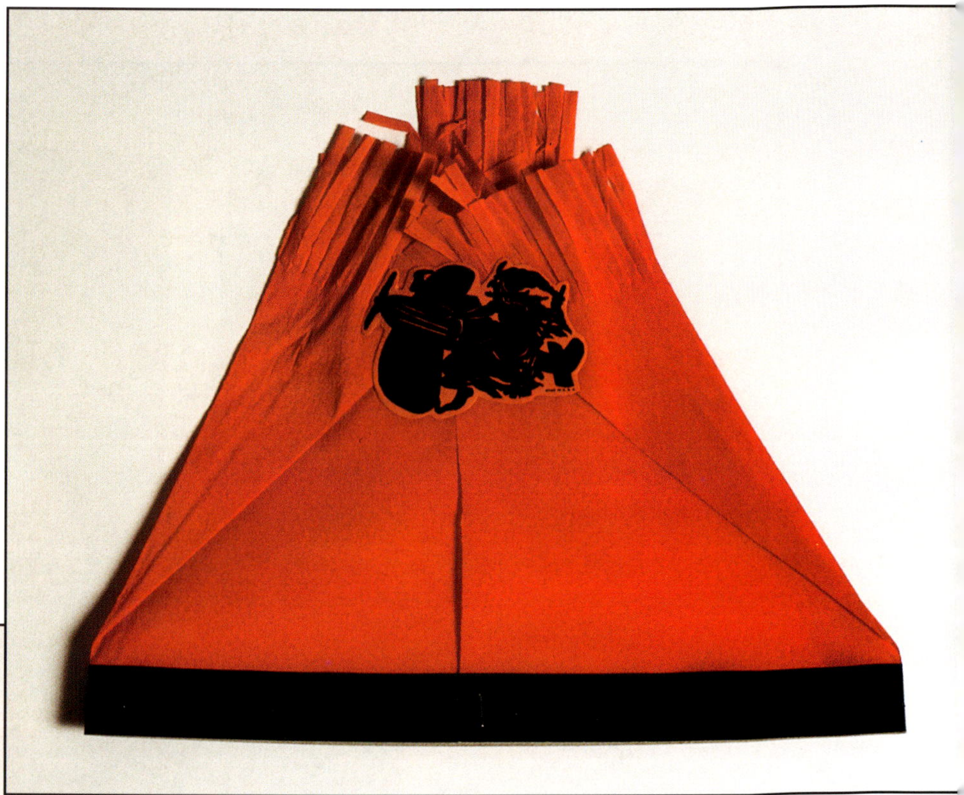

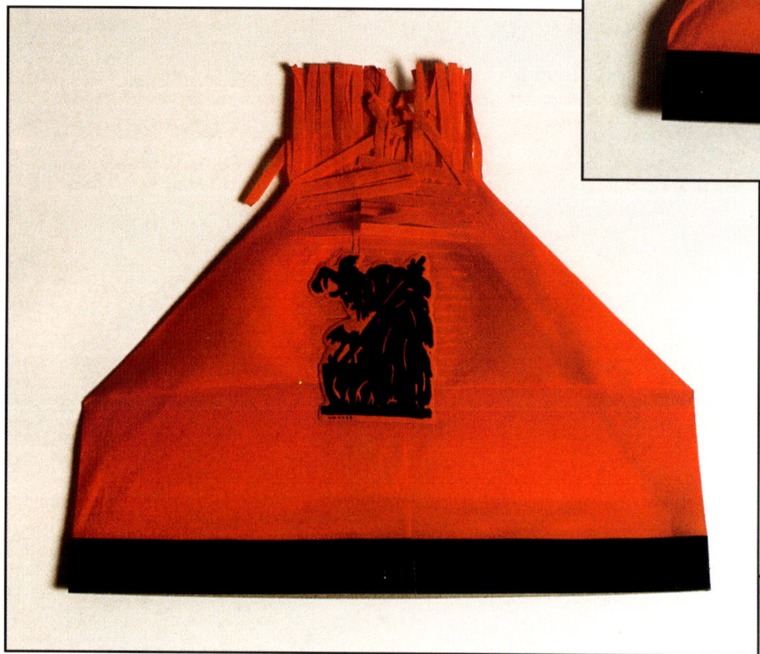

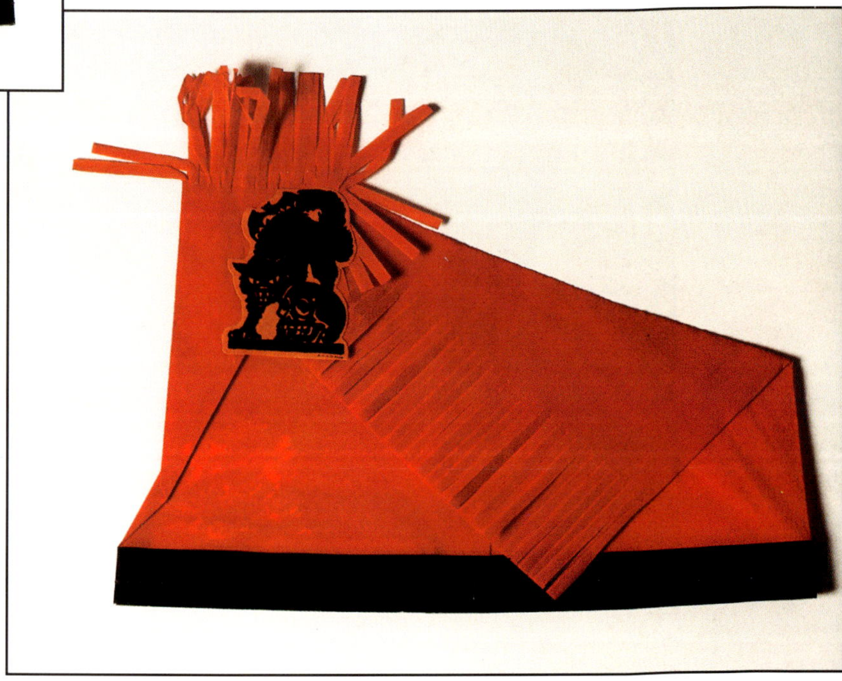

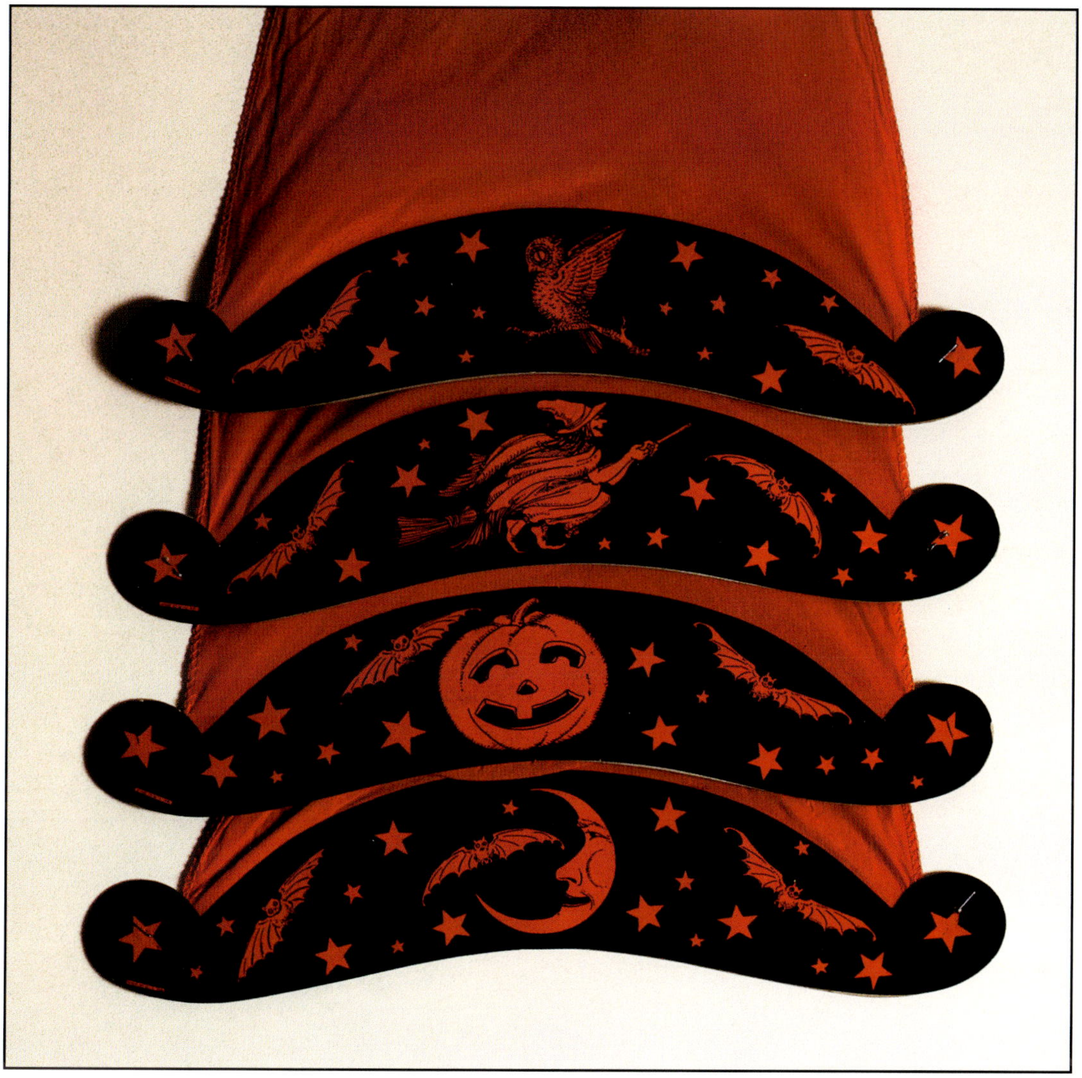

COSSACK HAT
Initial Release: 1936
Production Run:
1936 – 1937
Sewed crepe – printed cardboard bands. 4 designs.
*All four designs shown here stacked one behind the other.
Value: $20 each

MINIATURE CLOWN HAT FORM
Initial Release: 1941
Production Run: 1941 – 1942
Designed particularly for volume sales! Five different Halloween silhouettes printed in black on the front of the hat. Elastic keeps them on. About 5" high.
Value: $5 each

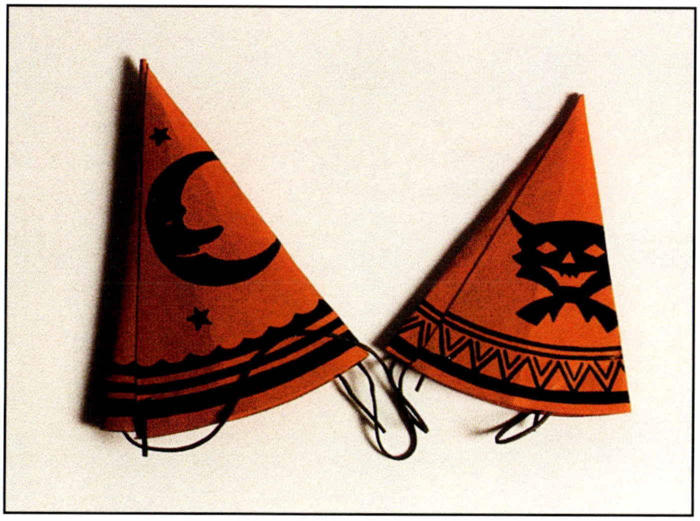

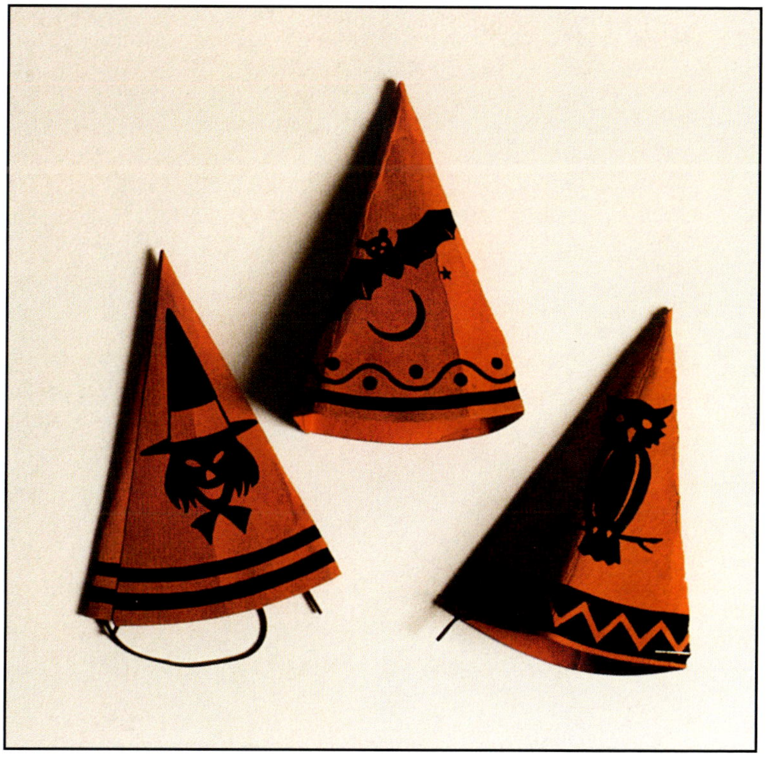

CHAPTER 5
Lanterns and Shades

TRANSPARENCIES
Initial Release: 1940
Production Run: 1940 – 1954*
Printed orange and black on cardboard with green crepe liner and candle holder on cardboard base. Owl, cat, witch and pumpkin designs.
*I hope the camera has picked up the subtle difference in the paper insert shading. In 1941, Beistle decided that the lighter green was just that – too light and so they deemed that tone obsolete. In 1942, the green darkened considerably (see the notations on the back of the owl transparency where the darker tissue paper has been affixed). Note the back of the cat transparency which models the lighter green paper insert.
Value: $165 each (for the lighter paper insert)
Value: $125 each (for the darker paper insert)

(Continued on following 4 pages)

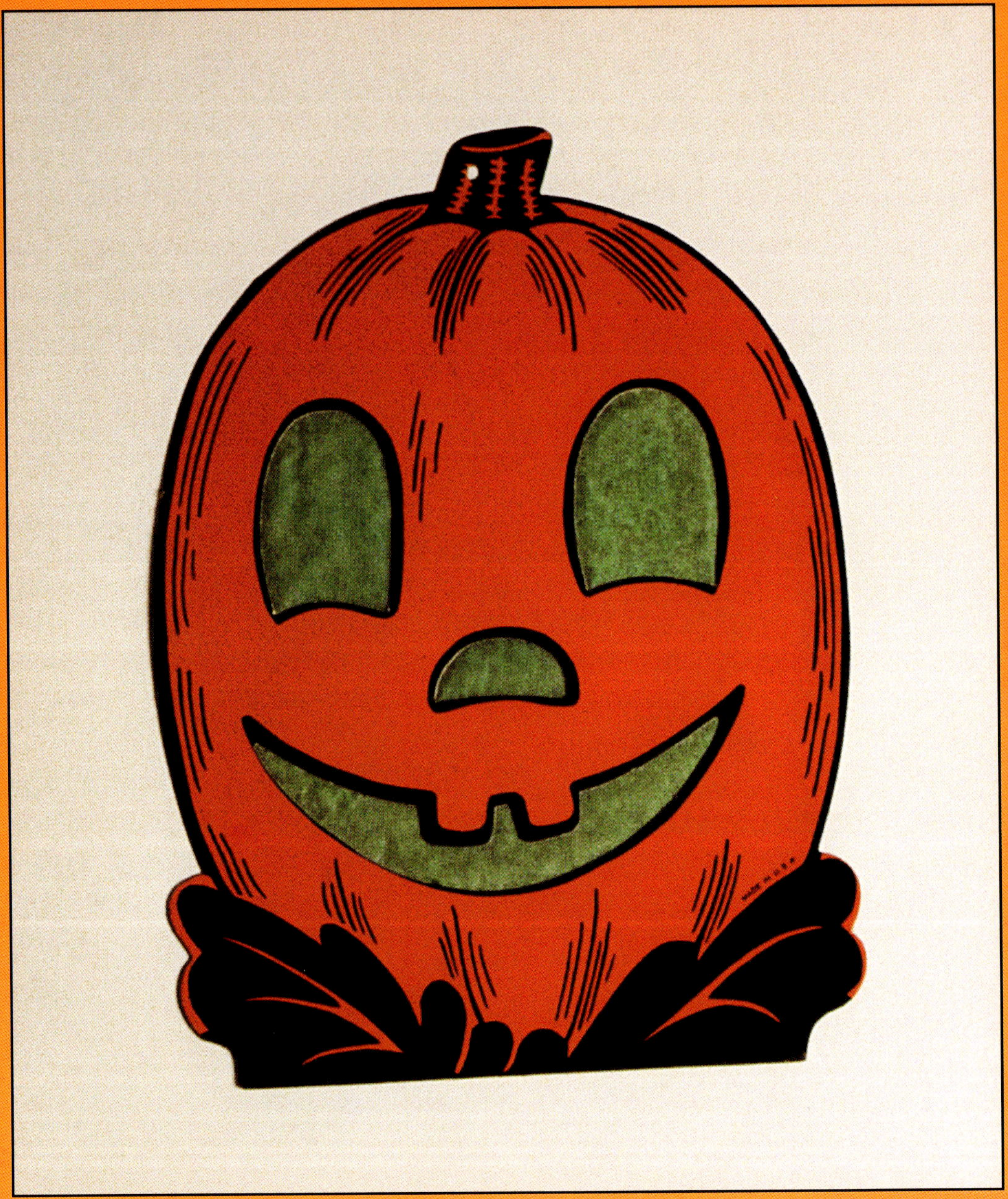

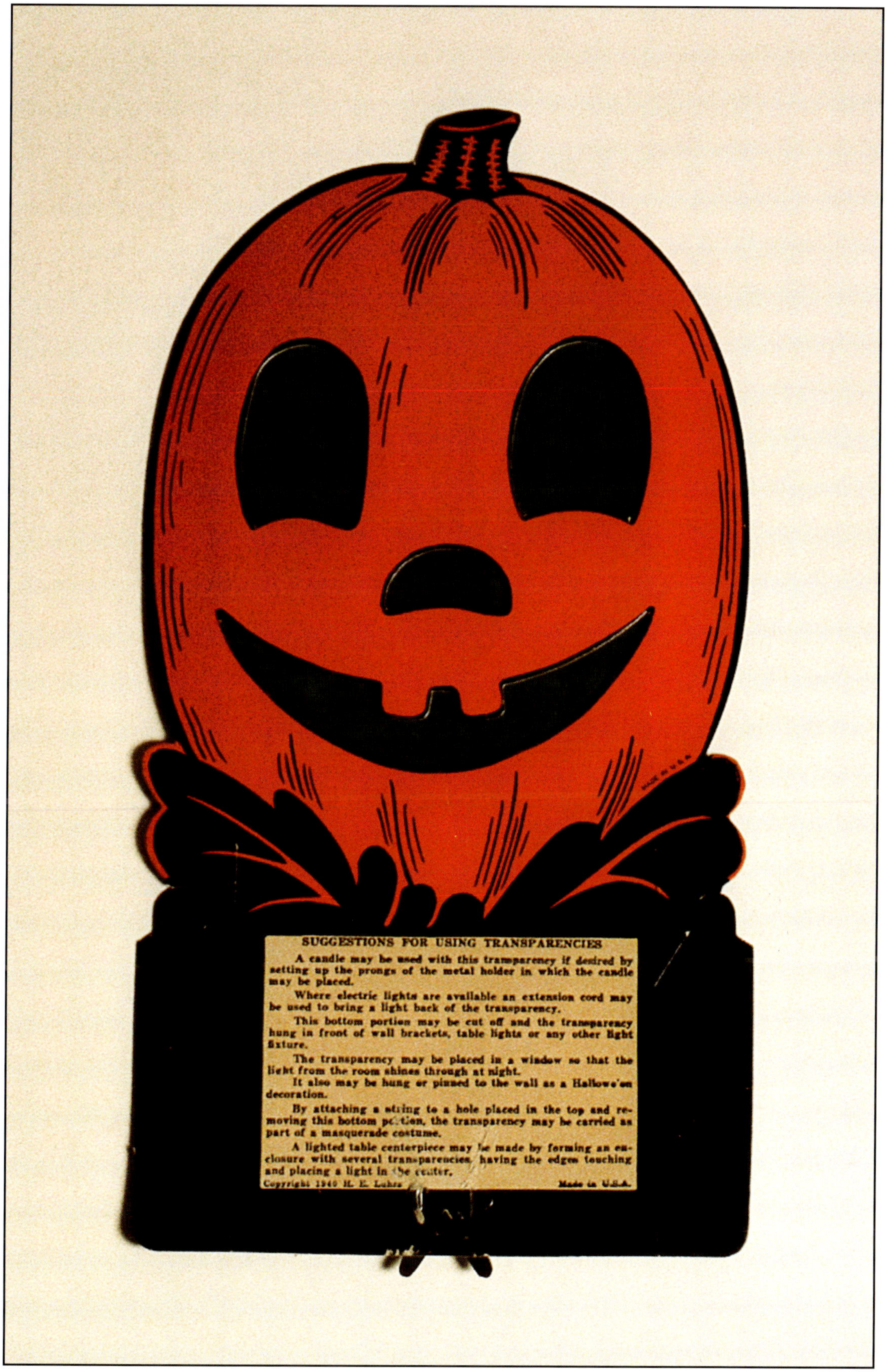
SUGGESTIONS FOR USING TRANSPARENCIES
A candle may be used with this transparency if desired by setting up the prongs of the metal holder in which the candle may be placed.
Where electric lights are available an extension cord may be used to bring a light back of the transparency.
This bottom portion may be cut off and the transparency hung in front of wall brackets, table lights or any other light fixture.
The transparency may be placed in a window so that the light from the room shines through at night.
It also may be hung or pinned to the wall as a Hallowe'en decoration.
By attaching a string to a hole placed in the top and removing this bottom portion, the transparency may be carried as part of a masquerade costume.
A lighted table centerpiece may be made by forming an enclosure with several transparencies, having the edges touching and placing a light in the center.
Copyright 1940 H. E. Luhrs
Made in U.S.A.

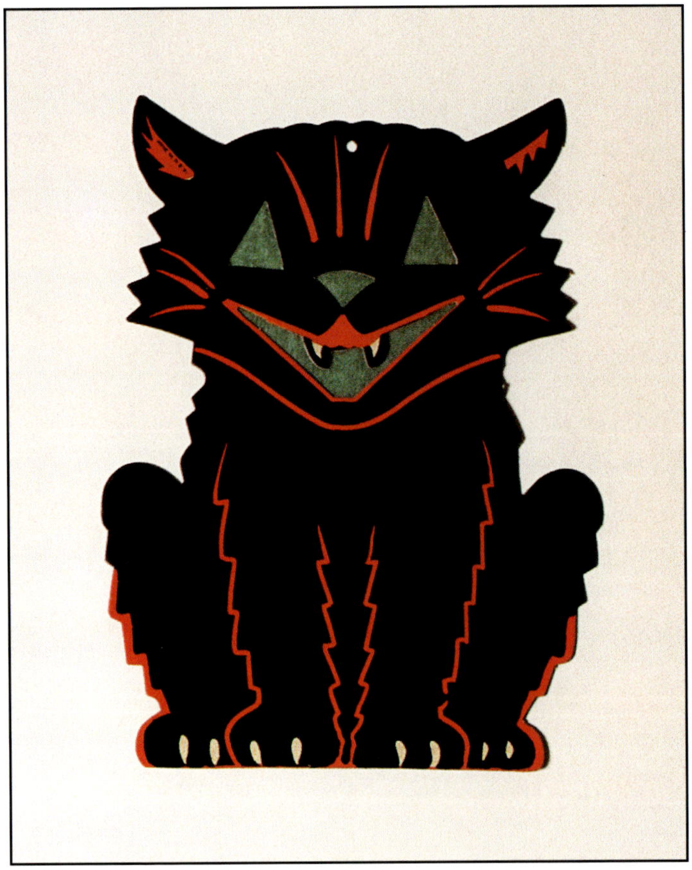

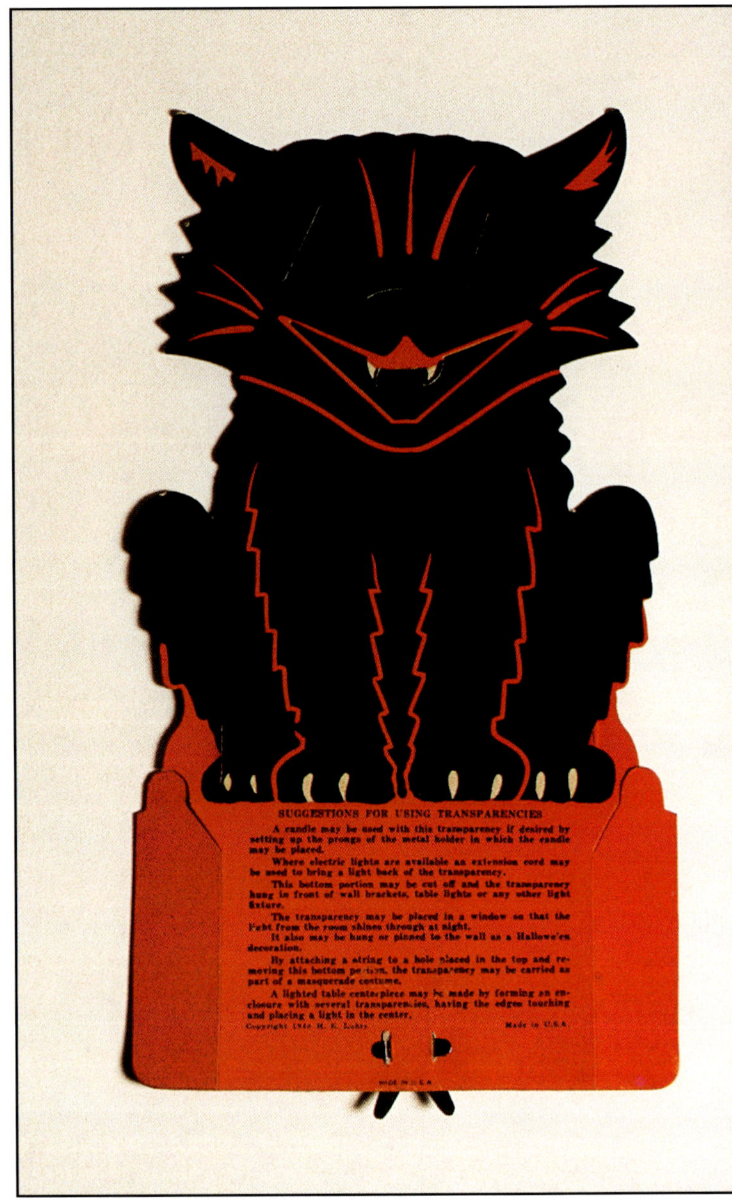
SUGGESTIONS FOR USING TRANSPARENCIES
A candle may be used with this transparency if desired by setting up the prongs of the metal holder in which the candle may be placed.
Where electric lights are available an extension cord may be used to bring a light back of the transparency.
This bottom portion may be cut off and the transparency hung in front of wall brackets, table lights or any other light fixture.
The transparency may be placed in a window so that the light from the room shines through at night.
It also may be hung or pinned to the wall as a Hallowe'en decoration.
By attaching a string to a hole placed in the top and removing this bottom portion, the transparency may be carried as part of a masquerade costume.
A lighted table centerpiece may be made by forming an enclosure with several transparencies, having the edges touching and placing a light in the center.
Made in U.S.A.

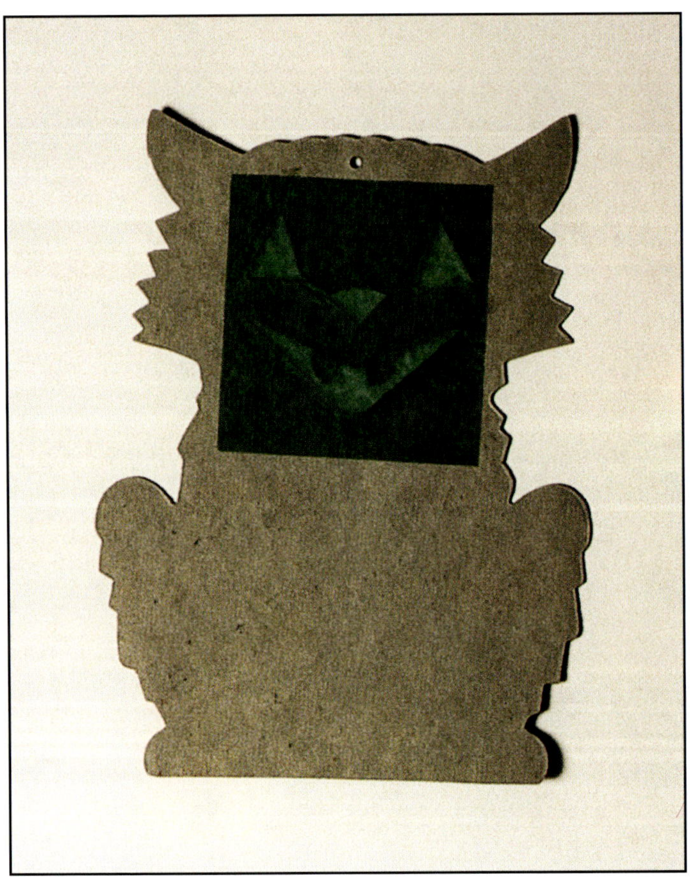

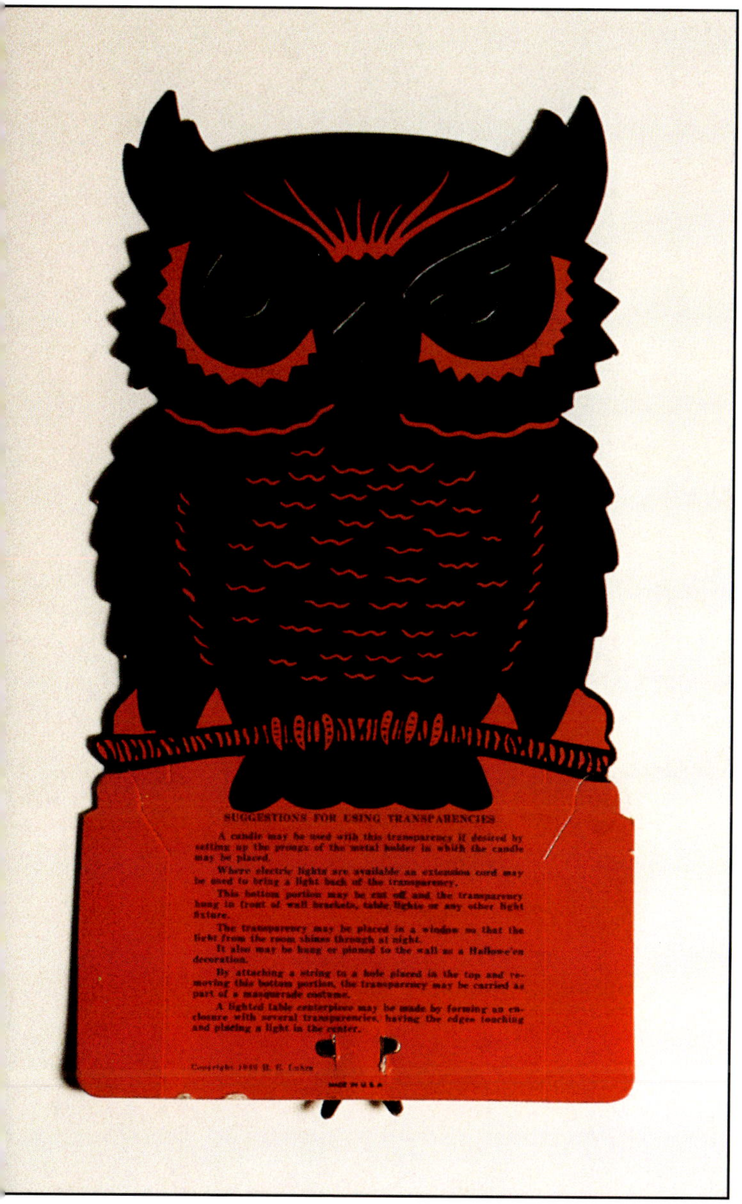
SUGGESTIONS FOR USING TRANSPARENCIES
A candle may be used with this transparency if desired by setting up the prongs of the metal holder in which the candle may be placed.
Where electric lights are available an extension cord may be used to bring a light back of the transparency.
This bottom portion may be cut off and the transparency hung in front of wall brackets, table lights or any other light fixture.
The transparency may be placed in a window so that the light from the room shines through at night.
It also may be hung or pinned to the wall as a Hallowe'en decoration.
By attaching a string to a hole placed in the top and removing this bottom portion, the transparency may be carried as part of a masquerade costume.
A lighted table centerpiece may be made by forming an enclosure with several transparencies, having the edges touching and placing a light in the center.

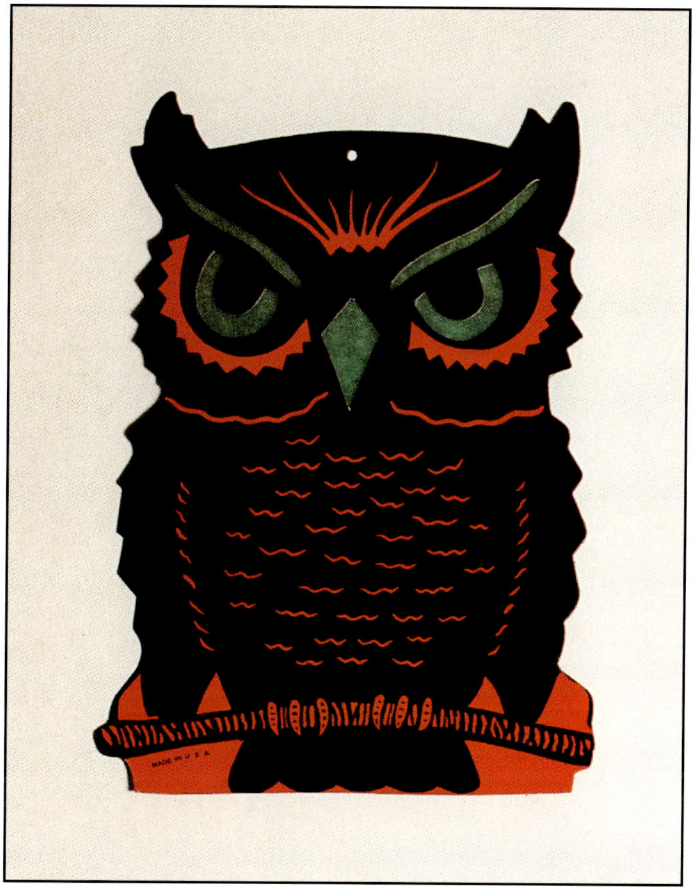

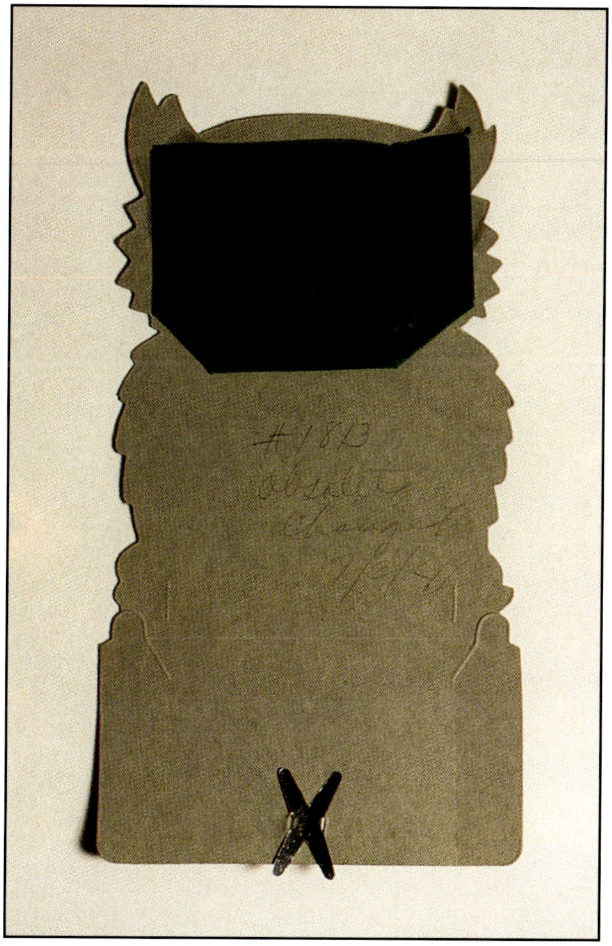

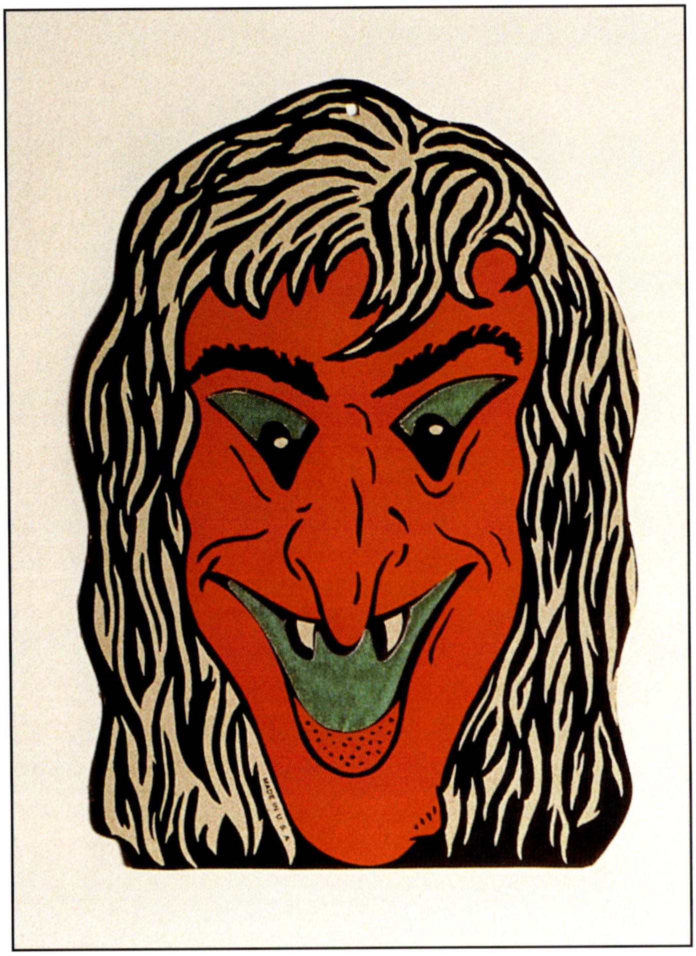

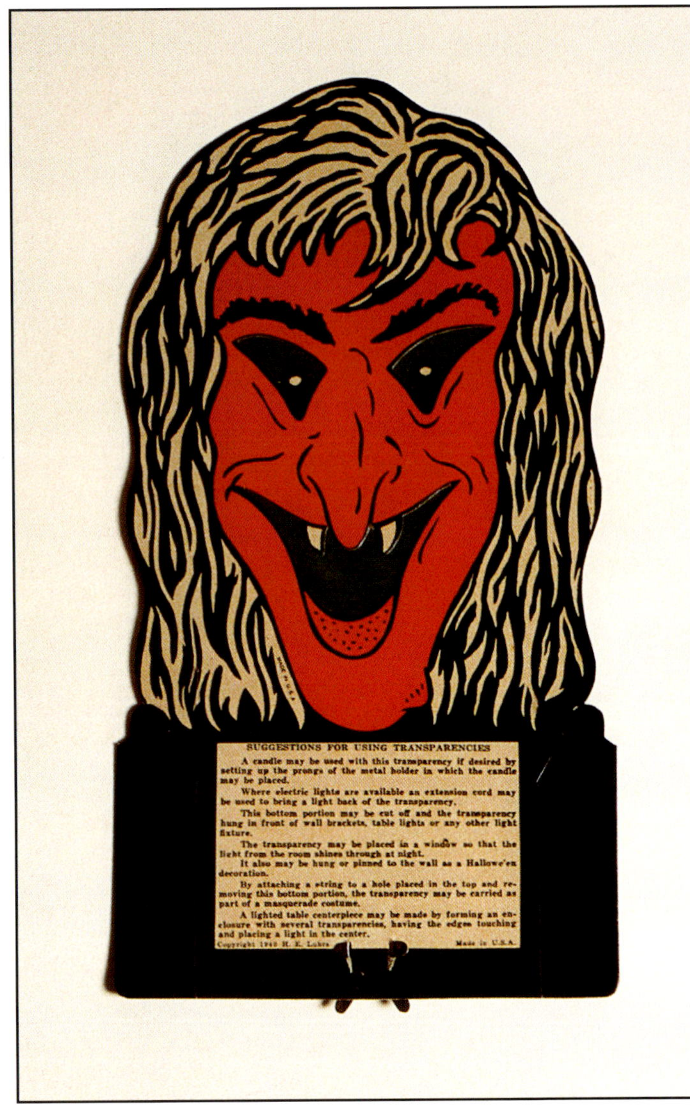

TOMMY WHISKER'S LANTERN
Initial Release: 1938
Production Run: 1938 – 1945
A new, lively-faced cat lantern printed on cardboard die-cut, with illuminated eyes, nose and mouth. Meshed tissue sides, candle holder in bottom, tissue liners, size 11" x 11.25". One design.
*The second photo gives a view of the meshed tissue sides.
Value: $185

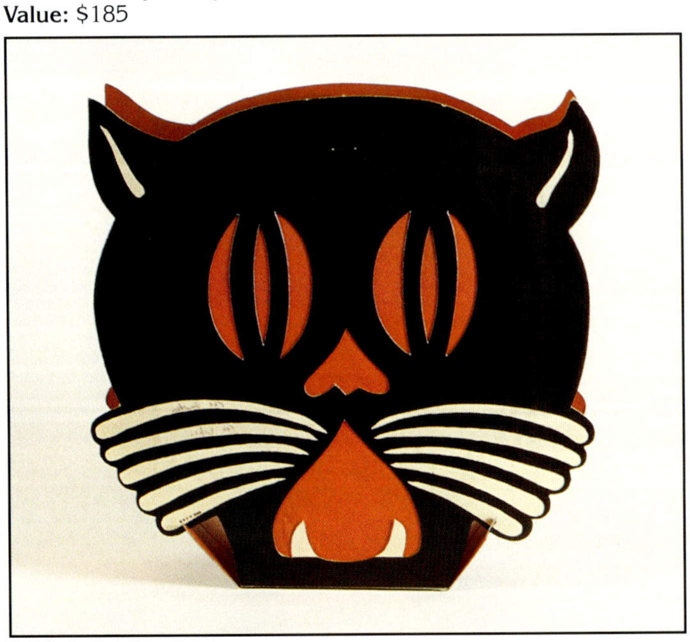

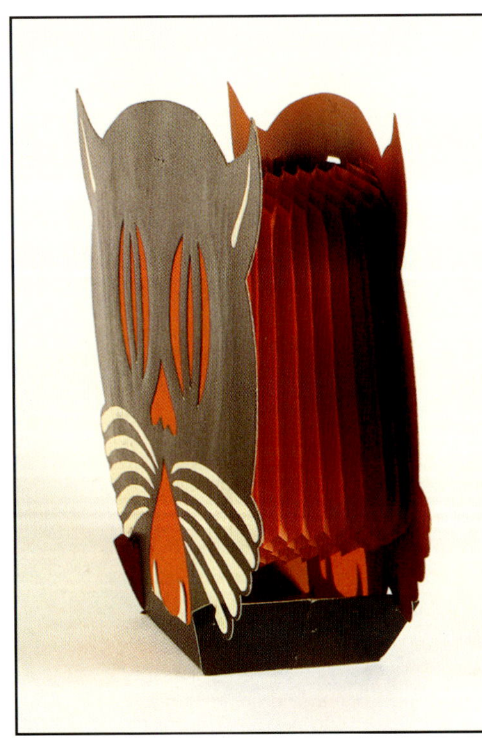

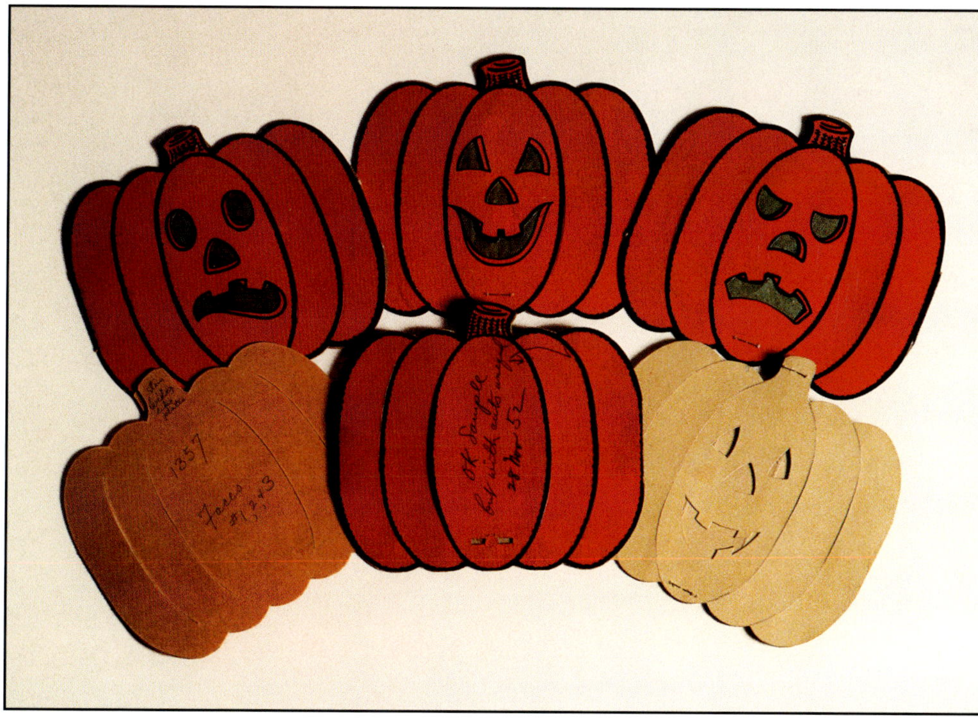

JACK-O-LANTERN
Initial Release: 1953
Production Run: 1953 – 1956
A novel lantern with slots that allow the pumpkin design to glow as well as the Jack-O-Lantern face. Printed orange and black, with green tissue transparency for the face. Complete with wire bail and candle holder. Size 5.5" high x 4.5" wide when open. Three designs, faces on one side only.
*The three lanterns are shown perched above the artist's models including notations.
Value: $65 each

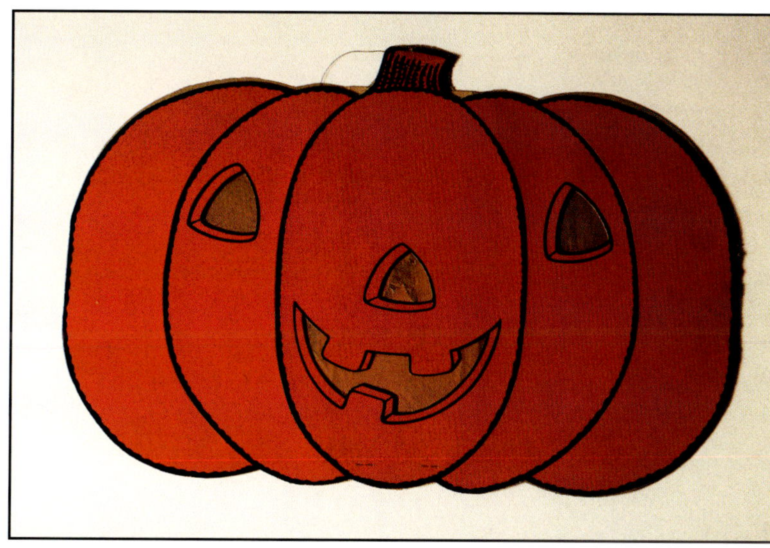

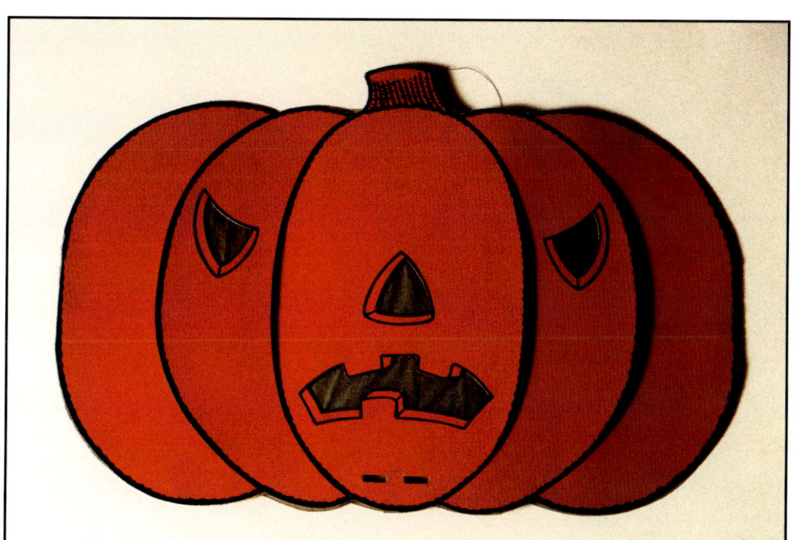

JACK-O-LANTERN
Initial Release: 1953
Production Run: 1953 - 1956
A feature attraction. Lantern is cleverly designed to allow the light to outline the pumpkin as well as its face. Printed orange and black with green tissue transparency. Complete with wire bail and candle holder. Size 6.5" high x 7.5" wide when opened. Two designs. Faces on one side only.
*Two models shown.
Value: $95 each

CHAPTER 6
Miscellaneous

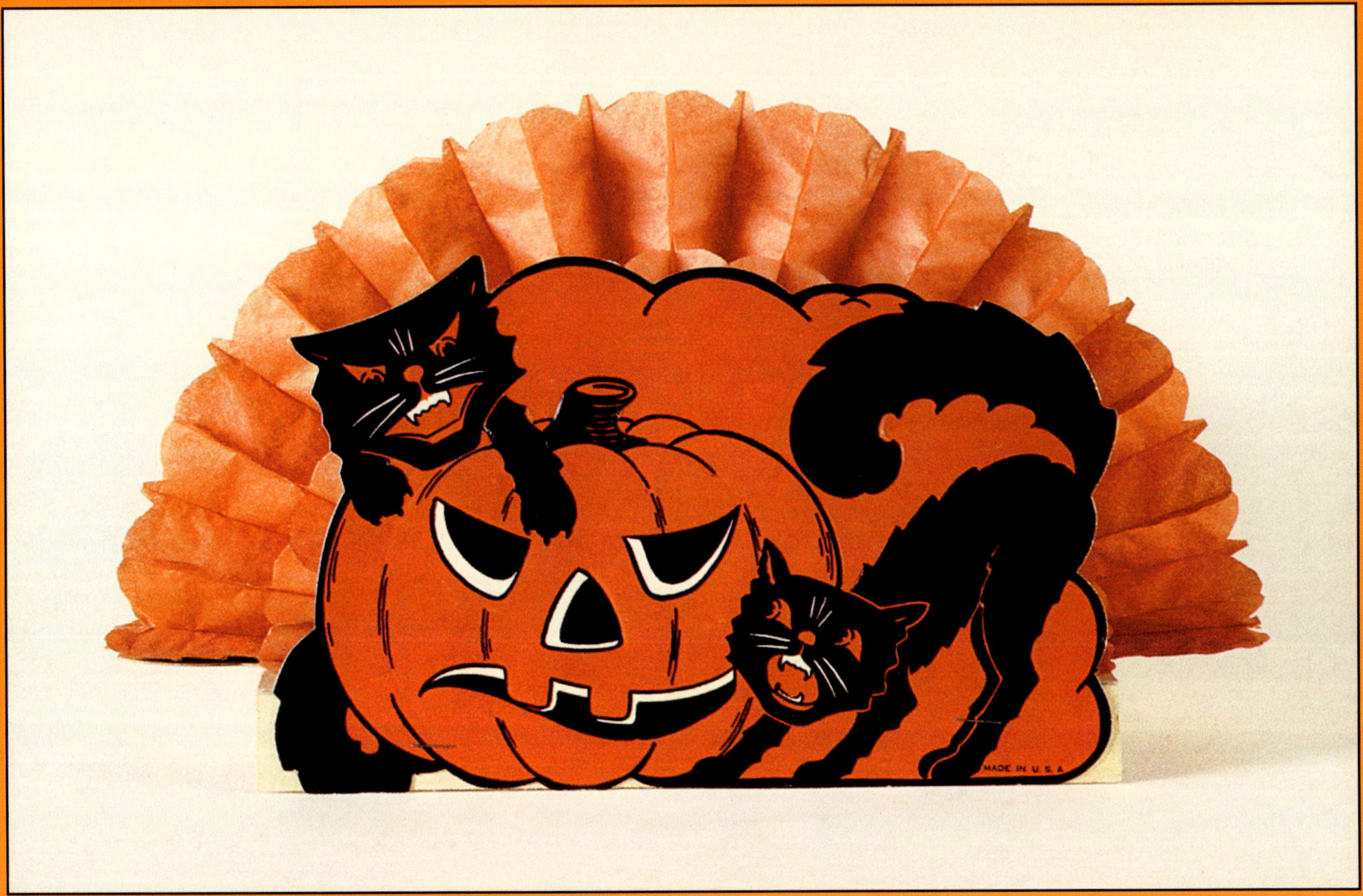

EMBOSSED CUTOUTS CENTERPIECE
*A wonderful, colorful and imaginative centerpiece that never took off. Several models with honeycomb tissue paper middle – both as a solid color (orange) and variegated (black and orange). The embossed cutouts premiered in 1952. The black cat came from the Halloween Stand-ups set which made its initial release in 1955. Sadly, these pieces were never marketed to the public.

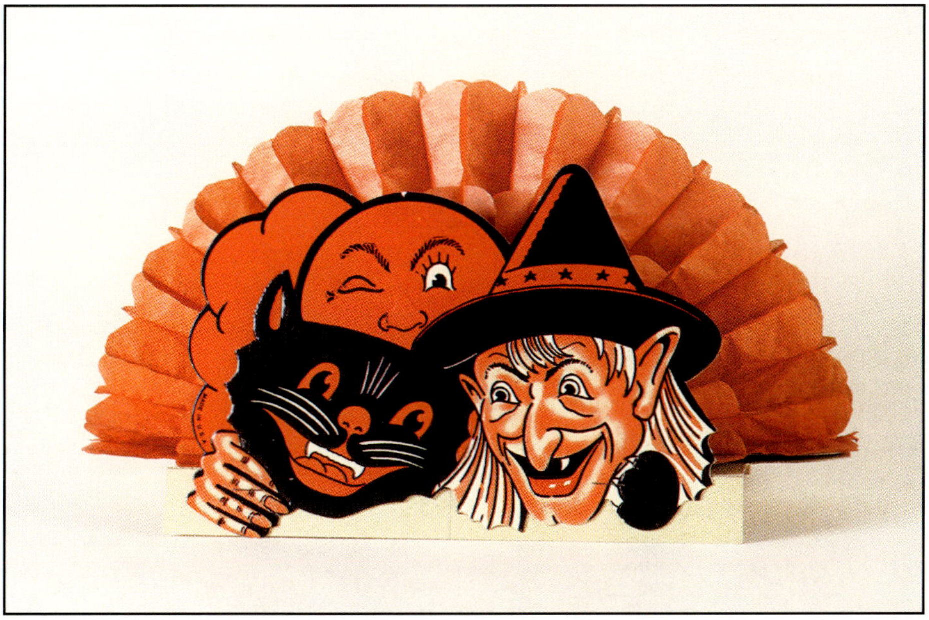

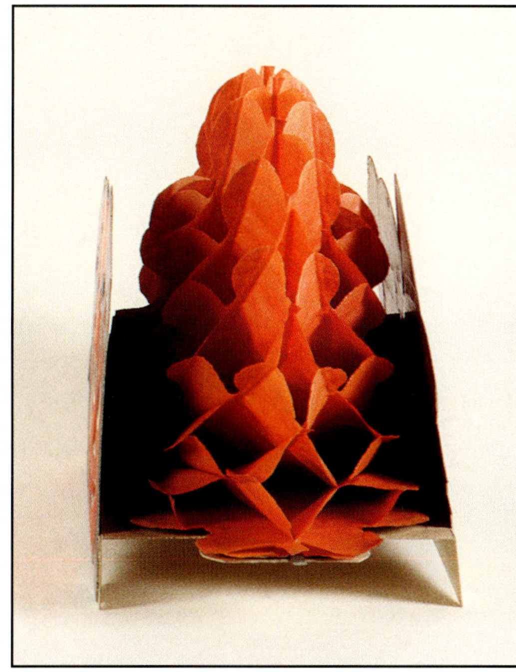

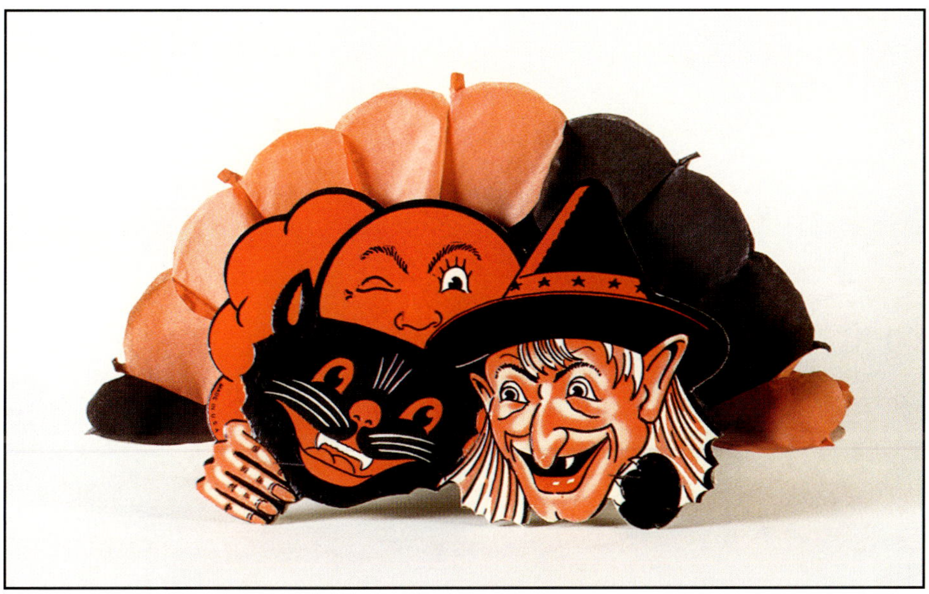

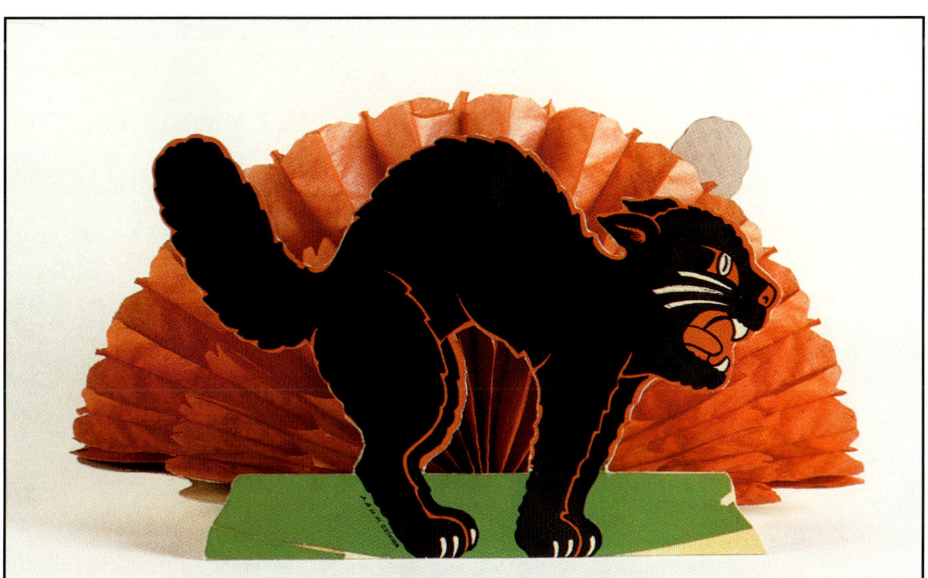

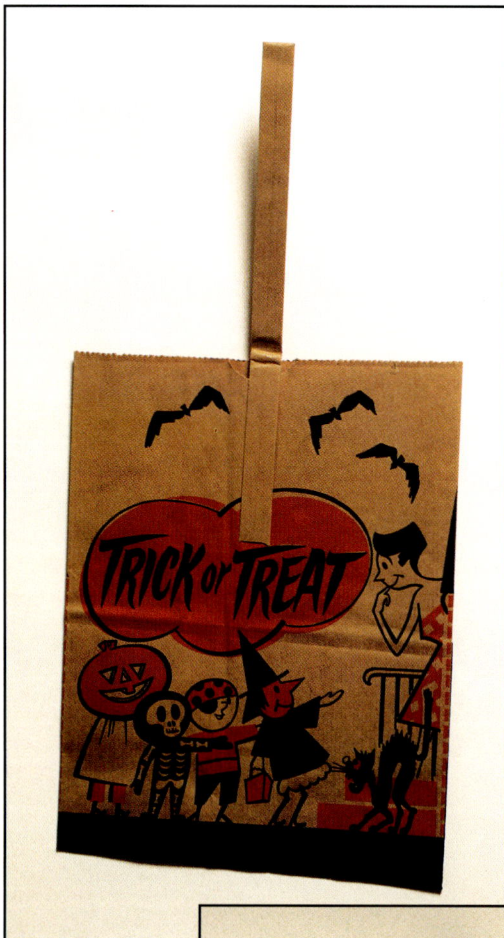

HALLOWEEN "TRICK OR TREAT" BAG
Initial Release: 1960
Production Run: 1960 – 1969
Build additional volume and new tie-in sales with these popular-priced "Trick or Treat" bags. Made of sturdy Super Kraft with reinforced handle for carrying. Printed as illustrated with orange and black Halloween design. Size 7.75" x 4.75" x 10.5". One design.
*I remember trick-or-treating with this bag! My mother purchased it at Furlow's, our neighborhood 5 & 10 (the same store where I purchased my first set of Halloween die-cuts). That bag held many a Reese's Peanut Butter Cup!
*I love the graphics on this bag. The front shows a group of children begging for treats while on the reverse the trick-or-treaters are eager to get to their next destination. It looks like it's the pirate's first Halloween venture – he can't keep up the pace!
Value: $15 – $20 range

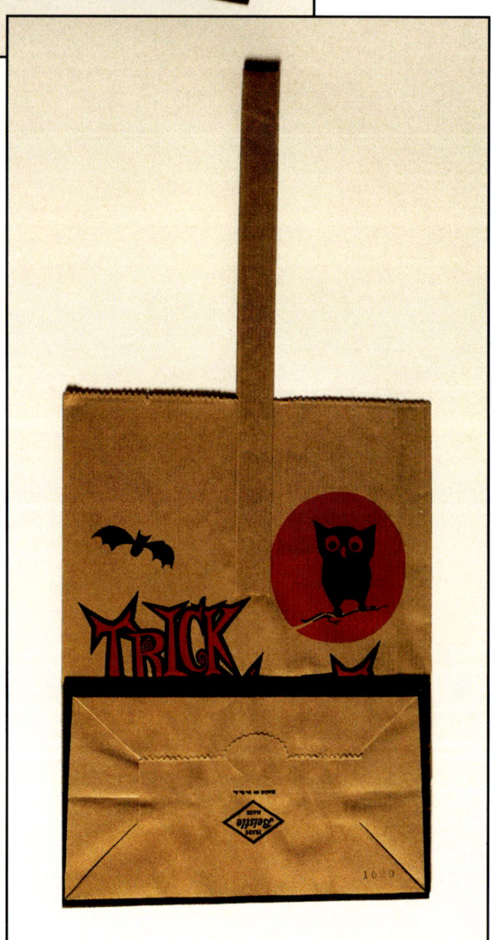

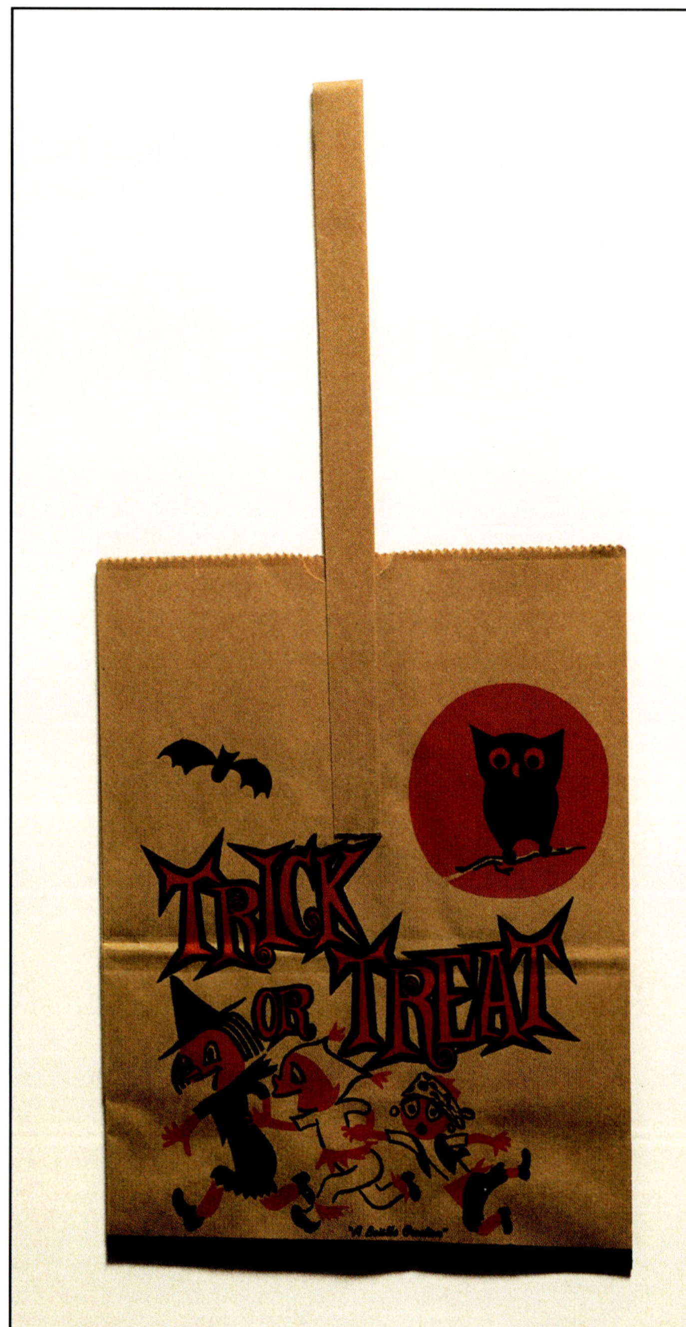

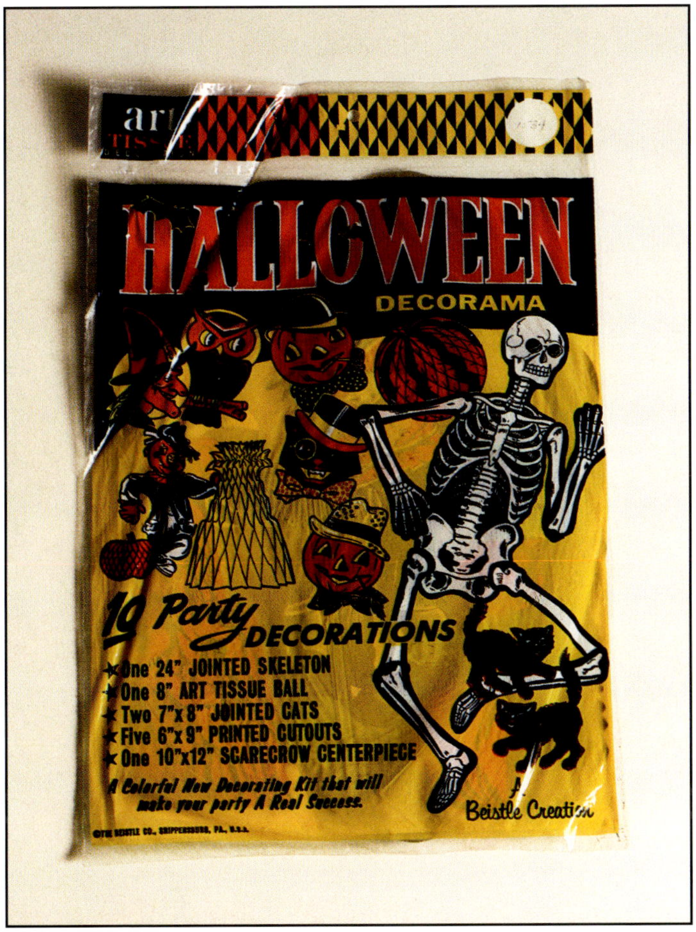

HALLOWEEN PARTY DECORAMA
Initial Release: 1964
Production Run: 1964 – 1973*
Now at a popular price, party planners can purchase a complete unit for decorating club or game room for that big Halloween party. A perfect tie-in sale with hats, horns, and other party goods that's sure to net a nice additional volume of sales on this popular seasonal line. Each kit is attractively packaged in a printed poly bag with full-color illustrations and descriptive copy.
*Included in each package: one 24" Jointed Skeleton, one 8" x 11" Tissue decoration, two 7" x 8" Jointed Cats, four 6" x 9" Embossed Wall Plaques, one 8" Art-Tissue Ball, and one 10" x 12" Scarecrow Centerpiece.
*In 1974, Beistle presented an updated version of the Halloween Party Decorama set. Both the package and the contents were new in design.
Value: $110 for complete packaged set

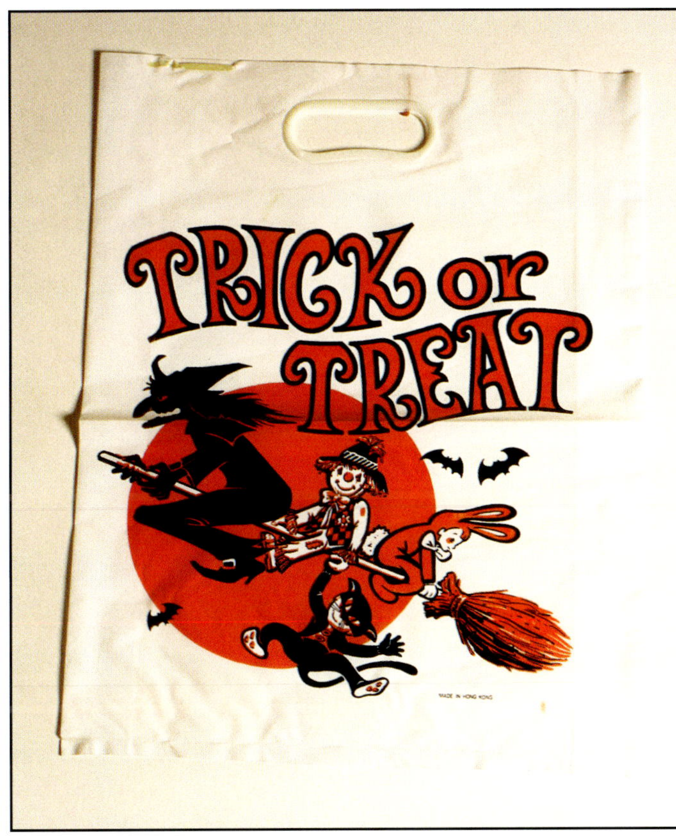

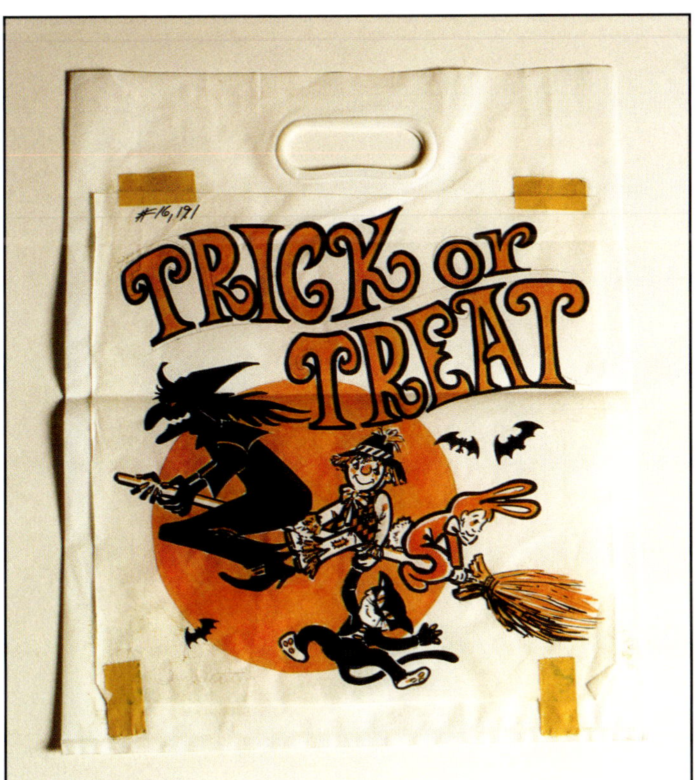

PLASTIC TRICK OR TREAT BAG
Initial Release: 1969
Production Run: 1969 – 1982
A new durable trick or treat bag constructed from 3 gauge white opaque plastic with reinforced inset handle for carrying. Printed in bright orange and black Halloween design. Size 12" x 15" x 3". One design.
*Here's another behind-the-scenes peek at a Beistle artist's prototype. I am ecstatic whenever I come across one of these finds!
Value: $15

FORTUNE STUNT PIE
Initial Release: 1948
Production Run: One year only: 1948
*In my latest excursion through the Beistle Company archives I came across a letter from H.E. Luhrs to the artist of the Halloween Pie game, Mary Clemmett. Again, this is rare opportunity to have a glimpse into the process of creating a new Halloween "treat." Mr. Luhrs was pleased with Ms. Clemmett's sketches and color suggestions for Beistle's most recent idea on a new Halloween party game and it is apparent from Mary's return letter that she was compensated accordingly and hopeful that she would be considered for future work. It is characteristic that artists who, on a company payroll, are rarely given acknowledgement for their individual work. I hope that the family members of Mary Clemmett have the opportunity of seeing this and knowing that one of her creations has become a much sought-after Halloween item for collectors.

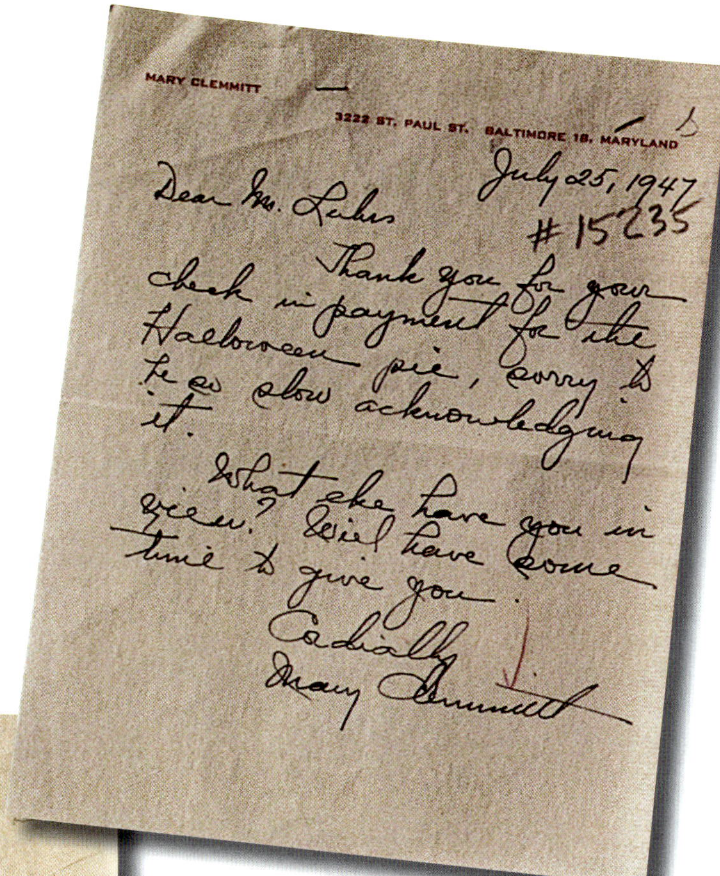

MARY CLEMMITT

3222 ST. PAUL ST. BALTIMORE 18, MARYLAND

July 25, 1947

Dear Mr. Luhrs

\#15235

Thank you for your check in payment for the Halloween pie, sorry to be so slow acknowledging it.

What else have you in view? Will have some time to give you.

Cordially
Mary Clemmitt

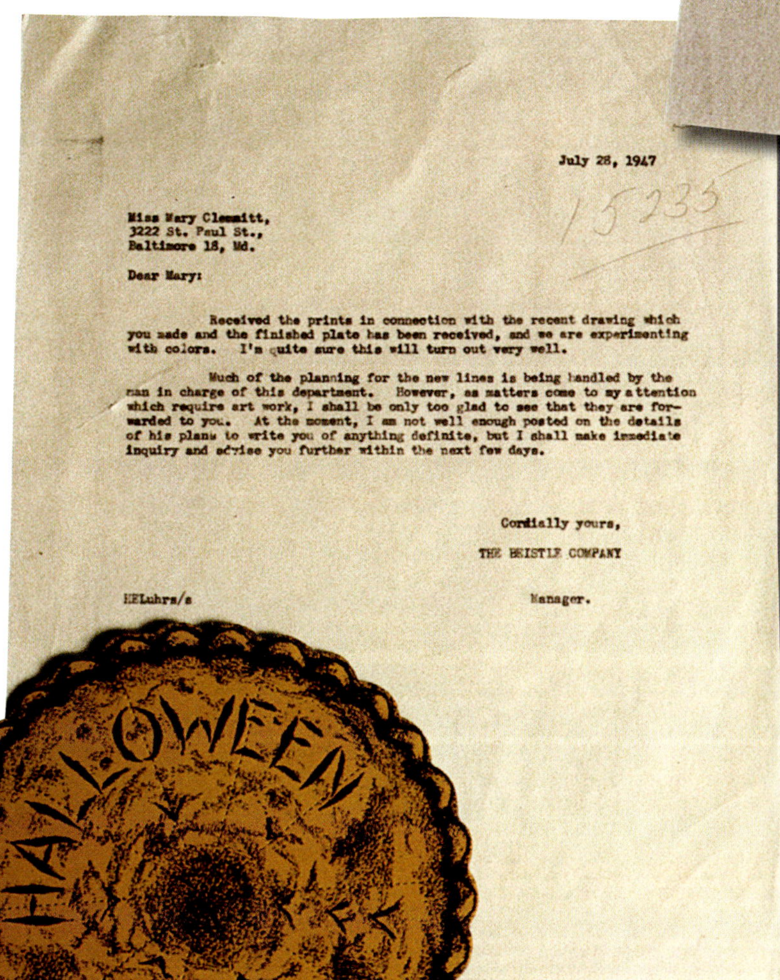

July 28, 1947

15235

Miss Mary Clemmitt,
3222 St. Paul St.,
Baltimore 18, Md.

Dear Mary:

Received the prints in connection with the recent drawing which you made and the finished plate has been received, and we are experimenting with colors. I'm quite sure this will turn out very well.

Much of the planning for the new lines is being handled by the man in charge of this department. However, as matters come to my attention which require art work, I shall be only too glad to see that they are forwarded to you. At the moment, I am not well enough posted on the details of his plans to write you of anything definite, but I shall make immediate inquiry and advise you further within the next few days.

Cordially yours,
THE BEISTLE COMPANY

HELuhrs/s

Manager.

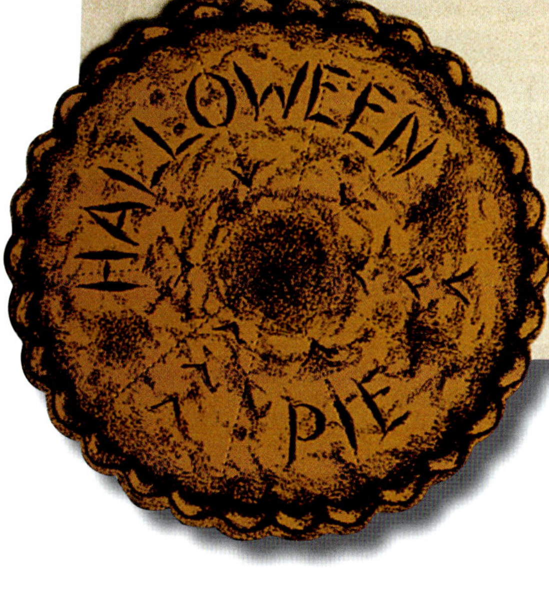

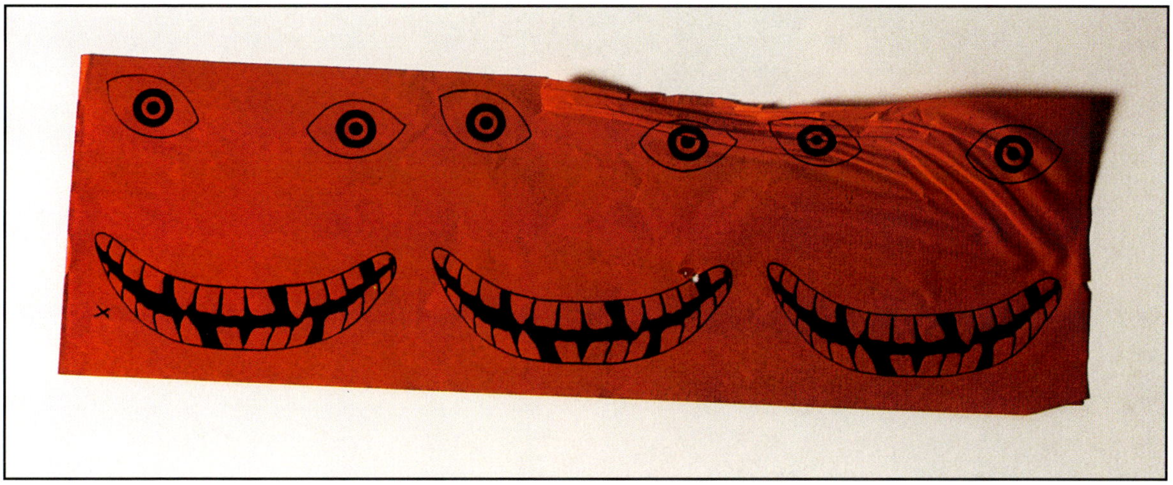

TISSUE PAPER INSERT
*Who does this Cheshire Cat-like grin belong to? It sure looks familiar!

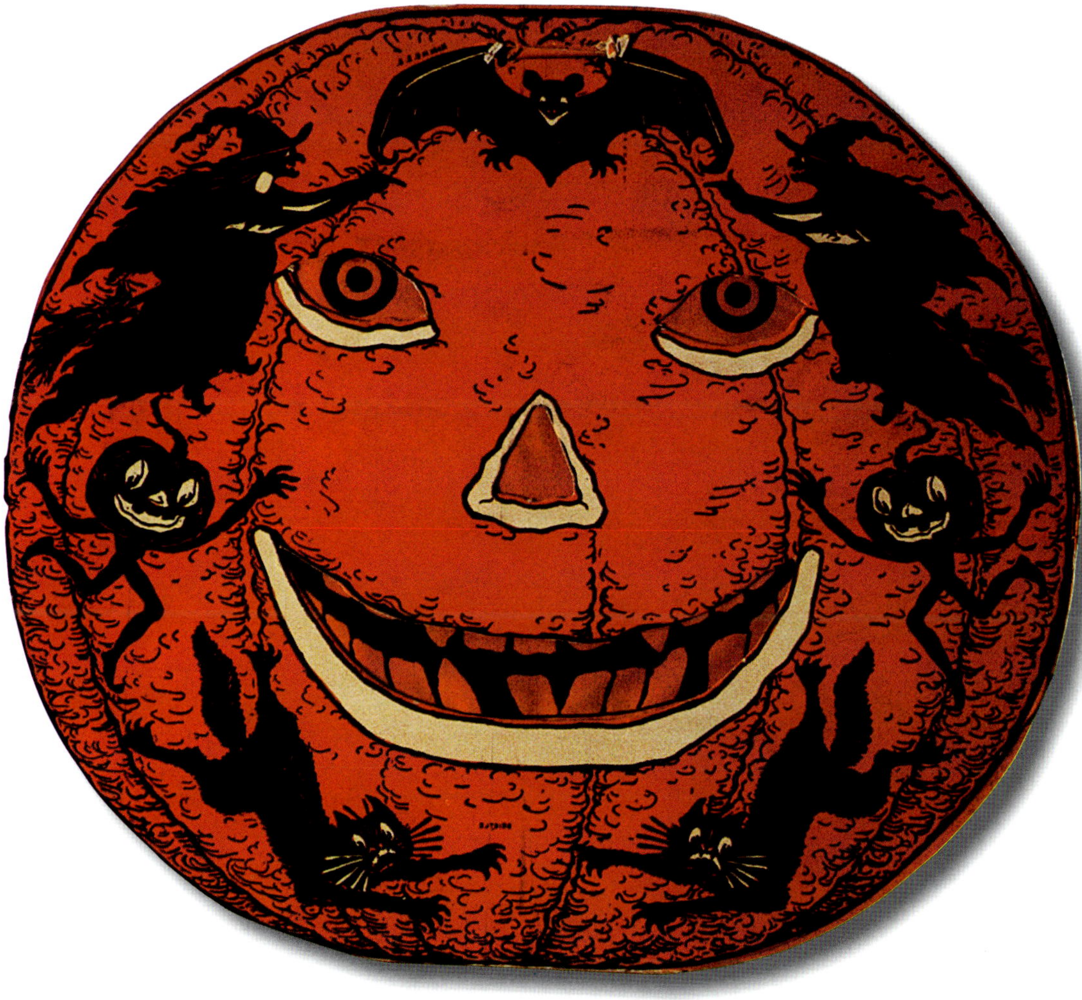

SURPRISE!
Why, it's none other than the renowned 1929 Beistle Jack-O-Lantern!! I found a sheet of the paper inserts before they were cut to fit the openings in the Jack-O-Lantern. I think this is one of the finest paper inserts on par with their German cousins. Surprisingly, this insert was never used for any other Beistle model.

BEISTLE BEAUTIES
*Foiled cardboard plaques from the late 1930s – early 1940s, to be used as ornamentation on crepe paper party hats. Quite a racy theme for couples' parties! I don't believe these were ever marketed to the public – can't picture too many wives snapping these up at the local party store!
*Four plaques flanking a sample party hat in the middle.

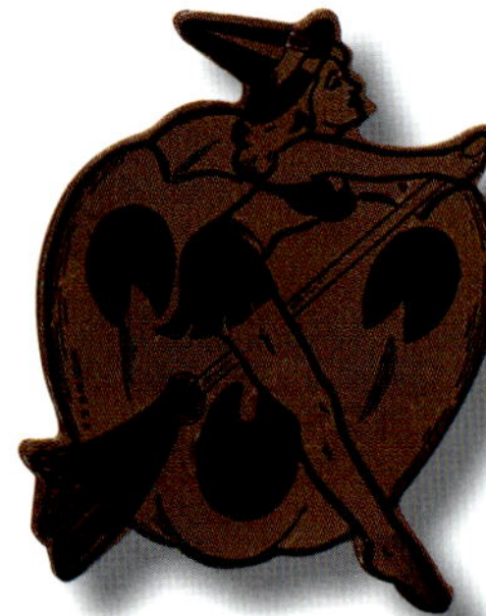

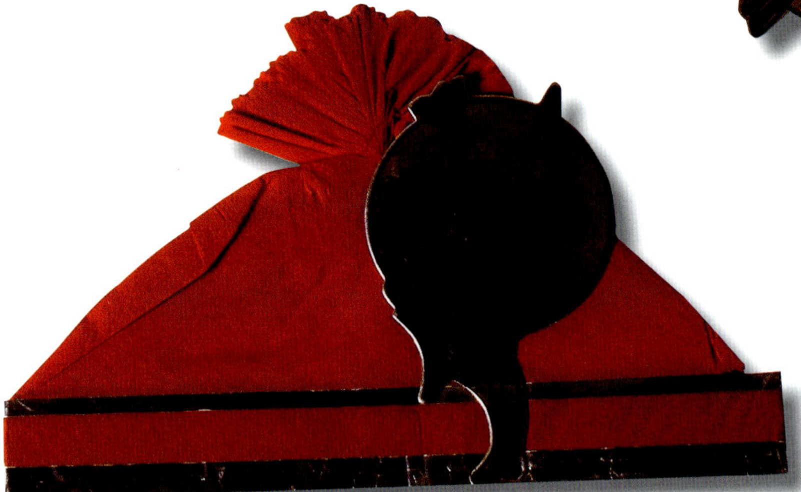

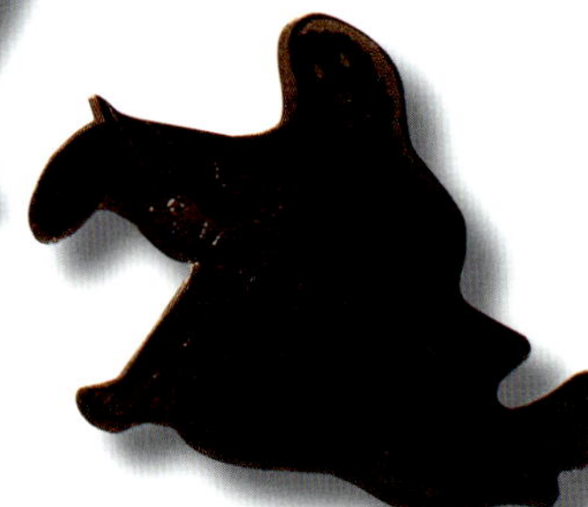

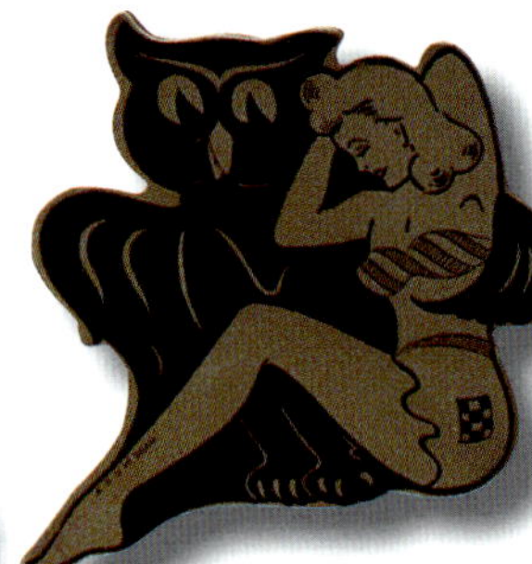

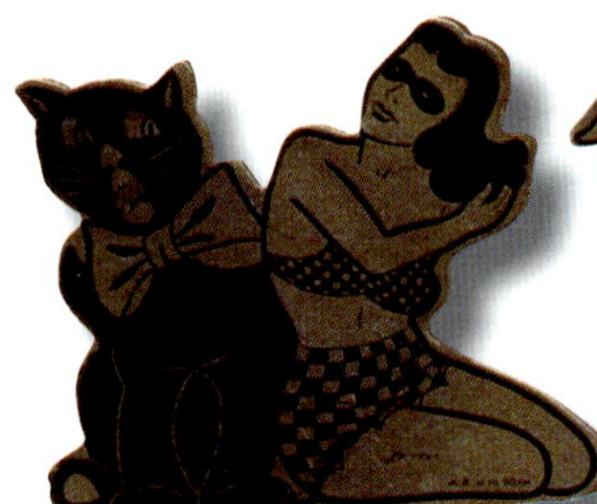

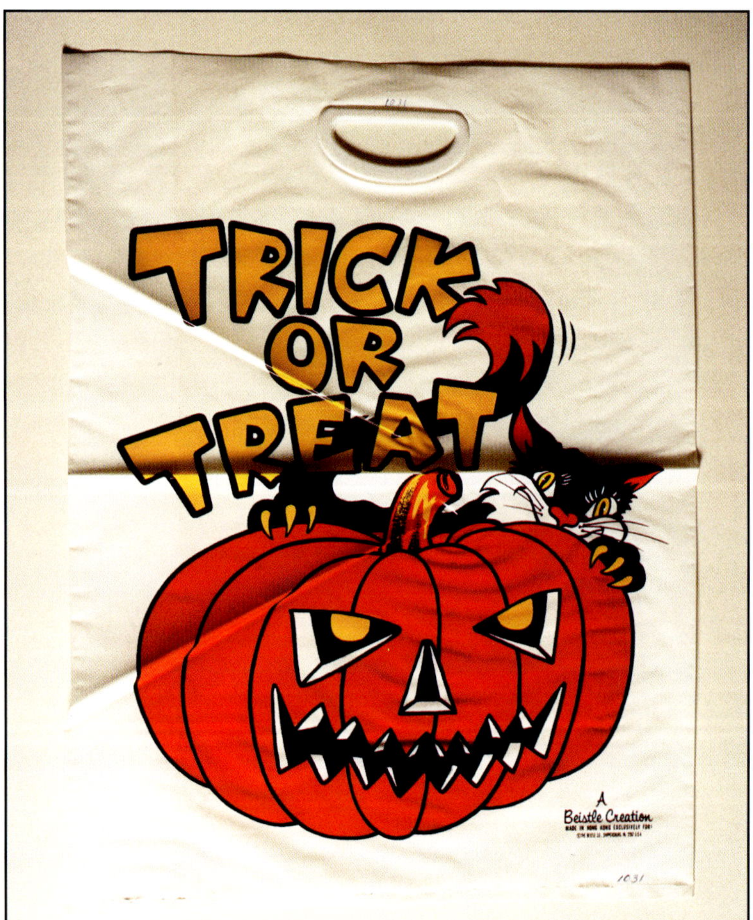

PLASTIC TRICK OR TREAT BAG
Initial Release: 1970
Production Run: 1970 – 1973
You'll discover new volume sales with this jumbo-size trick or treat bag. Made of durable 4 gauge plastic with reinforced inset handles. Printed in a bright three-color design on solid white opaque background. Size 15" x 20" x 5". One design.
Value: $20

CHAPTER 7
Other Manufacturers

THE DOLLY TOY COMPANY
MAKER OF FIBRO TOYS
DAYTON, OHIO

I was lucky to have in my collection copies of the Dolly Toy Company Halloween sales catalogue pages, that feature their introductory offerings of candy containers and lanterns in 1934 and (supposedly) ending in 1938. The tab-and-slot construction pieces, better known as "Fibro Toys," are quite recognizable to the collector of vintage Halloween. I was informed by a former employee of Dolly Toy that Halloween production lasted only those five years, yet I have in my collection a two-sided Jack-o-lantern clearly marked "Manufactured by The Dolly Toy Co. – Tipp City, Ohio U.S.A." along with two tiny candy containers, again marked with the Tipp City address, all of which are post-1938, since they do not appear in these catalogue pages. The early pieces were manufactured at 125 Bacon Street, Dayton, Ohio, until 1936. In 1937, Dolly Toy moved their production to 320 North Fourth Street, Tippecanoe City, Ohio (now known as Tipp City, Ohio).

There lies a mystery in the case of identifying marks – either the pieces had them or they didn't (referring exclusively to the 1934-38 production line). The candy containers shown on the following pages all are clearly marked, except for the model "Pumpkin Boy". A photo of this candy container was sent to a Dolly Toy Company expert to clear up the discrepancies in design. It was most identified as definitely a Dolly Toy piece, but he could not offer an explanation for the variations in ornamentation. Could it be an artist's model, like ones I found in the Beistle Company archives? We may never know.

The lanterns are another puzzle. The early ones (pre-1939) are not marked at all; those from the Beistle Company, at the very least, were stamped "Made in U.S.A.". Yet the lanterns and candy cups manufactured at the Tipp City address are marked. More investigation may uncover more definitive information. Dolly Toy Company is still in operation today, but their line of sales have changed from novelties to baby-related items.

I have learned that, for the most part, the company records were either destroyed or thrown away. I found this situation to be true especially with the smaller manufacturing companies, but not totally inclusive. I tried to find information on the Halloween production line of the Gibson Art Company, that was bought by American Greetings. A representative from their legal department confirmed that when American purchased Gibson, most of the files were incomplete. Such a loss!

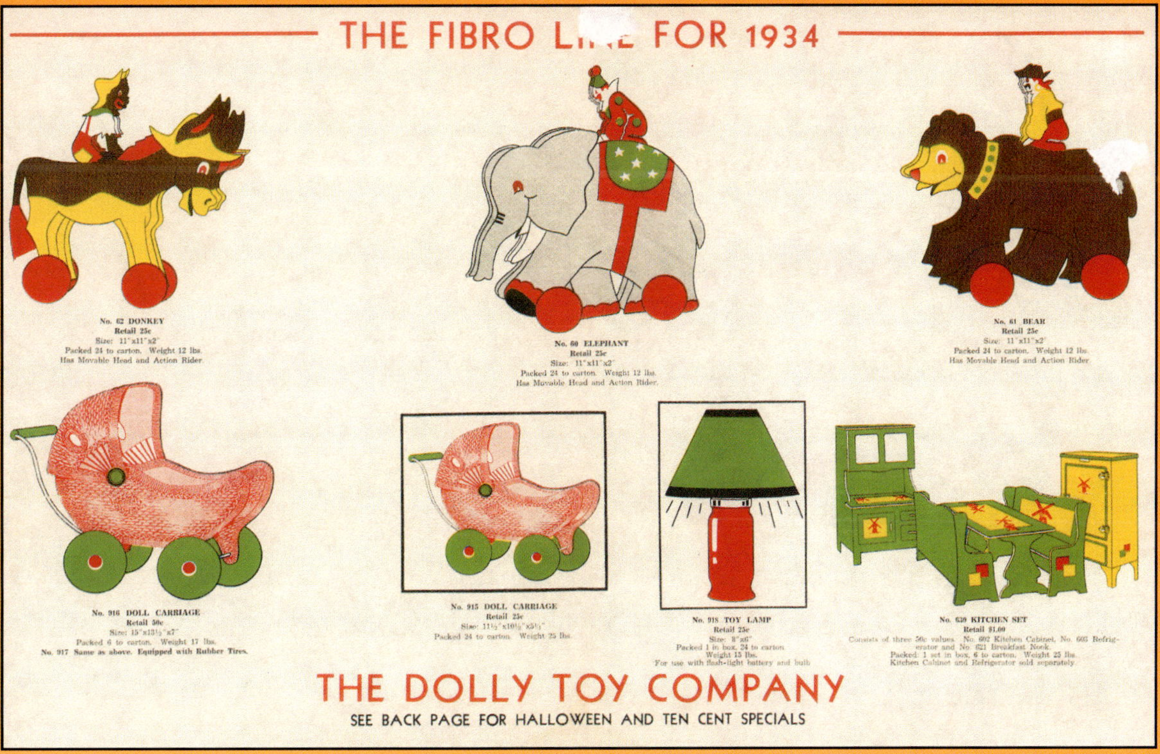

No. 63 HALLOWEEN CART
Initial Release: 1934
Production Run: 1934 – 1935
Retail $.10 – Size 9" x 6.5" x 4".
*This candy container was clearly marked: A FIBRO TOY – Mfg. by The Dolly Toy Co. – 125 Bacon St. – Dayton, O., U.S.A.
*I need to mention here that I've seen reproductions of this Cat & Cart. The newer pieces were made with a glossy/shiny paper finish. Very easy to spot.
Value: $185

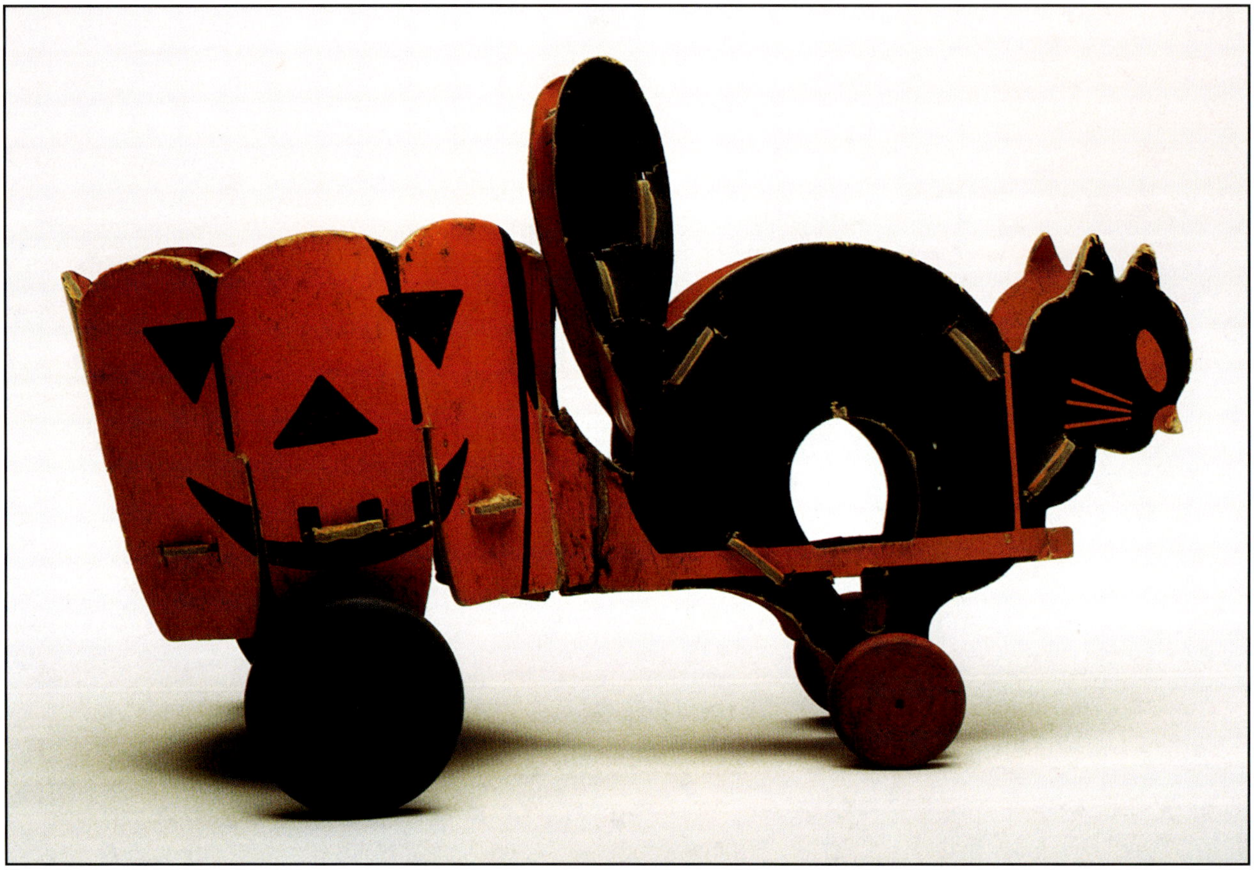

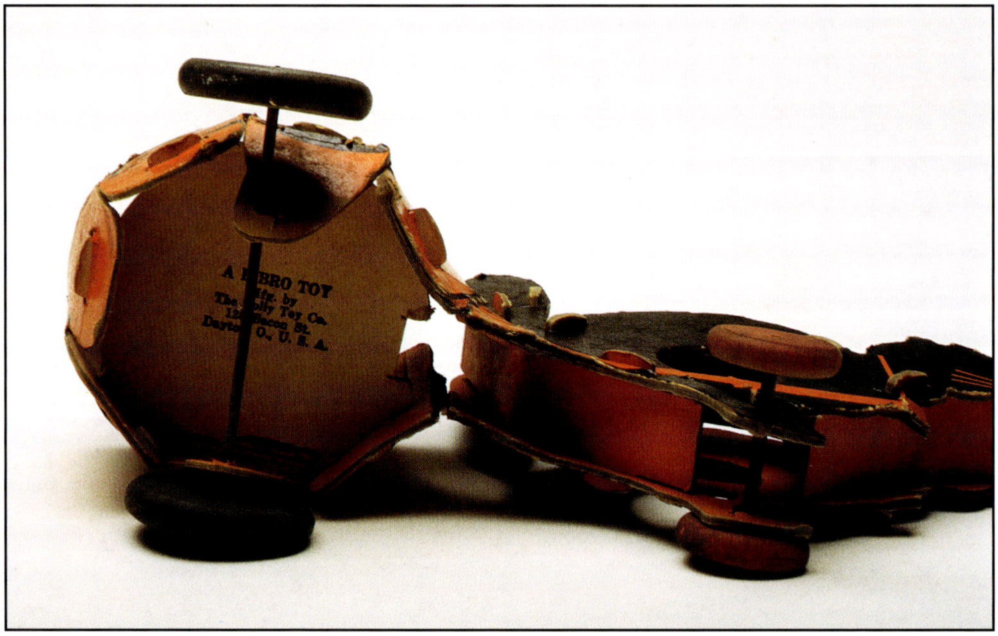

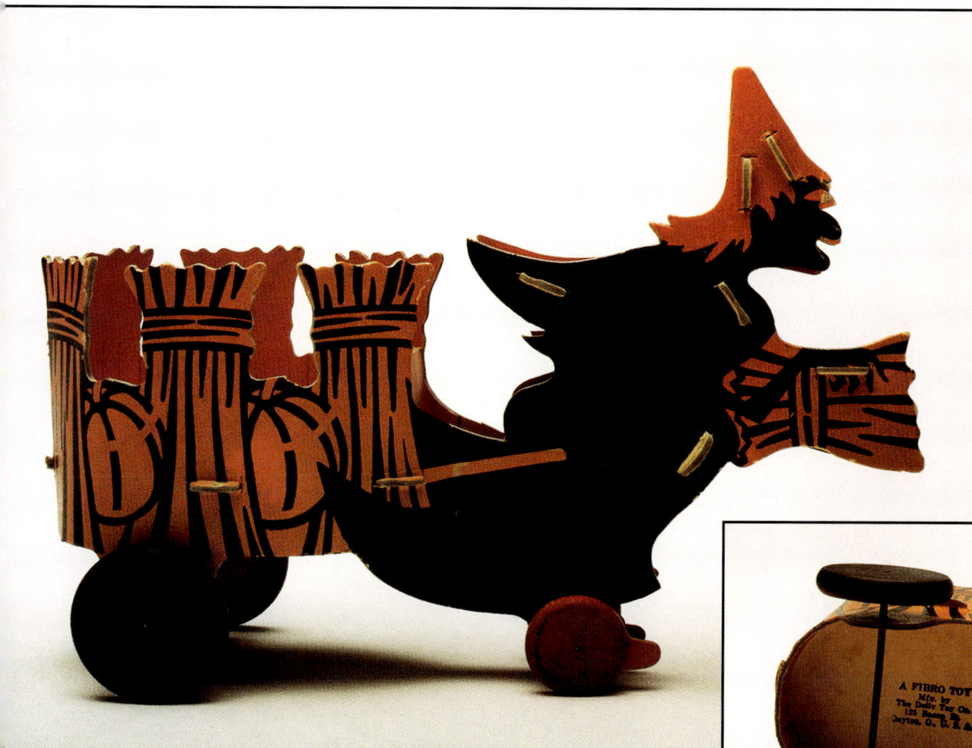

No. 64 HALLOWEEN CART
Stock No. 64
Initial Release: 1934
Production Run: 1934 – 1938
Retail $.10 – Size 9" x 6.5" x 4".
*As in the Cat with JOL cart, this item was clearly marked. It is stamped on the bottom of the wheat sheaf and pumpkin cart: A FIBRO TOY – Mfg. by The Dolly Toy Co. – 125 Bacon St. – Dayton, O., U.S.A.
*This candy container has been reproduced but the paper used has a very distinctive glossy finish. Quite discernible when placed next to the genuine vintage article.
Value: $185

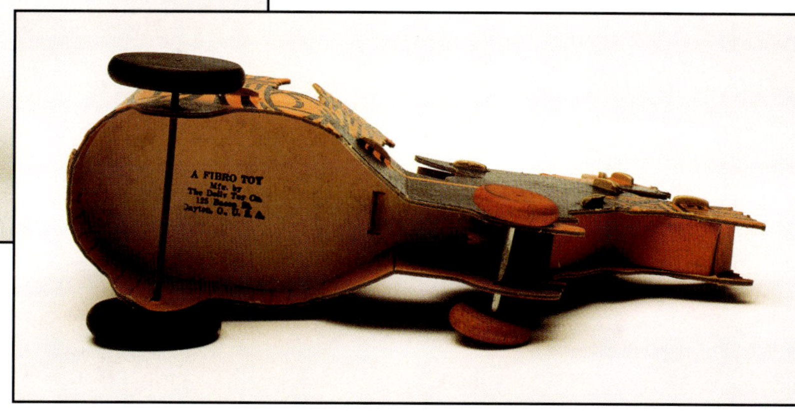

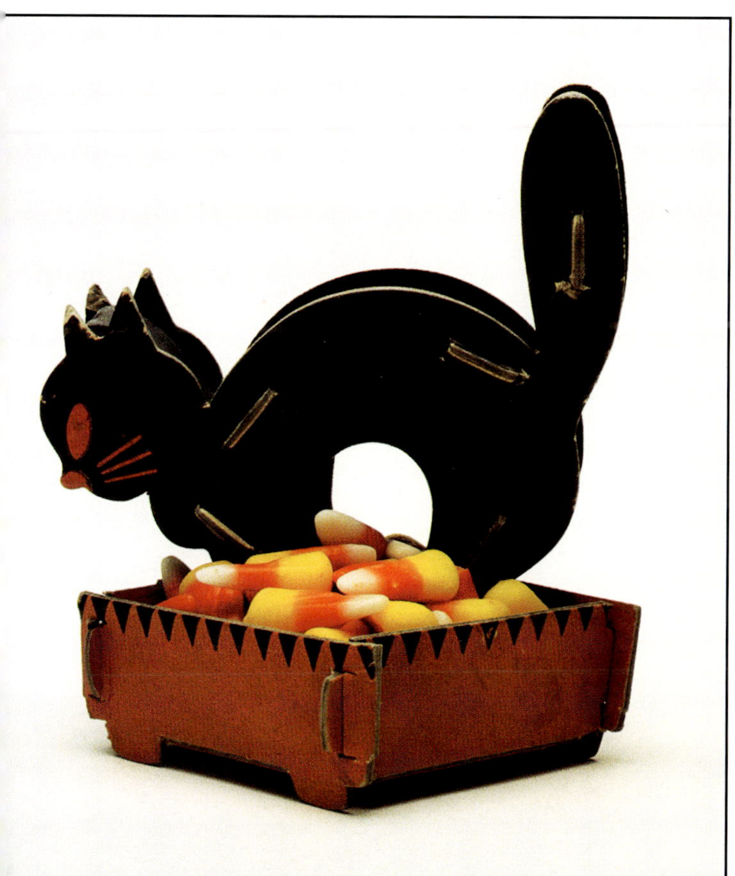

No. 65 HALLOWEEN FAVOR
Initial Release: 1934
Production Run: 1934 – 1936
*Candy container along with a photo of the mark on the bottom of the piece.
Value: $85

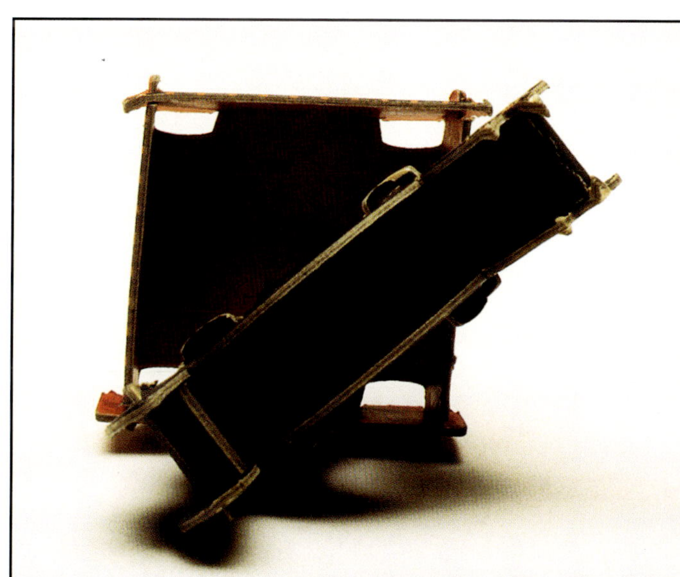

No. 66 HALLOWEEN FAVOR
Initial Release: 1934
Production Run: 1934 – 1936
*Candy container along with a photo of the mark on the bottom of the piece.
Value: $85

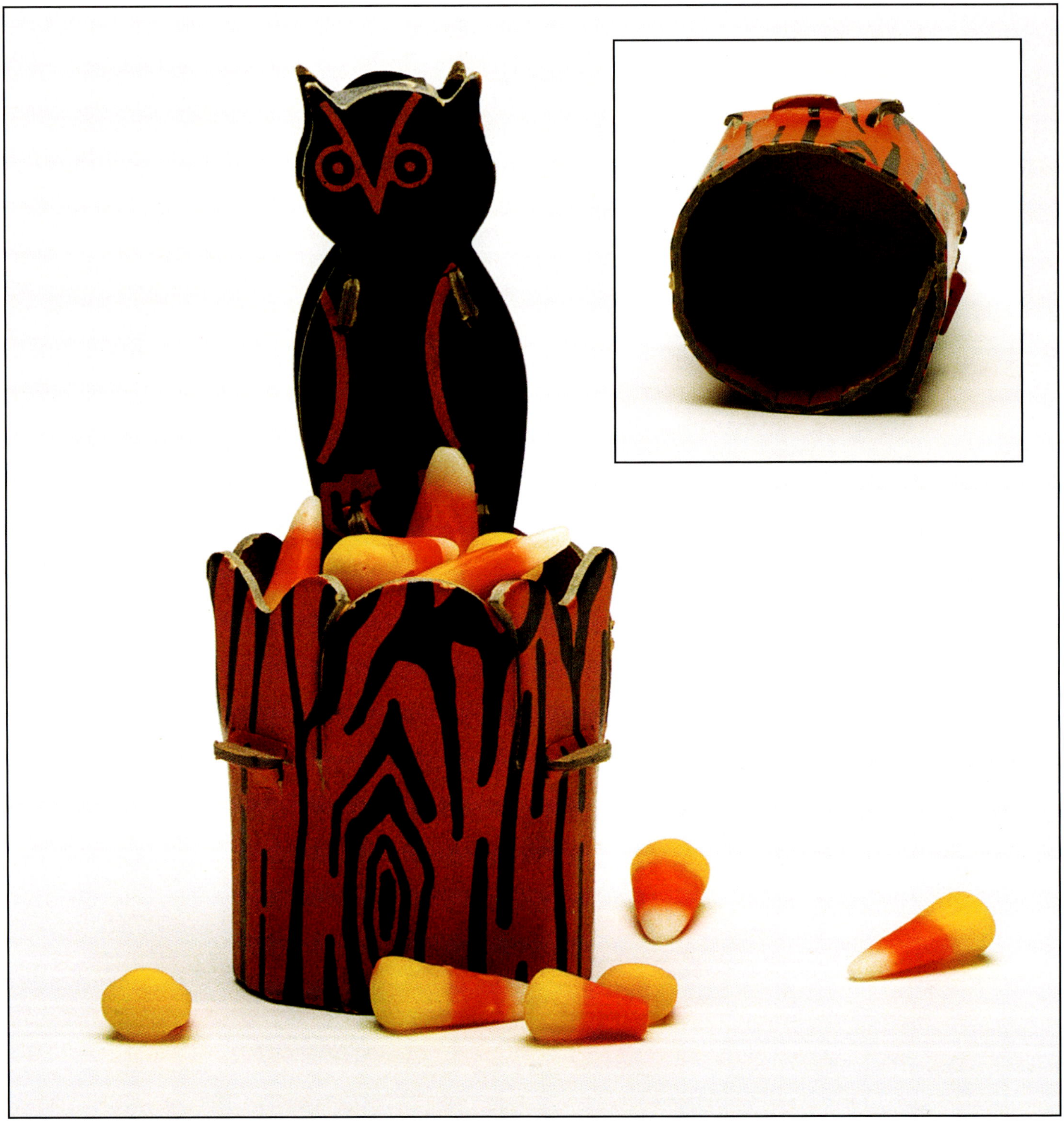

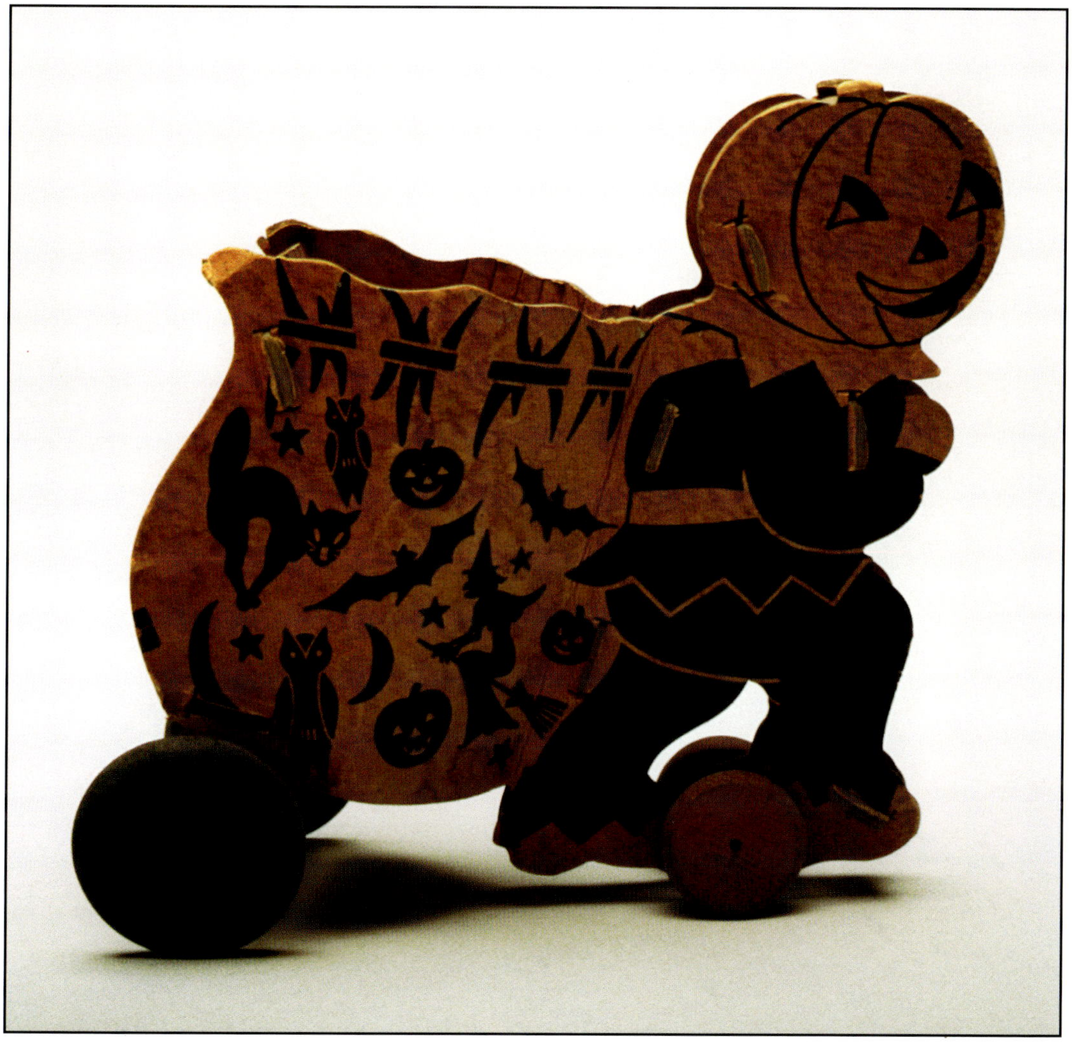

No. 86 PUMPKIN BOY
Initial Release: 1935
Production Run:
1935 – 1938
*Notice how this candy container in photo differs from the example from the sales catalogue. Another bafflement is that this is the only candy container that does not carry a Dolly Toy mark.
Value: $225

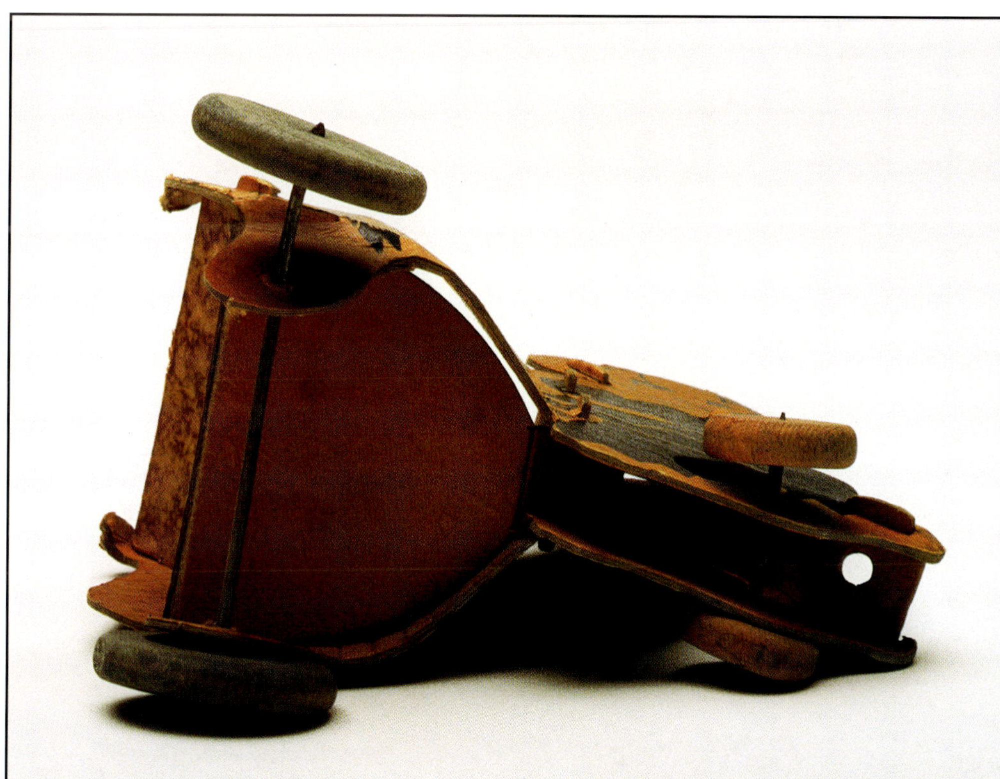

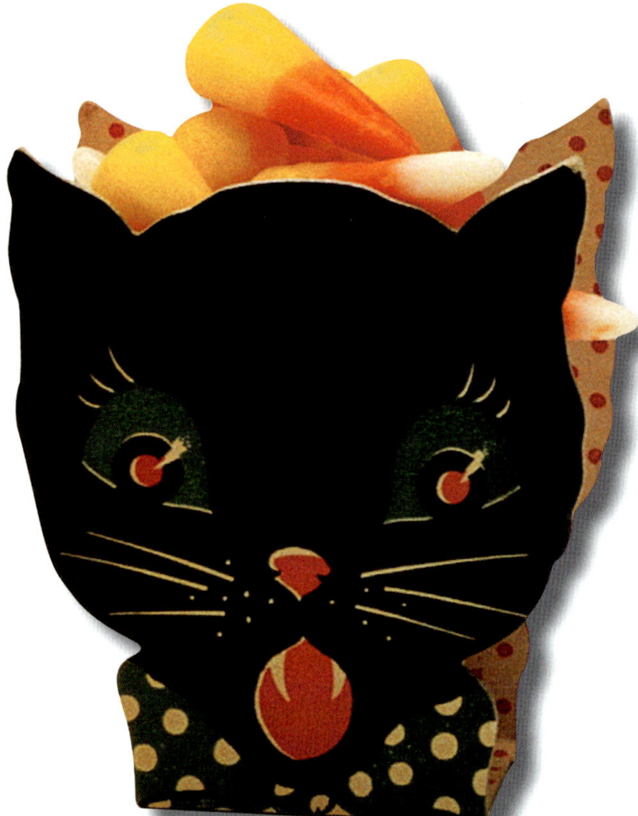

POST-1938 CANDY CONTAINERS
*There were three candy containers to this "set" – the black cat head, the black cat on a Jack-O-Lantern and an Owl. All marked with the Tipp City address.
Value: $65 each

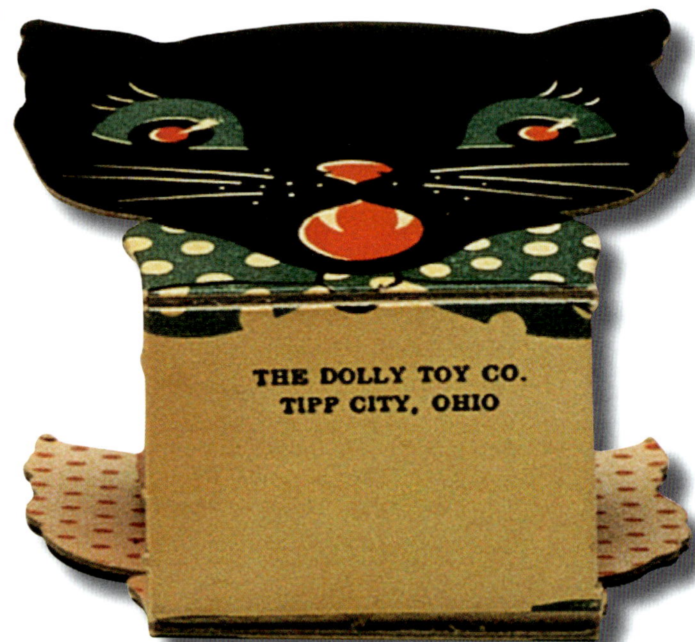

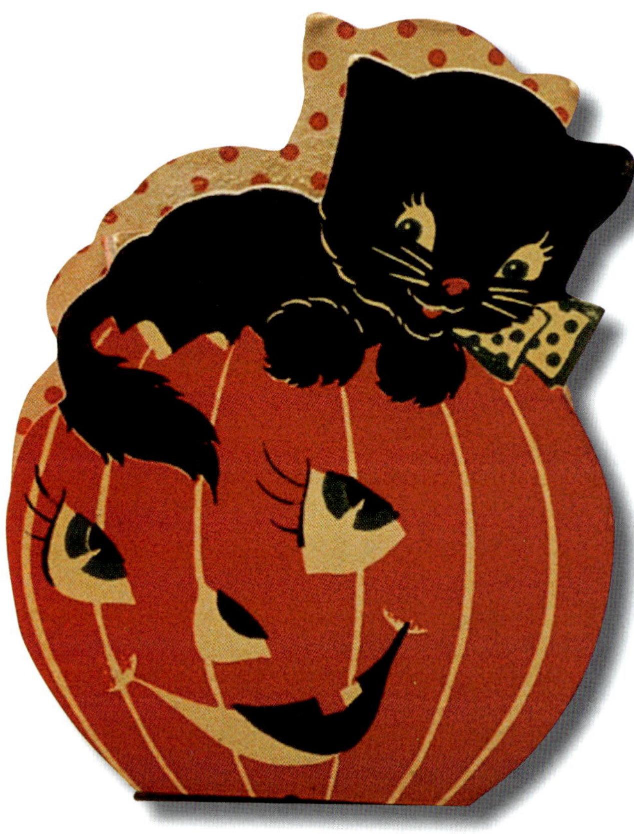

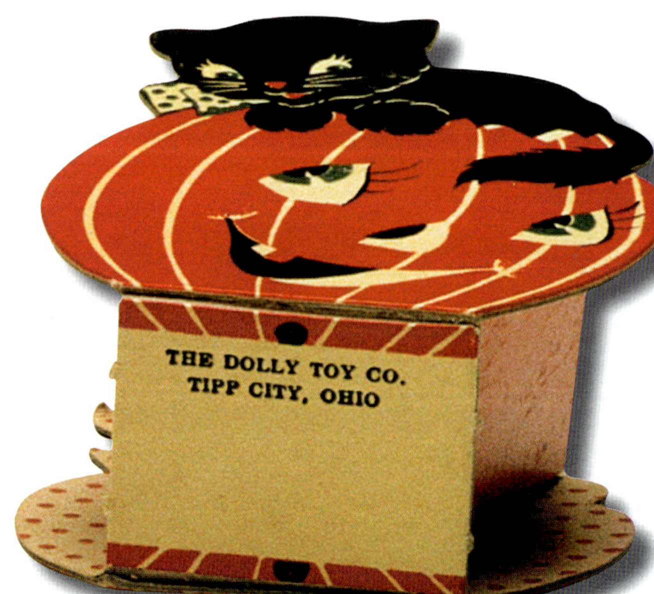

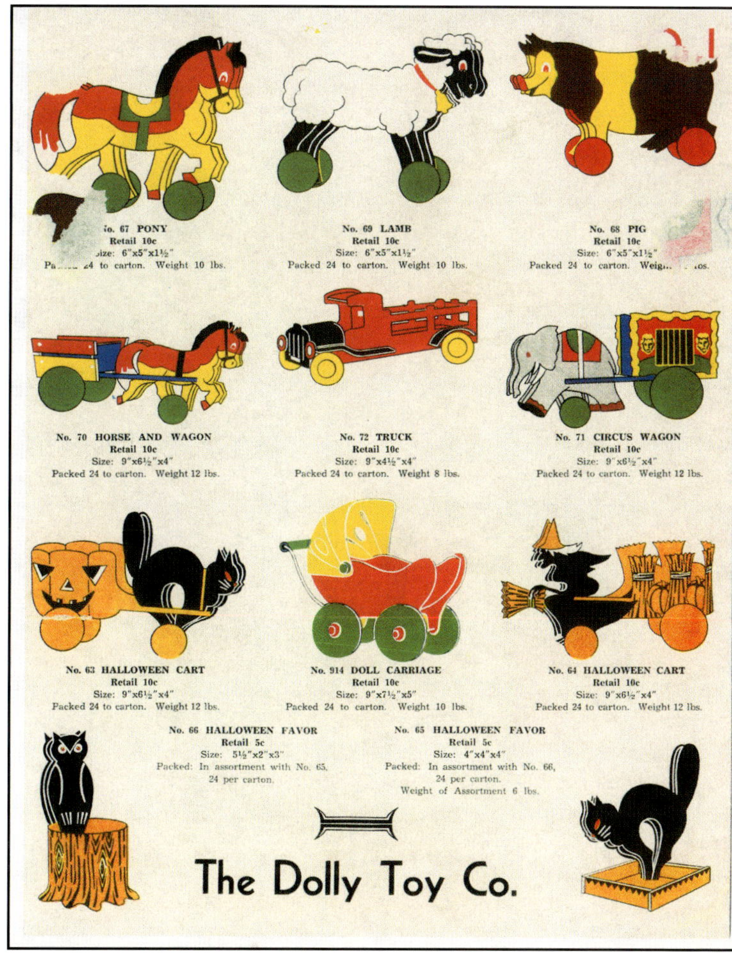
No. 67 PONY
Retail 10c
Size: 6"x5"x1½"
Packed 24 to carton. Weight 10 lbs.
No. 69 LAMB
Retail 10c
Size: 6"x5"x1½"
Packed 24 to carton. Weight 10 lbs.
No. 68 PIG
Retail 10c
Size: 6"x5"x1½"
No. 70 HORSE AND WAGON
Retail 10c
Size: 9"x6½"x4"
Packed 24 to carton. Weight 12 lbs.
No. 72 TRUCK
Retail 10c
Size: 9"x4½"x4"
Packed 24 to carton. Weight 8 lbs.
No. 71 CIRCUS WAGON
Retail 10c
Size: 9"x6½"x4"
Packed 24 to carton. Weight 12 lbs.
No. 63 HALLOWEEN CART
Retail 10c
Size: 9"x6½"x4"
Packed 24 to carton. Weight 12 lbs.
No. 914 DOLL CARRIAGE
Retail 10c
Size: 9"x7½"x5"
Packed 24 to carton. Weight 10 lbs.
No. 64 HALLOWEEN CART
Retail 10c
Size: 9"x6½"x4"
Packed 24 to carton. Weight 12 lbs.
No. 66 HALLOWEEN FAVOR
Retail 5c
Size: 5½"x2"x3"
Packed: In assortment with No. 65, 24 per carton.
No. 65 HALLOWEEN FAVOR
Retail 5c
Size: 4"x4"x4"
Packed: In assortment with No. 66, 24 per carton.
Weight of Assortment 6 lbs.
The Dolly Toy Co.

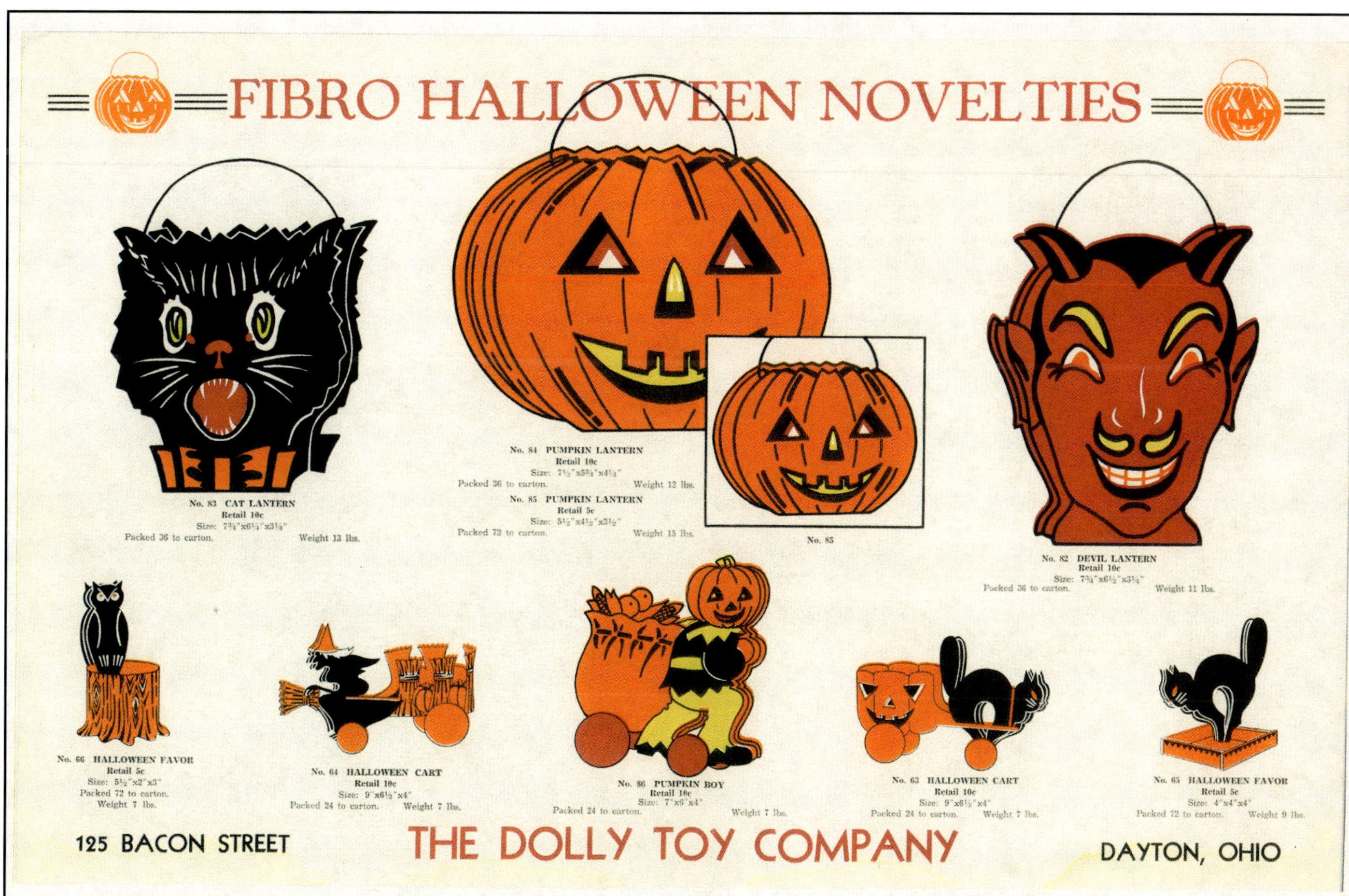
FIBRO HALLOWEEN NOVELTIES
No. 83 CAT LANTERN
Retail 10c
Size: 7¾"x6¼"x3¼"
Packed 36 to carton. Weight 13 lbs.
No. 84 PUMPKIN LANTERN
Retail 10c
Size: 7½"x5¾"x4¼"
Packed 36 to carton. Weight 12 lbs.
No. 85 PUMPKIN LANTERN
Retail 5c
Size: 5½"x4½"x3½"
Packed 72 to carton. Weight 15 lbs.
No. 85
No. 82 DEVIL LANTERN
Retail 10c
Size: 7¾"x6½"x3¼"
Packed 36 to carton. Weight 11 lbs.
No. 66 HALLOWEEN FAVOR
Retail 5c
Size: 5½"x2"x3"
Packed 72 to carton.
Weight 7 lbs.
No. 64 HALLOWEEN CART
Retail 10c
Size: 9"x6½"x4"
Packed 24 to carton. Weight 7 lbs.
No. 86 PUMPKIN BOY
Retail 10c
Size: 7"x6"x4"
Packed 24 to carton. Weight 7 lbs.
No. 63 HALLOWEEN CART
Retail 10c
Size: 9"x6½"x4"
Packed 24 to carton. Weight 7 lbs.
No. 65 HALLOWEEN FAVOR
Retail 5c
Size: 4"x4"x4"
Packed 72 to carton. Weight 9 lbs.
125 BACON STREET
THE DOLLY TOY COMPANY
DAYTON, OHIO

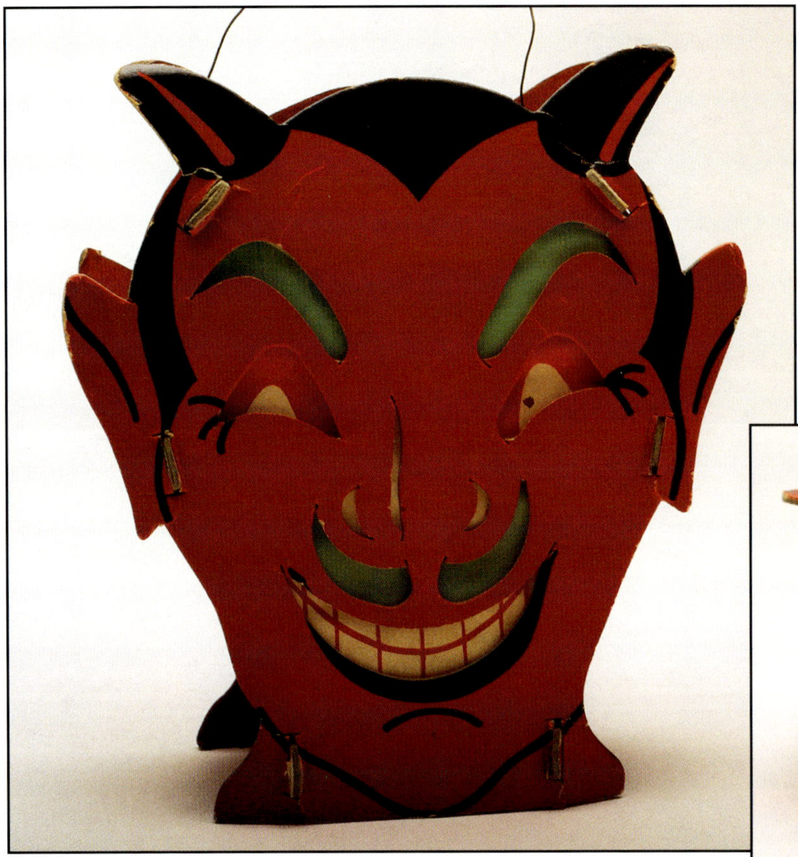

No. 82 DEVIL LANTERN
Initial Release: 1935
Production Run: 1935 – 1938
*Showing the lantern with no mark on the bottom.
Value: $185

No. 83 CAT LANTERN
Initial Release: 1935
Production Run: 1935 – 1938
*See sales catalogue sheets for example.
Value: $185

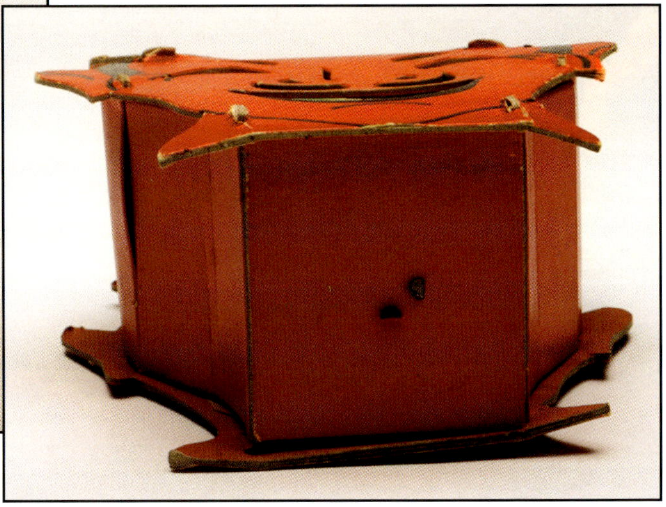

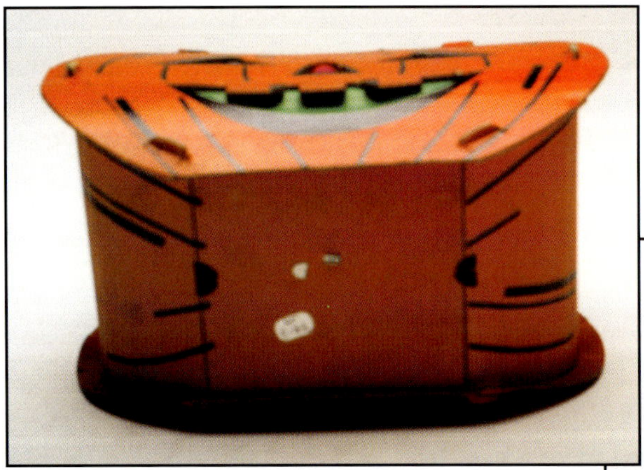

No. 84 & No. 85* PUMPKIN LANTERN
Initial Release: 1935
Production Run: 1935 – 1938
*This is a set of three Jack-O-Lanterns, although the sales catalogues only feature two. No. 84 is the largest at 7.5", No. 85 is the smallest at 5.5" and the middle one, not listed, is 6.5".
Value: $75 - $135 range

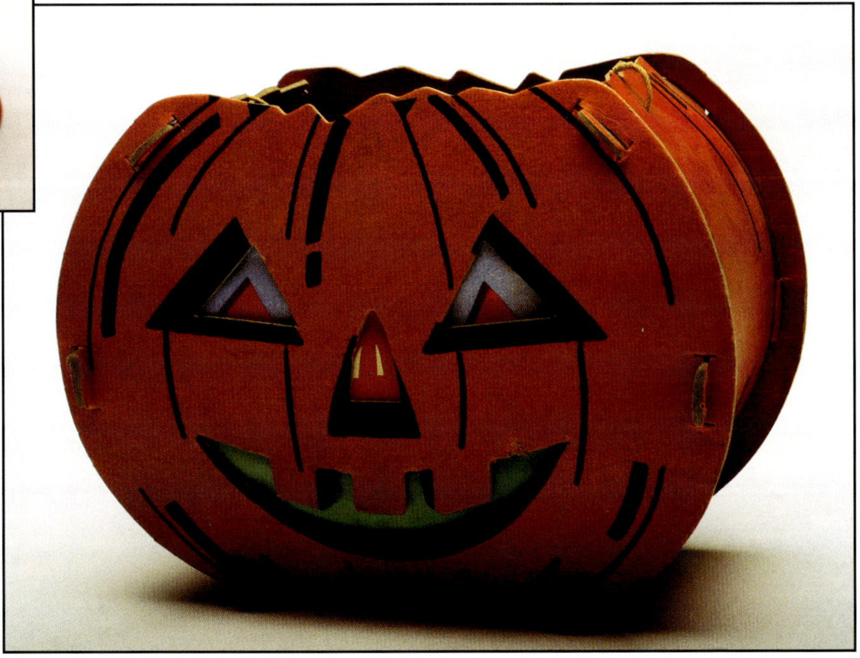

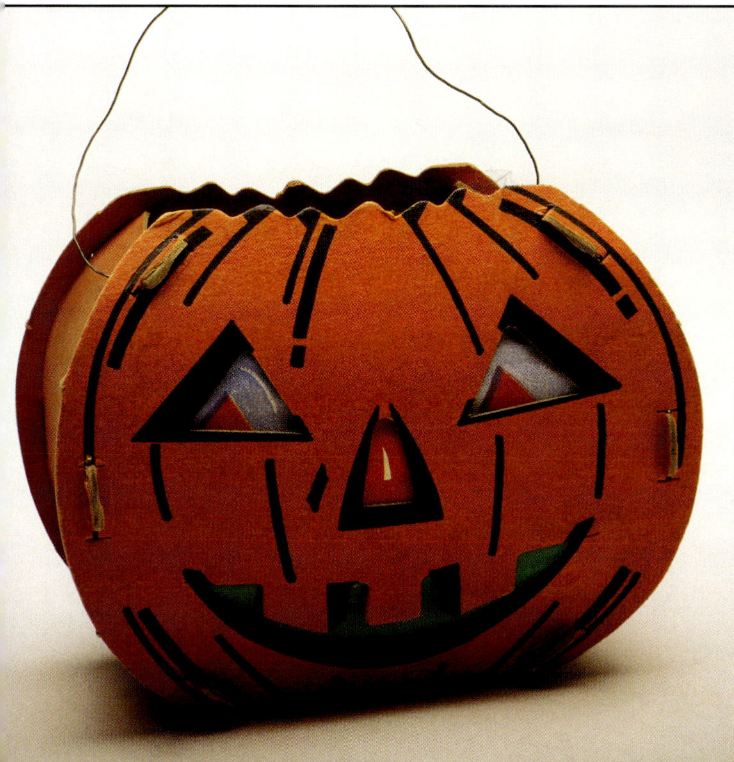

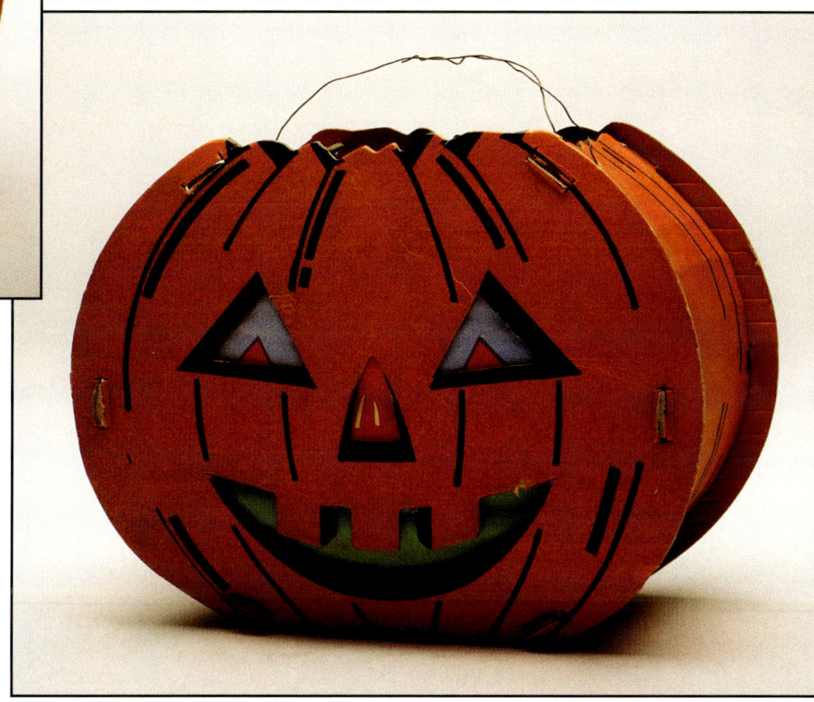

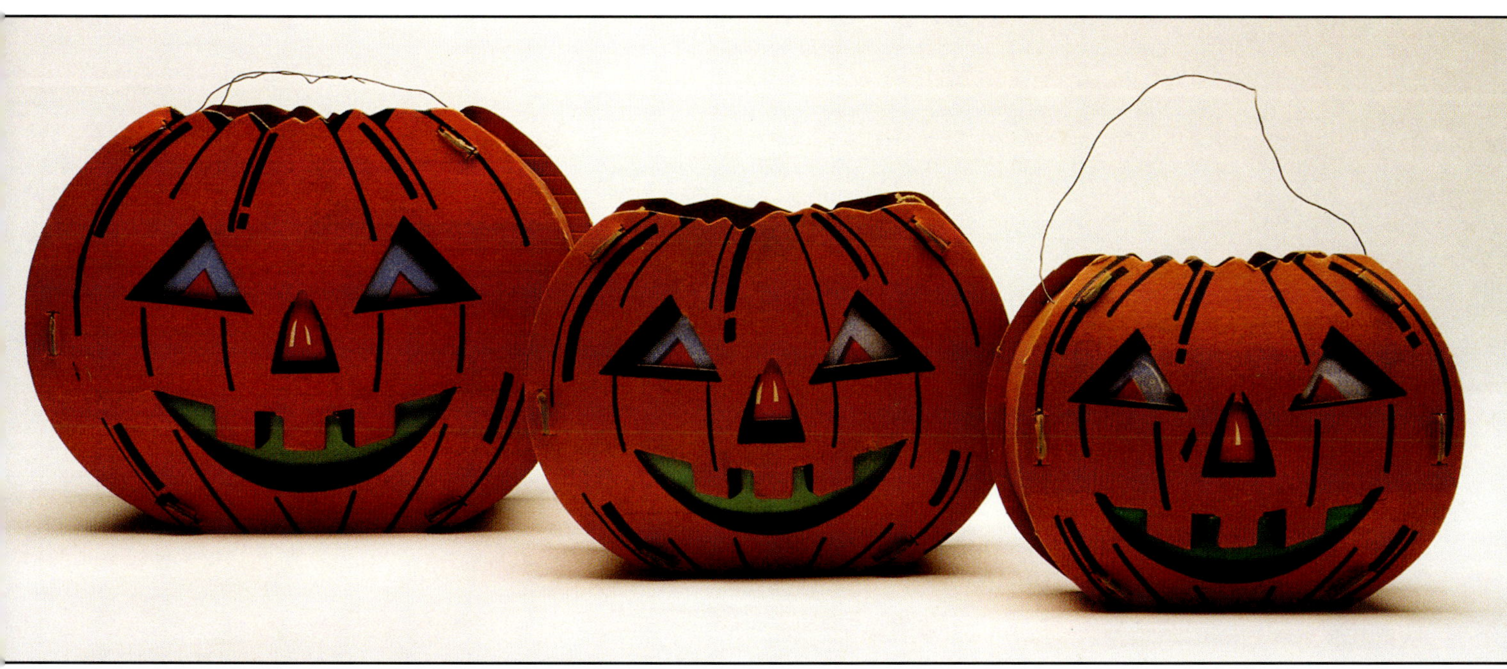

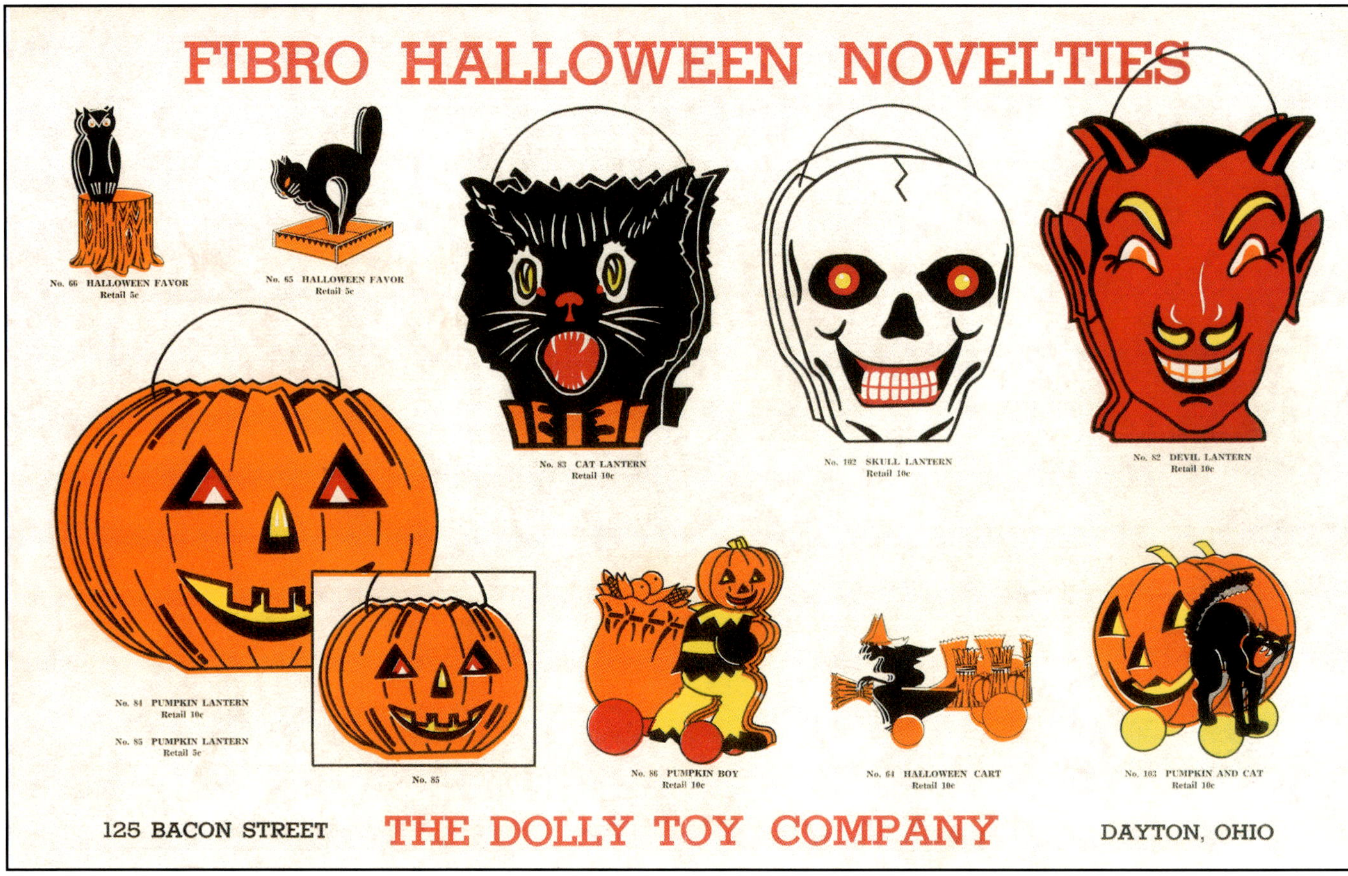

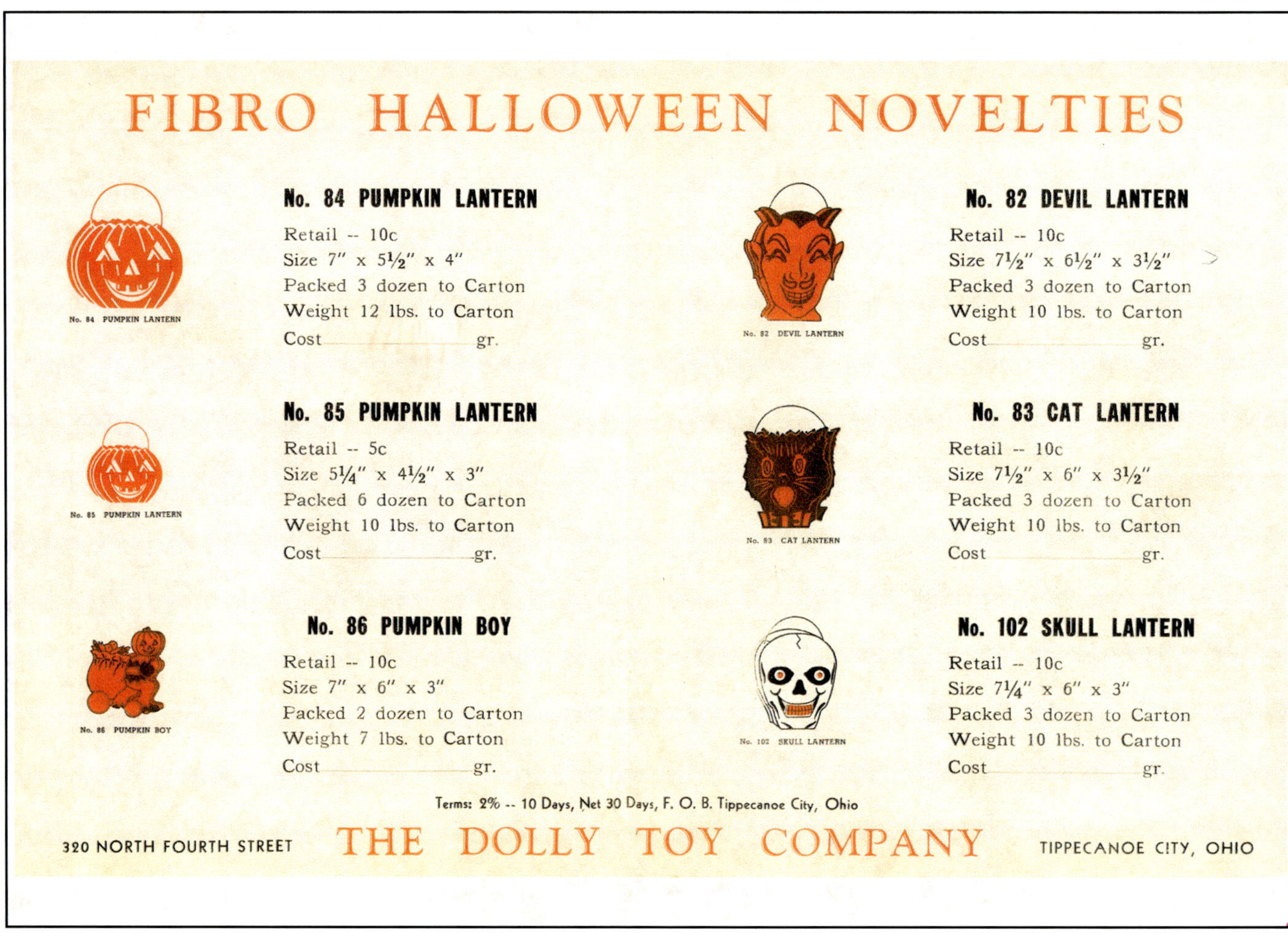

FIBRO HALLOWEEN NOVELTIES

No. 84 PUMPKIN LANTERN

No. 84 PUMPKIN LANTERN
Retail -- 10c
Size 7″ x 5½″ x 4″
Packed 3 dozen to Carton
Weight 12 lbs. to Carton
Cost ____ gr.

No. 82 DEVIL LANTERN

No. 82 DEVIL LANTERN
Retail -- 10c
Size 7½″ x 6½″ x 3½″
Packed 3 dozen to Carton
Weight 10 lbs. to Carton
Cost ____ gr.

No. 85 PUMPKIN LANTERN

No. 85 PUMPKIN LANTERN
Retail -- 5c
Size 5¼″ x 4½″ x 3″
Packed 6 dozen to Carton
Weight 10 lbs. to Carton
Cost ____ gr.

No. 83 CAT LANTERN

No. 83 CAT LANTERN
Retail -- 10c
Size 7½″ x 6″ x 3½″
Packed 3 dozen to Carton
Weight 10 lbs. to Carton
Cost ____ gr.

No. 86 PUMPKIN BOY

No. 86 PUMPKIN BOY
Retail -- 10c
Size 7″ x 6″ x 3″
Packed 2 dozen to Carton
Weight 7 lbs. to Carton
Cost ____ gr.

No. 102 SKULL LANTERN

No. 102 SKULL LANTERN
Retail -- 10c
Size 7¼″ x 6″ x 3″
Packed 3 dozen to Carton
Weight 10 lbs. to Carton
Cost ____ gr.

Terms: 2% -- 10 Days, Net 30 Days, F. O. B. Tippecanoe City, Ohio

320 NORTH FOURTH STREET THE DOLLY TOY COMPANY TIPPECANOE CITY, OHIO

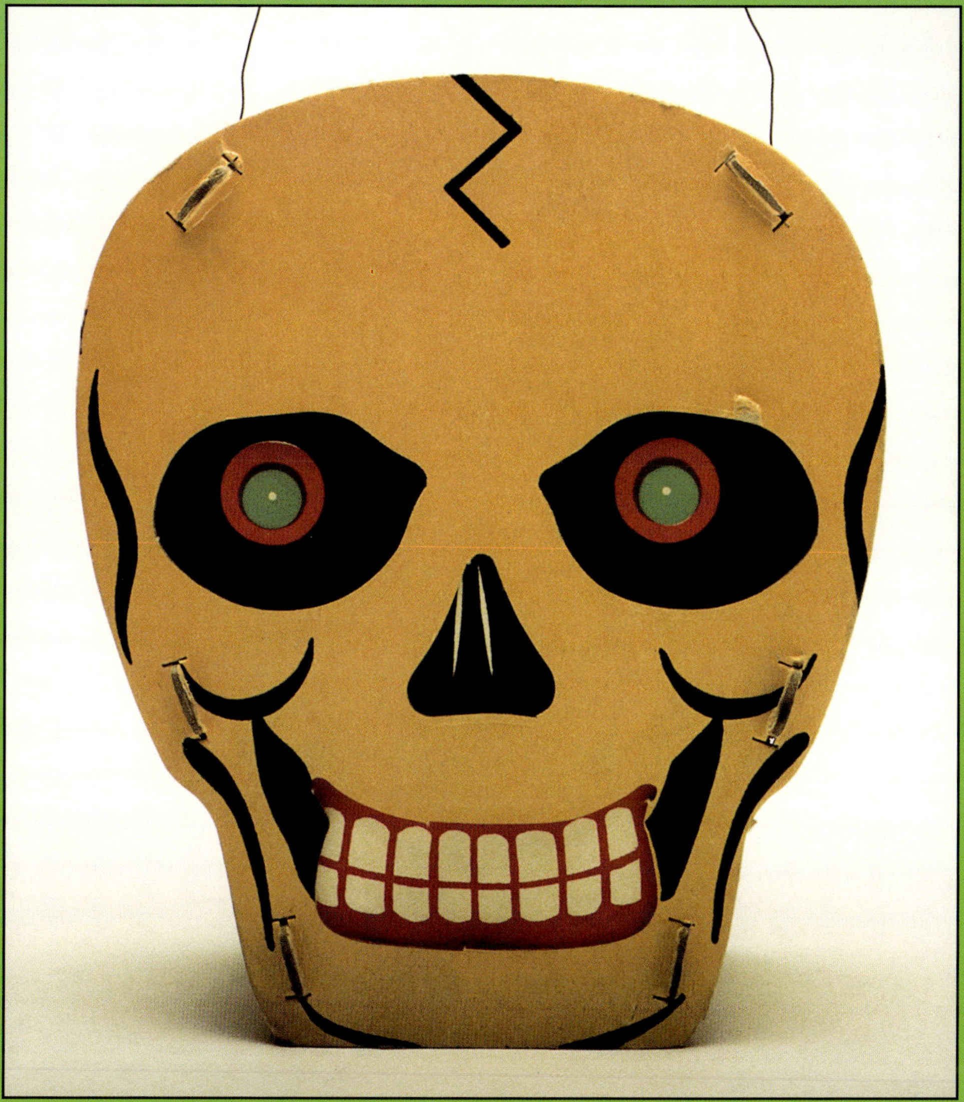

No. 102 SKULL LANTERN
Initial Release: 1936
Production Run: 1936 – 1938
*Showing both the lantern and the unmarked bottom.
Value $185

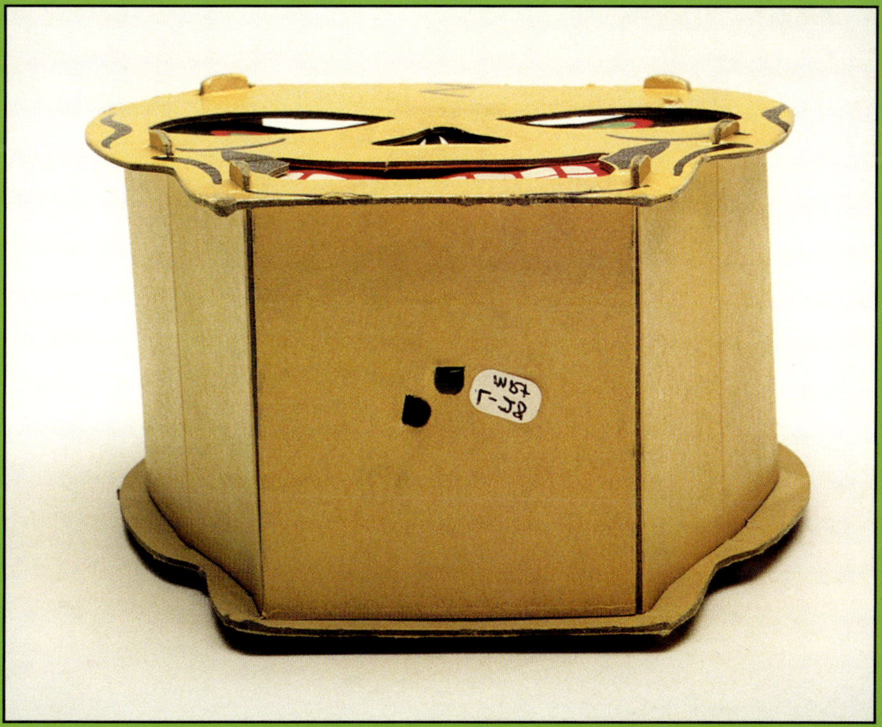

Two-Sided JACK-O-LANTERN
*Post 1938 lantern with the Tipp City mark on bottom.
Value: $145

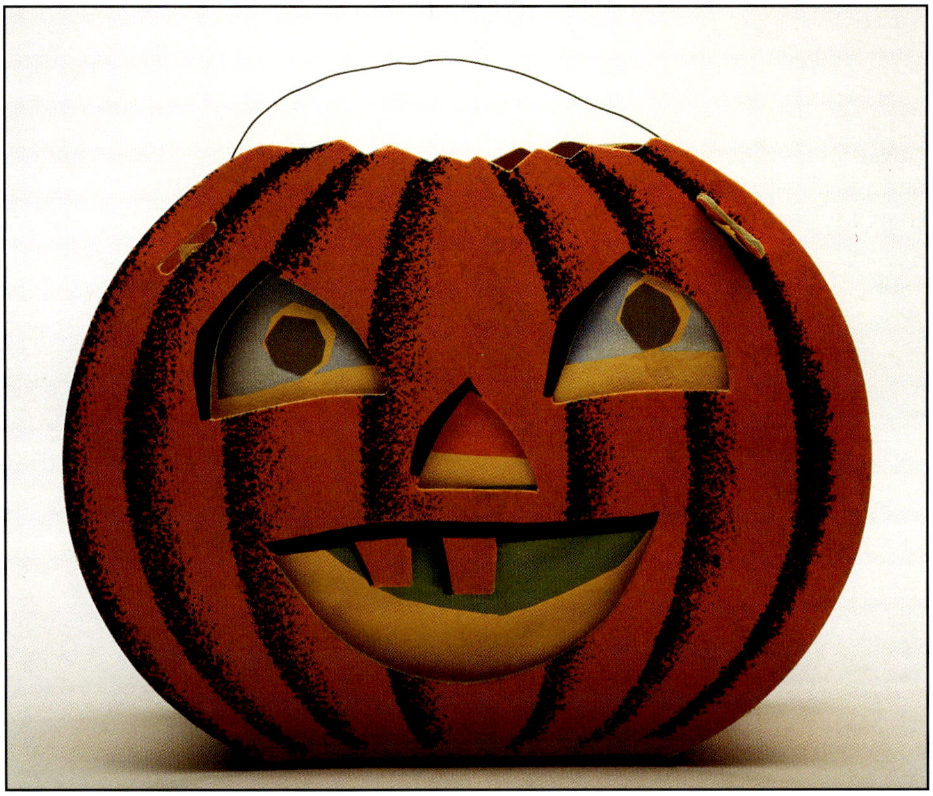

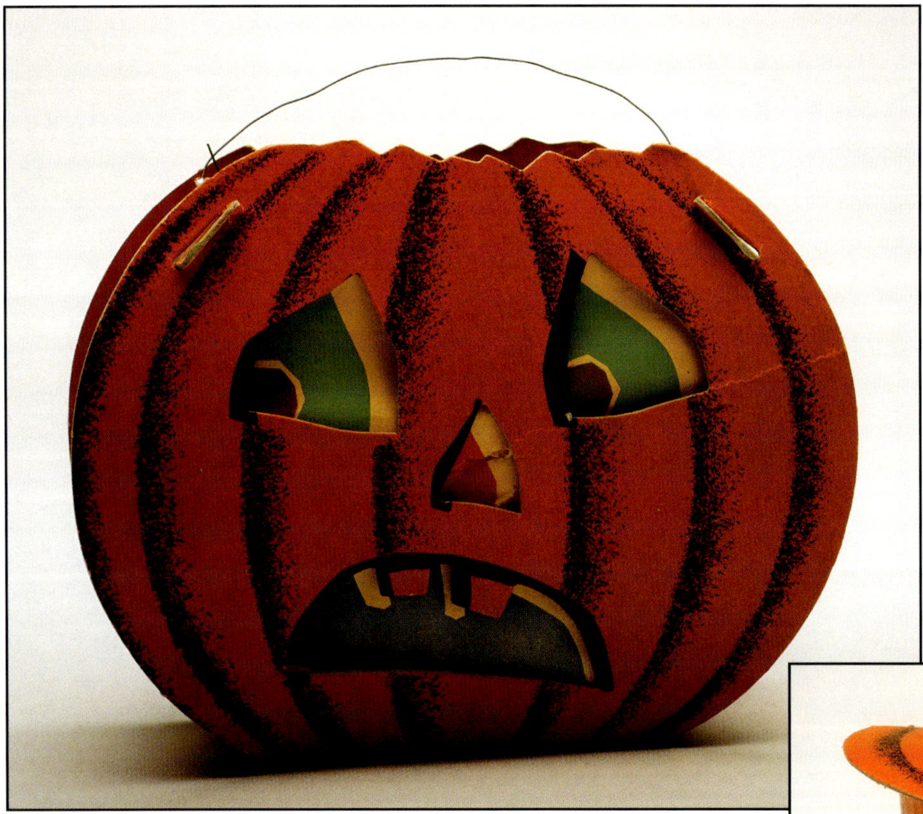

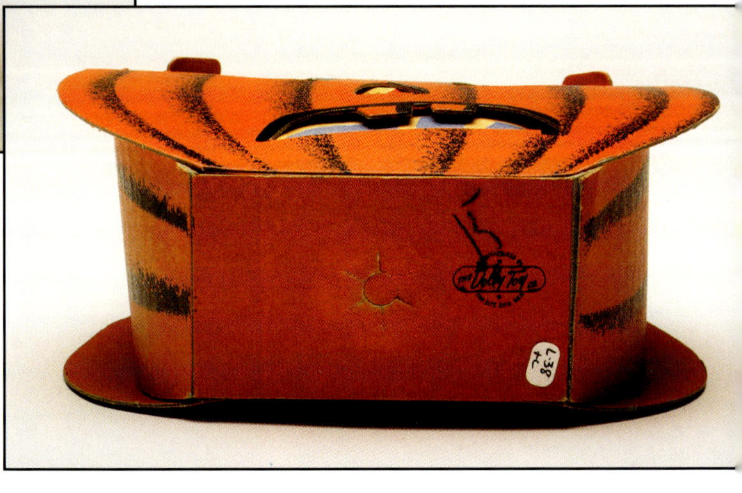

MERRI-LEI COMPANY
Brooklyn, New York

Do you recognize these wonderful pieces? I wonder how many other pieces made by Merri-Lei exist. I've never seen a more wonderful party favor/candy container as this black cat. Who would have thought of dressing him in crepe paper trousers and then filling each pant leg with candy! If someone owns a sales catalogue or was employed by this company, please contact the author.

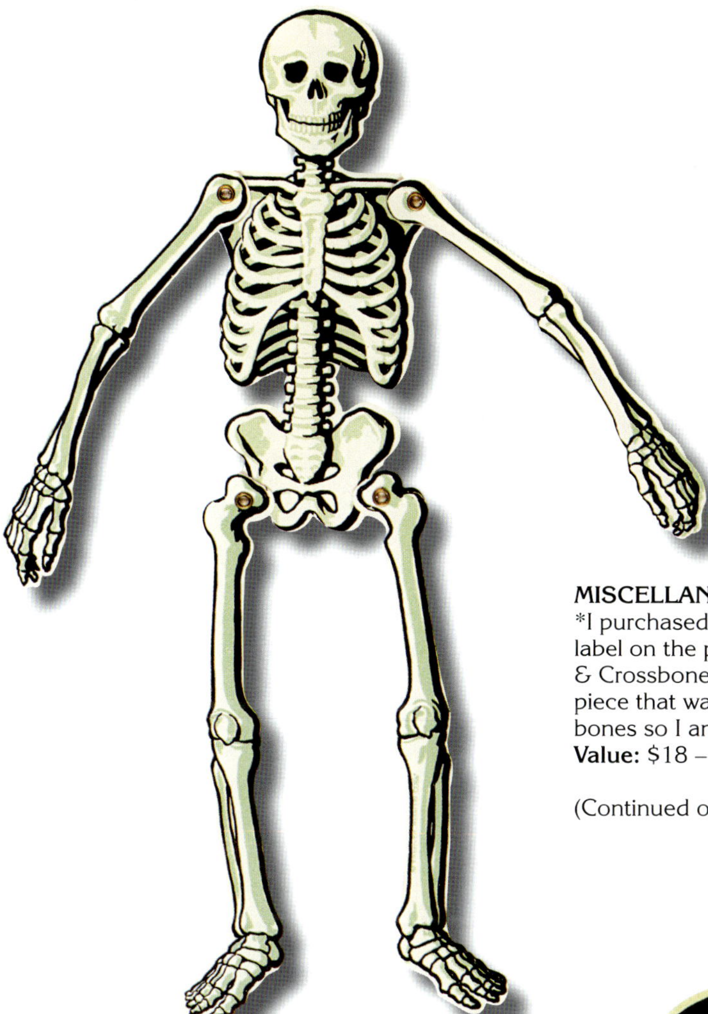

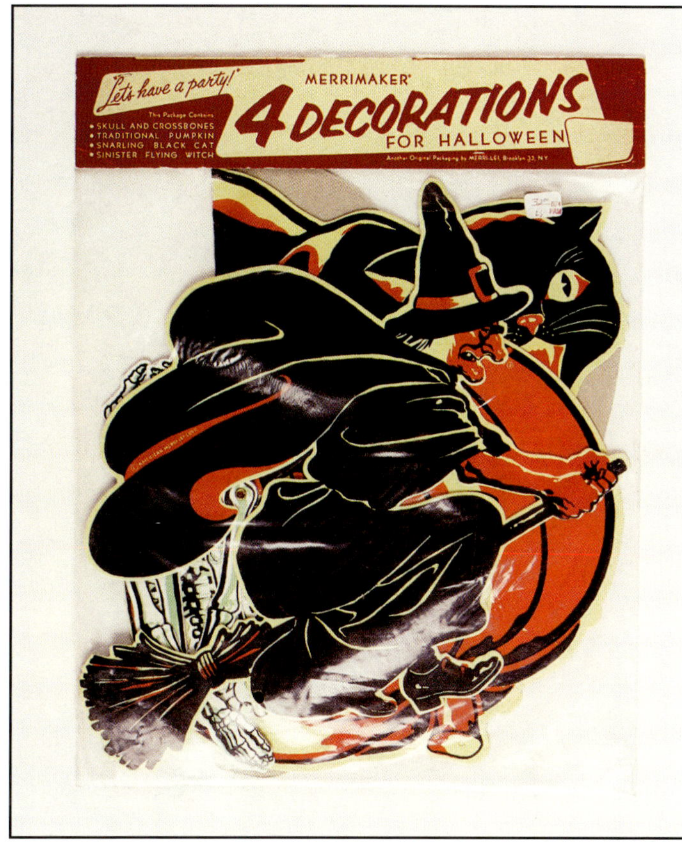

MISCELLANEOUS DIE-CUTS
*I purchased this package of Merri-Lei die-cuts unopened. If you read the contents label on the package banner, you will see that among the four decorations a Skull & Crossbones is listed. The funny thing is, this jaunty little skeleton was the actual piece that was packaged. Fortunately, I happen to have the Merri-Lei Skull & Crossbones so I am presenting both pieces.
Value: $18 – $75 range

(Continued on following page)

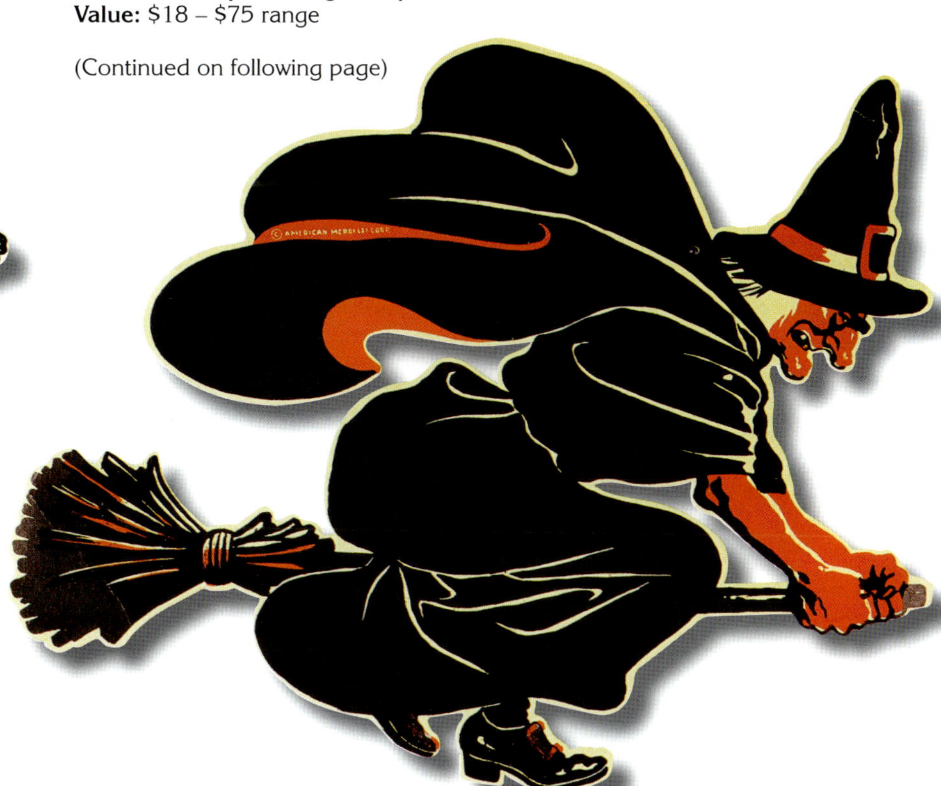

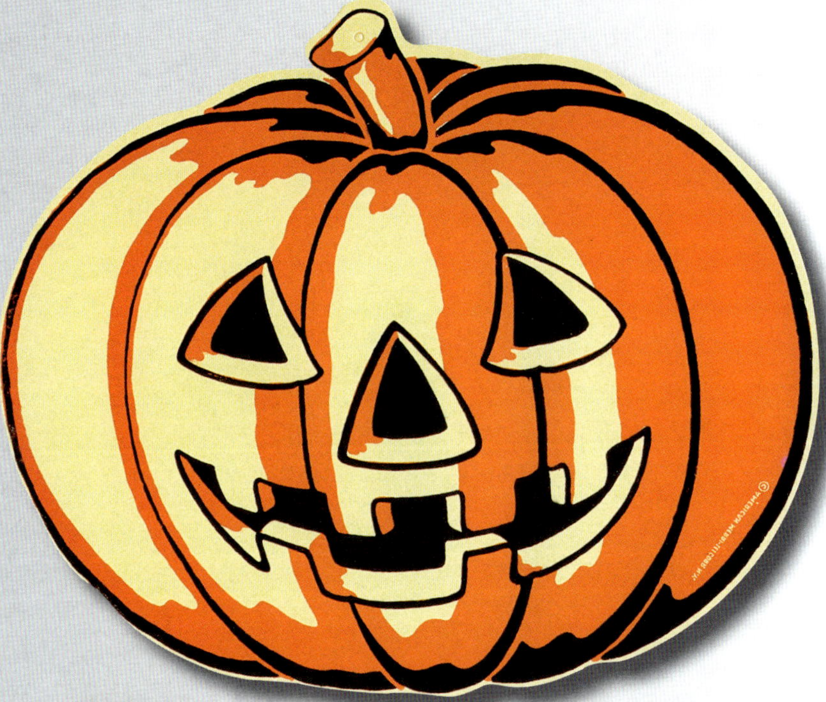

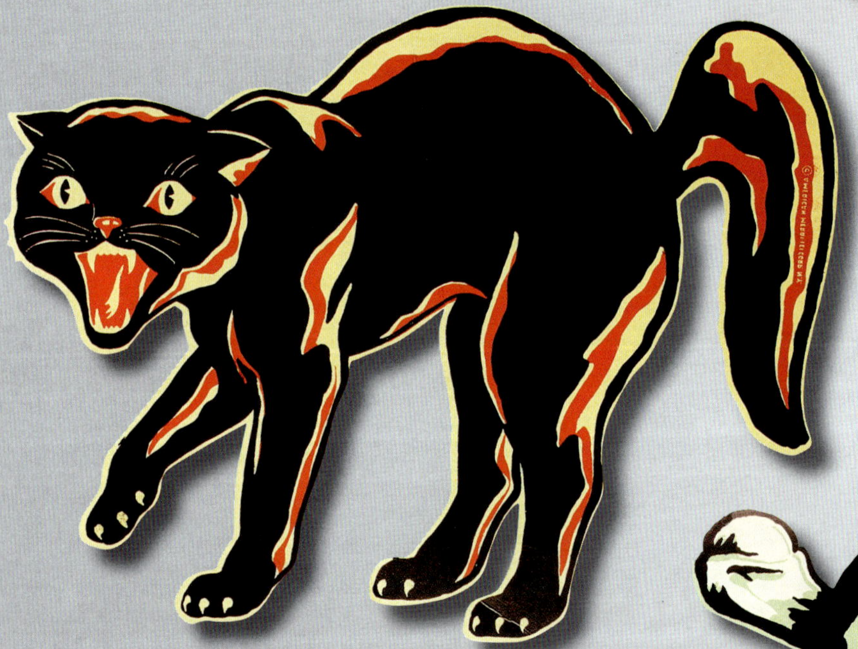

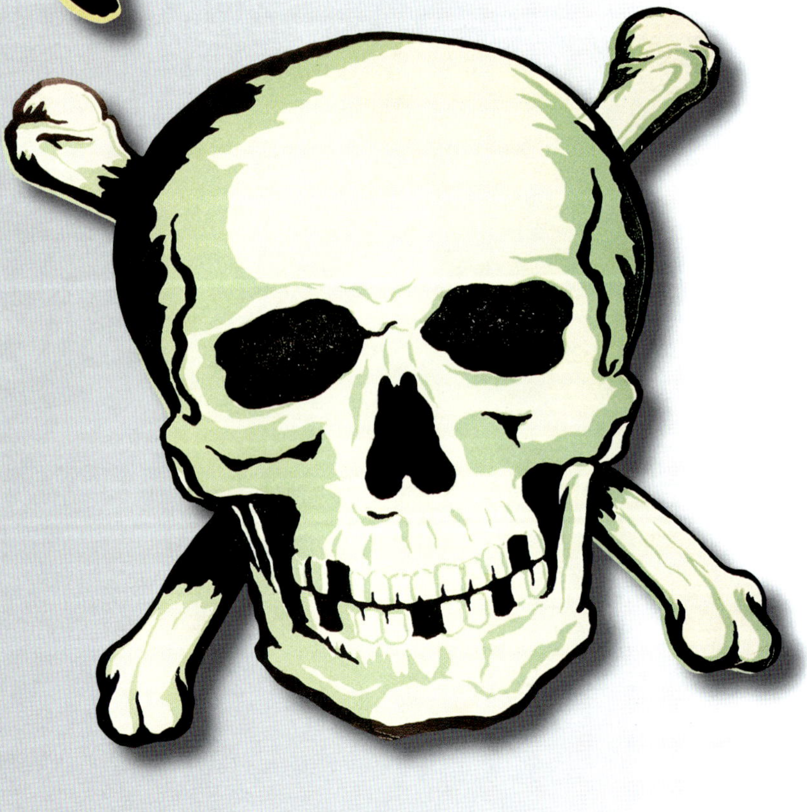

"MERRIKINS" CANDY CONTAINER

*This piece is an absolute delight! The Merri-Lei Halloween Black Cat is outfitted in orange crepe paper pants with a black stripe going up each pants leg. The legs are hollow so they can be filled with candy! The frustrating thing is that supposedly there are more pieces to this line but it seems I can't track down any more information on these treasures at this time.

*I filled the legs with all the candy corn I had, but as you can see from the photo you can barely see the tip of one piece of candy corn on the right leg. I've also included a side view along with the company's mark on the bottom of one leg.

Value: $135

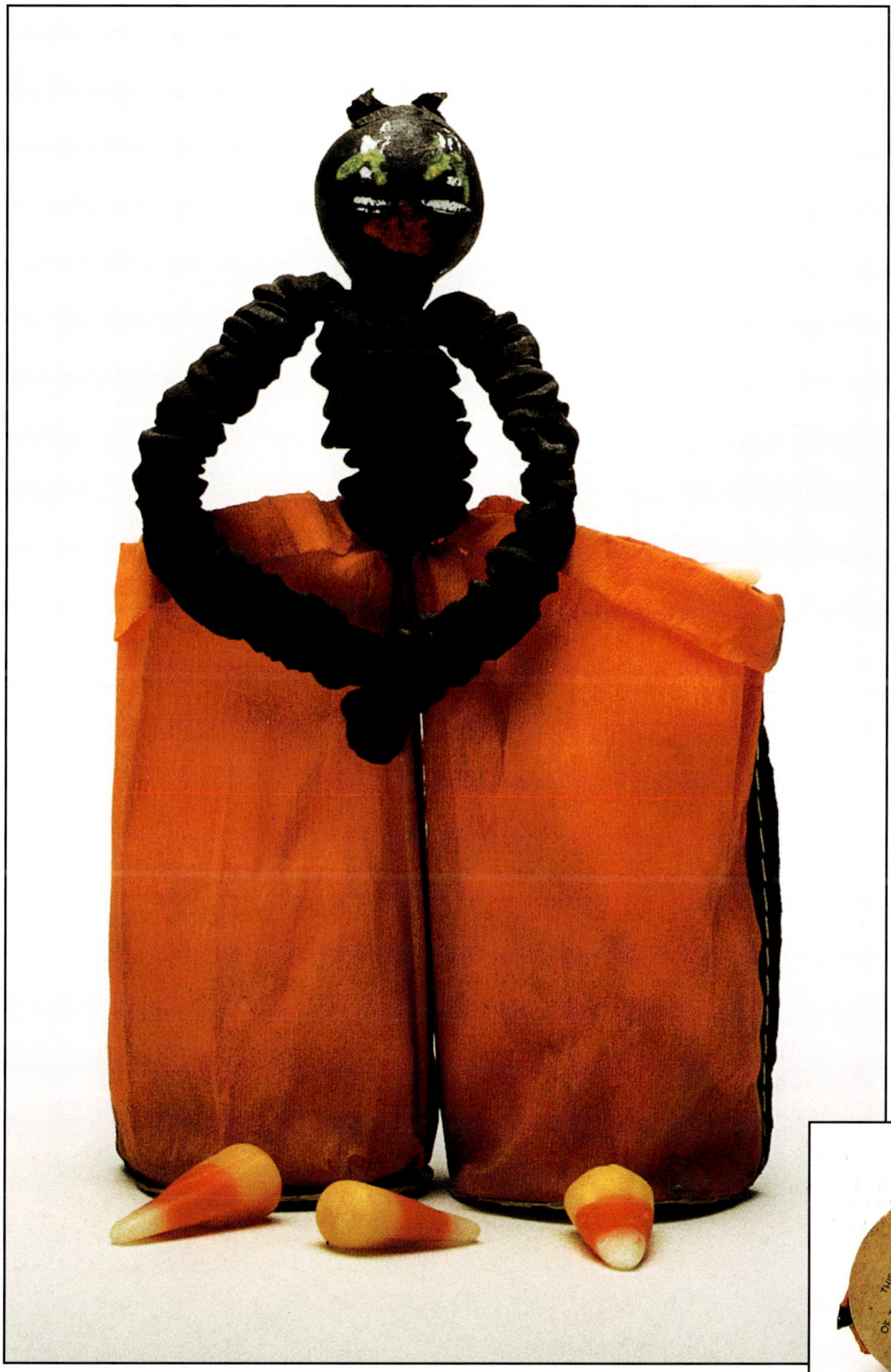

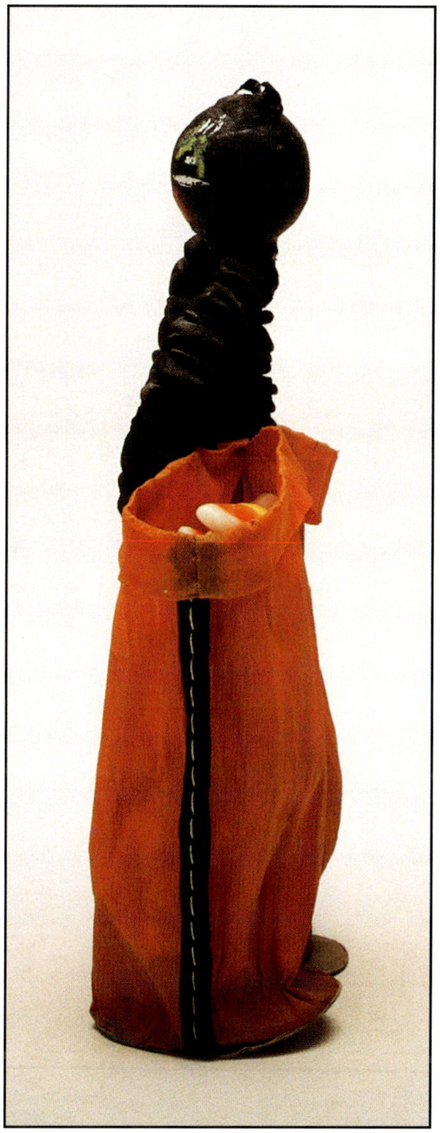

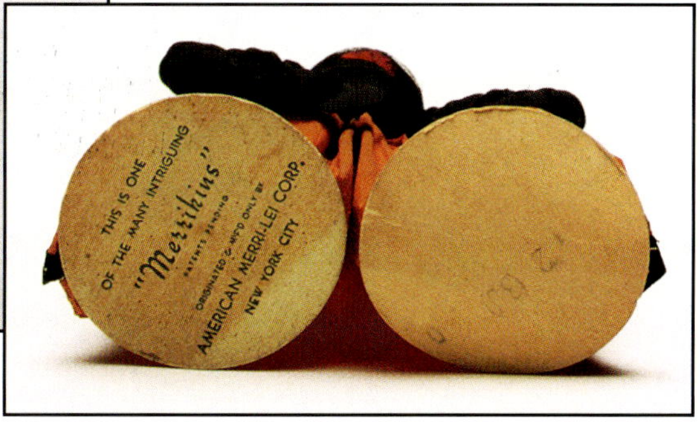

HALLOWEEN LANTERNS
Unknown Maker

Another great set of vintage Halloween lanterns. These lanterns are of unknown make and may be recognized by collectors of vintage Halloween. There are no markings. Any information would be appreciated.

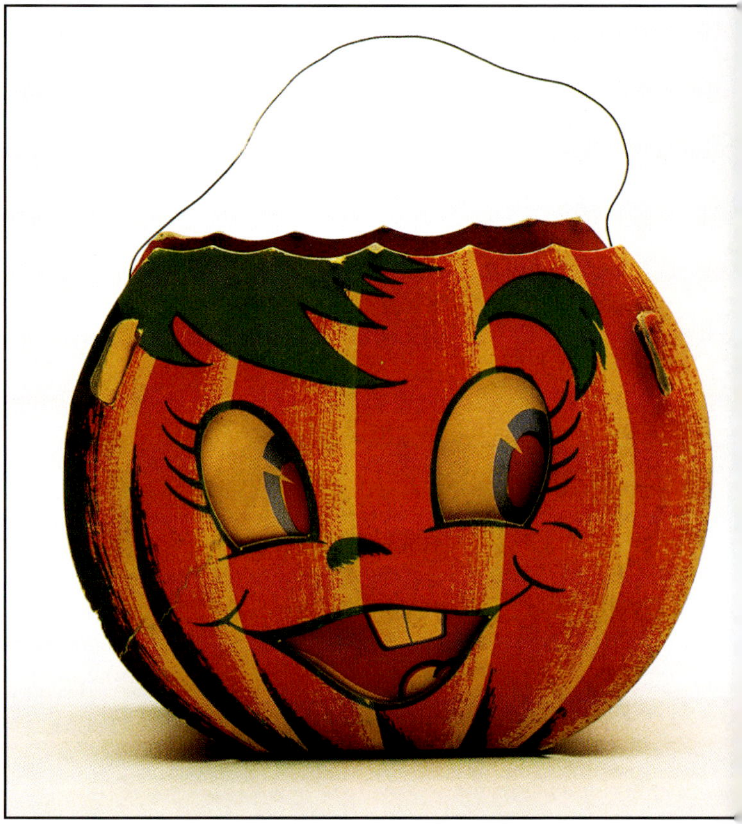

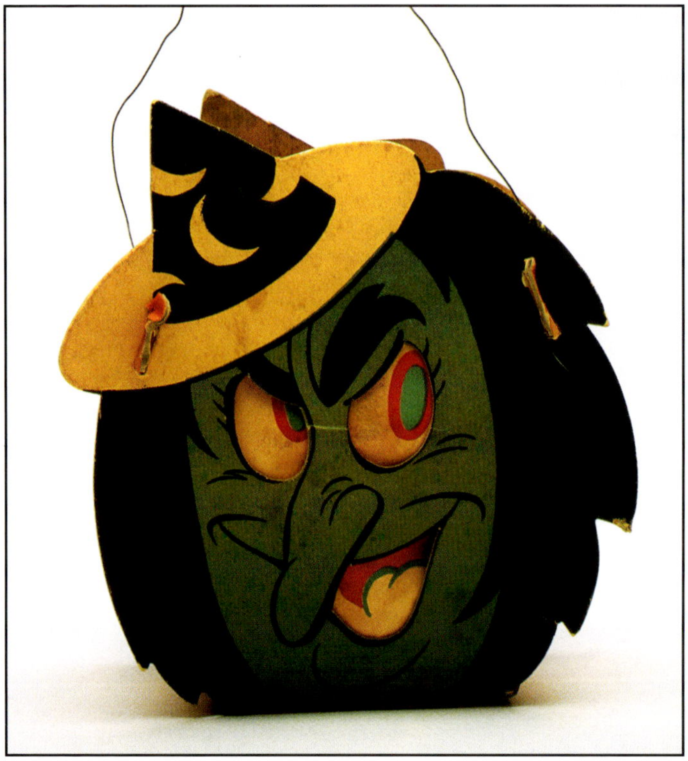

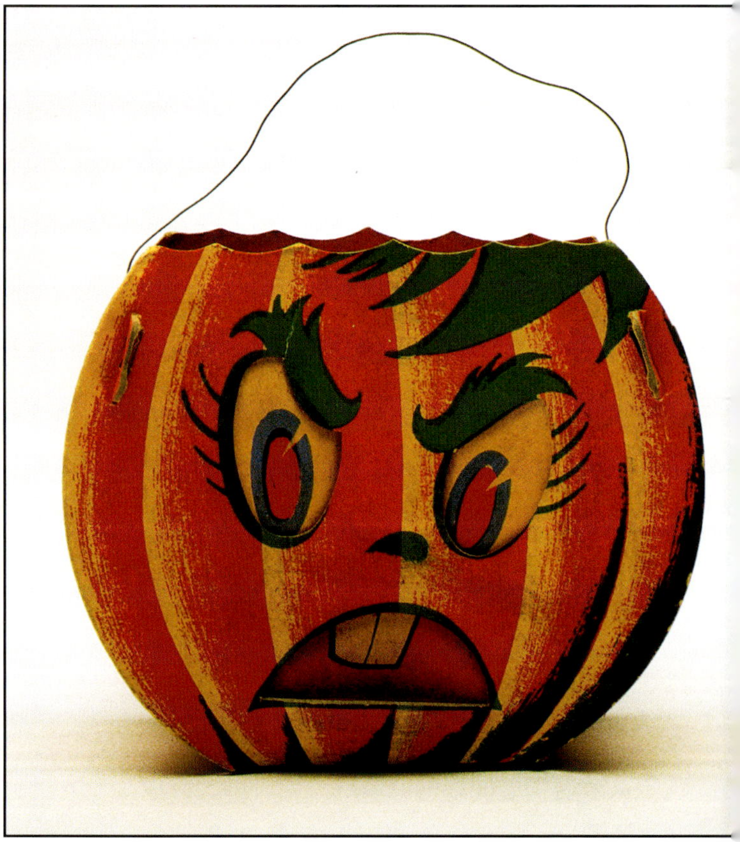

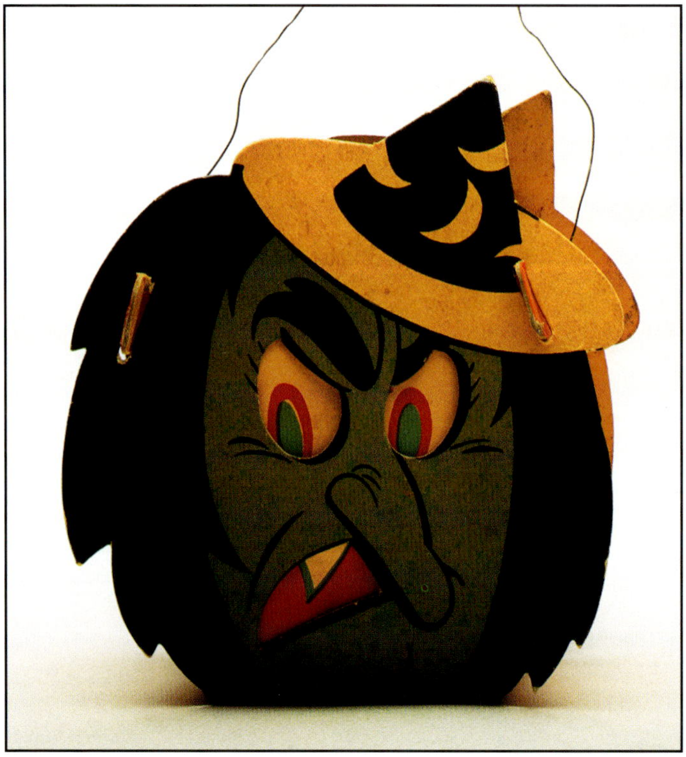

2-SIDED LANTERNS
This set of three two-sided lanterns (Witch, Jack-O-Lantern, and Black Cat) feature a sad/happy side. There were a small number of companies that made the tab-and-slot construction Halloween novelties so these pieces were not exclusive to the Dolly Toy Company.
Value: $135 each

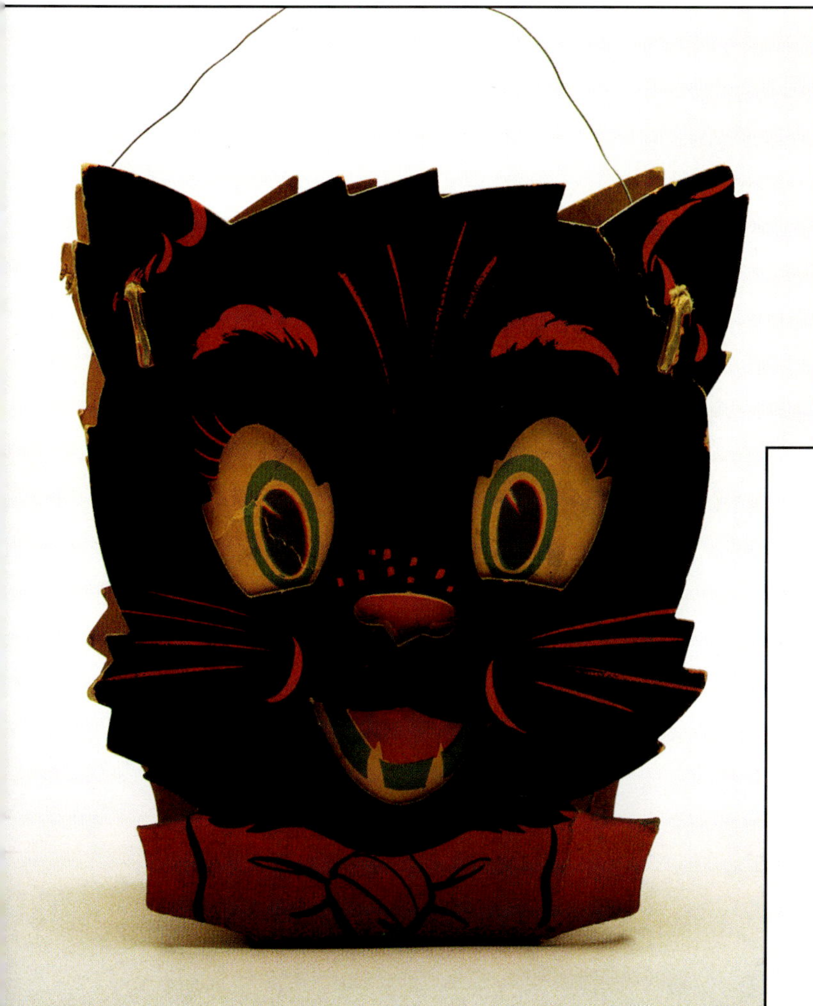

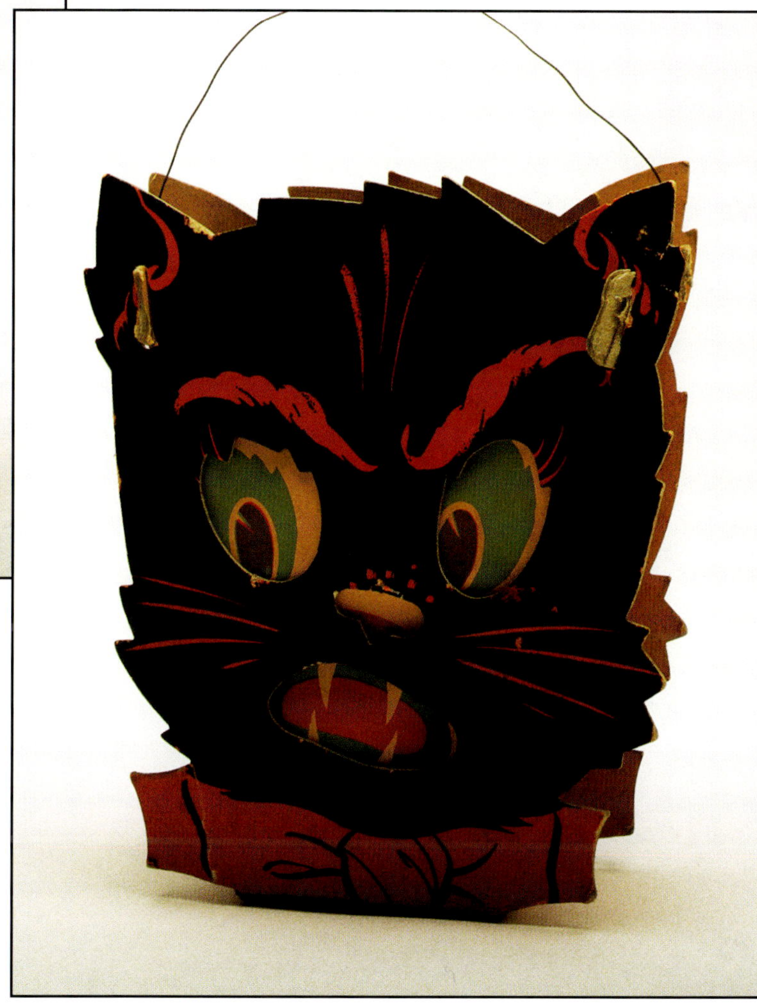

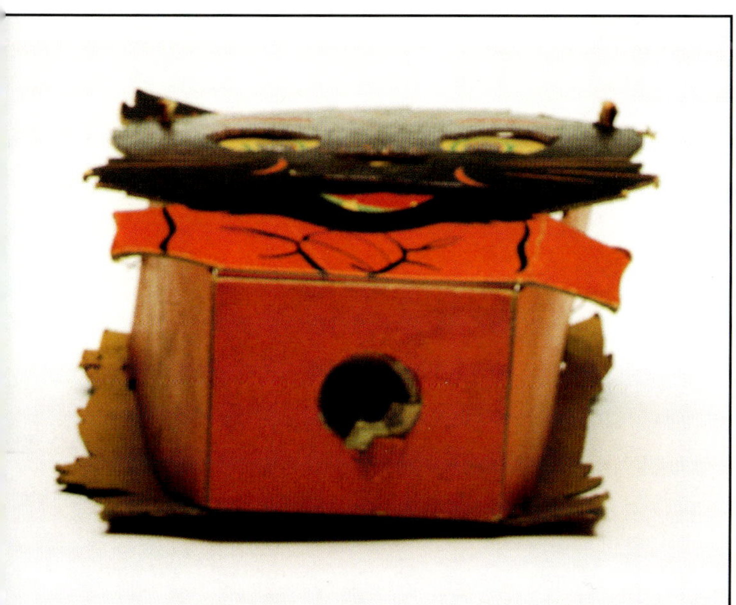

FIBRO HALLOWEEN NOVELTIES

No. 84 PUMPKIN LANTERN

No. 84 PUMPKIN LANTERN

Retail -- 10c
Size 7" x 5½" x 4"
Packed 3 dozen to Carton
Weight 12 lbs. to Carton
Cost ____________ gr.

No. 85 PUMPKIN LANTERN

No. 85 PUMPKIN LANTERN

Retail -- 5c
Size 5¼" x 4½" x 3"
Packed 6 dozen to Carton
Weight 10 lbs. to Carton
Cost ____________ gr.

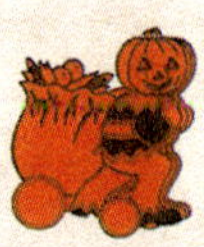

No. 86 PUMPKIN BOY

No. 86 PUMPKIN BOY

Retail -- 10c
Size 7" x 6" x 3"
Packed 2 dozen to Carton
Weight 7 lbs. to Carton
Cost ____________ gr.

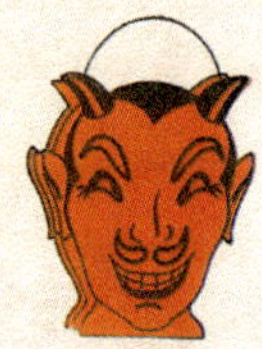

No. 82 DEVIL LANTERN

No. 82 DEVIL LANTERN

Retail -- 10c
Size 7½" x 6½" x 3½"
Packed 3 dozen to Carton
Weight 10 lbs. to Carton
Cost ____________ gr.

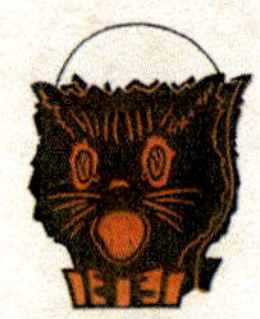

No. 83 CAT LANTERN

No. 83 CAT LANTERN

Retail -- 10c
Size 7½" x 6" x 3½"
Packed 3 dozen to Carton
Weight 10 lbs. to Carton
Cost ____________ gr.

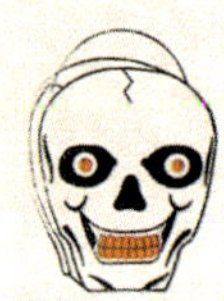

No. 102 SKULL LANTERN

No. 102 SKULL LANTERN

Retail -- 10c
Size 7¼" x 6" x 3"
Packed 3 dozen to Carton
Weight 10 lbs. to Carton
Cost ____________ gr.

Terms: 2% -- 10 Days, Net 30 Days, F. O. B. Tippecanoe City, Ohio

320 NORTH FOURTH STREET **THE DOLLY TOY COMPANY** TIPPECANOE CITY, OHIO